JUST-IN-TIME
FOR AMERICA

KENNETH A. WANTUCK

JUST-IN-TIME

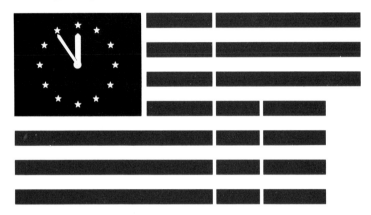

FOR AMERICA
A COMMON SENSE
PRODUCTION STRATEGY

THE **FORUM** LTD
3333 N. Mayfair Rd.
Milwaukee, WI 53222

The Forum, Ltd.
3333 N. Mayfair Road
Milwaukee, WI 53222

Library of Congress Catalog Card Number: 89-080110
ISBN: 0-9621982-0-X

Cover designed by Wm. Eisner & Associates, Milwaukee, WI.
Typeset in Times Roman by LTD Graphics, Inc., Wauwatosa, WI.
Printed and bound by Edwards Brothers, Inc., Ann Arbor, MI.
Printed in the United States of America.

To My Parents
Frank and Carole Wantuck
Who Gave Me Life, Love and Values

CONTENTS

PREFACE

The objective of this book is to provide you with the perspective, understanding and enough tools to begin implementing JUST-IN-TIME. That is a lot to ask from a single volume but, after much head scratching and many revisions, I believe *JUST-IN-TIME for America* meets that goal. It wasn't easy. During the early stages of this undertaking, a friend told me that writing this book would be like "trying to give birth to a square egg." In retrospect, I believe that was an *understatement*.

There were three main reasons for initiating this project. First, most of the JIT management books I had read did not cover all of the elements needed for a successful implementation and did not, in my mind, show how the pieces fit together and reinforce one another. Without a complete perspective, it's difficult to accept new ideas. Second, many of the "how to" JIT books didn't contain enough hands-on detail to get people started in actual JIT implementation. While it's good to know about JUST-IN-TIME, it's the *doing* that provides the payoff. Finally, too many people I've worked with seem to think JIT is complicated. It isn't really, but maybe it's the way it has been explained in the past.

While JIT is not complicated, it is broad in scope and it is important to appreciate how the various elements interact. Like a good recipe, you must use *all* the ingredients in the proper proportion to get the expected results. It can be your recipe for success.

It is my hope that you'll read the book from cover to cover because each chapter builds on previous ones and there's a lot of "good stuff" there that you should know about. If, on the other hand, you're in a big hurry to get the gist of the contents, you can read Chapter 1 and the summaries at the end of the remaining chapters. That will give you a fairly decent perspective of JIT from only 39 pages of reading.

Each chapter starts with an explanation of what that JIT element is all about and why it is an essential part of the whole strategy. I've used a lot of examples to reinforce key points and make them as understandable as possible. As you get further into the chapter, more detailed case studies and more real-world variations are introduced. In some cases I've included formats that can be used in your JUST-IN-TIME implementation. These are "how to" tools to get you started.

The information in the book was collected from a wide variety of sources, mostly from companies I've worked for or with during the last decade. They are among the American JIT pioneers whose successes have shown conclusively that JUST-IN-TIME, which started in America, is still a viable, "common sense" production strategy for building a world-class manufacturing business. It was people like Jim McDavitt, General Manager of Automotive Seating Mechanisms for Johnson Controls, Inc., who showed that it could be done. Jim was a newly appointed plant manager when we started working together. He came to the job from the sales department so he didn't know that JIT wouldn't work in a U.S. plant. He just went out and made it happen. Several examples in this book are taken from the work done at Jim's Linden, Tennessee facility.

Len Ricard, Vice President and General Manager of Harley-Davidson's Engine and Transmission Operations, had a major influence on my JIT thinking during the formulative years. He lived in Japan for four years and had some keen insights on how JIT was being applied there. Back in the early eighties when we were promoting JUST-IN-TIME for the Automotive Industry Action Group with the "Ken and Len Show," we had many lively debates on what would or wouldn't work in America and why. Some of his General Motors "war stories" have found their way into this text.

Six technical reviewers worked their way through draft copies of the book and made valuable suggestions for improvements, most of which were incorporated in the final product. I'm most grateful to:

- Herb Block, Director-New Products, AT&T Network Systems
- Alan Callet, Director-Human Resources, Dresser-Wayne
- Al Krohn, JIT Education Coordinator, Caterpillar
- Duane Lakin, President, Lakin & Associates
- Dick Spicka, Vice President-Finance, Kuhlman Corp.
- Mike Tillander, Vice President-Marketing, Bendix Transportation

Barb Sellers, Client Service Manager for The Forum, Ltd., had the unenviable task of editing the text in an effort to make it grammatically presentable. She did a masterful job of sorting through the shop slang, coined expressions and my inordinate use of commas to come up with a readable manuscript. Thanks are also due to Kent Ehly for his inputs on the quality subjects and to Terry Schultz, President of The Forum, Ltd., for two years of patience and for giving me the latitude to it my way.

My co-workers at Ken Wantuck Associates deserve special thanks for their contributions and for putting up with me during this project.

John Kinsey served as a technical reviewer and compiled the Index. Pamela Wantuck, my niece and Administrative Assistant, made reference searches, "paste-ups," copies, trips to the graphics and photography houses and more revisions than we would have believed possible at the onset of the project. My deepest gratitude goes to Howard Weston, Vice President-Consulting Services, not only for his advice and counsel during the writing of the book but also for keeping KWA afloat during the times I stole away to develop the manuscript. Howard worked himself to a "frazzle" last year and I suspect he's even happier than I am to see this undertaking come to a conclusion.

I also wish to acknowledge the many family members and friends who supported and encouraged me when the "creative juices" didn't want to flow, especially my dear friend, Louise DeMaggio, whose "eagle eyes" caught errors that everyone else missed and who contributed many creative ideas that enhanced the presentation of this material.

For all the help I received, I must confess that I did not accept every suggestion made. Therefore, any errors you find or points you wish to dispute are my responsibility. Your comments, good or bad, will be welcomed. How well I may have succeeded in providing you with the perspective, understanding and enough tools to begin implementing JUST-IN-TIME will be for you to judge.

Ken Wantuck
Southfield, Michigan
January 1989

JUST-IN-TIME
FOR AMERICA

MANAGEMENT
OVERVIEW

CHAPTER 1

"Common sense is not so common."
- Voltaire

This is a book about change. Our world is constantly changing. It always has. Since the dawn of creation the human race has survived as a species and prospered because it could adapt to those changes.

Today, American industry is faced with a rapidly changing world that includes global competition and increasingly difficult customer demands. In the last decade, certain sectors of American industry have gone bankrupt. Over 1000 companies have closed their doors. More than two million American jobs have been lost in manufacturing. America, once the maker of one-half of the world's steel, now imports one-third of its needs. We import 25% of our cars, 40% of our vacuum cleaners, and 100% of our video cassette recorders.

We have a choice. We can bury our heads in the sand and deny that we have a problem. We can blame somebody — management, unions, the work ethic, governments or unfair practices by others. Or, we can face up to the challenge for what it is — competitive survival — and resolve to conquer it in the manner that has always made America great, using our ingenuity, industry and willingness to try a better way.

A NEW PERSPECTIVE

JUST-IN-TIME offers us the opportunity to recapture our leadership, but the ideas involved are so different from today's traditional practices that you should hear the whole story before making a judgment. I am asking you to open your mind and revisit the business you know so well from a totally new perspective. For example, consider the JUST-IN-TIME emblem on the title page of this book.

The American flag is traditional. Everyone sees the stripes in the traditional way. Even though they appear sort of "funny," most people will not look any further because they have been conditioned to recognize what they see as the "flag." This is a phenomenon which physiologists call a *scotoma,* a "mental blind spot for the problem before one's eyes." Embedded in our flag are the letters J, I and T, the initials of JUST-

IN-TIME. It is easy to see when someone explains it, but you have to view it differently to see it from "scratch." It is the same with the problems facing us in our companies. The answers are clearly visible if we can take a fresh look from a new perspective. JUST-IN-TIME offers us that opportunity.

Similarly, we can all see that the blue field contains a clock, but why are the hands positioned at five minutes to twelve? They tell us that time is short. Most of us are facing broader competition from producers all over the world today, whether we realize it or not. Too many companies have ignored this reality until it was too late. If we expect to compete effectively we must become world-class producers, and now is the time to take action. JUST-IN-TIME can give us the means to make it a reality.

Business Objectives

How do these new ideas apply to our business? Why are we in business? We need to recognize that we are in business to make money. It's the basis of the free enterprise system. But first, we have to survive. A small businessman thoroughly understands that. Eighty percent of all new businesses in America fail within the first two years, according to the Small Business Administration. Even the largest organizations may face that issue, as did the Chrysler Corporation in the early 1980's. (It is interesting to note that much of the credit for their rapid recovery has been attributed to the implementation of JUST-IN-TIME.)

Beyond the survival threshold we want to profit from our endeavors. Making profit is what it's all about. It provides us with the funding to run our businesses and to be good corporate citizens. No manufacturing company that I know of is a "not for profit" organization - at least, not on purpose.

Finally, there is growth. Growth is the fun part of business, providing opportunities for promotion and expansion. Interestingly, we have to grow at least as fast as our market is growing, just to survive. Otherwise, we're going to *lose market share* and give business to the competition. Conversely, to grow faster than our markets we must take shares away from the competition. That's the battle, let there be no doubt. There will be winners and losers in this struggle, and our job is to assure that we are among the winners.

Business Strategies

To really make money, we have to translate our general goals into quantified objectives that make sense. We have to determine how fast we can grow. What profit percentage can we actually anticipate earning? How much return on our investment do we need to attract vital capital to our company, so we can support the growth? Then, we have to balance those objectives with the proper strategies, or game plans, to achieve those goals. We have to determine which markets we're going to serve and how we're going to penetrate the markets. We must define the products we're going to develop, or the improvements we're going to make, recognizing that all of these plans are constrained by the available resources. This is the Strategic Business Planning process. It's a classic balancing act, as shown in Figure 1-1.

What's missing, however, is a ***production strategy.*** We presume we will somehow build the products the way we always have. Typically, we strive to get more market and/or to improve margins. To increase market share, many people would propose building a higher quality product because quality sells. But, traditionally, higher quality always meant higher cost. Conventional wisdom told us that product quality had to be "good enough" but not "too good" or we'd price ourselves out of the market. Sometimes the strategy called for "acceptable quality" coupled with better service. Everybody knows that better service will sell more product. But, service parts cost money, warranties cost money and service departments cost money, all of which decrease the margin.

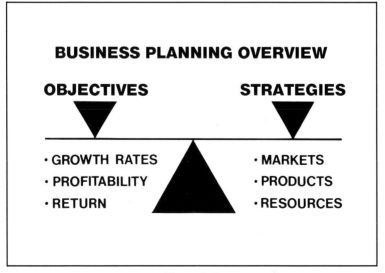

Figure 1-1

Eventually, the sales department would come up with the ultimate answer, "Let's cut the price and we'll make it up on volume." But we all know that unless we sell enough additional product to more than make up that difference we're not going to make more money, which should be our ultimate objective.

Then the accountants would get into the act, telling us, "You're looking at it from the wrong side of the equation. What you want to do is increase the price and make more margin per product." The problem is we can't arbitrarily set prices. The market sets the price, so we were constrained there, too. Invariably, all eyes finally turned towards manufacturing cost. And where did we focus our attention? On direct labor, that segment of our total cost which is usually less than 10% of the cost dollar. We have become experts at squeezing the last one-tenth of a minute out of our processes. But, while we've concentrated there, we've missed the bulk of the cost input. We've missed the indirect cost, the management cost, the general and administrative cost, equipment and building capital, and purchased material cost, to mention just a few. It is the summation of all of these elements that comprises our total cost input. Thus, we need to minimize the total input relative to the output. That's productivity, getting *more salable output for less total input.* Therefore, to make more money we must become more productive. To do that, we need a production strategy.

A New Production Strategy

Productivity is important in every aspect of the business. It is the production process, however, from raw material acquisition through finished product delivery to the end customer, that has been most neglected in our strategic thinking. Manufacturing provides us with the means to achieve real wealth through the production of tangible goods. America doesn't have to depend on information or services for its future survival, as some have predicted. A renaissance in manufacturing is within our grasp if we are willing to try a different way. It is called JUST-IN-TIME.

> *"JUST-IN-TIME is a production strategy*
> *with a new set of values*
> *to continuously improve*
> *quality and productivity."*

To many, that may sound like "having your cake and eating it, too." Your experience may tell you it can't be done, but with JUST-

IN-TIME, both quality and productivity can be simultaneously improved, as will be demonstrated in this book.

ORIGIN OF JUST-IN-TIME

Much has already been written about JUST-IN-TIME. Magazine articles and books abound, many of which are excellent. The most amazing book I've read on the topic is one in which the author described a manufacturing plant where raw iron ore was unloaded from a ship, transformed to steel, converted to finished automobiles and shipped to the customer in a span of less than 48 hours. You may be thinking, "Here it comes, another one of these Japanese manufacturing miracles." But, interestingly enough, this was an American plant, located in Dearborn, Michigan. Entitled, Today and Tomorrow, the book was published in 1926 and authored by Henry Ford!

My copy was obtained from the public library because the book was not sold in America. Printing had ceased decades ago. When I looked at the check-out history on the back cover, I found I was only the eighth person to borrow the book during the last 35 years. Meanwhile, our friends from Japan had reprinted it in their language and until recently, one could purchase a copy in Tokyo. The Japanese embraced Henry Ford's principles and put them into operation in the modern era. They have shown us these things still work today, even in our sophisticated manufacturing environments. What was their motivation? Why did they do it when we did not?

JIT Motivation

The nation of Japan is a string of islands, located off the East coast of the Asian mainland, containing fewer square miles than the State of California, as shown in Figure 1-2. It's highly mountainous. The only places where people can live are the flat spots, which comprise about 20% of the land area. More than 115 million people live there, approximately one-half the population of the United States. They have almost no natural resources. They have to import over 95% of their raw material and more than 99% of their energy. In fact, the only thing they have in abundance is people, which is another of their problems. They have to import some 25% of their food. Every Japanese child learns early in life that, unless they can develop foreign exchange in order to buy food, one-quarter of the population will have to move away or die. That's what you call a survival issue.

Looking at it on a global basis, Japan's disadvantages are considerable. They are remotely located. They have long lines of supply from raw material sources and long distances to their world customers. They have little space to accumulate goods. Yet, despite these drawbacks, they have become formidable world-class competitors.

By comparison, the United States is much larger, and indeed, has much more in the way of natural resources and raw materials. In fact, we've always been called the "land of plenty." We can trace our approach to manufacturing to this environment and the events that transpired just after the Second World War. At that time we had the world's largest undamaged industrial complex and a huge domestic market that was starved for commercial goods. Volume became the byword. Quality was never an issue because for every customer that complained there were a dozen more waiting in line.

Very few of us in the workforce today were around prior to that era. We've been trained to believe that "more is better" when it comes to manufacturing. Mass production has been seen as the way to achieve the competitive edge. But, Japan found out that the opposite could be true, that small could be better, that conservation was the key to productivity and quality, and that *simplicity could actually be beautiful.*

JIT Impact on U.S. Markets

America did, and still does, excel in the development of new

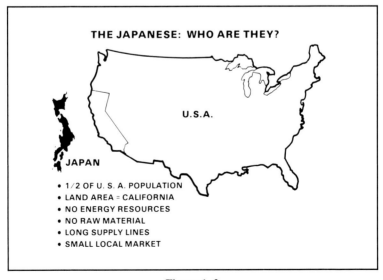

Figure 1-2

technology. So, rather than trying to "reinvent the wheel," Japan imported that technology and concentrated their efforts on production systems. This resulted in a vast array of products in which they became world leaders: products like machine tools, steel, television, video cassette recorders, radios, stereos, cameras, motorcycles, automobiles, semiconductors and even musical instruments, like guitars and pianos. From the smallest microchip to the largest super tanker, Japan has assumed world production leadership in the previously recognized domains of other nations. Remember Swiss watches, German cameras and American electronics?

How did the Japanese get to be so good? Some people say they cheated. That makes good rhetoric for the politicians, but why do you suppose we Americans buy their products? Invariably, it's because they work better and the price is right. From a consumer's viewpoint,there's nothing unfair about a high-quality, low-cost product, and that's what we're dealing with in this global competitive arena. The automotive industry has experienced major impacts from Japanese imports and is struggling to meet this competitive threat. In 1980, Japan succeeded the U.S. as the world leader in car and light truck production. The underlying reasons were better productivity and quality. The sad part is we had all kinds of evidence well before that to spur us into action, but we chose to ignore or disbelieve the information.

Consider quality, for example. Back in the late 1970's, the Hertz

---

CUSTOMER REJECT RATES
Mitsubishi Himeji

- **Starters** . . . . 60 ppm

- **Alternators** . . . . . . 100 ppm

- **Distributors** . . . . . . 50 ppm

TARGET . . . . 40 ppm

Figure 1-3

Corporation conducted a study to determine the number of repairs required for its fleet of vehicles during the first 12,000 miles of operation. The American cars in the fleet required six to eight times as many repairs as did the Japanese-produced Toyotas. Now, it's one thing to worry about a competitor who is percentages better than us, but here we're talking about multiples! That's pretty impressive, but that was a decade ago. What about now? Today, our competition is measuring their defect rates in parts per million, as shown in Figure 1-3. To put that in perspective, 100 parts per million (the highest figure on the chart) is one failure in 10,000 products! And yet, our competitors don't think that's good enough. Following the concept of continuous improvement, they have already set a new target to achieve 40 parts per million. That's what our customers are seeing and expecting from us.

What about productivity? According to the U.S. Bureau of Labor Statistics, North American productivity gains have lagged behind our major European and Asian competitors for the last quarter-century! In fact, as shown in Figure 1-4, France has almost doubled U.S. gains and Japan's figures are close to triple our numbers. As a result, it is becoming increasingly difficult for North American companies to compete on a world-wide basis. In fact, Japanese auto companies make most of their profits in ther U.S. market, thanks to their low production costs and the high prices set by our domestic producers.

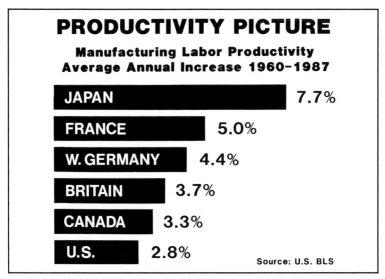

PRODUCTIVITY PICTURE

**Manufacturing Labor Productivity
Average Annual Increase 1960-1987**

JAPAN	7.7%
FRANCE	5.0%
W. GERMANY	4.4%
BRITAIN	3.7%
CANADA	3.3%
U.S.	2.8% Source: U.S. BLS

Figure 1-4

JIT in America

There are those who claim that the Japanese have lower wage rates or unfair tax advantages. Others say that they were able to make Henry Ford's ideas work in their country, but they could never work in America because of "cultural" differences. These are myths and excuses. JUST-IN-TIME works very well in America in Japanese owned and managed companies which are subject to our tax laws, labor rates, and employment culture. One of the first indications that we had of this was at an electronics firm purchased in the late 1970's. A Japanese company bought the U.S. plant, retained the same work force, yet doubled the productivity per person in two years. At the same time they reduced in-house repairs by a factor of 20:1 and the warranty costs went down by at least 8:1 (see Figure 1-5).

Today, there are hundreds of Japanese-owned companies operating in the United States. In the automotive market, as shown in Figure 1-6, Honda is in Marysville, Ohio; Nissan is in Smyrna, Tennessee; Mitsubishi is in Bloomington, Illinois; and Mazda is in Flat Rock, Michigan. Toyota's joint venture with General Motors in Fremont, California (NUMMI) has been so successful, employing American UAW workers, that they have erected a plant in Lexington, Kentucky. Upon completion, the Japanese will have the capacity to build more than two million units a year on our shore. Coupled with the imports, it will add up to 4.5 million vehicles a year, or 45% of our market in a good year.

U. S. PLANT PRODUCTIVITY EXAMPLE

	OWNERSHIP	
	U.S.	JAPAN [1]
Direct Labor Employees	1,000	1,000 [2]
Indirect Employees	600	300
	1,600	1,300
Daily Production	1,000	2,000
Assembly Repairs	130%	6%
Annual Warranty Cost	$16M	$2M

Notes: [1] 2 Years Later   [2] Same People

Figure 1-5

Those are automobiles that American owned companies aren't going to build. They are going to be using a great number of components that American suppliers won't be manufacturing.

This is not to say the American automotive industry has been standing still. They have been learning that JUST-IN-TIME techniques can help them become competitive again, although progress has been slow and uneven, at best. Yet, despite false starts, conflicting signals from the same company at times, and a desperate lack of JIT understanding in many quarters, we are seeing improvements in productivity and quality. In the late 1970's, Japanese auto workers outproduced ours by almost two-to-one. One worker in Japan produced 14.5 cars per year, while in the U.S. and Canada each person made only 8.3 cars. Six years later, we improved to about 12.5 cars per person per year, a tremendous gain. But, we are chasing a moving target because Japan went to almost 15.5 cars per year. However, the message is clear: JUST-IN-TIME, with its emphasis on quality, productivity and continuous improvement, makes it possible to become ever-increasingly competitive, right here in America with American workers. The issue is — can we do it with American management?

JUST-IN-TIME COMPONENTS

In order to utilize JUST-IN-TIME as a strategic competitive weapon,

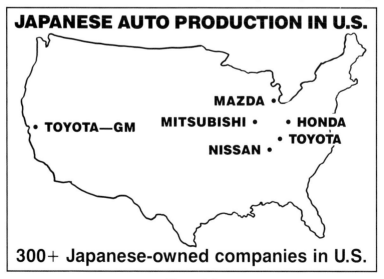

JAPANESE AUTO PRODUCTION IN U.S.

MAZDA •

• TOYOTA—GM   MITSUBISHI •   • HONDA
                                  • TOYOTA
                     NISSAN •

300+ Japanese-owned companies in U.S.

Figure 1-6

management must first **understand** what JIT is and how all the pieces fit together. This structure can then provide the context within which all the "how-to's" will make sense. Otherwise, JIT may appear to be a jumble of loosely related programs. JUST-IN-TIME is not a program, it's *a way of life!*

Simultaneous Quality and Productivity Improvement

When people do consider JUST-IN-TIME as a way to become more competitive, they often ask the question, "Which should I do first— the productivity things or the quality things?" The answer is that you have to do them both. It's much like a coin, say a U.S. quarter. The two faces are inexorably intertwined and cannot be separated. You can't have one without the other. As shown in Figure 1-7, we can equate the head to the JUST-IN-TIME Strategy and the tail to Quality at the Source.

The *JUST-IN-TIME Strategy* includes seven principles which can guide us toward world-class productivity. It requires that we:

1. *Produce to exact demand.*
2. *Eliminate waste.*
3. *Produce one-at-a-time.*
4. *Achieve continuous improvement.*
5. *Respect people.*
6. *Allow for no contingencies.*
7. *Provide long-term emphasis.*

Figure 1-7

These principles are explored in detail in Chapter 2. This may be considered a risky strategy by some when compared to traditional approaches because it is built on the premise that nothing shall go wrong.

That is why **Quality at the Source (Q@S)** is so necessary to make the JIT Strategy feasible. Q@S establishes the framework to make it possible to "do it right the first time and every time."

In Chapter 3, the seven principles of Quality at the Source are defined and explained. They include:

1. *Perfect parts every time.*
2. *Operator responsibility.*
3. *A new customer definition.*
4. *The new Q@S Tool Kit.*
5. *Stop and fix the problem.*
6. *Visibility management.*
7. *Machines always ready.*

JIT Core Elements

If we could peel the faces of the JIT coin apart and expose the inner core, it would reveal the fundamental elements of JUST-IN-TIME, the tactical "nuts and bolts" that make implementation of the JIT Strategy possible. A two-dimensional representation is shown in Figure 1-8. In the center are the intermixed outer surfaces of the coin, the JUST-IN-TIME Strategy and Quality at the Source. Around the outside are the

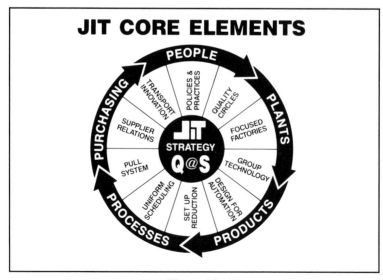

Figure 1-8

five "P's" of production: *People,* the most important part; *Plants and Equipment,* the physical things to support production; *Products,* including the design and producibility needed to sell them for a profit; *Processes* to manufacture and schedule the product; and *Purchasing,* our "outside shop," the link to the rest of our network to complete the cycle. Within these five "P's," each of which blends with the other, there are ten Core Elements of JUST-IN-TIME that can be examined separately, though all of them need to be addressed to become a complete JUST-IN-TIME operation.

The first element covers the ***People Policies and Practices*** required to make JIT work. Chapter 4 explains why people are the only source of the needed quality and productivity improvements. It outlines new management policies that are needed to provide stable work environments and to build employee motivation and trust. New management practices, methods and organizational concepts are also discussed to explain how to make the policies and practices work.

Quality Circles should be the tools for implementation, not necessarily the way you may have heard about them before, or maybe even practiced them. They are proposed in Chapter 5 as the ideal mechanism to introduce, on an experimental basis, the new JIT policies and practices and to provide a forum for learning the new management style. Also covered are some insights as to why Quality Circles are probably misnamed and why they have often failed to meet expectations in the past.

On the hardware side, the ***Focused Factory*** (Chapter 6) addresses the physical arrangement of plants to most effectively concentrate the minimum amount of resources needed to do a world-class job of manufacturing. It is a radical departure from the decentralization and functional specializations commonly practiced today.

Group Technology zeroes in on the manufacturing areas. Chapter 7 describes the configuration of individual pieces of equipment to change the production of both final assembly and component parts from a focus on operations to a focus on integrated processes, even in a low-volume shop.

Design for Automation (Chapter 8) reveals the four progressive steps of automation and the proper role of robotics in that scenario. It emphasizes process simplification and the understanding that is necessary to design products on a timely basis that are competitively producible, while providing a smooth transition to Computer Integrated Manufacturing (CIM) and the factory of the future.

Chapter 9 covers ***Setup Reduction,*** the JIT starting point. It explains why Setup Reduction is the key to small-lot production, and why it is the easiest and fastest element to implement. A three-step process, by which any setup can be reduced by 90% or more, is described, using some detailed examples.

When lot size is no longer an issue, *Uniform Scheduling* can be employed. Chapter 10 covers a new planning method for resource allocation, based on smooth, homogenized production flow and fast communication of support requirements. The relationship between JUST-IN-TIME and Manufacturing Resource Planning (MRP) is explored, including a way to really make MRP pay off.

Execution of the plan in JIT is accomplished through a separate system. Chapter 11 describes the *Pull System,* which is driven by actual consumption and uses synchronized replenishment signals (some people call them KANBAN) to provide real production control. This system can better coordinate the activities of both the inside shop and outside supply points, while substantially reducing indirect costs.

In Chapter 12 we cover *JIT Supplier Relations.* The new role for suppliers in the world of JUST-IN-TIME delivery is described, as are the new relationships that will exist between customers and suppliers. New customer responsibilities, which are necessary to make JUST-IN-TIME supply work, are also reviewed.

The execution portion of JUST-IN-TIME supply is transportation. Chapter 13 addresses *Transport Innovation* — creative approaches to provide more frequent deliveries to JUST-IN-TIME customers at less total cost. This includes more effective containerization and material handling strategies to make it possible. Interim approaches to overcome the distance problem, should you happen to be located a long way from your key suppliers or customers, are also covered.

The relationships between the Core Elements are shown on the JUST-IN-TIME anchor chart. It gives us the needed perspective for this multi-faceted production strategy. But, knowing about them won't do a bit of good unless you implement them. That is what JUST-IN-TIME for America is all about.

Accordingly, Chapter 14 addresses *JIT Implementation.* It describes some alternate implementation sequences, including one for the bold and another for the timid. A ten-step game plan for pilot project implementation is presented to give you a clear framework for your action plan.

JIT implementation will have a profound impact on our historical measurement system, which can make things appear to be getting worse when they're really getting better. Chapter 15 discusses the problems with traditional cost accounting approaches and offers some alternate *JIT Measurements,* which not only give us a truer short term picture of what is happening and more accurate product costs, but also motivate us to do the "right" things.

JIT Links to Other Strategies

Where does JIT fit in the management process? Let's take a look at the Management Process Pyramid in Figure 1-9. The capstone is Business Requirements Planning (BRP). This is the strategic planning process we use to set the company objectives for growth, profitability and return on investment, and to quantify them. Next, specific strategies must be selected to achieve those objectives. A popular strategy today is Manufacturing Resource Planning (MRP). It is a good system, but it doesn't always meet our expectations. Why? Because it accepts our present manufacturing processes as if they were right, but are they? How many outdated practices are we accepting as gospel in our plants? JUST-IN-TIME attacks those givens and emphasizes process improvement. We simplify the operations by eliminating all non-value added activities and stressing quality improvement. This makes MRP easier, and really makes it pay off. JUST-IN-TIME also results in a better understanding of our manufacturing processes, which gives us a bridge to Computer Integrated Manufacturing (CIM). Only when we really know what we are doing does it make any sense to invest the huge sums

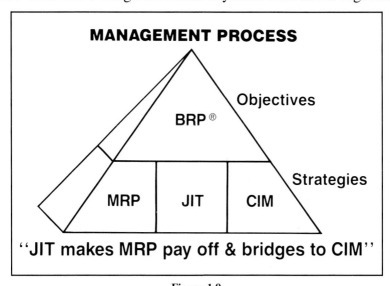

MANAGEMENT PROCESS

BRP ®

Objectives

MRP | JIT | CIM

Strategies

"JIT makes MRP pay off & bridges to CIM"

Figure 1-9

of capital required for the factory of the future. That's why JUST-IN-TIME is the centerstone of the Management Process Pyramid and will be with us for years to come.

JIT BENEFITS

If we do all of the things JIT requires, what's in it for us? What are the benefits, in quantifiable terms, that we can expect? Let's start with the two surfaces of the JIT coin, quality and productivity. If you cannot improve your quality by a factor of ten, you're not even beginning to do the job that is possible by using JUST-IN-TIME. You should improve your productivity by at least 10% per year, and most people do far better than that, especially at the beginning. JUST-IN-TIME results in leadtime reductions of 50% or more, substantially improving customer service. JUST-IN-TIME gives us better utilization of our plants. You can get up to one-third more output from your present facility without adding a single brick. Standardization will improve as more human resources are directed towards process simplification. Transportation costs and performance are enhanced, as is the total flexibility of the shop, to meet customer demands.

These improvements are accompanied by many reductions. The most obvious is reduced inventory. Here, we are talking about huge numbers — 90% of work-in-process and 50-60% overall. Lot sizes and leadtimes will decrease in direct proportion to the inventory reduction. Unit costs go down as well, which increases profits. In the design area, both the design time and the amount of time it takes to implement an engineering change will be reduced, thanks to shorter leadtimes, simpler processes and less inventory to rework. Space and energy reductions also occur because of the emphasis on better utilization of existing facilities.

These benefits, summarized in Figure 1-10, are being realized today as JUST-IN-TIME comes back to America. In addition to the many Japanese-owned companies in the USA, American-owned and operated companies are beginning to adopt the JIT strategy. AT&T, IBM, General Motors, Ford, Chrysler, General Electric, Harley-Davidson, Westinghouse and Xerox are among them.

Both large and small companies are beginning to experience eye-opening improvements. Productivity gains of 40%, scrap reductions of 60%, inventory reductions of 90% and 10 times quality improvements have been reported. How is this possible if JUST-IN-TIME is culturally dependent? The answer, of course, is that there is no such dependency.

Remember, JIT started in America. All the Japanese did is demonstrate that it still works today in our complex, technological world like it worked 60 years ago in Henry Ford's era. We can give the customer any color desired, not just black!

IMPLEMENTING JIT

Successful implementation of JUST-IN-TIME requires substantial change from most of today's accepted practices. Although most of the changes are good "common sense" moves, the biggest obstacles are our traditional management beliefs, organization concepts and protection of the status quo. In the words of Walt Kelly's Pogo the Possum, "We have met the enemy and he is us." Why? Because change is uncomfortable, to some it's even painful. But change is necessary if you expect to establish a new standard of excellence for your company to assure world-class competitiveness. Paul Fortino, Dean of Dana University, hit the nail on the head when he said, "If you always do what you always did, you'll always get what you always got!"

You can't make JIT happen at your facility if you study it to death! After the initial awakening (finding out it exists), and an intensive period of initial education to develop an awareness of JIT principles, you have to do it in order to acquire the knowledge that only experience can give you. It doesn't have to be perfect the first time, just better than it was.

MAJOR BENEFITS OF JIT

IMPROVED	REDUCED
• Quality	• Inventory
• Productivity	• Lot Sizes
• Service	• Leadtimes
• Capacity	• Unit Costs
• Standardization	• Design Time
• Transport Systems	• Space
• Flexibility	• Energy

Figure 1-10

Ongoing education at all levels will help keep the ball rolling. Remember the basic tenet of JUST-IN-TIME: *continuous improvement of quality and productivity.*

The payback can begin in months, sometimes even weeks. The savings can then finance further improvements, which is why JIT is a "pay as you go" strategy.

Finally, it must be emphasized that *people* are the source of quality and productivity. *People* will come up with the answers. *People* will give you a gold mine of innovation, provided you make a serious effort to respect them and earn their trust. That's the secret of JUST-IN-TIME.

These things are possible because JUST-IN-TIME is the best production strategy to meet today's challenge of competitive survival. The first company that fully implements JIT can become Number One in its industry in the world. The last company to think about it won't have to worry! Now is the time for your company to proceed.

THE JUST-IN-TIME STRATEGY

CHAPTER 2

*"JUST-IN-TIME is a production strategy
with a new set of values
to continuously improve
quality and productivity."*

In the Management Overview, you were presented with a challenge to establish your company as the Number One competitor in your industry by becoming the highest quality, lowest cost producer in the world. It is the only way to insure long-term survival in today's economy. In order to meet that challenge, there must be a game plan and the JUST-IN-TIME Strategy provides the foundation for that game plan. Consider again the coin analogy from the Management Overview (Figure 2-1). The JUST-IN-TIME Strategy is the top surface of the coin. It consists of seven key principles which will be explored during this Chapter. They are:

1. Produce to exact customer demand
2. Eliminate waste
3. Produce one-at-a-time
4. Continuous improvement
5. Respect people
6. No contingencies
7. Long-term emphasis

The JUST-IN-TIME definition, ". . .a production strategy with a new set of values to continuously improve quality and productivity," may seem contradictory to some. Yet, it will be shown that we can achieve quality and productivity improvements *simultaneously.* We are no longer going to consider these as trade-off objectives. First, however, we must adopt new values, many of which are directly opposite the way we have managed our businesses in the past.

The old values may have been quite adequate to meet yesterday's standards. Today, however, these standards are changing and we must adapt to them if we intend to be competitive. That means re-examining previously accepted "givens" for the business. "We've always done it this way," or "That is the way it's done in this business" are unacceptable conditions when we're looking for continuous improvement. Tradition is comforting, but it's also inflexible and sometimes unfathomable.

The JIT world emphasizes simplicity and flexibility as the ultimate weapons in the manufacturing arsenal. It is the ticket to improved customer satisfaction and increased market share. As shown in Figure 2-2, we intend to forge a physical linkage between every activity in the production process, from the customer through the plant to the outside suppliers, to make the entire network simple, flexible and responsive. This is the essence of the JUST-IN-TIME Strategy and the seven principles that make it possible. It starts with a new manufacturing attitude toward the customer, without whom we would not be in business.

JIT 1: PRODUCE TO EXACT CUSTOMER DEMAND

Today's customers are demanding faster deliveries, better quality, lower prices and better service than ever before, especially as those things become available from the competition. Our choices are to change the customer (not likely) or change ourselves (difficult, but "do-able"). So, no matter what flavor of our product the customer wants, we will learn to produce it as required with near zero leadtime. Instead of wishing the customer would order what we can comfortably build, we will revise our processes so that we can respond to the customer's needs. That is a new value.

Historically, manufacturing people have felt themselves to be "slaves

Figure 2-1

of the system" because of unreliable sales forecasts. Despite today's sophisticated forecasting mechanisms, there is still a lot of "windage factor" involved, primarily because even the customer doesn't usually know for sure what is needed until the eleventh hour. As one wag put it, "Forecasting is a sporting term. It's origins are golf, where *fore* means *look out,* and fishing, where *cast* means *throw out!"* Rather than wishing for the impossible, the principle of "Produce to Exact Customer Demand" reverses conventional wisdom and resolves to contend with the real world. Instead of trying to make long runs at fixed rates for long periods of time, we are going to organize our shop to place a premium on flexibility, short runs and minimum notice time from the customer. Ideally, every process would be physically linked.

An Example of Producing to Exact Customer Demand

Imagine, for a moment, a room full of people seated at tables, each close enough to touch the person on the right or the left. Suppose the group is making a product and that the process we have developed is so good that everyone's work cycle is exactly 30 seconds long. Each person has only one piece to work on at any given stage of production. Everyone is idle because there is no customer yet. When a customer does arrive, we hit a gong to signal everyone to begin one work cycle after which the completed piece will be moved forward. The response time to the customer is 30 seconds because the whole process indexes

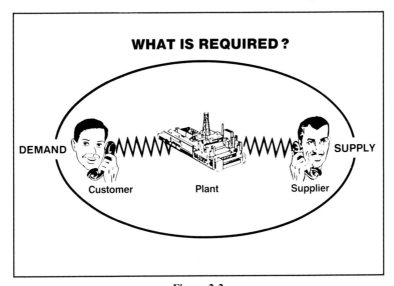

Figure 2-2

forward in that period of time. No more work will be done until another customer arrives. Then the process will be repeated. This example depicts the responsiveness, flexibility, reaction to short leadtime and the physical linkage we need to achieve the ideal balance and synchronization.

Of course, the example is oversimplified. Every operation in the real world cannot be physically linked, especially when we start with raw material from outside suppliers. We have to consider product options as well. On the other hand, does that mean it can't be done? Absolutely not. Techniques can be developed to compensate for breaks in the direct linkage and to handle product variety. Consider again Henry Ford's accomplishments. We remember him for the assembly line, but what most of us forgot is that his process started with raw iron ore and integrated every single process, including component manufacturing, right through to the customer delivery, as shown in Figure 2-3.

JIT 2: ELIMINATE WASTE

Production to exact customer demand sets the stage for what may be the most important principle in the JUST-IN-TIME Strategy, which is to totally eliminate waste. Under JUST-IN-TIME, waste is anything more than the minimum amount of plant, equipment, materials and workers which are absolutely essential to production.

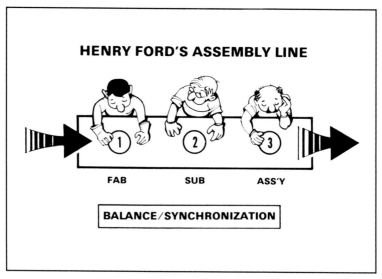

Figure 2-3

Causes of Waste

There are many causes of waste, such as *imbalances* between workers and processes. Industrial engineers spend a lifetime trying to balance our shops. For them, it is almost like seeking the Holy Grail. Every time they almost make it, somebody changes the schedule and sends them back to the drawing board. Yet, these imbalances create excesses or shortages, which are wastes.

Everyone recognizes *production problems* as a waste. They can prevent us from meeting schedules by causing work stoppages and result in idle workers. Nobody wants to see idle workers; that's a waste for sure. But, what about *surplus workers?* How many of us have extra people on the payroll in anticipation of Monday or Friday absenteeism? How many of us have a couple of extra people just in case there may be a budget cut? Those surplus workers are a waste. They are a cost that doesn't add value to the process.

Excess equipment capacity is another waste. Most plants have more capacity than needed, even though it may not look that way at first glance. Many plants are "capacitized," not for today's needs but rather, for tomorrow's hopes. That extra capacity is a waste from a cost standpoint. But, we also do it from a capability standpoint. How many times do we buy a machine intended for a specific application, only to load it with extras, just in case we might need them some day for another undefined application? That's a waste, and it introduces variability as well. The simpler version has fewer things to go wrong or go out of tolerance.

Insufficient preventive maintenance is another waste. We have extra machines on hand because we expect them to break down. Then, we fail to properly maintain them and, sure enough, they do break down. It becomes a self-fulfilling prophecy. Excess equipment is an excess investment that we should not need, provided we could keep the minimum number of machines running properly. In fact we can, as shall be discussed in Chapter 3.

Defects and rework are wastes we all recognize but don't do enough about. They consume resources but don't add value to our production system. When we *employ people in areas where machines are better,* it's a waste, not just from an efficiency standpoint, but because we are not making the proper use of people's real talent, their brain power. Machines should do the dull, routine jobs, not people. Conversely, *using a machine where a person is better* is also a waste. We spend untold sums of money trying to create complex machinery that can't begin to duplicate a human being. So why do it? Let people think and the machines grunt!

Of all the wastes we might observe in manufacturing, the **greatest waste of all is overproduction**. In all of my years in manufacturing, no one ever faulted me for overproducing. Being short or behind schedule got me in trouble, but if I was ahead of schedule or produced a few extra units, I actually received "positive strokes." Now, after all these years, I've learned that overproduction is a great waste. Why? Because it is a total misallocation of resources. In the JUST-IN-TIME shop, since we don't have any extra anything, it means we would consume resources that should be applied somewhere else. This would cause a double problem: *too much* of something we don't need and *too little* of something we want!

These wastes must be eliminated from our shop if we are ever going to produce to exact customer demand. Then, we can progress to the ultimate principle in the JUST-IN-TIME Strategy, which is to produce one-at-a-time.

JIT 3: PRODUCE ONE-AT-A-TIME

In final assembly we have always produced one-at-a-time, but not so in manufacturing. With JIT, we will produce one-at-a-time everywhere in the shop. We are going to create a real world plant that can function like the simplified example introduced under JIT Principle #1. In our plant, we will always strive to meet two basic JIT production objectives:
  1. Produce only the necessary units in the necessary
     quantities at the necessary time.
  2. Eliminate unnecessary inventory.

Anything more than Item 1 is a waste. Item 2 is a special waste because in JUST-IN-TIME, the value of inventory is disavowed. To understand why, we need to examine why we have inventory in the first place.

Inventory and Leadtime

Consider your own manufacturing process. It takes time to do all of the tasks that have to be accomplished to produce and ship your products. It takes time to purchase material and accumulate it. It takes time to manufacture component parts. It takes time to assemble and test the final product. It even takes time to pack it and ship it out the door. The summation of all these times is your cumulative leadtime. In most companies, that amount of time is much longer than the customer is willing to wait for your product. So, what do you do? You compensate for some of that leadtime with different kinds of inventory, as shown in Figure 2-4.

In a *make-to-stock* business, the inventory is almost all finished goods, in order to ship off the shelf. In an *assemble-to-order* business, some partially assembled units are put on the shelf and then final configured to the customer order. This takes less inventory, but final assembly is limited by capacity. In a *make-to-order* business, there is still some inventory, mostly raw material, and capacity is the key issue. Each of these production approaches makes use of some inventory to shorten delivery leadtime, trading that off against capacity.

But, where is it written that the cumulative leadtime has to be that long? Why presume that leadtimes are fixed? In JUST-IN-TIME we attack the givens. For example, there is a fallacy in the premise that inventory shortens leadtimes. It certainly does when it is available to use in finished form, either as a part or as an assembly. But work-in-process inventory actually lengthens leadtime because it forms queues in front of operations, just like lines at the store. By shortening the lines, we can get checked out faster. By eliminating inventory, we can reduce the cumulative leadtime until it begins to approach the delivery time the customer will accept. To get there, we have to squeeze out all of the unneeded inventory, because it is a waste. In addition, when we

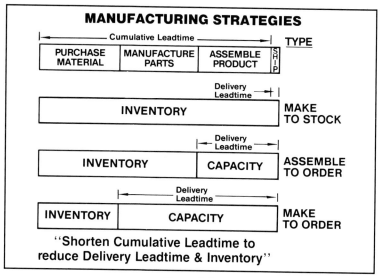

Figure 2-4

lower the inventory, it leads us to higher productivity because of improved visibility on the shop floor.

Benefits of Reduced Leadtime

When inventory reduction results in shorter leadtimes, it makes us more responsive to our customers. With shorter through-put time in the shop, we can react faster to changes, especially engineering change orders (ECO's). How many of us, when faced with an ECO think to ourselves, "Oh, my gosh, there's three months worth of material out on the floor that we are either going to have to "work off", rework or scrap in order to adopt this change." Yet, the ECO should be viewed as an opportunity for improvement. Without excess inventory, it will! Best of all, when we lower the inventory we can uncover problems. When we solve those problems, we improve the process.

Think of the material flowing through your shop as if it were a river, and think of yourself in a boat on top of that river, riding the current and hoping to move as quickly as possible, because your *travel time represents your through-put leadtime.* Below the surface of that river are rocks, as shown in Figure 2-5. Those rocks represent the problems you have in your shop. If there is sufficient water in the river, you won't see those rocks, those problems. But, they are causing you difficulties, whether you realize it or not, because they create eddies and still, stagnant pools that slow down the flow of the river.

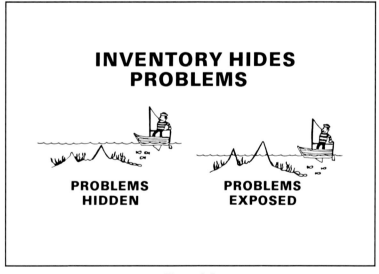

Figure 2-5

To speed up the flow, you must purposefully lower the water level in a controlled manner until you expose the first rock, which is the first and biggest problem. Next, you want to solve that problem, blow up the rock and get it out of the river. Now, you can flow down the river with less water (lower inventory), your speed will be faster because that rock (problem) has been eliminated, and the process will have been improved. Then, you will lower the water level a second time and expose the next biggest rock (problem). You are going to fix that one, too, and continue to do this until you have the water level so low, it barely clears the keel of the boat. You will then have maximum speed, which will *minimize the leadtime or through-put time in the shop.*

This procedure will only work if you are prepared to allocate the necessary resources to solve the problem once it has been identified. Otherwise, you'll feel terribly frustrated. Similarly, don't try to expose all the rocks (problems) at once. It is too big a task and the resulting stoppages could put you out of business. Gradualism is the secret. The reason, then, that the JUST-IN-TIME Strategy tells us to lower our inventory is to get it out of the way, so we can gradually improve the process until we get it "near perfect."

JIT 4: CONTINUOUS IMPROVEMENT

Incremental, continuous improvement is a vital JIT principle because it counters two typical tendencies found in our traditional practices:
1. Looking for the "magic formula" to make a big score.
2. Wanting to be finished with a "program."

Most of us in the U.S. are enamored with the home run. The home run hitters in baseball get the big paychecks. Yet, you win ball games with lots of singles. Check the statistics. For JUST-IN-TIME, we need lots of singles hitters so we can make continuous improvement every day, not just make one big score and then rest on our laurels. Each day needs to be better than the prior day, and it should continue to get better until we reach perfection. Continuous improvement is not a program in the traditional sense. It is a never-ending process because, until we reach the ideal of perfection, we are not yet good enough.

Continuous Improvement at Work

A small company in southern Michigan uses the principle of continuous improvement to improve productivity very effectively. They select parts from 128 varieties and repackage them, in a specified sequence, for delivery to their customer. They got the job based on a target pick rate of 100 units per hour, which was substantially better than their predecessor had done. Everyone in the company knew that the rate had to be met to break even and exceeded to make money. A visual display board was hung on the wall to show the target and each day's actual performance. Many improvement suggestions were made by the employees to increase the pick rate, while maintaining 100% sequence accuracy. Within two months, the target was achieved, so a new goal of 138 per hour was set. That, too, was accomplished and a further objective of 160 per established. It will never end.

Overcoming Postponed Perfection

Continuous improvement also beats "postponed perfection," which is another traditional tendency in many shops. As shown in Figure 2-6, rather than waiting until everything is perfect before taking the first step, we want to start now and make incremental improvement steps. If you had to drive from your home to work, but insisted upon waiting until you knew every single traffic light was going to be green before leaving, you'd never leave! This may sound silly but apply it to your work environment. How many times have you seen wonderful new ideas die on the vine because people were unwilling to consider them until every single possibility was accounted for with certainty? Postponed perfection

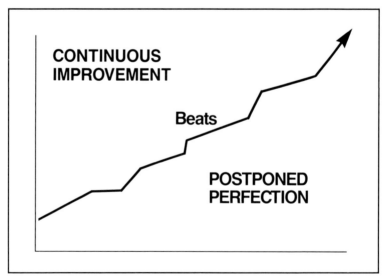

CONTINUOUS
IMPROVEMENT

Beats

POSTPONED
PERFECTION

Figure 2-6

is just a ploy used by some to avoid trying something new. Starting now and getting better every day is the key to continuous improvement.

JIT 5: RESPECT PEOPLE

The source of the continuous improvements we seek is our people. There is a gold mine of innovation available if we learn how to uncover it. The key is respect. An American graduate school offers a course in "Managing Research and Development," which describes how scientific and technical people must be treated with respect because they are contributing their brain power. In JUST-IN-TIME, everyone utilizes their brain power, not just an elite group.

While all people are important, *the most undeveloped source of improvement potential is the shop floor,* where 80% of our personnel spend 99% of their time. Since JIT is a production strategy requiring a rethinking of traditional processes and practices, these are the people who will be a major source of the quality and productivity improvement ideas we seek.

Resource Distribution Study

As shown in Figure 2-7, a study at one company showed that top management people represent only about 2% or so of the total personnel and spend no more than about 1% of their time on the shop floor.

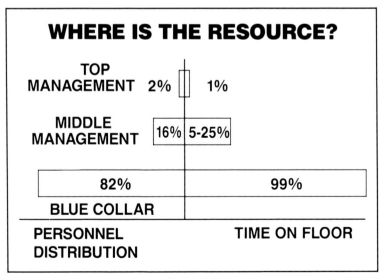

Figure 2-7

Can we get enough ideas for continuous improvement from them? Not likely. Middle management and technical people comprise 15-16% of the personnel but only spend between 5% and 25% of their time on the shop floor. Can we hold them responsible for all of the improvement ideas we need in JUST-IN-TIME? There's not enough resource there, even though that has been the source of most of our improvement ideas in the past. But, the blue collar workers represent 82% of the population and are on the shop floor 99% of the time. There's the untapped resource. And that's the reason why we have to respect everybody, not just certain classes of people.

Accounting for the People Resource

Most of us intuitively recognize that people are a valuable asset. We often say they are the most important asset, but our scorekeeping system belies that statement. Where do you find people on the Balance Sheet? You don't. You will find them indirectly on the Profit and Loss Statement as an expense! We report inventory as an asset, but we've already established that inventory is a liability. We report plants and equipment as assets, but plant and equipment depreciate over time. Only people can appreciate in value, but for that to happen, new values will be needed to nurture and harvest this resource. People must be given the respect, stable environment and motivation to contribute their ideas to the organization. This will be explored at length in Chapter 4.

JIT 6: NO CONTINGENCIES

The JUST-IN-TIME Strategy calls for a production organization that is so finely tuned there is no margin for error. As shown in Figure 2-8, the tolerance objective is plus or minus **ZERO,** which flies in the face of all our practical experience. While most of us will agree that we should eliminate waste, many of us still feel the need for a little "insurance" to provide for the unexpected. This is the basis for our traditional "Just-In-Case" practices. We have extra inventory Just-In-Case something doesn't arrive on time. We have extra capacity, Just-In-Case a machine breaks down. We have extra people, Just-In-Case somebody doesn't show up for work. All of these are wastes. The trouble with insurance is that we are constantly paying premiums to cover events we hope will never happen. These premiums represent a substantial cost which makes us less competitive and could drive us out of business.

There was a time when every mother wanted her child to grow up and become a doctor, for status and financial security. Today many doctors are "taking down their shingle" because they cannot afford the malpractice insurance. Neither can we. *Contingency planning,* whereby we know exactly what to do if a disaster occurs, is a prudent management tool. *Contingency investment* is a waste that world-class manufacturers cannot afford to spend.

The Value of Good Stress

If we don't provide for contingencies, doesn't that put too much stress on the organization? Everybody knows stress is "bad," especially when it involves impossible goals and unacceptable alternatives (like getting "fired"). Actually, there is good stress as well as bad stress. We want good stress to help us do our best. If the boss asks you to do something "when you get a chance," how often do you never get the chance? But, given a deadline, isn't it amazing how, even though you are a little uncomfortable, you always seem to get the job done? Without a little discomfort, we are never going to learn or improve.

Consider, for a moment, a simple rubber band. It has no value when laying loosely in a box. But, if you stretch the rubber band and place it around some straws or a deck of cards, it is doing useful work. This is what is meant by good stress, producing just enough discomfort to overcome the inertia of the status quo, so we can move ahead.

Notice that the stress in the rubber band example was uniform. We

JUST-IN-TIME PRODUCTION

OBJECTIVE

± Zero

**PERFORMANCE
TO
SCHEDULE**

Figure 2-8

We don't want to put unequal stress on the system, because it creates weak links in the chain. Stress needs to be smooth and uniform all over. That's why this JUST-IN-TIME principle tells us to *"draw out our capabilities to the very limit by placing all people, equipment and material in a state of uniform stress."* This is another new value. Even though many of us often look to the sky, asking for "just one easy day," we shouldn't really want that comfort because it won't help us improve. The principle that prods us toward continuous improvement is to provide for no contingencies.

JIT 7: LONG-TERM EMPHASIS

Think about the six principles we have just established. We are going to produce to exact customer demand and totally eliminate all of the waste in our system. We are going to learn to produce one piece at a time with near zero leadtime, so we can respond to whatever flavor the customer wants, and we'll get from here to there through continuous improvement, starting now. We are going to learn how to make those continuous improvements by respecting all of the people and we are going to provide for no contingencies in the system; so if one thing does go wrong, everything will stop. If you are willing to accept these principles, can you expect to implement them overnight? There isn't any possibility of that, which is why the final principle of the JUST-IN-TIME Strategy is that we have to go about it with a long-term emphasis.

Traditionally, most of our measurements have concentrated on short-term objectives. Daily, weekly or monthly production targets to get parts out the door and capital equipment justifications requiring paybacks in six months or a year are typical. We measure things like labor efficiency and machine utilization, which often drive us to suboptimal decisions because we are trying to make the numbers look good for the short-term. What we have to remember about JUST-IN-TIME is that we cannot settle for instant gratification. We cannot mortgage the future just to make today look good. This is going to require a major change in our thinking.

I said at the beginning that JUST-IN-TIME is a strategy, and strategies take time to implement. They are long-range game plans, not short-term tactics. The horizon must change from today, this week, this month or this year to decades and beyond. In fact, the JIT Strategy calls for us to *survive as a company forever.* We need to establish new standards of excellence and must have the time to achieve them. For many, that may be the most difficult new value of all.

SUMMARY

The JUST-IN-TIME Strategy encompasses seven basic principles to improve productivity and facilitate better quality. The principles, summarized in Figure 2-9, comprise one surface of the JIT coin introduced in Chapter 1. They represent some new values when compared with traditional practices, but they are working in many companies today.

The JIT principles will promote a flexible manufacturing organization which can *produce to exact customer demand* and totally *eliminate all waste in the system.* The ultimate goal will be to learn to *produce one-at-a-time* with near zero leadtime, so you can respond to whatever flavor the customer wants. The pathway to get there is through *continuous improvement* and the source of those improvements can be cultivated by practicing *respect for people.* To match world-class productivity levels, your strategy will *provide for no contingencies,* so if something does go wrong, everything will stop. Since it will take time to incorporate these new values into your company culture, JIT will have to be implemented with a *long-term emphasis.* It is not a "magic pill." Finally, the principles are interdependent, so all seven must be embraced to make the strategy an effective game plan for your company.

Figure 2-9

The basic goal will always be to improve quality and productivity simultaneously through the total elimination of waste. You will get some nice bonuses, like capital conservation, because now you will be able to make more with less. Significant inventory reduction will occur, even though that is not the driving force, and you can use that money to fund additional improvement. That's why JUST-IN-TIME is a "pay as you go" strategy. You don't have to ask for millions of up-front dollars to implement JIT or wait for years to see any results. Remember, though, that the JIT Strategy does introduce a very important caveat. It says that there will be no margin for error, so it must be done right the first time and every time. This concept is called *Quality at the Source,* the other side of the JIT coin. Without Quality at the Source, you cannot implement the JUST-IN-TIME Strategy.

QUALITY AT THE SOURCE

CHAPTER 3

*"Quality at the Source (Q@S) is meeting
customer expectations by the value adder
doing it right the first time and every time"*

When we follow the JIT Strategy described in Chapter 2, we can achieve more rational, predictable processes which have been simplified, resulting in higher-quality, lower-cost products. The challenge is that the JIT Strategy provides for no contingencies. They are considered to be a waste. Instead, JIT establishes a system that is totally dependent upon linked operations performing as planned and for which there are no "just-in-case" provisions.

Thus, it is vital that we produce a quality part every time. This concept is called Quality at the Source. It requires that the value adder have total quality responsibility and be given the needed tools and management backing to "make it happen."

Many people call this concept TQC or Total Quality Control, but TQC does not fully define the ultimate objective. TQC suggests that we have some sort of overview program or system that makes quality possible. Quality at the Source, on the other hand, is a grass-roots approach. The whole idea is that there is only one person who can assure that good work is being done consistently, and that is *the person who is adding value.* Anything less is inadequate. Quality at the Source is the flip side of the JUST-IN-TIME coin, as shown in Figure 3-1. And, like a coin, you can't have one side without the other. The benefits of JUST-IN-TIME will only be realized when the seven principles of the JIT Strategy are combined with the seven principles of Quality at the Source.

Q@S 1: PERFECT PARTS EVERY TIME

The first principle of Q@S is to make perfect parts every time. Years of experience may tell you that making perfect parts every time is impossible. Most of us have never seen an operation where all of the parts come out exactly the way they are supposed to. At the very least, we expect to scrap some parts until the process is properly adjusted. In JUST-IN-TIME, we want every piece to be good, including the first piece, because when we get to one-at-a-time it's the only piece we're going to make!

Some might say there is no such thing as a perfect part. This may be true of our past manufacturing processes, but perfection is not impossible. In fact, we often expect it in our daily lives. Suppose you were visiting your newborn child in the hospital and the nurse dropped it on the floor! Would you take any comfort in the knowledge that this only happened one time out of 10,000? I doubt it. Why, then, can we not begin to think like a customer and transfer this same standard to the shop floor? Every manufacturing process is a combination of variables which can be controlled to assure the desired output. Of course, we have to learn what those variables are. Too many of us, however, take refuge in the belief that we are dealing with an *art* instead of a science. This may be convenient to explain today's reject rates, but it has no basis in fact. When we identify the critical variables, establish standards for them, and install the right process controls to manage them, we can begin to produce "perfect" parts every time.

Do we really mean perfect parts or just good enough? After all, should we invest time and money to make the parts better than the specifications? The answers to these questions require a new viewpoint, like most of JUST-IN-TIME. The principle of Perfect Parts Every Time has two important corollaries. First, *total perfection must be the goal.* The fact that we can't achieve it now does not make it impossible. But,

Figure 3-1

by consistently striving to achieve that goal, we can make quantum leaps in our present quality levels. Many of those who have taken this approach are now measuring reject rates in *parts per million.*

We have a client here in the U.S. who was doing an analysis of one competitor's products and was amazed to learn they were so good they were beyond the precision capabilities of the measuring devices. In fact, the inspector thought his gauges were broken and sent for a repairman. That's how good it can be. We don't really have much of a choice because our competition is doing it today. The quality demands of the marketplace are changing as new performance levels are experienced, and yesterday's standards simply no longer apply. In JUST-IN-TIME, then, "perfection" means as good as it can be. When coupled with continuous improvement, "perfection" is a practical, achievable, moving target.

The second corollary of Q@S Principle #1 is that *quality improvements need not be more expensive.* We don't intend to expend vast sums of money to make incremental process improvements that can't be recovered. That approach could put us out of business. However, by shifting our emphasis from catching defects to preventing them from happening in the first place, we can steadily improve our product quality while simultaneously reducing the total cost of manufacuring. This is done by eliminating the waste of non-value added functions, which are used for detection while building up the capabilities of the value adder, the operator.

Q@S 2: OPERATOR RESPONSIBILITY

Quality at the Source can only be achieved when the operator has total quality responsibility. Is that shocking? If you believe that operators are not smart enough, or that they will goof off every chance they get, or that they don't want to know or care enough about their jobs to take on this responsibility, then you will have a big problem with Q@S. On the other hand, if you can accept three major attitude adjustments, we can build on the premise that the operator can accept this responsibility.

The first of these is the belief that *defects and machine breakdowns can be prevented* from happening. They are not ordained from on high as some seem to think. How else could Murphy's Law have been invented? You remember that one, don't you? It says, "If anything can go wrong, it will. . .and at the worst possible time." It is defeatism at its worst and a "cop out" at its best. The trouble with Murphy's Law is that it becomes a self-fulfilling prophecy because it encourages us to give up and succumb to the status quo. This is another "given" that must be attacked and, as shown in Figure 3-2, Murphy's Law must be evicted from our plants to establish the foundation for Q@S Principle #1.

Next we have to believe that our operators are capable of accepting and implementing the quality responsibility. Here, again, many will decry the poor education levels of their employees. Statements like, "In our part of the country, most people don't get past the third grade," are common. But, we're not talking about education here, we're addressing intellect. The fundamental intelligence is there. It's our responsibility to provide the necessary education and training to teach the operators the things they need to know (and aren't taught in most schools anyway). They can absorb and apply that information to a new role in JIT, the **source of quality.**

Third, our *workers can be trusted.* They are not trying to sabotage the operation to make life difficult for others or to avoid doing their job. In fact, it's a basic human trait to want to do a good job, provided there aren't an abundance of negative motivators around. Trust is nurtured in a positive environment, and that's our job.

Problems With Inspection

Today, the presumption is that the operator *won't* make good parts, and therefore we have to sort the good from the bad in order to prevent

QUALITY @ SOURCE ATTITUDE

DEFECTS AND BREAKDOWNS
CAN BE **PREVENTED**

Figure 3-2

shipping bad parts to our customers. Unfortunately, inspection *happens after the fact* and the damage has already been done. Even the best inspector will only find about 80% of all the defects that he or she visually inspects. This means if you do double inspection, *some bad parts will still reach the customer.*

Inspection introduces an adversarial, Big Brother kind of situation to our shop. On the one hand, we tell the operator to make lots of parts and make them fast. On the other hand, we tell the inspector to screen those parts to make sure no bad ones are shipped out the back door, a task we already know is impossible. If the inspector rejects a lot of parts, it reflects badly on the operator, which invites a visit from supervision. If the operator makes a lot of bad parts, some reach the customer and the inspector gets blamed. This is an *adversarial environment created by management.* I've never seen operators and inspectors having coffee or lunch together. In JUST-IN-TIME, we want to create a team relationship, with everyone pulling in the same direction.

Inspection also *lets the operator abdicate quality responsibility.* Let me explain that with a story. My mom is probably the best back seat driver in the world. When I drive her somewhere, she tells me where to turn (never the final destination), when to start, look out for this, look out for that, and when to stop! As a result, I sit behind the wheel, oblivious to what is going on around me, because I know she is going to cover for me. Yet, when I drive alone, I have to become a much better driver. I have to watch the road, the traffic, the signals, and know the directions to my destination because I am responsible, and I can't rely on anybody else. I'm the same person in the same car who has somehow become a more responsible operator. That's the condition we need for Q@S.

Inspection is reactive. Since it happens after the fact, the damage has already been done and all we can do is try to put out the fire. JUST-IN-TIME calls for a pro-active process that fosters continuous improvement. To correct and improve a process, we must have immediate feedback. Only the operator, the value adder, can do that. The inspection personnel and equipment we use today to screen completed work *add time and cost to the process but don't add value.* When we assign this responsibility to the value adder, we get operational advantages, real process control, and a more positive environment for improvement.

The bottom line of this principle is that ***the quality of our product is determined at the instant the product is made, and no amount of inspection will ever make it any better.*** Knowing that and doing it are two different things. The mind set that says we are going to make a perfect part every time and we are going to hold the operator, and that person alone, responsible for making it happen is still insufficient. There are additional principles which we must follow.

Q@S 3: NEW CUSTOMER DEFINITION

When we mention our customer, most of us think of the person or company receiving our final product. In fact, we have banners on the wall proclaiming "The Customer Is Always Right." But, how many people actually see that customer? Is that really the customer of the person running Operation 20? Not at all. His/her customer happens to be the person in Operation 30. This is a vital change in thought process because, until we get that sense of understanding on the shop floor, we won't be able to *personalize* quality responsibility. We have to eliminate the "they" from our process and reduce all relationships to "you and me." Under these conditions, the next operation is always the ultimate customer for the prior operation.

An Operations VP, named "Joe," once told me about a personal experience which may help illustrate this point. He said he had just started work on his first job as an apprentice machinist many years ago and was placed in a group machining motor armature shafts. They were on a group incentive rate and were only paid for good parts produced. Around mid-morning of the first day on the job, he reached the point where he knew he should shut down the grinder he was operating to dress the wheel because it had worn down. But, in his zeal to make more parts, he continued to run. Very soon thereafter, the machinist from the next operation came walking toward him, holding one of Joe's recently completed shafts in his hand, like a war club. The machinist was very big, and had a scowl on his face when he asked, "Did you grind this shaft?" Joe gulped and admitted he did since he was the only grinder in the group. "Well," said the machinist, "make me one more just like it and you'll eat it for lunch!" That certainly personalized the quality responsibility for Joe, and he never forgot who his real customer was.

Q@S Applies to Everyone

While the foregoing discussion has centered on the shop floor, quality can't stop there. Everyone in the organization must follow the same principles: Perfect Work (Parts) Every Time, Individual (Operator) Responsibility and Personalized Customers (new definition). This means the order entry person intends to process every new order perfectly so his/her customer can ship that order on schedule without error or delay. The design engineer needs to produce perfect drawings and specifications, without the aid of a checker (inspector), so his customer in Manufacturing can build the product. The production scheduler must strive to publish perfect schedules which are do-able every time by the customers who must allocate resources accordingly or promise deliveries to others. Everyone has personal customers. When each of us meets those customers' needs and specifications, the principle of Quality at the Source will be a reality.

Q@S 4: THE Q@S TOOL KIT

The first three Quality at the Source Principles, Perfect Parts Every Time, Operator Responsibility and a New Customer Definition, give us the underlying foundation for Quality at the Source. Next, we must give the operator the necessary tools to do the job. This is the fourth Quality at the Source principle, the new Q@S Tool Kit. As shown in Figure 3-3, the Q@S Tool Kit has two layers. The first contains the needed items to achieve process control, instead of inspection. It includes the use of statistical techniques, which we call Statistical Process Control (SPC) and some failsafe methods to reduce the chance of human error. The second layer contains problem-solving methods to help us recover from difficulties, which often arise, and make improvements.

QUALITY @ SOURCE TOOL KIT

- ## Process Control, Not Inspection
  - ### - Statistical Techniques
  - ### - Failsafe Methods
- ## Problem Solving Methods

Figure 3-3

Statistical Process Control (SPC)

First, let's examine the top layer. Why should we even care about Statistical Process Control? For one thing, we know that Dr. W. Edwards Demming taught SPC to the Japanese in the 1950's, and we are competing with high quality levels today which are a far cry from the "cheap junk" image Japanese goods had back in those days. But, is SPC difficult? Can we teach this science to our operators, who don't have advanced mathemathics degrees? Actually, it can be simple if we stick to the basics.

How do statistics help us improve quality? First, we have to learn how to define a total population (like all the parts we're making), without measuring every single unit. To do that, we take advantage of a phenomenon called the normal distribution. Suppose we had a room full of people, say 100 or so, and we measured all of their heights in inches. By summing the inches for everybody and dividing by the number of people, we could get the average height for all the people in that room. Interestingly, if we counted all of the people who were exactly the average height, and we had a *normal* population, the largest number of people in the room would be at the average height. If we counted the number of people one inch taller and one inch shorter than the average height, each group would be slightly smaller in number than the average group. If we continued to group people in one-inch increments, in both directions, until we finally ran out of people, we would have defined our group of people by height. By plotting these numbers on a chart, with the number of people in each group on the vertical axis and heights on the horizontal axis, and drawing a line through the points, we would create a "normal distribution" curve for that population, as shown in Figure 3-4. Some people call that a "bell" curve because it certainly is shaped like a bell. In most normal populations, that is the way the picture always looks. This is not only interesting, but very important to us in manufacturing, because we can apply it to the shop floor. The curve gives us a visual picture of how the process is working and how widely we should expect it to vary.

Imagine that we are performing a lathe operation and want to turn a three-inch outer diameter on a part. If we tried to make 100 pieces with that outer diameter, every piece would not be exactly the same. Some would be slightly larger and others would be slightly smaller, like 3.001 or 2.999 inches. If we grouped our measurements and plotted the points for this population as we did for the people's heights, we would end up with a similar bell-shaped curve. If our drawing tolerances are outside the ends of our bell-shaped curve, we are in good shape because our whole population is within the specification limits. But, when the process begins to drift, the real value of the normal distribution becomes apparent. For example, if the tool started to wear and got smaller, the piece we are trying to turn would get a little bigger. The distribution curve would begin to drift toward the right. When the tail of our curve falls outside of the specification, we are beginning to make some bad parts. We might not know it because the samples we are taking for the measurement might well be from parts within specifications, the largest part of the curve. That's how we begin to get into trouble. To avoid that problem,

1) we have to find ways to keep the curve right in the middle of the tolerance band, which is called "centering the process," and

2) we want to squeeze the bell-shaped curve down until it's a narrow as possible. The squeezing down is what our competition is doing today. As we approach perfection, the curve will become a single vertical line right in the middle of the tolerance band.

Understanding the distribution curve, centering the process, and narrowing the curve through continuous improvement are the basic building blocks of Statistical Process Control (SPC).

Using Control Charts

The tool we use to actually implement SPC is called a control chart.

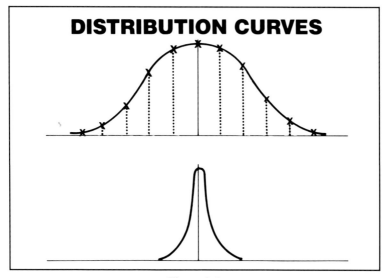

DISTRIBUTION CURVES

Figure 3-4

It is a basically simple device that any operator can be instructed to use. In Figure 3-5, the normal distribution curve is shown on its side along the vertical axis. The number running through the middle of the curve is set at 80. That's the average number that we have experienced for this process. It is obtained by collecting data. We start by measuring several sample parts and averaging those measurements. In this case, let's say the average for three samples turned out to be about 78. An hour later, we take three more samples, and this time the average is 81. We continue to do this every hour over a period of time, plotting the averages for each set of samples.

Eventually, we will have enough data to calculate our process capability. Although it is not difficult, the operators don't have to do this. It can be assigned to our quality engineers. They can plug the data into a simple formula which will tell us, based on what we have already done, what we are capable of doing. That creates the two dashed lines on the control chart. They are called control limits. The top one is the upper control limit (UCL) and the bottom one is the lower control limit (LCL). If our averages ever fall outside of those lines, our process centering has moved beyond normal variations. Forget the specification! Forget the normal distribution! We now have defined our demonstrated process capability.

When our data points do fall outside the control limits, it is time to investigate, to verify the readings, and to make the necessary correction

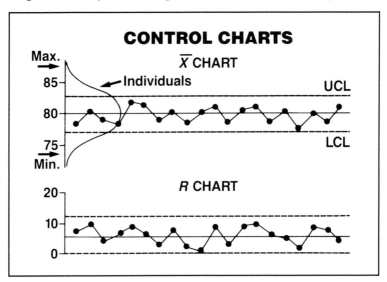

Figure 3-5

to bring us back inside the dotted lines. At this stage, we still haven't made a "bad" part because we have caught the shift in the process before we've ever produced a part outside of the tolerance limits. That's how you can make every part good every time.

The bottom part of the control charts describes the measurement range. For each group of samples we measure, we take the difference between the biggest reading and the smallest one, and plot it right below the average for that group. It tells us how widely the group of measurements were spread and whether the curve is geting "fatter" or "thinner."

In addition, we sometimes make mistakes when we take a measurement, or sometimes we encounter a real strange one that is way out of line and needs to be verified. We want to be confident that the measurements we are taking are truly representative of the total population. Remember what they say about averages, "If my head is in the freezer and my feet are in the oven, on the average I am comfortable!"

The Value Adder is Vital

Could your operators learn to do that? Of course they could. Do they need an advanced mathematics degree? Absolutely not. Every successful shop which has implemented SPC to truly control its processes has the operator take the data, make the calulations, and maintain the control charts. What does a real one look like? Figure 3-6 is a chart

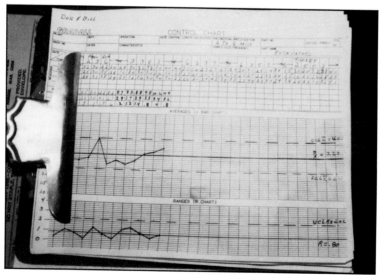

Figure 3-6

that was prepared and maintained by an operator. If you look at it carefully, you'll see it is full of finger smudges. That's good! If it's not dirty, it's probably not useful. *If it's nice and tidy and hanging on a wall, it makes good wallpaper.* Control charts are good tools for process control only when the operator does the work and gets immediate feedback. Only then is the value adder controlling the process.

Control charts can also be used as a tool to monitor continuous improvement. As we think of new ways to improve the process, we can watch the control limits compress as they approach the target, that single straight line which is the perfect part, the ultimate goal of Quality at the Source.

Fail Safe Methods

Statistical Process Control, alone, would give us an incomplete Tool Kit. We also must compensate for some basic human weaknesses to minimize the opportunities to make careless mistakes. We call this category "Fail Safe" Methods. It recognizes that even the most conscientious people can be distracted or will slip into periods of low attention, due to natural, cyclic variations during the course of a day. After examining the production process and identifying the critical points, we can build in positive reinforcements to help the operator.

For example, the *use of color* is a powerful tool. We can match sets of tools by painting the handles the same color so any intermixing would be obvious, even to the subconscious mind. Color coding right-hand versus left-hand parts is another excellent application. To *raise the attention span* of an operator, we can ring a bell or sound a gong just prior to an important step in the process. We can help insure correct part orientation by building *checking features* into the holding fixtures or the containers that we are using. In other words, we made it impossible to switch or reverse the part, which could result in drilling a hole in a piece upside down. We can place *limit switches* on our machines to stop them if we exceed our control limits when the operator is distracted. In each case, we are backing the operator up with a fail safe mechanism. which makes it more difficult to make a mistake.

Sometimes an operation may be so important we will install a *double signal,* like a limit switch and a *buzzer,* to alert the operator. The best way, however is to incorporate fail safe concepts in the *production process design.* When the holding fixture not only orients the part, but also serves as a checking device, you know that it's going to be done right the first time.

Summarizing the Top Layer

The top layer of the Q@S Tool Kit, then, is aimed at positive control of manufacturing processes by imperfect humans. It employs Statistical Process Control, or SPC, to assist the operator in the quest to make a perfect part every time. The operator, the value adder, uses the power of a control chart as the mechanism to insure that the process stays in control and to monitor improvements. Fail safe methods are also employed to give the operator added back-up, to help insure a good job every time.

For all of that, there will still be problems. The Q@S Tool Kit would not be complete if it did not contain provisions to cope with those problems. The bottom layer of the Tool Kit contains methods and techniques to evaluate each problem as it arises, to prioritize it, to solve it, and to consequently improve the process.

Window Analysis

The first step is to determine whether we have a real technical problem or a people problem centering on communications or training. The evaluation technique we use is called Window Analysis. It is analagous to looking at a problem condition through a set of window panes. Each pane represents an interaction between two people or groups of people for certain conditions, as shown in Figure 3-7. The Roman Numerals in the upper left-hand corner of the figure represent

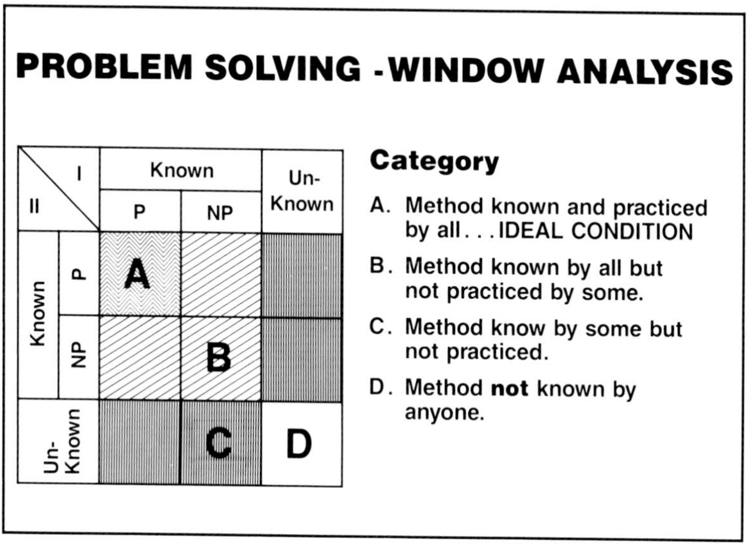
PROBLEM SOLVING -WINDOW ANALYSIS
I
II
Known
Un-Known
P
NP
Known
P
NP
Un-Known
A
B
C
D
Category
A. Method known and practiced by all. . . IDEAL CONDITION
B. Method known by all but not practiced by some.
C. Method know by some but not practiced.
D. Method **not** known by anyone.

Figure 3-7

Person or Group I and II. They might be a supervisor and an operator, a day-shift person and a night-shift person on the same machine, or even two interfacing departments. For simplicity, we'll discuss the interaction between Person I and Person II. Each person either knows the process by which the job should be done or doesn't know it. This is a "go/no-go" or binary condition. However, even if the person knows what to do, he or she may Practice (P) what is known or may Not Practice (NP) what is known. This gives us three possible conditions for each person:

1) A known process which is practiced,
2) A known process which is not practiced,
3) An unknown process.

The possibilities for Person I are at the top of the Window and those for Person II are on the left side.

Examining the interactions, it is easy to see that the best circumstance is when both people know and practice what they know, which is Condition A: the ideal condition. Unfortunately, that's only one window pane. A more prevalent condition in most operations is represented by the three panes in Condition B. Here, although both people know what to do, somebody is not practicing what is known. This often happens when people fall into bad habits or try to take short cuts. This situation can be corrected, however, by redirecting the non-practitioner back to the original process. We already have a known solution for Condition B, so it's a communications issue, not a technical problem. When one of the people doesn't know what to do, a new variable, the unknown, is introduced. This is represented in the figure by the four panes of Condition C. This is often caused by inadequate training of new people or by not keeping people informed of process changes. It's a training issue because those who know and practice can teach those who don't. That leaves us with only one pane, Condition D, where nobody knows what to do. That's a real technical problem.

It is rather interesting to note that, of the nine panes in the window, only one of them represents the ideal condition. The other eight represent some kind of problem condition, of which only one is a technical problem. That's one out of eight, or 12.5%. Shop studies have shown that only about 15% of the problems that we encounter on the floor are real technical problems, which is very close to the proportion in the Window Analysis. The rest, some 85%, are information exchange (communications) or training problems which can be solved relatively easily because *somebody* already knows the answer to those problems.

Our job is to track them back to the information source to get them straightened out rather than to "reinvent the wheel."

Pareto Analysis

For all the sorting done in the Window Analysis, we seldom, if ever, come up with only one technical problem. In fact, we usually have a whole plateful of them. How should we decide which one to work on first? We should work on the most important ones first. To identify them, we use a technique called Pareto Analysis.

Pareto was an Italian economist who lived in the late 1800's. His economic studies showed that the vast majority of wealth in every country he studied was controlled by a small number of people (which is no suprise to most of us) and that the same phonomenon applied to other populations which had value associated with individual members. He wrote a book on the principle and later retired in great wealth to an island in the Mediterranean Sea (not from the book proceeds, but from a large inheritance). The Pareto Principle has been used for many years in materials management for inventory control. It turns out that a few part numbers (usually less than 20%) account for most of the value of the inventory (usually more than 80%). Sometimes called the 80/20 Rule or the ABC System, it lets us control most of the inventory value by concentrating on a small portion of our part numbers (the "important few") instead of diluting our efforts by

PROBLEM FREQUENCY

PROBLEM	TALLY	TOTAL
1	₩₩ ₩₩ II	12
2	₩₩	5
3	₩₩ ₩₩ ₩₩	15
4	II	2
5	III	3

Figure 3-8

spending a lot of time managing the "trivial many."

The Pareto Principle can be applied to the problems on the shop floor by using the frequency of occurrence as the value measure. The more often a problem occurs, the more likely it will cost us more time, money and rejects. While you can probably think of an exception, it is still a valid general assumption and helps us prioritize our problem solving.

Applying the Pareto Principle

Suppose we were faced with five seemingly big problems in a work center and wanted to prioritize them. The first thing we'd do is collect some information about how often those problems occur. We'd place a clipboard in the work center and, as each problem arose, we'd tally it on a chart, as shown in Figure 3-8. At the end of a week, we'd add them up. In this case you can see that Problem One happened 12 times; Problem Two was seen 5 times; Problem Three occurred 15 times; Problem Four surfaced only twice; and Problem Five was encountered 3 times. Next, we'd arrange the problem frequency in a bar chart, by descending value, as shown in Figure 3-9. It clearly shows us that Problem Three is the most frequently occurring and should be solved first. Next, we would go after Problem One. As you can see, Problems Two, Five and Four are not the big problems right now and won't be significant until we get rid of Problems Three and One. This

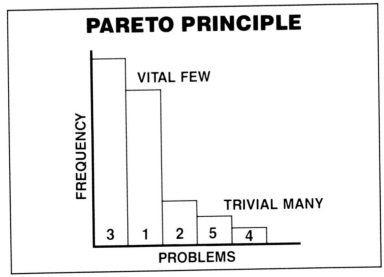

Figure 3-9

is a very practical application of the water and rocks analogy introduced in Chapter 2. It is also a valuable way to demonstrate to others just why one problem should be solved before another. Otherwise, it's usually the loudest shouters in our plants who get the attention, even when their problem may not be the most productive one to solve first.

Cause and Effect Diagram

Having selected the most important problem, we can solve it by a method known as Cause and Effect Diagramming. It is a systematic way to get at the root cause of a problem instead of trying to solve the symptoms. It helps to envision a problem as if it were a tree. The trunk, limbs and foliage are what we see but are only the symptoms, or the effects, of the problem. The roots, which are hidden under the ground, and not visible, represent the real causes of the problem. Our job is to dig down to the potential root causes, as shown in Figure 3-10, and sort them out to isolate the most probable cause of the problem.

If we rotate the tree image 90 degrees clockwise so it's laying on its side, we get the schematic diagram shown in Figure 3-11. The effects of the problem (the foliage) are listed in the box on the right and the causes (the roots) are placed in the network on the left. We follow a five-step process to solve the problem:

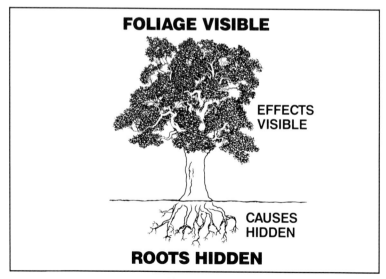

Figure 3-10

1. *Describe the Problem (Effect).* In as much detail as possible, we list all the information we can accumulate about the problem we see, which are really symptoms, or effects of the real problem.

2. *Define the Cause Categories.* In this step, we establish the broad categories of potential causes to help us organize our ideas into logical groupings. People, Material, Methods and Machines are commonly used categories.

3. *Identify Potential Causes.* Here, we try to identify potential causes in more detail. Brainstorming techniques can be very effective in this step. We want to "free wheel" ideas and get them on the chart in the appropriate category. Often, one idea leads to another and stimulates creative thinking. We don't have to justify ideas at this point, just list the possibilities.

4. *Prioritize the Causes.* Each potential cause is evaluated and prioritized to find the most likely cause. Often, the easiest way to do this is through the process of eliminating the least likely causes.

5. *Refine the Causes.* The probable causes isolated in Step 4 will have to be refined even further to get to the real root cause. To do that, we take advantage of the most powerful tool in our arsenal, asking the question, "Why?" Its power comes from attacking the "givens" and taking nothing for granted.

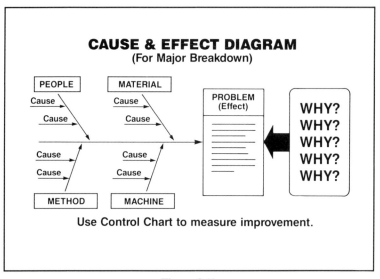

Figure 3-11

The Value of Asking Why?

Most of us learned more during the first five years of our lives than during any other five year period, including college. We learned a language, customs, basic sciences, self-care, and even some philosophy, mostly by repeatedly asking the question, "Why?" In fact, when you're the parent, isn't that a tough one to answer? When you respond with a shallow "quickie" answer, children come right back with another, "Why?" Then you have to give a more detailed answer, and they come back with still another "Why?," forcing you to dig deeper and deeper. When we apply that to problem solving, it helps us get to the real root causes. The secret is to ask, "Why?," as many as *five times* before you are satisfied with the answer.

Cause and Effect Example

Let's review these steps, using an actual example. When we were filming our JIT for America video tape course, there was one segment that employed a simple prop with a lamp that was to illuminate when I pushed a hidden switch. It didn't work the morning we were to start filming. The whole crew was standing around waiting, the "meter" was running, and we had to find the cause of that problem, *real fast!*

The first step tells us to describe the problem in as much detail as possible. Well, the lamp wouldn't light, that was pretty clear. It worked the previous day, so something must have happened in the interim. There was a bulb in the prop so it wasn't a question of somebody removing it, and every time I pushed the switch I heard it click. That was all the information we had to describe the effects that were observed.

The next step is to outline the possible categories of causes that might relate to this problem. Well, a lot of people handled the prop, so maybe we had a "people problem." That was one category. There could have been material deficiencies, so we selected that as a category. Then, we speculated that something in the method by which I was using the prop might be wrong, or it might have been the prop itself, the "machine." These categories defined our best guesses of the four major trunks of the causes of our problem.

The third step tells us to define specific potential causes, so we tried a little brainstorming. Under the Material Category, we thought the bulb might have burned out, a fuse may have blown, a socket may have been faulty, or that we had a bad switch. In the Machine Category, we thought about a loose socket, poor solder joints, erroneous wiring, etc. We also came up with ideas for the other two categories.

The next step tells us to prioritize the causes, so we did. The first thing that was easy to check was the burned-out bulb idea. When we removed the bulb and tested it in another socket, it worked, so that wasn't the cause of our problem. Next, we pulled the fuse, and sure enough it had blown.

At this point, we might have been tempted to stop the process and identify the blown fuse as the cause of our problem. However, we still had to do Step Five, which is refining the first probable cause. So, we asked ourselves, "*Why* did the fuse burn out?" Well, the only thing that makes fuses burn out is too much load or too little fuse. In this case, no other fuses had blown, so the chances were the fuse was undersized. But if so, *why* was it undersized? It turned out the prop maker didn't know the right size, so he guessed. Again, we asked, "*Why* didn't he know?" The answer turned out to be that the prop designer never specified a value for the fuse. Great! Now we could blame Engineering! But, one more time, we asked, "*Why* didn't the designer specify a value?" His answer? He thought the prop maker knew the right value without being told. Because of this misunderstanding, there wasn't a piece of paper anywhere that defined the fuse rating. (By the way, *presumed knowledge* is often the reason for many of the problems we encounter.) That was the root cause of our prop problem. The symptom was a burned out bulb, the first probable cause was a blown fuse, but it took four why's to get to the root cause, insufficient information given to the prop maker. The solution was an agreement that every sketch submitted to the prop room would include values for every component specified. This way, we didn't just cure the symptom by replacing the fuse, but rather improved the process by eliminating a repeat of the incident due to lack of information.

Taking C&E Diagrams to the Workplace

With Cause and Effect diagramming, you are going to be able to solve problems that have been plaguing you for years. But what happens when you run out of ideas and haven't yet solved the problem? You may need to tap other resources to get more ideas. The ideal way to do this is to take the chart containing all your efforts to date and tape it on the wall near the spot where the problem occurred. Then, people who might know something about the problem can examine the analysis and think about it. Place a self-stick note pad and a pencil alongside the chart so people who stop by can jot down their idea and place it wherever they think it fits. As more people come by, get an idea, jot it down, and stick it on the chart, you are going to get a wide array of new input. A number of American companies are trying this technique and they are finding that it not only works, but they are also getting excellent results in a matter of weeks, so we are not talking about a lengthy time investment to take advantage of this tool. It is a powerful way to solve nagging technical problems by accessing heretofore untapped resources.

Q@S Tool Kit Contains the Basics

The Q@S Tool Kit doesn't contain very many things. The bottom layer has only a few techniques for problem solving, but they are all critical because each leads to the next. The top layer of the Tool Kit is also very basic. It establishes our ability to control our processes with "fail safe" back-ups for the operator. While there are many other techniques that can be employed, this is all we need at the beginning. You can think of it as a "starter set." Later, once our operators are actually using these techniques to make good parts, we can add more techniques to further improve the process so we can make every part the same as every other part.

The bottom line of the Q@S Tool Kit is it gives operators the wherewithal to meet customer expectations. Conversely, we can't meet those expectations when the product varies even if it is within tolerance. We really don't have an alternative because the competition is getting better all of the time which is increasing the expectations of our customers. Each improvement we make will eliminate some of the variations in our manufacturing processes, producing greater uniformity between parts. Ultimately, this will lead to every part being like every other part, allowing us to uniformly meet our customer expectations.

Q@S 5: STOP AND FIX THE PROBLEM

When we do find a problem, we must immediately stop the process and fix it. Otherwise, we'll be sending a very clear signal to our employees that we're not really serious about quality. This is a significant departure from traditional practices, whereby making something, even if it was marginal, was preferred to waiting until the process was "right." By stopping the process, we purposely make things uncomfortable for ourselves and force a solution to the problem. The caveat is that we must immediately fix that problem, at least on an interim basis, or we could be out of business.

Stopping an operation to fix a problem is hard to initiate in many industries. When I first entered the automotive industry, I was told, "Ken, there are really only two sure ways to lose your job. One is to do something dumb like hitting your boss on company property. The other is to stop an automotive customer's assembly line, and we think that's worse than the first one!" Everybody "knows" that if you stop production it is going to cost us a lot of money. Some of us even know how many dollars each minute of shut-down will cost. But, the first principle of Quality at the Source says we must never make a bad part. Therefore, if something happens to the process to cause a deviation from our capability, we *must* stop it.

Origin of Stop and Fix

Stop and Fix is one of the few JIT elements that came to us from overseas. In the 1920's, Mr. Sakichi Toyoda, the founder of Toyota Motor Company, manufactured power looms for the textile industry. These machines wove cloth from many spools of thread, which were fed from all directions. If a spool of thread broke, the machine didn't know the difference. It kept right on weaving cloth with flaws in it. (We've seen a lot of that material on the "fire sale" counter at fabric stores.) Toyoda's goal was to build a machine that could never make bad cloth. He placed sensors on every spool of thread to detect when a thread broke or a spool ran out of thread. The sensors then triggered the power switch to shut down the machine. A signal light alerted the operator to come fix the problem and restart the machine. It was a very successful product improvement.

Later, at the Toyota Motor Company, he was faced with the same problem, but it was more difficult. His Vice President of Manufacturing, Taiichi Ohno, accepted the challenge. The difficulty was magnified by the fact that automobile manufacturing was not a closed loop mechanical system. It entailed many people and disconnected operations, a very complex process. Starting at final assembly, Ohno instructed every operator to work on only one part at a time and to take action if they found something wrong, like a defective part, or production moving too fast to complete the work in-station, or a safety hazard. A push button or pull cord was activated by the operator to stop the process. Ohno called the process, "Jidoka."

At that point, a light would flash, a gong would ring and a pre-assigned team would descend on the spot, much like a volunteer fire department, and production came to a halt. The team solved the problem on the spot or came up with a temporary fix before the process would be restarted. This avoided the reproduction of bad parts. The worker became the quality source and there was no need for quality control inspectors. Wherever they could, they used automatic monitoring of operations, so people didn't even have to take redundant measurements, but the important thing is that the workers' judgment was trusted.

During all of this activity, the production workers were "idle," in that they were not producing cars. On the other hand, they took the opportunity to clean up their areas and restock, if necessary, to prepare for the line restart, but nobody made any product. This is the part that shocks most of our financially-oriented managers. How could they justify that much lost time?

Cost Consequences of Stop and Fix

A few years ago, Toyota stated they stopped their lines between 15 minutes and 30 minutes per shift as normal practice. For a 2000 person assembly plant, this would result in 1000 person hours a day of lost time under the worst condition. Not many of us would like to face the consequences of submitting those kinds of numbers to our management. On the other hand, for a 2000 person plant, we typically have 250 line inspectors and repair operators on the payroll to "catch and fix" the errors that we are unwilling to stop the line to correct. We are paying 250 people 8 hours per shift, or 2000 person hours, to do it "our way." We're paying twice as much to do a less effective job when we insist on keeping those lines running.

There are cases in the United States where Stop and Fix has been successfully employed. When it was installed in a Chevrolet Engine Plant a few years ago, it produced some very interesting results. The very first day Stop and Fix was initiated, an operator stopped the line because a piston and ring assembly scored the cylinder wall on one of the engines. It turned out to be an old, recurring problem. The rings had sharp edges on them and often picked up burrs during manu-facturing. The "volunteer fire department" could not come up with a quick fix, so a call was made to the product engineer, who was located in another building across town. (When he arrived, one wag claimed it was his first visit to the plant in some seven years.) In any event, he recognized the problem and offered to write an engineering change order to add a little chamfer on those sharp edges. The plant personnel were pleased with the fix but wondered why their complaints about the problem had not been addressed earlier. The product engineer said, "I didn't know you had the problem." For whatever reason, the needed communication was missing. But, with Stop and Fix, we force attention on the problem and force ourselves to solve it because we can't restart the process until we do so.

That's why Stop and Fix is really very cost effective. As shown in Figure 3-12, it is going to look terrible on the short-term P&L when you shut down an operation. But, as soon as you fix that problem, you improve the process, which produces long-term savings. When the operator is the source of quality and is empowered to stop the process upon finding a problem, we can begin to produce better products at lower costs. It hurts in the short-term, but results in permanent "fixes" which improve the process for all time.

Q@S 6: VISIBILITY MANAGEMENT

Stop and Fix is a powerful Q@S principle because it forces problems to the surface. Hidden problems, complex shop layouts and

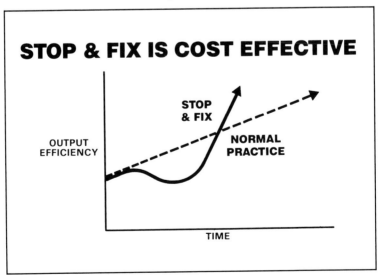

Figure 3-12

general disarray hinder quality production. Deviations from the norm must be clearly visible to everyone if we are to know what needs to be done to maintain the current process and then to improve it. That's why Visibility Management is a vital principle of Quality at the Source. We need to be so well organized that an *outsider* can tell whether things are going well or are amiss, without the help of a tour guide.

Housekeeping

Visibility Management starts with five basic housekeeping concepts:

1. *Simplification:* Keep only what is needed in the work area to perform regularly scheduled activities. Remove seldom-used or never-used tools, dies and gauges. Remove excess stock and equipment. Get down to the basics needed to do the job. Make it simple and easy to understand. If you need a hammer in your work center, have a proper place for it. If you don't need a hammer on a regular basis, don't keep it in the work center. Send it to a remote storage area.

2. *Organization:* Designate a specific location for everything you've decided to keep and identify it clearly. This way, you can tell when the right thing is in the right place, as well as what is missing if it's gone. With hand tools, as shown in Figure 3-13, you could paint profiles of the tools in their allocated locations. You can see when

Figure 3-13

a tool is in the right place, what is missing if tools are removed; and upon finding a loose tool without a painted profile underneath it, you know it is out of place and where to put it back. Everything is simple and very visible.

3. *Discipline:* Keep everything in its designated location. Now that you know where it belongs; keep it there. This may be the most difficult housekeeping concept to maintain. Too often, we start out with the best of intentions; only to lapse into previous habits after the "bloom" of the start up has worn off. The practical reality of this concept is that we can only respond to exact customer demand (JIT Principle #1) when everything we need is available for instantaneous use. We cannot afford to spend time looking for missing material, tools or people.

4. *Cleanliness:* Clean everything immediately so it is constantly ready for use. Clean and seal your floors so person-moveable roller carts can be employed to free your operators from dependency on material handling services. Keep contaminants, including tobacco, drinks, food and leisure reading material out of the workplace so you don't introduce alien elements which can degrade your process control. A JUST-IN-TIME shop is absolutely spotless. I have been in an engine plant where I had to take off my shoes and don cotton "footies" so I wouldn't mar their floor. Figure 3-14 shows an American JIT plant. This shop has presses, welders, grinders, heat treat and platers in it,

Figure 3-14

yet it is extremely clean. There is no manufacturing process, including foundry activities, that *has* to be dirty.

Cleanliness is emphasized in Quality at the Source because it sets the stage for people to do high quality work and to maintain a quality workplace. When a machine is absolutely spotless, the first time a drop of hydraulic fluid, coolant or lubricant shows up where it ought not be, we can see it and recognize it as a symptom of a potential problem. We can trace it to the source and fix it before it becomes a catastrophe. If, on the other hand, the machine is covered with oil and debris, we'll never see the initial symptom and probably won't know about it until it becomes a rupture. Cleanliness enhances visibility and quality.

5. *Participation:* Everyone cleans their own areas and observes the housekeeping rules, including sales and management people who are escorting outside visitors. It makes no sense to pay people to clean up messes made by other people. That's a waste. When everyone cleans up after himself or herself, they tend to create less mess in the first place. When everyone participates, it establishes a total visible commitment to the new quality ethic you are trying to instill throughout the company.

Visibility Management presents information to employees and all passers-by, in the clearest possible way, as to what should be, what is, and deviations from expectations. The information board shown in

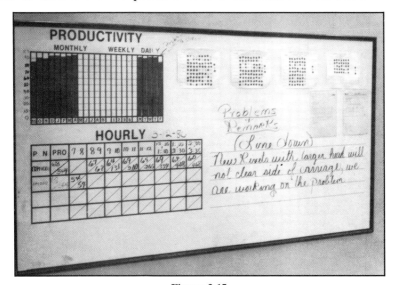

Figure 3-15

Figure 3-15 is typical. One of these is displayed in every department at this American company. In the upper left-hand corner are the productivity levels achieved for the day, week, month and the year to date. The lower left chart displays an hourly manufacturing schedule with actual completions by the hour for the day. In the upper right is a cross-training chart, displaying both capabilities and needs. The lower right portion carries today's number one problem, the biggest *rock* that has surfaced. Rather than clutter up the board with the top five or top ten problems, all attention is focused on solving number one. Nobody has to guess or read a report to know how this department is doing.

Figure 3-16 demonstrates how employees are made aware of potential end-customer problems with their product, an automobile seat track. Everyone can see how the portion of the product which they produce can affect total performance. It helps to focus attention on the ultimate goal — meeting customer expectations.

Visibility Enhances Productivity

Visibility Management can also be used for continuous improvement. Suppose an operator was trying to control a production process using the three gauges shown in the top portion of Figure 3-17. There are three different variables to monitor and control. The operator has a basic tool, the gauge, but doesn't have the necessary backup

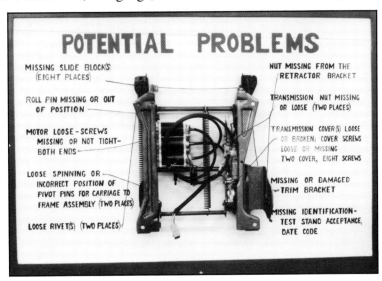

Figure 3-16

to insure that the job is done correctly every time. What could be done to make that job easier? The readings that have to be maintained are written on a specification, which is probably in a drawer. If we could display those numbers below the gauges on masking tape, we could improve the operator's visibility. As shown in the lower portion of the Figure, the first gauge should read 20 plus or minus 1, the second should be 35 plus or minus 3, and the last gauge should read 10 plus or minus 5. Now, the operator is constantly reminded of the proper readings, and that's an improvement.

But, we can do more. Rather than requiring the operator to mentally translate the numbers on the tape to the needle position, why don't we put the information where the operator can use it? Using masking tape again, as shown in the bottom half of Figure 3-17, we can simplify the task by outlining the acceptable tolerance ranges.

That's better, but how could we improve it even further? If we don't really care about reading the brand name on the gauges, let's rotate each of them in their mounting holes until the desired reading is a vertical needle, as shown in the top part of Figure 3-18. Now, a brief glance will tell the operator if the process is within limits. Even a passer-by could see how things were going with this combination of visual aids.

We could still do one more thing. Recalling the fail-safe methods discussed in the Q@S Tool Kit, we could add a second signal, like a

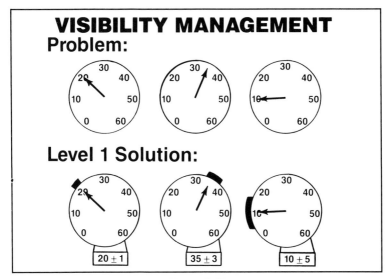

Figure 3-17

bell, which would activate if any of the gauge readings exceeded the tolerance limits, as shown in the bottom portion of Figure 3-18. Each of these steps added value to the process because we helped insure that it could be maintained. That's what Visibility Management is really all about.

Q@S 7: MACHINES ALWAYS READY

The first six Q@S Principles are people related. Manufacturing, however, is a blend of people and machines. For the JIT Strategy to work, there can be no contingencies allowed for "balky" equipment, any more than for "uncontrolled" processes. There is no greater inhibitor to high quality production on schedule than machines that don't work when they are supposed to. The performance and reliability of machinery, then, is critical. The machines must always be ready when we need them.

This is not to say we can expect our equipment to operate 24 hours a day forever (although some of us seem to try). If a machine is to be operational when scheduled, it must be maintained properly. We cannot afford an unscheduled shut-down because the JIT Strategy provides for no extra inventory, people or machines to cover these possibilities. That would be a waste. Thus, preventive maintenance, which might be better called *Productive Maintenance*, needs to become

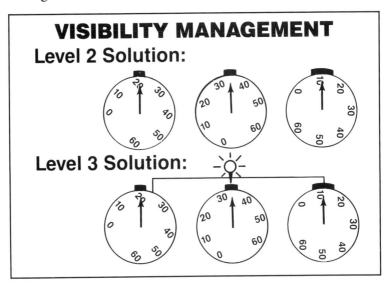

Figure 3-18

a *religion* in our plants, not just something we wish we had time to do. In traditional operations, we often push the equipment too far, forcing a breakdown to be the indicator that we must now repair the machine. Breakdowns aren't scheduled, so we usually aren't ready for them. The only alternative is to purposely take down a machine to perform the necessary maintenance at our convenience, not Fate's convenience.

When we initiate this kind of PM program, we want to improve our machines, not just fix breakdowns or replace worn parts. We want to employ Cause and Effect Analysis, as discussed in the Q@S Tool Kit, to determine the cause of the problem and then fix that cause. For example, if a bearing burns out on a machine, rather than looking to the maintenance manual for the replacement bearing size, we have to ask ourselves *why* the bearing burned out. Maybe it didn't get enough lubrication or maybe the journal is scored and needs to be reground. Maybe our application of the machine is different than was originally intended and we need a heavier duty bearing. There are all sorts of possibilities. But, when we put the machine back together it ought to be a better machine than it was before we took it apart. With this kind of productive maintenance, a machine, like fine wine, should actually *improve with age.* How's that for a new thought? No more should we accept appropriations requests with justifications that say, "machine wore out." An old, old machine, thanks to the continuous improvements made during scheduled maintenance periods, should be better than it was the day it was purchased.

A Sense of Urgency

This kind of preventive maintenance cannot be done in a "laissez-faire" fashion, as often happens today. When there are no contingencies, scheduled maintenance must be accomplished quickly at the planned times. While most maintenance people rightly complain that they are often denied access to equipment because of production priorities, they seem to take forever to complete the job once they get it torn apart. PM must be treated with a sense of urgency by everyone, much like an Indianapolis pit stop. It's been said that the races at Inianapolis are won or lost in the pits. The crews can fuel the car, change tires, clean the windshield, give the driver a drink and get the car going again in 11 to 14 seconds! It takes organization, trained personnel, procedures and pre-staged material to accomplish it. That's the way we have to do our maintenance. We'll get organized, go in on schedule, quickly do the job and get out in a hurry to minimize the machine down time. As we get better at it, we'll learn to anticipate problems and fix them before a breakdown occurs. Over time, we will continuously improve our entire complement of machines to insure that they are always ready for duty, as scheduled for production.

Productive Maintenance Responsibilities

This is too big a job to "pawn off" on the Maintenance Department. Nor can we afford to hire a larger maintenance staff. The only way to get the additional resources needed is to have many others participate in PM, as shown in Figure 3-19. For example, we can offload many basic tasks from the specialists by getting the operators involved in productive maintenance.

Operators should clean, check and lubricate their own equipment so they can sense when something is amiss. Many of us employ oilers to lubricate machines. An oiler is supposed to know the location of every lube port on every machine in the plant. It is a routine function with little incentive to excel. An operator needs to know his or her machine intimately and usually has only a small number of lube ports to memorize. In addition, the operator has more to gain if that piece of equipment is working properly, with the new responsibilities of Q@S Principle #1. This vested interest can help insure that proper

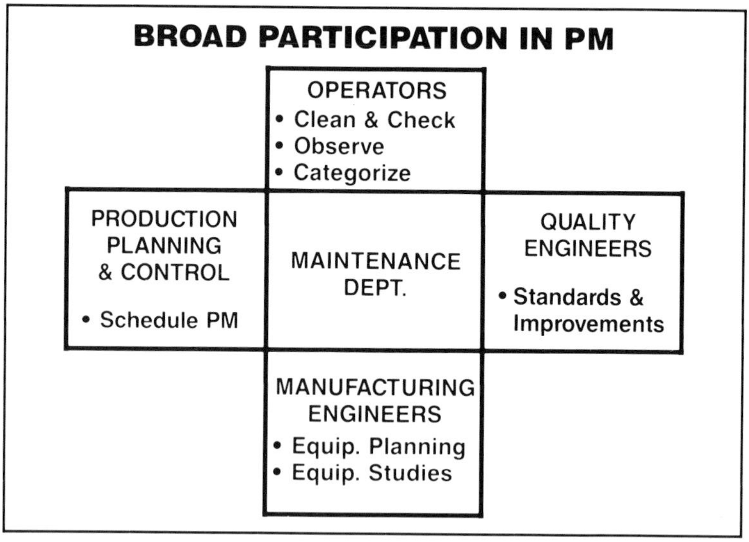

BROAD PARTICIPATION IN PM

	OPERATORS • Clean & Check • Observe • Categorize	
PRODUCTION PLANNING & CONTROL • Schedule PM	MAINTENANCE DEPT.	QUALITY ENGINEERS • Standards & Improvements
	MANUFACTURING ENGINEERS • Equip. Planning • Equip. Studies	

Figure 3-19

lubrication is done in a timely fashion.

Operators should be the first line of defense against potential disaster by using their powers of observation. Few of us are automotive mechanics, but every one of us can tell when our car sounds differently than it did the previous day. We describe those symptoms to the mechanics when we take the car in for service. The same thing should apply in the shop. Operators should know their machines, notice when they are starting to sound differently, and recognize potential problems. When they describe the symptoms to the specialists, they give Maintenance a head start to save valuable time. They also free skilled maintenance people from doing many mundane tasks so they can concentrate on the important things they were trained to do.

One of the biggest problems we have in preventive maintenance today is getting anybody to agree that we have the time to do it. *Production Control* is usually the biggest obstacle. Every time Maintenance wants to work on a machine, Production Control says, "We can't shut that equipment down now. We have hot customer orders and have to ship parts out the door." The best way to solve that problem is to place the responsibility for scheduling productive maintenance in the hands of Production Control. The Maintenance Department is a finite resource and the maintenance orders are treated just like customer orders. The trick is to develop a schedule that will do both. That's tough, no question about it, but our professional schedulers are in Production Control. Who is better qualified to do this job? The best part is that it works. The resulting published schedule considers the limited capacity of the Preventive Maintenance Department, while fitting scheduled maintenance in with production jobs.

When the machine is shut down for PM, it is the ideal time to install improvements. The Quality Department, especially *Quality Engineering,* should accumulate the improvement ideas that people have suggested and work with Maintenance to incorporate them during regular PM times. It doesn't make sense to take a machine down one time for preventive maintenance and another time for improvements. Coordination is required, but now it is feasible since the schedule is published and known to all.

As improvements are made, they should be reported to those who specify new equipment, like *Manufacturing Engineering* or whoever does it in your shop. When a whole series of improvements has been made to a machine over a period of time, do we want to buy another one like it that doesn't work as well? We want our engineers to pass these improvements on to the machine manufacturer and have them incorporated before shipment. If the manufacturer refuses, we should incorporate the improvements ourselves, before we commission the machine on the floor. That way we have two better machines than were originally shipped from the equipment manufacturer.

Productive Maintenance Case Study

Does it really work? Let me share with you the experience of a Chevrolet Engine Plant in Flint, Michigan. They had the same problems so many of us do: too little "up time" on the machines, insufficient production output levels to meet scheduled demands, and all sorts of unplanned disruptions. In cooperation with their UAW local, they decided to look beyond the obvious and try an novel approach. They realized that running three shifts a day, six days a week, they had no time for preventive maintenance, yet they couldn't meet production demands, either. As shown in Figure 3-20, to provide time for the needed maintenance, they decided to go to two nine-hour production shifts instead of three eight-hour stints. The first shift started at six o'clock in the morning, and ran until about 3:30 p.m. There was a two and a half hour break before the second shift started at six o'clock in the evening. It lasted until 3:30 a.m., after which there

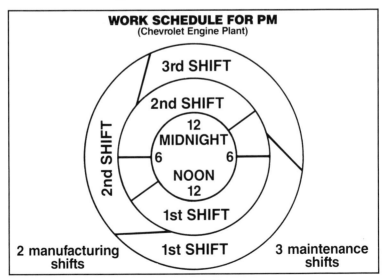

Figure 3-20

was another two and a half hour break. These breaks were purposely set aside to do preventive maintenance and even some tool changes. Maintenance continued to work three overlapping shifts, as they had done before. This way each Maintenance shift could hand off to the next to provide continuity.

The results are shown in Figure 3-21. As you can see, when the plant was running three shifts a day, five days a week, plus Saturdays, it averaged 64 to 70 units per scheduled hour out of the three machining lines. With the new approach, the average hourly production increased to between 95 and 104 units, almost a 50% improvement. With only two production shifts instead of three, they got better productivity because the machines worked when they were supposed to!

SUMMARY

It is only by following the seven principles of Quality at the Source that you can make the JUST-IN-TIME Strategy work. Like two sides of a coin, you can't have one without the other. You have to strive to make *perfect parts every time,* hold the *operator responsible* for producing those parts, *change the customer definition* for each value adder, employ the *new Q@S Tool Kit* to give the operator the necessary control mechanisms, *stop and fix each problem* immediately as it occurs, install *visibility management* aids to help make

OUTPUT IMPROVEMENT - 2 SHIFTS (Chevrolet Engine Block Line)			
	OUTPUT IN PARTS PER HOUR		
	LINE #1 MILLING	LINE #2 ROUGH TURNING	LINE #3 FINISHING
March 1981 3 Shifts + Sat.	70	66	64
March 1982 2 Shifts (9 Hrs)	104	97	95
Improvement	49%	47%	48%
	AUTOMOTIVE INDUSTRIES, July, 1982		

Figure 3-21

the job easier for the "doers" and the status obvious to everyone, and have *machines always ready* because there are no provisions for contingencies in the JIT Strategy. These seven principles are summarized in Figure 3-22.

The Q@S principles reject the popularly accepted "excuse" called "Murphy's Law." The starting point and the finish line for Quality at the Source are the same; we must convince ourselves that it is possible to prevent defects and breakdowns from ever occurring so we can truly make a "perfect" part every time.

QUALITY @ SOURCE

- **Perfect Parts Every Time**
- **Operator Responsibility**
- **New Customer Definition**
- **New "Tool Kit"**
- **Stop and Fix the Problem**
- **Visibility Management**
- **Machines Always Ready**

JIT STRATEGY

Figure 3-22

PEOPLE POLICIES
AND PRACTICES

CHAPTER **4**

*"JIT People Policies and Practices build
the environment, motivation, respect and trust
that promote continuous improvement"*

Having explored the two faces of the JUST-IN-TIME Coin, the seven principles of the JIT Strategy and the seven principles of Quality at the Source, the next step is to address the question, "How do we actually make these good things happen?" We have to peel back the surfaces of our coin and take a close look at the center core, which contains the elements that make it possible to continuously improve quality and productivity simultaneously. These elements are essentially the *tactics* that will be employed to implement the overall strategy. Tactics, according to Noah Webster, are *"the actions or methods employed to gain an objective."* Since continuous improvement can only be achieved through the efforts of people, it makes sense that we begin our journey around the core elements with the People Policies and Practices that are necessary to establish the basis for the improvements.

The Trouble With People. . .

Why such an emphasis on people? Think of your company operating like a set of gears, with JIT as the main gear meshing with Marketing, Engineering, Manufacturing, Material Management, Information Systems, Finance and Human Resources — all of the departments required to make an organization function efficiently. When everything is properly meshed, as shown in Figure 4-1, JIT can provide the drive and direction to keep all the gears moving together toward common goals. The problem is that these departments are made up of many individual people, so we have to get them working together to make the gears move in the first place. That is not necessarily easy, is it?

People Disadvantages

People are emotional. They seem to get upset over the smallest things. They come into work one day on a "high" and the next day on a "low." We are never absolutely sure just how they are going to handle their jobs because it depends on today's environment and their most recent experiences. People have limited load capacities. Unlike robots, which can lift huge amounts, we have to limit the amount that people carry or move around. The output of people is not always uniform either. It varies over the course of a day, from day to day, and through the course of time. It also varies as emotional levels change. So, even though we develop standards, every person doesn't necessarily do the job exactly the same way all the time.

Furthermore, people are fragile. You cannot expose them to hazardous environments. You can't assign them to dangerous areas or places where they're going to have to breathe toxic fumes, without careful precautions to protect them. Thus, there are limitations to the placement of people in the workplace.

On top of that, people get tired. They can't work continuously like machines. Consequently, we have to work people in shifts, so they can spell one another. They want to go home and sleep at night. They take time off for illness and vacations. They have other interests besides their jobs, which can cause distractions.

People Advantages

With all of those disadvantages, why would anyone want people around? Indeed, there are those who say, "If I didn't have to deal with people, I would have no problems whatsoever." Yet, despite some visionaries' concepts of workerless factories, people are vital

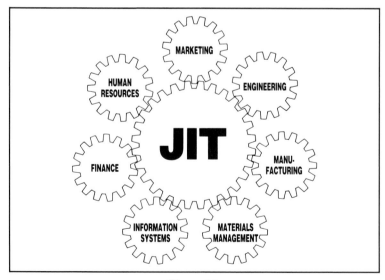

Figure 4-1

and necessary to achieve the JIT goal of continuous improvement. To do so, we must recognize that there are many people advantages.

People are very creative. They can think of new ways to do things in better ways if we provide them with an environment which fosters creativity.

People are versatile. Unlike a machine that is limited in its functions, people can do many different things if given the opportunity. They are adaptable and able to respond to changes in requirements.

People are intelligent, able to use deductive and inductive reasoning as they face problems and to apply that reasoning to unfamiliar situations which arise in the workplace. Using highly developed sensory perceptions, they can integrate observations with logic to make sound decisions.

Even though people do get tired, the maintenance and repair required is low, because they fix themselves. People don't require a huge maintenance department to care for them constantly, as is needed for robots. They go home at night, have something to eat, get a little sleep, and come back the next day refreshed and ready to go (at least most of the time).

People can also be extremely flexible when it comes to learning new things. Their reprogramming cycle is short compared to machines. As our business changes and the demands change, they can change with them.

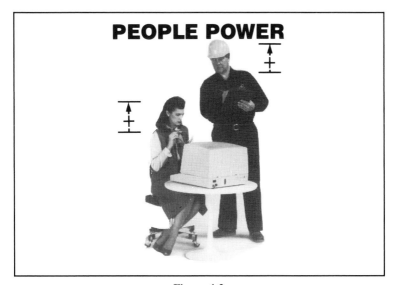

Figure 4-2

People disadvantages are primarily physical in nature. Most of the advantages that we discussed are mental. The real people power is that portion of the human being from the neck up; it's the neck down portion that presents most of the liabilities (See Figure 4-2). Yet, in the past, we have often hired people for their weakest features, their physical abilities. To implement JUST-IN-TIME, we must harvest people's strength, which is their brain power, because people are the source of all quality and productivity improvements.

People Needs

To accomplish this, we have to recognize and satisfy people's needs, as shown in Figure 4-3. Based on Maslow's Hierarchy of Needs, it demonstrates that people's expectation levels keep rising as lower level priorities are satisfied. Creativity will only occur when the higher level needs are met.

The ground level represents the *basic needs,* such as food, shelter and the other necessities for day-to-day survival. Most of our traditional compensation plans: wages, salaries and basic fringe benefits, have been directed toward these needs. For people raised during the Great Depression it seemed enough. For people expected to think and contribute improvement ideas, it is inadequate. Pure monetary compensation, even when tied to Suggestion System Programs, does not satisfy the higher

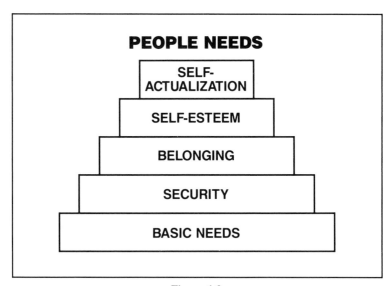

Figure 4-3

levels of people's needs. It is just a start.

The next level of needs addresses *security.* As soon as we've satisfied the survival issue for today, we humans want that state to be extended as long as possible into the future and to be protected against catastrophe. Our health and major medical programs, retirement plans and seniority systems are all aimed at this level of needs. They fall short, however, because of economic uncertainties. All of the foregoing can be terminated suddenly by the dreaded layoff. As long as people face this specter, the need for security will never be fully met.

POLICIES FOR A STABLE WORK ENVIRONMENT

Yet, our company policies must recognize and address the need for security if we expect to unleash the creative energies that our people can contribute. The objective should be to create a stable work environment, the foundation of which is to provide our employees with the highest level of job security that is possible. Most employees want this desperately, and it is becoming an increasing vital issue in union contract negotiations. Not only do we need to provide employment security, we want it to evolve to some form of lifetime employment.

Stability Through Lifetime Employment

Many executives "panic" when they hear such a suggestion. "That's impossible," they say. "That's not the sort of thing that is done in America." To the contrary, it is often done in America. IBM and Xerox, to mention just two companies, have been practicing it for generations. They just don't advertise it. And many small companies in America have found that full employment makes economic sense because it gives them a consistent, knowledgeable work force all of the time. This is a tremendous benefit, from management's perspective, because it provides stability and predictability. The average turnover rate in manufacturing in America is between one and one and a half percent per month. This means that, on the average, we are dealing with a new team of players every eight years. How are we going to implement all of the new JIT and Q@S principles needed to achieve continuous improvement if we must constantly bring brand new people "up to speed?" We can't.

Highly Qualified Hires

On the other hand, if we're going to have our people around for life, then we'd better be extremely careful about whom we hire. We can't afford to qualify new hires by seeing if they can "fog a mirror" when they breathe on it. We must concentrate on attracting highly qualified people for our JUST-IN-TIME operation. Their education, training and work experience, while still very important, only represent part of the qualifications. Of equal importance are their attitudes, intelligence and "fit" into our company culture, because we know they're going to be with us for life. We're looking for people who are going to be team players, who will work together, and who can work with other people to accomplish a common objective.

Extensive Training

Having very carefully selected whom we are going to hire, we must then give them the extensive training that is necessary for them to make the JUST-IN-TIME principles work. For example, at the NUMMI plant in Fremont, California, they give new operators between 200 and 700 hours of training before they'll even let them touch a vehicle. That's extensive but not unique.

Many years ago when, as a new graduate, I joined Westinghouse Corporation, I was put through a training program that lasted about four months. Starting in a training center, for the first four weeks, I was exposed to the company history, the company philosophy, the company goals, the company organization, its products and geographic locations. That gave me a real understanding of what the company was all about. Then, after taking a solid week of tests, I went through a series of one-month job assignments at three different locations before they decided I was ready for a permanent assignment. That's extensive training, here in America, and it happened more years ago than I care to admit.

The training can't stop with new employees. It has to be continued over the years so that the longer an employee is on the payroll, the more valuable he or she becomes to the company.

Pay for Capability

The incremental training received by the employees throughout their careers helps them widen the scope of their contributions. It then makes sense for us to pay those employees for their capability, not for the job they happen to be doing at any given moment. Today, we seldom do that. If we have a person who can do ten jobs sitting next to one who can do only one job and both are doing the same thing today, we pay for the job, and both people make the same amount of money. But, as far as the company is concerned, the person who can do five or ten jobs is worth more because tomorrow he or she can do many other things, if needed. Conversely, the person who can do only one job limits our flexibility. Therefore, by paying for capability, we reward flexibility and the scope of abilities. It also simplifies bookkeeping, since we no longer have to record the minute detail of who is doing what every moment of the day.

In JUST-IN-TIME, since people are thought of as an investment or a "sunk cost" rather than a variable cost, this concept not only makes heavy training a wise investment, it gradually equates capability with longevity. The longer you are here, the more you are going to be worth, because there are more things you will be able to do. Another way of saying it is that capability **should** be synonymous with seniority, provided that the senior employee has twenty years of experience, not one year of experience twenty times.

Job Flexibility

We pay more to a senior employee in a JUST-IN-TIME shop, not only because of that person's ability to do many different jobs, but also because of a willingness to do them. Job flexibility is extremely vital in a JIT environment. We are seeking flexible generalists, as opposed to specialists (who oftentimes must be idle while waiting their turn to implement their specialties).

There have been some false starts in a number of American companies. One of them created a "pay for knowledge" program. As an employee became qualified in a new skill, that person received a higher increment of pay because he or she should have become more valuable to the company. Unfortunately, their union contract included bumping privileges, based on seniority. Thus, a person could learn five new skills, bump into a preferred one and never be moved again, not even with TNT! That accomplished nothing except raising costs. The training skills were wasted. Pay for capability is important, but it has to be coupled with job flexibility. The two go hand in hand.

What About Surplus Workers?

Job security, a stable work force, highly qualified hires, extensive training, pay for capability and job flexibility will help build a stable work environment to satisfy people's fundamental needs. But, you may be wondering, at what cost? Many companies have a genuine fear of this aspect of JUST-IN-TIME. They ask, "If I go to lifetime employment and then make all of the productivity improvements that have been described, what am I going to do with all the surplus workers?" It's a fair question and there are two parts to that answer. First, it isn't going to happen overnight, so you won't be faced with an instant problem. Any surplus will build up gradually. Second, we have to be creative in this area and use our brainpower, just like we're asking our people to do. Some approaches are shown in Figure 4-4.

We start by reminding ourselves that the primary objectives of JUST-IN-TIME are to improve our quality and productivity so we can make more money, primarily by increasing sales. If our markets are increasing and all we do is hold our own, then our sales will increase, providing needed jobs for those "surplus" workers. If the market stays the same, we can still increase our sales because we can take some share away from the competition. In fact, there are even cases where the market will go down and we can still increase our sales because we will have a powerful, competitive advantage. In all of those circumstances, we won't have to worry about absorption of surplus workers; we could easily end up doing some hiring.

On the other hand, suppose that we cannot increase our sales.

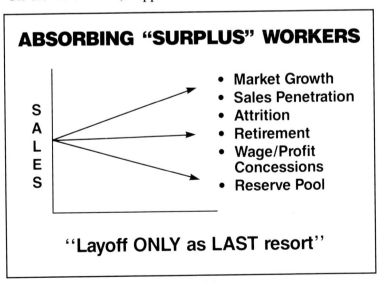

Figure 4-4

What if sales stay level, regardless of what happens to the market or our penetration percentage? There are some natural reduction factors working in our favor, like attrition. While we're going to work towards reducing attrition, it won't happen overnight either, so it can ease some of the problem. Then, there are retirements. We don't have to replace everybody who retires, so that gives us another option. In a real crunch, we can offer early retirements, as many companies have already done.

When all of the natural things have been done and we still have some extra people, we have to start getting creative. One of the painful things we can do is to seek profit and wage concessions. Not just wage concessions from the employees, but also profit concessions on management's part. We have to talk to each other, bite the bullet, and work together to find a way to get over this "hump," so we don't have to let people go.

There are other ways, too. Have you thought about a reserve pool? When you have a small number of surplus workers, you can assign them to a pool, usually in Manufacturing Engineering, and give them the opportunity to mingle with the engineers to contribute their perspectives of potential improvements. Some people call them Tiger Teams.

How Others Did It

A Michigan company did this and it proved to be very successful. The surplus employees were given desks in Manufacturing Engineering and told they had no specific assignments except to think about better ways of doing things. Many of them came to work wearing shirts and ties because, after all, they were part of Engineering now. Most of them began by reading magazines and newspapers, possibly feeling like they were getting away with something. But people, especially manufacturing people, quickly get bored with inactivity. So, they started to wander around the shop (showing off their white shirts and ties) they began to look at the processes they knew so well from a new perspective. When they came up with an improvement idea, they would go back into the Engineering Department and say, "Hey, George, (they could call him George now because they were working in the same department) let me show you something out on the floor." Together they would talk about the problem, often developing unique solutions. As time went by and the need for this person out on the shop floor redeveloped, he or she went back to the shop. While the operator was temporarily prevented from doing his or her normal job due to reduced demand, there was still an opportunity to help improve productivity and quality for the future. Upon returning to the original job, the operator became a better employee, due to the broader perspective acquired during this Tiger Team assignment.

Kawasaki, in Lincoln, Nebraska, was even more creative. When they were implementing JUST-IN-TIME, they anticipated that the productivity improvements and normal attrition would pretty well offset one another. It turned out, however, that productivity increased much faster than planned and the attrition rate slowed down, resulting in some 40 surplus employees. After doing all the things they could think of to keep the people occupied, like rearranging equipment, painting and even cutting the grass, they just ran out of things to do. They didn't want to lose these highly skilled employees, so they approached the City of Lincoln and offered the services of the 40 people as a civic contribution. They remained on the Kawasaki payroll and, as business picked up, they all gradually returned to the plant. A little far out? Certainly, but that's a measure of the creativity that can be exercised to solve this type of problem when and if it ever occurs. Strictly an "oriental" solution? The same thing was done by Digital Equipment Corporation in Alberquerque, New Mexico, when their plant experienced an economic downturn.

The LAST Alternative

By now, it should be apparent that you have many options available to handle the issue of surplus workers. But, suppose after exercising *all* of them you still have a problem? When the only alternative is to lay off workers or shut the doors, then, of course, you're going to lay off. You really don't have any choice. You are going to save the business because the first rule of business is survive. But, there is a very important reason why we try to avoid layoffs until there is no alternative. We have been asking people to contribute ideas which eliminate many unnecessary jobs. They will do that if they know their employment is not jeopardized. The minute they see that they or their teammates are going out the door, it will put an end to your productivity improvements unless *it is clear to them you had no choice.* Otherwise, it will be a long time before those wounds will heal and you can ever expect to resurrect your program. But that happens only a small percentage of the time. Let's not make a mountain out of a molehill. You have many things to work your way through before you ever get to the point of having to really shut the door. The important thing to remember is *layoffs should be the LAST RESORT, not the first option.*

How You Can Do It

You can begin by developing a local plan to keep your people. This starts with local senior management accepting the responsibility and exercising hands-on leadership to communicate with everybody in the organization to develop such a plan. You can't count on Corporate Office to do this. It has to be done by you and your people at your location. Ask for input from everybody, getting them to use their brain power. Figure out ways to increase your market share. You can do this by implementing the JIT Strategy, Quality at the Source, and the Core Elements of JUST-IN-TIME to reduce your costs so you can, in turn, reduce your prices to the market. In some cases, once you have a specific plan underway, even before you have actually experienced the full benefits of JUST-IN-TIME, you can anticipate the timing of those benefits and lower your prices accordingly, to gain more market share.

Above all, though, remember that you will have substantial retraining to do. As you implement JUST-IN-TIME, people must learn new ways and new thoughts. As they are displaced from non-value adding jobs, they must be taught new skills to do new jobs. None of these things can happen automatically. It requires a carefully orchestrated plan, a local plan.

DEVELOPING MOTIVATION AND TRUST

Even after we decide that management policies aimed at building a stable environment make sense, we must address another set of people's needs to draw out the ideas needed for continuous improvement. Referring again to Figure 4-3, there are three more levels which must be satisfied to achieve a creative atmosphere. First, there is *belonging*. Human beings have a driving need to belong to a group of other human beings. We are social creatures and crave peer acceptance. Once that is satisfied, the next thing we want is *self-esteem* or status in that social group. We want to see some sort of visible recognition of our accomplishments and our contributions to the social group. Finally, the highest level of all is *self-actualization*. At this point, we just feel good about ourselves, because all of the lower level needs have been satisfied, things have come to-gether and we are proud of ourselves and proud of the organization (family) to which we have attached ourselves. Our people policies, then, have to motivate the work force and develop mutual trust among them so everyone can reach the top plateau of self-actualization.

Family Atmosphere

To encourage belonging, you need to develop a family atmos-here in your company. Why family? The family is the ultimate group. It is the one we started out with in life. It is the one we are closest to and trust the most. We want to transfer this family feeling to the place where we work. After all, we spend more of our waking hours at work than anywhere else. If we can make that group seem like an extended family, we can motivate people to want to be accepted by the group. People must want to belong to our organization.

The first step is to develop a company tradition because tradition helps build the family feeling. But we have to work at it. We can't just say, "We've been around for 50 years or 100 years, and there-fore we have a tradition." Who knows that? Have you ever told the people where you're coming from, the history of your company, what your values are, what you are trying to achieve, how you are going to do it, and what part they need to play to make it happen? This must be conscientiously pursued if you expect to convince people that you believe they are an important part of the company family.

In Marysville, Ohio, Honda has an interesting ceremony that helps promote the family feeling. When an employee has been with the company for one year, they plant a tree together. The company President, along with the management people who relate to the em-ployee, attend the ceremony. It's very moving, because the employee looks at that tree as a physical representation of his or her relation-ship to the company. As the years go by, they watch their trees and all the other trees grow, reflecting their own growth and that of the organi-zation. It is very dramatic, but no different from some of the initiation ceremonies we conduct in our social and fraternal organizations. There are many things you can do to engender a family feeling, but it requires conscientious development.

Loyalty and Mutual Dependence

Within the family environment, you want to create bonds between the people. Bonds lead to loyalty and loyalty is a critical ingredient of belonging. Loyalty builds as we begin to trust each other and rely on one another. Loyalty is not something you can buy with dollars. You can buy people's time with dollars, but *you can't buy loyalty.* That's a mental mind set, and it only occurs when you begin to satisfy their need to belong.

Loyal family members who trust each other will work to achieve mutual goals instead of "going for themselves." It is natural and it is rational. Imagine two people in a lifeboat after a shipwreck. It is a big lifeboat and the oars are so far apart that one person couldn't possibly manage both at once. If the two people work together with coordination, they can not only survive, they can point the lifeboat in the right direction, their mutual goal, and make it take them where they want to go. But, neither one can do it alone. Think of that lifeboat as the company, and of the people in the boat as labor and management in the company. They have to work together to make anything worthwhile happen. And, either one would be foolish to drill a hole in the bottom of the boat.

Mutual goals require mutual dependence and trust, which can be risky. There are many managers who will ask, "Are you seriously suggesting that I should risk my career by relying on other people?" The answer is, yes. There is no such thing as a free lunch. You have to give a little to get a little. So, this is going to be very difficult for a lot of traditionalists. But, developing these mutual goals and becoming dependent on one another is absolutely crucial if we ever expect to develop teams and teamwork.

Building Teams

A few years ago, William Ouchi wrote ***Theory Z,*** a book about the differences between Oriental and American business cultures, especially when it comes to teamwork. His analogy used the growth of primary grains in the two countries — rice in the East and wheat in America. In the Orient, one person, working as hard as possible, can't grow enough rice to feed his own family because of the necessary farming techniques. He has to build dikes and flood the fields and drain them at critical times in the growing season. It is too big a job for one person, but ten people working together can actually grow enough rice to feed their own families and 100 more. (That's why you see clusters of houses surrounded by rice paddies in Asian farming areas.) That is *synergism,* where the whole is greater than the sum of the parts. It is exactly what we do in Manufacturing. No one person can cost effectively build a car or a refrigerator, but all of us working together can make the product and sell it for a profit.

Ouchi went on to say this is natural for the East, but Americans are different. If you fly over a wheat farm in Kansas, you will see one farmhouse, one barn, and acres and acres of wheat in all directions. It is supposed to be characteristic of our technology and our independence, reflecting our tendencies to want to do things by ourselves. In essence, it suggests that it's not natural for Americans to be team players.

Do you believe that? I don't. There are no more team-oriented people on the face of the earth than Americans. Look at our sports teams. In school, it's always the team sports that are the most popular. Historically, consider the wagon trains. Would we have ever opened the West if people hadn't banded together in a team to accomplish a mutual objective? What about barn raisings or our responses to natural disasters, when people came together to help one another to overcome adversity? We've even created team sports from individual sports, like tennis, golf and swimming. Never let it be said that we are not team-oriented. But, we have to be motivated. It has to be a team that we *want* to join, and Americans love to join a winner. We'll work tirelessly to build and be part of a winning team.

Peer Pressure

When a real team spirit is established and everyone wants to achieve the mutual goals, the team policies itself. Peer pressure becomes a natural force to make sure that the job is done and done right. Go to any old line manufacturing plant in America and you'll often find several generations of the same family working there. Rarely, will you see one of those people disrupting the organization because it would bring discredit to their personal family as well as to the company family. Couple that with a reward system that addresses group performance instead of individual accomplishments, and the team members will do a better job of assuring that everyone contributes than any supervisor can do. There have been some very successful experiments tried in U.S. companies in which the team had no supervisor, shared administrative duties, and outperformed the traditional groups.

Peer pressure is also effective because people have an inherent desire to do a good job, to succeed. The vast majority, over 95%, not only want to belong, but also want to do well. Yet, isn't it interesting that the personnel administration systems in most of our companies are aimed to the less than 5% who might not. It's a negative system. Why do you have timeclocks for the hourly people? Aren't they as good as your salaried people or as trustworthy? Most companies going into JUST-IN-TIME throw their timeclocks out the door because there is no such thing as second class citizens in a JIT environment. A visible sign like that makes it clear to the employees that they are trusted. This is just one motivational step, but it helps.

Gainsharing

Another way to motivate the teams is to share our success with them when we achieve our mutual goals. Since we are in business to make a profit, the best thing we can do is share some portion of those profits with the employees. In fact, we would like to make an increasingly larger portion of their earnings dependent upon our ability to make a profit, as the years go by, to reinforce our common goal. It helps improve team performance because we are all sharing the same reward system.

If you have individual incentives on your shop floor today, they are counterproductive to JUST-IN-TIME goals. Individual incentives drive people to do things that may put short-term money in their pockets but can hurt the team effort, department efforts and plant goals. Individual incentives often drive people to do the wrong things, like make easy parts as fast as possible, even if the parts aren't needed, or to over produce. Individual incentives should be at the top of your list of things that you want to negotiate out of your existing labor contracts, or to gravitate away from in a nonunion shop. You can replace them at first with team incentives, eventually enlarging the base until the "team" is the profit center, where profit sharing makes the most sense.

Donnelly Mirror, in Holland, Michigan, has used a gain sharing program more than 15 years, and it is amazing how their employees relate to earning profits and know how every dollar of profit is going to be shared with them. The applicant waiting list at Donnelly is several times greater than their whole payroll, and their turnover is absolutely one of the lowest in the State of Michigan — not just because of gain sharing, although it is a big piece of it, but because they practice what we have been discussing in this chapter.

. Pride

The ultimate, highest level of people's needs that can be reached is self-actualization, or pride. Here, I use the word pride in the context of doing a good job and feeling good about it. This level, reached only when all lower levels have been satisfied, is the one that spurs the continuous improvement required by JUST-IN-TIME. Pride is the glue that binds the team together and the fuel that drives the idea machine.

General Motors closed its Fremont assembly plant some years ago, declaring it was too far away from its supply base and too costly to operate. In actuality, the plant had lower productivity, lower quality, higher absenteeism, and more labor problems than any other plant in the GM system. Both management and the union considered the other side to be totally unreasonable. *Wards Automotive Magazine* quoted one employee as stating, "We were building garbage. When people asked me where I worked, I told them I was self-employed."

Then, GM and Toyota created NUMMI, a new company at the old location which introduced very significant changes. The top management team, provided by Toyota, brought with them a new people management system based on the issues discussed in this Chapter. New American middle management was assigned to NUMMI from GM, to be trained in the "new way." Most of the workforce was comprised of the same the same UAW workers who were there before, and the bargaining unit was recognized. Yet, NUMMI was able to produce over 240,000 cars a year with 2,400 people (including the body stamping operations) compared to more than 5,000 people at the old plant for the same number of vehicles *without* the body stamping activity. Product quality went from last to first. During the first quality audit, conducted shortly after NUMMI started producing cars, they received the second highest rating in all of General Motors. The were unhappy with that and worked hard to improve. On the very next audit they equaled the highest quality rating of any plant in GM.

What was different? The people were the same. The plant layout was changed to implement some of the JUST-IN-TIME elements that will be covered in subsequent chapters of this book. But, the key differences were the management attitudes, policies and practices that motivated the old work force and changed the negative environment, replacing it with the positive factors that led to personal pride and pride in their company. Recently a NUMMI employee (one of the same people who was there before the changes) said, "I thank God this place was built." That's pride, and only enlightened management can bring it about.

Building motivation and trust, then, satisfies the highest level of people's needs, which engenders the continuous improvement we are seeking with JUST-IN-TIME. You may not believe it, but the competition, your competition, is doing it today. You need to understand it, know how it works and learn to apply it to improve your operation, because it does work. It is the capstone of the management policies that are necessary to build the foundation of JUST-IN-TIME.

JIT Compensation Strategy

To reinforce these policies, our JIT compensation strategy should be comprised of two parts:

1. *Pay for Capability* — the **INDIVIDUAL** is rewarded for learning new skills and willingly applying them where needed to attain workplace flexibility. In the spirit of continuous improvement, the learning never ends, so capability can eventually be equated to seniority in a JIT operation.

2. *Gain Sharing* — the **TEAM** is rewarded for helping the company earn a profit. This means building "perfect parts" to "exact customer demand" at the lowest possible cost. While every individual has responsibilities, only the team can earn money and this form of compensation provides an incentive for team members to help one another achieve their common goal.

When we couple compensation with policies that provide a stable environment and motivate the people, all incentives are working in concert with one another to achieve the real company goal — making money. We eliminate "local" incentives which can actually detract from our profit goal by emphasizing suboptimal measurements. These are covered in greater detail in Chapter 15.

JIT MANAGEMENT PRACTICES

Good policies and a commensurate compensation plan will give us the necessary foundation to develop our main source of quality and productivity improvements, our people. But, policies alone won't get the job done. New management practices are also needed to implement and administer the policies. These practices fall under three general classifications:

1. Our *attitude* toward the people who work for the company.

2. *Bottom round decision making,* which is quite different from the way many of us do it.

3. A change in the *organization structure* and the delegation of responsibilities within that structure.

Management Attitude

First, let's consider our attitude toward people and their abilities. Attitude has been addressed often in this book already, but now we want to step back just a little bit and examine the broader perspective of how we perceive other human beings. We have to accept the premise that workers are very important as people. Earlier, we reviewed the many disadvantages of people and how hard it is to try to manage them when they are so variable. Because people are never the same, many managers believe that the easiest way to supervise is when you have a labor contract. In that case, everything is "black and white." Either it is in the contract or it isn't in the contract. But relationships with human beings are not black and white. They are shades of gray, and those shades will vary from day to day, depending on the attitudes, the backgrounds, the environments and the aspirations of the individuals with whom you are working. That's not easy.

I was trained as an engineer and was taught to work with "things." I understand things better than people. I admire those people who can read body language or can sense what people are trying to say without hearing the words. Yet, this is an important requirement for management in the JUST-IN-TIME environment. It isn't easy for me and it may not be easy for you either, but it is vital because we have to learn to manage the whole person if we expect to harvest the creative abilities that are so important to our JIT Strategy.

Worker Capabilities

Just how good is that "whole person" we're trying to manage? For Quality at the Source, we have already determined that he or she has the capability to do self-inspection, use the Q@S Tool Kit, and perform minor maintenance functions. But now, we need to go one step further. Think about all of the abilities of that person from the broadest possible perspective. Every worker has a very high degree of ability, much of which has never had the opportunity to surface.

That may be hard to accept at first. Undoubtedly, you can call to mind one or more exceptions. After all, hasn't everybody heard about the *"Peter Principle?"* It says that everybody gets promoted until they eventually reach their level of incompetence! Are you there? I doubt it. Most people I know don't believe they are there. Well then, let's think about it a different way. Do you know any *other* people who have reached their level of incompetence? Maybe a subordinate, or a peer. How about a boss who got there two levels ago? I suspect you can come up with quite a list. Why is it that we're so good and they're so bad? I submit to you that the reason is, that we know ourselves, but everybody else sees us through a set of filters that we create. It is a product of our environment and our life experiences. It lets others see only what we allow them to see. It means that even a really "tough" human being, a grouch that nobody likes, one that people want to stay away from, has considerable talent buried deep inside but hasn't revealed it yet. You have to believe it is there, because that's the *"gold mine"* of creativity and innovation that makes continuous improvement of productivity and quality possible.

Management Responsibilities

Nobody ever said mining for gold was easy. As a matter of fact, it is pick and shovel work, which brings us to another management attitude issue. If we really believe the mother lode is there, then we have to help it emerge. We have to provide those workers with the wherewithal to display their full capabilities. The management task in JUST-IN-TIME is not just to "allow" it to happen, but to provide the people with the tools, the encouragement, and the motivation to make it possible.

One final attitudinal consideration is that those workers who have that great ability also want to do one heck of a good job. The vast majority of all workers, well over 95% in all companies, are very conscientious. The work ethic is still here in America, but every one of us is very susceptible to environmental influence. The management challenge is to create and maintain a positive environment which will nurture human capabilities.

Bottom Round Management

The next thing we have to do is take some risk and give up a little power by employing a technique called *Bottom Round Decision Making*. Just as the name indicates, it's a two-part (bottom and round) approach. The "round" part addresses the development of JUST-IN-TIME team players. These people must have an opportunity to participate in the decision making process, especially when it directly affects their work activities.

In some places, they call this consensus decision making. Other companies in America call it participative management. That's a good term, too. We are not talking about management by committee nor are we suggesting taking a vote of the whole company every time we want to do something, especially if it's an operating decision. We are saying that significant decisions which affect a person or a group should include inputs from them. Even if the recommendations that those people make are not adopted, the very fact that we asked them, listened to them and explained why we made a different decision than the ones they recommended, will help them "buy in" to whatever decision is made, and therefore help with the implementation.

True consensus decision making is very slow because it takes a long time to get everybody to agree. Have you ever tried to reach a unanimous decision at a club meeting? There is always at least one major dissenter, so it's difficult. The key is to avoid having winners and losers, so we don't want votes. If somebody dissents, it means that the group doesn't have enough information or the individual doesn't have enough information to allow everyone to come to the same conclusion. As a rule, group decisions tend to be better decisions than individual decisions. Anyone who has ever done the "lost in the desert" exercise can attest to that. The price you pay, though, is a long, slow, decision-making process.

Managers who can make quick decisions are admired today. Conversely, when someone takes "forever" to make a decision, we look down on that person. Unfortunately, this encourages "hip shooting," which is harmful in many cases and almost always takes more time when implementation is considered. When a good group decision is made, implementation is very fast because everybody involved has already "bought into" it. All of the pros and cons have been investigated, including the obstacles that might have to be overcome. On the other hand, when we make a snap decision, implementation is usually difficult and lengthy because nobody took the time to consider all the obstacles that could be encountered, and we often have to keep "selling" the decision to people who weren't consulted in the first place. Worst of all, we sometimes even have to abandon our decision because we encounter an obstacle that is so large we can't overcome it. Then, it's back to the drawing board to start all over at square one!

Which way is best? Let's examine a combination of quick decision making and long implementation -vs- long decision making and quick implementation. If both combinations take the same total time, the latter is best because every decision we make can be implemented when we have the whole team behind it, working to make it happen. That's why it is so vital that we learn the consensus approach to decision making to build the framework for Bottom Round Management.

The most difficult part of Bottom Round Management for most of us is to rethink our operating procedure so we can literally force decisions as far down the organization as possible. We want operating decisions to be made *at the point of action*. For managers and supervisors who have achieved job satisfaction and a sense of personal achievement by making operating decisions, even to the point of defining jobs that way, this can be traumatic. The problem is that too many of us make decisions about activities that are far removed from our day-to-day involvement. If we aren't living the problem, we're probably not the right person to make the decision. That person is the one at the point of action on the firing line, who is usually held responsible for the outcome anyway.

Many of us have been breaking the cardinal rule of "Management 101" because, while we've delegated responsibility, we've usually been a little hesitant to delegate the commensurate authority. Under JUST-IN-TIME, we want to let the "doers" run their own business. It shouldn't be important for a plant manager to know whether a given machine is running or not running at this point in time. Yet, I have friends who have computer terminals on their desks and take great pride in knowing this level of detail, as if that were the measure of a good plant manager. That's not a plant manager's job. That's the job of the people on the floor, running those machines and running those departments.

This applies to all parts of the organization, especially at the first and second levels of supervision. It is hard to accomplish because it strips away the security blanket of authority that has comforted us in the past. Yet, we already know that "comfort" is an inhibitor to continuous improvement so this should not be unexpected. By the same token, we must be prepared to deal with the fear of lost status (a form of job security plus self-esteem), and the historical mistrust of the workers by some managers. This change to the "company culture" requires patience, accompanied by intensive training, to achieve the transformation.

Traditional Organization Structure

The place to start is a re-examination of our present organization structure, which is typically archaic. The classic management organization used by most major corporations, and small companies as well, was employed by Alexander the Great. It is the classic pyramid with top management at the apex making decisions, passing them down to middle management where they are interpreted, "refined" and passed down through subsequent levels for more refinements until the "doer" is finally told what to do. It is the autocratic approach that has been used for centuries.

But, there are a lot of problems with that structure in today's competitive environment, especially in a JUST-IN-TIME manufacturing business. Using the graphic shown in Figure 4-5, let's explore whether it makes sense in an atmosphere of continuous improvement. At the apex is top management, whose function in life, according to many management magazine surveys, is to *make decisions*. Most top managers see themselves as decision makers. Harry Truman, former President of the United States, had a sign on his desk that said, "The buck stops here," inferring that he was the only person who could (or

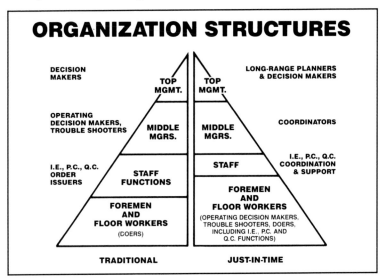

Figure 4-5

would) make a decision. This attitude is commonly found in business and it sets the tone for how the rest of the organization behaves. This is not to say that today's business executives don't involve themselves in other important things as well, like strategic planning and financing. The important thing is that they see themselves primarily as decision makers. And, as the leaders go, so do the rest of us follow.

Consider the next level, middle management. What is middle management's primary goal? Realistically, it is to get *themselves promoted* to top management. So, what do they emulate? Decision making. In fact, they're not just demonstrating how "well" they make decisions, they are jealously guarding the right to make them! It's a territorial prerogative. And woe be to the person who comes along and suggests we change all that and push decision making down to the action level. See the problem? We are flying right smack in the face of tradition, and we have to change it. If we don't, if management continues to decide how everything is to be done, we are telling our people, "don't think, just do. Basically, you are arms and legs. If we wanted you to think, we would have put that in your job description."

We figuratively chain the people to their work places, measure their contribution by pieces per hour, and tell them not to stop for any reason because it will reduce production. Consequently, we have to employ a virtual army of people to help them, like schedulers to tell them what to do next, material handlers to bring material to them and take it away, inspectors to look at the material and decide if it is good or not, machine set-up people to help them change products, and the list goes on. This is one of the reasons that supporting operations costs are so much higher in traditional plants than they are in JIT facilities. The organization structure is the driver, and we can improve it.

The JIT Organization Structure

In the JUST-IN-TIME organization structure, we want to start at the bottom, at the foreman and the floor workers' activities. Look again at Figure 4-5. The relative size of this part of the organization is much larger when compared to the traditional one. As has been said before and will be repeated, we want the "direct labor" people, the value adders, to absorb more and more of the activities that we normally associate with staff functions. Whenever you have specialists performing support functions, it's a waste: a waste because somebody is always waiting for somebody else, and a waste because specialization spawns lines of demarcation, which inhibit flexibility.

Staff should be a knowledge resource, not a group of "doers." It is written, "Give a man a fish, and you'll feed him for a day. Teach a man to fish, and you'll feed him for life." That's the role of staff in a JUST-IN-TIME world. When we need to know how to prepare SPC charts, Quality Control will show us how to get started, how to maintain the charts, and how to interpret them. Then, they are going to leave and we'll carry on with the day-to-day operations. They're not going to do it for us. Without "doers" on the staff, we don't need as much staff, which reduces their proportion in the organization.

The next level in the organization, middle management, is theoretically unnecessary in a JUST-IN-TIME shop. If every worker is truly independent, capable of doing the job and able to make the needed decisions in his or her operation, additional layers of management inhibit the process. All we really need is a cadre of "doers," some knowledge resource and top management (ideally, just one person, the President). From a practical standpoint, this is not going to happen in our lifetime, if ever. However, a number of American plants are working toward this goal. For example, a million square foot Consolidated Diesel plant in North Carolina has just four layers in its reporting structure: the plant manager, seven department managers, first line supervisors and workers. The plant manager has stated that this is the easiest plant he's ever had to manage. Four isn't the ultimate number of levels but, just like the perfect part, we must set our objective so that we can begin to head in that direction, and every subsequent organizational decision can be made to bring us closer to that goal.

With this greatly reduced management team, there won't be enough resources to do all the decision making at the top level, so this will promote the redeployment of operating decisions to lower levels. Top management's role in a JUST-IN-TIME shop will be to chart the course of the organization. Many people, including our customers, employees, suppliers and investors, are dependent on our "ship" of wealth production and somebody needs to be at the helm. This means a longer range plan with longer range strategies. We are in a global market now and the world is changing so fast that we can't just do a strategic exercise once a year.

How many of us today go through a frantic six week "blitz" to prepare our strategic plan, present it to some Vice President, have a cocktail party afterward to congratulate ourselves, and then put the plan on the shelf where it will gather dust until next year? That is not the way we are going to survive in tomorrow's environment. Strategic planning has to be an ongoing process. It is the most important thing our top management can do. And, beyond this, the shift in thrust by top management will have a significant impact on the motivation of middle management in the organization. With new signals coming from the top, the way will be opened to change middle management behavior.

The Role of Middle Management

As was stated earlier, we're going to need our middle management for quite some time to come, especially during the transition to JUST-IN-TIME. The changes will be influenced by less available time to make operating decisions, a new role model by top management, and the need to learn the skills required to provide leadership in this new environment. Middle management will need to discover how to become holistic managers and how to relate to people who are all different but who have untapped brain power to contribute. The needed time to achieve these skills can only be gained by off loading routine decision making, changing the focus to becoming better people managers and, more important than that, to becoming better developers of teams in the organization to achieve the company goals. Middle management will be measured in the future much like a coach is measured in team sports today. The ability to develop a team and the achievements of that team will be the measure of the manager's contribution. The best coach is recognized as the one whose team wins, regardless of his or her personal credentials.

OVERCOMING CONCERNS

The People Policies and Practices described in this Chapter are vital to the success of JUST-IN-TIME because they establish the environment to develop and nurture continuous improvement. They are, in essence, the "Table Stakes" of JIT. You can expect to meet resistance to some of these concepts from a number of fronts, especially middle management, first line supervision and, if you have a labor union, the union leadership. While union leaders may strongly object to being included with "management," the fact remains that they are the management team which conducts union business and are subject to the same stresses that create resistance among company managers and supervisors.

Management Fears

Those stresses create genuine fears, which include:

1. *Fear of Change:* Nowhere is the comfort and security of the status quo more entrenched than among these groups. Change, especially when it affects management style and human interaction, disrupts the historical baseline that has been established and opens the door to the unknown. Even though most of us have quoted Franklin D. Roosevelt's line, "We have nothing to fear but fear itself," it is harder to buy into it when it applies to us personally, and to what we perceive as jeopardy to our careers.

2. *Fear of Failure:* Management hates to fail and very few "new" things are 100% certain to succeed. How many times have you heard a person say, "It sounds like a good idea, but let someone else try it first." Even when failure is not career threatening, nobody wants the blemish on his or her record. This is the condition that gave rise to the old saw, "The turtle only moves ahead by sticking its neck out."

3. *Fear of Power Loss:* A sense of power is a sense of self-esteem. Managers and supervisors who have worked for years to attain their current positions don't want to see this status eroded. Bottom Round Management is often eyed suspiciously as "giving away authority, taking a vote on everything or telling people more than they need to know." After all, knowledge is a base of power, too, especially in the technical and financial areas. This fear is rarely openly expressed but is often the motivator for obstructionist or "foot-dragging" behavior (See Figure 4-6).

Although these management fears are real, their severity is usually blown out of proportion. To counter them it is necessary to answer two key questions from those concerned:

1. Do I have to do this?
2. How do I benefit from this?

The "have to" issue is contingent upon how top management addresses the JIT People Policies and Practices. If you're going to "stick your toe in the water and see how it feels," you'll provide no motivator to help overcome the fears. The "turtle" syndrome will prevail. On the other hand, "plunging in head first" doesn't make any sense either. These changes to the company culture must be evolutionary in nature. What is needed is a clear top management signal that these changes **WILL** take place in an orderly fashion and that the future leaders of your company will be the ones who demonstrate the the ability to manage this "new way." This is a top down policy decision, but one of gigantic strategic importance because it will set the tone for human interactions for decades to come.

Personal benefits, aside from continued employment and promotional opportunities, will come from the self esteem that is associated with creating something new that actually works. We've all heard about those "crazy inventors" who drive themselves unmercifully in their quest for discovery. The "creation high" can be an unmatched human experience. Few managers, however, get such an opportunity. They inherit an organization and are expected to "run it" as well or better than their predecessors. Size and power in a rigid structure are their hallmarks of success. But, these things can also be depressing and debilitating. Creation can be fun! Ask any of the core team members who helped start a new enterprise that blossomed through their efforts, like Apple Computer or Electronic Data Systems (EDS). The best part is that those people actually like one another.

Worker Fears

The "labor force" has almost always been very receptive to the

"Hang on, Griswold! Don't give up the turf!"

COPYRIGHT 1987, USA TODAY. Reprinted with permission.

Figure 4-6

concepts of JUST-IN-TIME in the JIT implementations with which I've been involved. The idea that somebody is finally hearing what they've been trying to say for years and that their opinions are valuable to the business provides positive motivation. There is, however, a genuine concern about loss of jobs. When taken in the context of those people currently on the payroll (i.e., the "family") these fears can be allayed by the steps outlined earlier in this Chapter (What About Surplus Workers?). If, on the other hand, you have a labor union which measures job security in terms of headcount it is another matter. This is just one of a number of concerns that seem to rise up in a union environment, although they aren't restricted to it. Alan Callet, Director of Human Resources for Dresser-Wayne, has been grappling with these concerns for many years and categorizes them as follows:

1. *Fear of Membership Loss:* The size of the Local is a measure of prestige and financial power. When the union leadership takes this perspective, it is concentrating on the same local optimums and protection of turf that were discussed under Management Fears. Yet, if bloating the membership roles means the company cannot compete effectively, there may be no membership at all. This is the most difficult dilemma that must be faced by the Local leadership.

2. *"What, Me Worry?" Syndrome:* Workers may not really believe that there is a competitive threat which could cost them their jobs. This is especially true in small towns where provincial thinking gives long term employees little perspective of external happenings or influences on the company's ability to compete. A history of Theory X paternalism or confrontation will amplify this syndrome when management first tries to share economic realities with the union. It will take repeated efforts to get this message across, but it is necessary. Otherwise, the prevailing attitude will be, "It can't happen here, so why should we embrace drastic change?"

3. *Unwillingness to Give Up Control:* Even when there is general acceptance that the company has a serious survival situation, union leaders may see JUST-IN-TIME as a threat to their power base and the influence they exert over members. In extreme cases possessive leadership will intervene to jam the direct boss — subordinate dialogue which involvement programs, and JIT, thrive on. Bottom Round Management, which takes the fear out of giving more decision-making responsibility and independence to the value adders, will reduce the need for the intermediary role (and commensurate control) that the leaders are

used to playing; even more importantly, the memberships' blind dependency on union leadership, which was based primarily on company indifference will evaporate quickly.

4. *The Happy Worker Myth:* The proliferation of job descriptions over the years has been fueled not just by the desire to create as many jobs as possible, but also by the belief that the "Happy Worker is *narrowly skilled and broadly idle.*" While there may be some truth to this premise in a traditional environment, it not only undermines ecomic security; it utterly ignores people's psychic needs, as described earlier. The JIT environment, on the other hand, provides the stability and motivation to appeal to their higher interests, their natural enjoyment of variety and the recognition that idleness is a waste which endangers competitiveness.

5. *Refusal to Surrender Past "Gains":* Until union leaders recognize that the JIT approach will provide workers with more satisfaction, opportunity, and security, there will be a fear that this is just a management ruse to "take away the hard won gains" of past negotiations. Nobody wants to give up something they have struggled to achieve, even if it doesn't make sense anymore. It will take candor, forthright communications, patience and possibly an economic quid pro que to pave the way for JIT.

6. *A "Death Wish":* Sometimes conditions are so acrimonious that the union is totally intransigent. Even though the need for change and the benefits of the new way may be evident, the years of battling and perceptions of past betrayals may result in an "over my dead body" position by the union leadership. While it may seem impossible that anyone could take such a position when the known result would be catastrophic to the workers, the number of U.S. plants that have been closed in recent years due to such an impasse is considerable. No one knows for certain why a responsible union would do such a thing, any more than we know what drives an individual to suicide. But, suicidal tendencies can be overcome with a lot of bridge building and education. We should also remember that this situation is relatively rare, and that most of the union reticence to JIT will be caused by one of the previously stated fears.

These fears will manifest themselves in many ways, but there are three very common ones. First, the union may block any efforts to initiate Employee Involvement or Quality Circle Programs (discussed in Chapter 5). This is a sure sign of a high level of mistrust and determination to prevent any change to the current order of doing things. More often, however, the union will give the EI program a trial but refuse to negotiate changes in job classifications. Here, even though the need to involve the employees in the drive toward increased quality and productivity in order to get more competitive is recognized, the fear of job loss or power loss is still very strong. In some cases, the union will actually agree to job classification changes but will then dispute every actual change and take it to arbitration. This is just a more sophisticated strategy driven by the same concerns as the refusal to negotiate at all.

Paving the Way for Change

With all these fears and road blocking maneuvers, one might wonder if there is any hope for JIT in a union shop. Yet, there are many examples already here in America, some of which have already been cited in this Chapter. What then can you do to bring about the necessary changes in your shop? Alan Callet suggests five steps that have helped him pave the way for change:

1. *Substitute data for rhetoric.* People are tired of hearing nice round words. As Sergeant Joe Friday used to say, "Just the facts" are wanted. This means sharing statistics and financial information that used to be kept secret from employees. People at all levels need numbers to decide if a change in habit is mandatory, yet it's companies most in need of change who are usually last in sharing financial data.

2. *Remember that, "actions speak louder than words."* Don't promise more than you can deliver, but do deliver everything you promise. It is good that people have a vision of the "Big Picture." But vibrant involvement programs won't flourish where managers can't act as vigorously on little ticket items promoted by workers as on big ticket items traditionally promoted from above. It is on these work-site to do lists published by the circle or Involvement Team that management must focus it's urgency; otherwise the seed of partnership trust whose nourishment comes from "doing things together" perishes from lack of visile achievement.

3. *Make safety the first topic for Employee Involvement.* Safety is a non-contentious subject that can get the ball rolling. It should be important to everyone and can provide a basis for initial agreement. When both sides get used to working with one another in a productive fashion, then more difficult topics can be addressed.

4. *Work together to juggle ALL the variables.* Historically, nego-

tiations between union and management representatives have been piecemeal. "Easy" issues were always addressed first to get them out of the way, but any concessions here led to hardening positions on the tougher subjects. The changes for JIT are so broadly based and there are so many trade-offs that all the variables need to be examined in relationship to the total picture. It is imperative that both sides feel that they are trying to come up with a real "win-win" agreement.

5. *Use JIT training to achieve a non-contentious plane.* The key to successful JIT implementation is understanding. When every union and company representative sees the economic and psychic benefits of JUST-IN-TIME, as well as the techniques, negotiations can move to a higher non-contentious plane where everyone will have the same data base and the same vision. Similarly, when agreement is reached employees need to be brought to the same level of understanding to alleviate any fears and concerns they might have. Everybody enjoys abandoning a contentious relationship and training is a good transition vehicle.

Pitfalls to Avoid

While there is rarely a sure-fire, guaranteed path to success, there are a number of things to avoid which are almost certain to sabotage JIT implementation. They include:

- A "ho-hum" response, especially by first line supervision.
- Failure to respond to employee ideas.
- Failure to adapt the firm's compensation and reward/punishment systems to the new culture. (Old measurements foster old ways.)
- Failure to evolve to Bottom Round Management.
- Unilateral, top down implementation of JIT techniques without changing the People Polices and Practices.
- Too much too fast, creating psychic overload. (All this and my old job, too?)
- Devaluing hard won experience. (Doesn't anything I've learned in the past apply?)

SUMMARY

Changing the company culture is not an easy task. It cannot be accomplished quickly. Yet, is vitally necessary to provide the environment to make JUST-IN-TIME work. The environment we seek is one which fosters the generation of ideas which will continuously improve quality and productivity. This innovation and creativity can only be achieved when the highest plane of people's needs are met.

Management Policies must establish a stable environment that is free from fear of job loss. They must be aimed at developing mutual trust, a team spirit, mutual objectives and dependency, sharing of both hardships and gains, and pride in everything the organization stands for and does.

Management Practices must begin with a holistic attitude about people, their worth and potential to contribute from an intellectual standpoint. Each person must be encouraged to be a flexible generalist and a team player, while shouldering individual responsibility. Decision making should be done at the lowest possible level, at the point of action. The organization structure should have the fewest possible levels and be team oriented instead of having a rigid, top down superstructure.

Top management must establish the vision, values and goals for the organization, continuously update them so the company can compete in world-wide markets and provide the inspiration and leadership to make the changes possible. As John Scully, CEO of Apple Computer said, "By providing the stability of a clear corporate identity, directional goals, values, a work environment where people can thrive and the resources they need, top management is adding *wisdom.*"

QUALITY CIRCLES

CHAPTER 5

"A Quality Circle is a method to implement
the people policies and practices required
to obtain continuous improvement
at the work place level."

People are the source of all the quality and productivity improvements we will achieve through JUST-IN-TIME. This is only achievable if we shift our emphasis in manufacturing from muscle power to brain power, as discussed in Chapter 4. In many companies, this represents a major change from established working relationships, one that won't come easily. We need a tool, a methodology, to enable us to try these new approaches on a small scale and to build the experience and self-confidence needed to move forward. There is such a tool available today. It is something we can implement gradually while learning and which will clearly demonstrate the advantages of cultivating "people power." It is called a Quality Circle. When used correctly, it is a proven method to implement the people policies and practices required to obtain continuous improvement at the work place level.

WHAT'S IN A NAME?

Quality Circles have a bad name in a number of American companies today. Some people will even bristle when they hear the term and refuse to listen any further. In fact, reactions have been so strong in some quarters that the International Association of Quality Circles, headquartered in Cincinnati, Ohio, actually changed its name to the Association of Quality and Participation (AQP) in 1988. Why is there such a negative feeling about something that can be so beneficial? Sadly, it's because too many Quality Circle Programs were implemented the wrong way and for the wrong reasons.

When the first Americans saw Quality Circles at work in Japan it was mainly the money saving results they brought back with them. Some thought it was the "secret weapon" to achieve a competitive advantage. American Quality Circle programs, which started in the 1970's, have had mixed reviews because too many of them seemed to be preoccupied with the financial results instead of the people aspects.

It's Not The Name, It's The Substance

Shakespeare once said, "A rose by any other name would smell as sweet." It isn't the name that's important, it's the substance. To fully understand and benefit from a Quality Circle Program, it is vital that we firmly establish the real objectives of this methodology and not get sidetracked by the siren song of "fast money." When we do, it will become apparent that the emphasis should be placed on individual growth, team building and management style, using continuous improvement as the agenda to provide a focus for everyone's development. Only then can Quality Circles be a mechanism to change the company culture.

There's no law that says you have to call them Quality Circles anyway. Many companies give other names to their programs to suit their needs. Quality of Work Life, or QWL, is a popular one, as is EI, or Employee Involvement. Digital Equipment Corporation's Alberquerque Plant calls theirs VIA, which stands for Volunteers In Action. Plasti-Line, Inc., in Knoxville, Tennessee named its program Common Sense Circles, which they are! (Their emblem is shown in Figure 5-1.) In addition, most of the improvements proposed by American Quality Circles turn out to be productivity or quality of work life oriented, so the title, "Quality Circles," probably isn't that descriptive.

To my way of thinking, any name that suits you should be fine,

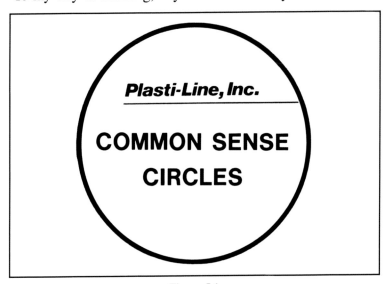

Figure 5-1

the word, *circle,* is very significant. The mathematical definition of a circle is "a single curved line, every point of which is equally distant from its center," but Webster also gives us another, very applicable definition, which is *"a group having a common tie."* It is also very natural for human interaction. Notice how people group themselves at a social function — they always form a circle. Every person has equal status and equal access to one another, which maximizes the interchange of information. This is the very essence of what we are trying to achieve through the Quality Circle methodology.

Origin of Quality Circles

Quality Circles is one of the few JUST-IN-TIME elements that did not originate in America, although some people say that the concept dates back to our town meetings. Modern day Quality Circles started in Japan in 1962 under the sponsorship of a magazine publisher. When Dr. W. E. Deming introduced statistical process control to Japan and started a quality crusade back in the 1950's, a number of magazines were published in support of the movement. Circulation was fairly small, however, as they were apparently only read by the "technical types." In an effort to broaden the applications of quality techniques to the factory floor, (and, undoubtedly, to increase readership) a special edition of the magazine entitled "Statistical Quality Control" was published in November, 1961. Written in everyday language, it was presumed that foremen would read it, understand it and teach their employees how to apply these quality methods to their work places. It didn't quite work out as expected. Something was missing.

The publisher turned for help to a man named Kaoru Ishikawa, a renowned professor at Tokyo University, recognized by many today as the "father" of the TQC movement in Japan and inventor of the Cause and Effect diagram discussed in Chapter 3. He suggested that the most effective way to create a new quality awareness and obtain quality improvements was to develop a mechanism for *group learning and application* of the new techniques, which would involve both foremen and workers. The groups were called QC Circles, and the concept was first proposed in the maiden issue (April, 1962) of a new magazine entitled "FQC" (Foreman's Quality Control). It triggered the QC Circle development in Japan.

QUALITY CIRCLE OBJECTIVES

The Quality Circle "Bible," published by the Union of Japanese

Scientists and Engineers (JUSE), lists three main objectives of Quality Circles: 1. Improve the enterprise.
                   2. Build a better workplace.
                   3. Develop individual abilities.
    Notice that nowhere in these objectives does it say "save money." It turns out, as will be shown later in this chapter, that substantial savings can be achieved, but this is a *by-product* of the process, not an objective. Let's look at the three in more detail.

Objective 1: Improve the Enterprise

Improving the enterprise means the entire business. It starts with focusing everybody's energies on the one thing that keeps us all in business, which is meeting our customers' needs and expectations. It recognizes that quality is not something that resides just on the shop floor, but applies everywhere in the organization. It calls for continuous improvement in every phase of our value added activities and the elimination of those that don't add value. It means that the new ideas and techniques available should be put to actual use throughout the enterprise, including the marketing, engineering, financial, and support functions. It is a *total, all-encompassing concept.*

Objective 2: Build a Better Work Place

Building a better work place has more localized objectives. It is aimed at building small teams that can learn together, work together and grow together. It provides a forum to practice, in a real sense, respect for one another, to utilize the wisdom and experience people bring from previous jobs, and to develop their brainpower for even higher levels of contribution. It establishes desirable peer groups, which people *want to join,* that promote the concept of continuous improvement by working "smarter, not harder" and provides self-esteem to individual members by recognizing their contributions to the team's achievements.

Objective 3: Develop Individual Abilities

Developing individual abilities applies to every person in the company, starting with supervisors who need a non-threatening environment in which to learn and apply the management methods so vital to JUST-IN-TIME. New leaders can also be identified by their deportment during meetings and projects. Most importantly, the Quality Circle should be a mechanism to help draw out the hidden abilities that we know reside within every human being, give them an opportunity to display those abilities, and provide them with on-going training opportunities so their capabilities can grow with their seniority.

HOW QUALITY CIRCLES WORK

Quality Circles are small groups of volunteer employees who meet on company time to identify, analyze and solve local problems of their choice and present their solutions to management for implementation authorization. A Quality Circle is a *permanent group* and is expected to grow in competence as the members become more skilled and display more initiative. Some companies organize temporary problem-solving, or productivity teams which address specific management-directed problems and disband after the task is completed. While they can be very useful, they should not be confused with Quality Circles which have a much broader charter and more far reaching objectives, as shown in Figure 5-2.

Volunteers

The Quality Circle is comprised of volunteer workers from an area that gives them a baseline of commonalty. It can be people from the same workcenter (including those who interface with that workcenter) or from a common discipline like engineering, production control or a steno pool. It is equally applicable in blue or white collar environments

---

DIFFERENT MEANS/ENDS

PRODUCTIVITY TEAMS	QUALITY CIRCLES
• Ad Hoc Group	• Permanent Family
• Multi-Disciplined	• Common Work Area
• Directed Focus	• Self Directed
• Problem Solution as an End	• Problem Solution as a Means
	• People Growth as an End

"Both are needed"

Figure 5-2

but must be voluntary so the participants will be receptive to new ideas, willing to learn, and interested in improving themselves and the enterprise. Initiative cannot be legislated.

Meet on Company Time

Quality Circles meet on company time, usually for an hour a week, for which members are paid. A good time to schedule the meetings is during the last hour of the shift. Oftentimes the circle members will elect to extend a meeting on their own time. If your manufacturing process makes it next to impossible to let members break away for meetings during regular hours, they can be scheduled on overtime (it's worth it). Once a circle has been formed, it is important that meetings be held regularly and that members be permitted to attend every meeting. This is management's visible commitment to support the program for the future good of the company.

Identify Local Problems

During their meetings Quality Circle members concentrate their efforts on identifying and prioritizing local problems. We don't expect or want them to try to solve all the problems of our company. In fact, one reason they were brought together from a common area was to utilize their familiarity with the problems under consideration. It is in the areas with which they are most familiar that they have the best chance for an early success.

Analyze and Solve Problems

Having selected the local problem that they (not management) have elected to solve, the circle members must gather and analyze the necessary data or information to find the solution. Employing techniques from the Q@S Tool Kit and others, such as brainstorming, flow diagramming, trend analysis and charting, circle members develop their answer to the problem. Some people think that Quality Circles just come up with lists of problems for others to solve, but that doesn't help anybody. It is low-cost *solutions* that are needed to achieve continuous improvement. And, in that vein, it is best for the Quality Circles to begin by working on small problems, graduating to larger issues as more techniques are learned and skills are developed.

Present to Management

The solution becomes a proposal which is delivered in a *face-to-*

face presentation to the appropriate level of management required to obtain implementation approval. Many times, the proposal can be approved by the supervisor who, conveniently, is also the circle leader. This can save miles of "red tape." When higher levels of approval are needed, the Quality Circle makes its proposal directly to the appropriate manager. This means that presentation techniques will also have to be taught to members of the circle. These people-to-people meetings help develop the personal relationships that are so fundamental to JUST-IN-TIME by providing new bridge-building opportunities.

KEY ELEMENTS OF QUALITY CIRCLE MEETINGS

The Quality Circle meeting provides an "artificial" environment that lets us try, on a small scale, what we hope will become our universal practice in the future. The "rules of the game" are designed to enhance self-initiative, interaction, free and open discussions, and team building by solving common problems. It is a Bottom Round Management Laboratory.

Self Initiative

The team leader is not a "leader" in the classic sense. In a Quality Circle, he or she is really a *catalyst* to help the team members reach consensus decisions, while ensuring that everybody abides by the "rules." This means giving everyone a chance to speak, often by going around the table in order for inputs, and preventing aggressive members from dominating the proceedings. It also means bringing people together when there are disagreements by defusing "hard line" positions and knowing when more information is needed in order to reach consensus.

Reticent individuals are encouraged to speak their minds. The "rules" prohibit laughing at anyone's input. A suggestion is presumed to be valid until proved otherwise. While no one has to talk, the meeting format encourages even the shiest person to get involved and, over time to display self-initiative. It is the first step toward uncovering the "gold mine" of innovation.

Interaction and Open Discussion

As circle members get more familiar and comfortable with one another, totally open discussions can be held. No subject to taboo except taking "shots" at other people. As the group begins to realize that management is not going to direct their topics of investigation, so long as they stay within the "rules," there is a growing sense of being "masters" of their own destiny. Mutual trust begins to build and group interaction becomes more synergistic. The whole becomes greater than the sum of its parts.

Common Objectives

The focus should always be on achieving common objectives. As successes are attained, the team welds together, experiencing a real sense of achievement. The Quality Circle becomes a "family," joined by choice, which fulfills members' needs for belonging, self esteem and pride. It is Bottom Round Management in action.

ORGANIZING A QUALITY CIRCLE PROGRAM

There are as many ways to structure a Quality Circle program as there are companies in America. However, there are some basic elements which should be common to any structure. As shown in Figure 5-3, the fundamental building blocks include team members, circle leaders, facilitators, and a steering committee. Each makes an important contribution to a successful program.

Team Members

The team members are the bedrock of Quality Circles. They provide

ORGANIZATION LEVELS

STEERING COMMITTEE

FACILITATORS

CIRCLE LEADERS

TEAM MEMBERS

Figure 5-3

the foundation for the program. Each circle should have between four and ten members. Fewer than four members have a much harder time synergising and more than ten members gets difficult to manage in a free flowing, problem solving session. Eight is an ideal number. Sometimes the circle will subdivide into smaller groups to work on specific problems, and individual members often do research or data collection on their own. When problem investigations affect two or more Quality Circles, representatives from each team can form a temporary circle to address that issue, returning to their original groups when the job is done. This can be very beneficial to the growth of these members as it expands their horizons. It is important, however, that each person have a "home base" with which he or she can identify.

Circle Leaders

The circle leader is the catalyst that draws the circle together and helps it reach consensus. The first leader for any new Quality Circle should be the foreman or supervisor from the area in which the circle is formed. This is consistent with one of the original objectives of the QC Circle movement in Japan, which was "to improve the leadership and management abilities of foremen and first line supervision." It also makes sense with respect to the people policies and practices of JUST-IN-TIME. If we expect to develop an atmosphere of mutual trust, especially in plants with a history of distrust and antagonism, then we must begin at the front lines.

Yet many American Quality Circle, Employee Involvement and Participative Management programs have consciously *excluded* first line supervision! What a waste. How can we build bridges between the workers and management when we *dig a moat* between them? Excuses like "we don't want to intimidate the workers," or "the union would object" are simply ways to avoid confronting the real issue, which is distrust. This is one problem we can't run away from. We have to tackle it head on.

Benefits of Supervisors as Circle Leaders

Leadership of a Quality Circle is an ideal way to help heal the wounds and transition "hard line" supervisors to holistic mangement practices. Remember, a circle leader cannot function as an autocrat. He or she must follow the "rules" of the game. And, at the beginning, it can be thought of just that way. After all, everyone is used to playing games by the rules, and we're only talking here about an hour per week.

Even the grumpiest, Theory X type of supervisor will agree to do that for "the good of the company."

Then an amazing thing begins to happen. While struggling with the "confinements" imposed by these "rules," the supervisor begins to see the circle members in a totally new light. As the Quality Circle begins to develop and grow, he or she discovers that people work well when they are trained and then trusted; they have good minds that can absorb new information and, given the opportunity and motivation, will develop them on their own initiative. The supervisor begins to understand that workers can think, not just "do," and that thinking is not a waste of time but rather the avenue to continuous improvement.

Back on the job, the workers do not necessarily demonstrate these abilities if the supervisor continues to manage the "old way." Sooner or later, the supervisor begins to figure that out, at least subconsciously. Then he or she begins to slowly transfer some of the methods used during circle meetings to the job and finds that they do indeed work in the real world just like they did in that "artificial" environment. Over time, there can be a complete metamorphosis. The key point is that it is evolutionary, not revolutionary. If that same supervisor was sent to a "charm" school and came back completely changed, nobody would believe it. The workers would be wondering, "What's he/she up to now?" With Quality Circles, the behavioral change is not only more subtle, but it's also no surprise to the workers as they have seen it during circle meetings.

Facilitators

The supervisors won't be able to "pull this off" without some help. That's where facilitators, the next level of the Quality Circle organization, come in. Facilitators train circle leaders and members, coach them during circle meetings (especially at the beginning) and administer the company program.

The training responsibilities of the facilitator are broad in scope. Management must be exposed to the concepts, informed about the mechanics of the process, and sold on the benefits to the company so they can support the Quality Circle program. Circle leaders receive instruction in human resource management, team building techniques, motivation, problem solving procedures, how to conduct circle meetings and, most importantly, *how to listen.* Team members must be taught both interpersonal skills and technical skills, starting with the basics (like those in the Q@S Tool Kit) and getting more sophisticated as the circle grows in ability. This is an ongoing function that never ends.

Facilitators sit in on Quality Circle meetings to coach and assist the team leaders. While they should not interfere during the meetings, the facilitators act as resources for the circles and provide critiques to the leaders afterward to assist in their development. When special needs arise, the facilitator may serve as the conduit to outside resources to meet those requirements.

Facilitators also have a big administrative responsibility, starting with basic issues like meeting locations, schedules and authorizations. They coordinate the activities of the circles and help them prepare reports and presentations. They actively promote the Quality Circle program and interface with top management and the steering committee to explain what's happening, give progress reports, and secure program resources.

The facilitator may well be the most vital person in the Quality Circle program. He or she must be a "people person" with good communication skills, yet technically competent and familiar with the work environments of the circles. Finding someone with all these skills will not be easy, but look for a person who seems to be a good integrator and recognize that significant training outside the company will probably be required to give him or her the necessary foundation to launch your program.

Steering Committee

The steering committee is the policy-making body of the Quality Circle program. It is usually comprised of the management group that controls the resources needed for the program (like key department heads) and a cross section of other people who represent the Quality Circle organization structure (like team members, circle leaders, and area managers). In a union plant, it should include a representative from the union's policy-making group (like the president or business manager).

Typically meeting once a month, the steering committee determines how the program will be organized and administered, how many circles should be established at the beginning and how fast the program can be implemented, selection of circle members (often, there are more volunteers than can be accommodated at one time), overtime payment, a reward system (if any) and how it should relate to an ongoing suggestion system. In other words, there is much to decide.

The steering committee also hears selected presentations on improvement proposals from Quality Circles. This provides an opportunity to gauge the quality of the work being done and to see the development of the people as the program grows. It exposes the policy makers to the evolutionary change that is taking place at the working level and brings them into the process so all levels can learn to operate the "new way."

IMPLEMENTATION TIMETABLE

It must be re-emphasized that the role of Quality Circles in a JUST-IN-TIME business is to provide a vehicle to evolve the company management culture from a "top down" to a "bottom round" style. Motivated self starters and thinkers are the key to continuous improvement, but they don't emerge over night. The speed at which you implement your Quality Circle program will pace your evolutionary adjustment, but don't try to go so fast that you out-pace your ability to organize, properly train and initiate effective circles in your company.

A few years ago, during a coffee break at a JUST-IN-TIME seminar I was conducting, a man approached me and disputed the value of Quality Circles. He said, "We tried them at our company last month and they just didn't work." *Last month!* Obviously, his expectations were "quick fix" oriented. Quality Circles are not a "secret weapon" that can be "plugged in" for instant results. Remember JIT Principle #7: Long-Term Emphasis.

On the other hand, starting two or three, or even a half dozen Quality Circles, and then allowing the program to stagnate or die represents the other extreme. While not everyone in your company is going to volunteer to join a circle, you need enough of them to generate the critical mass that can spill over to the regular work environment. The best indicator of your progress is the growth in numbers of your Quality Circles. A plateau should be a signal to "stir the pot" again.

What, then, is the "right" pace? There is no hard rule, but you should know that it will take years, not months to effect the transition. It takes six months to get just one circle operating effectively. Let me share with you two examples of companies who have made Quality Circles a high-priority objective.

Westinghouse Experience

Westinghouse Corporation started its Quality Circle program in 1978. Management not only supported the program but also took the lead in promoting it. Booklets were produced to explain Quality Circles and invite employees to join them. They also included signed commitments to the program from the top executives. Within 18 months the company had organized over 200 circles.

At the Defense Group — Baltimore Divisions, there were seven circles in the pilot program, comprised of employees from all the major manufacturing functions, plus the purchasing department. The circle leaders were first line supervisors. They received two days of preliminary training which emphasized "developing an atmosphere within the circle which encourages the free interchange of ideas and suggestions among the circle members in solving work-related problems." Two full-time facilitators were assigned to the pilot effort. The first six to eight circle meetings were devoted to training the team members.

Within months after the start-up, the circles began to make improvement recommendations, including work area rearrangement, improved work flow, safety, paperwork simplification and more effective tooling, that resulted in "significant dollar savings to the company." Members of each Quality Circle (except for the leaders) shared cash awards granted through the Westinghouse Suggestion Award program.

Company-wide surveys on types of proposals generated showed that more than half of the improvement ideas proposed by the Quality Circles were really productivity related. About 35% were related to quality improvements and the balance, some 15%, covered safety and other subject areas. They also found that their best facilitators were females with a liberal arts education and prior experience working in a blue collar job.

Perhaps the most significant results, however, were in the reawakened employee interest and enjoyment in their jobs. Nine out of ten team members surveyed said they devoted some of their own personal time, either at lunch or at home, working voluntarily on projects for their Quality Circles. In one case, a laid-off worker asked for permission to come into the plant to attend his circle meetings because "they needed his input." (I know of another case in which an employee who had requested early retirement, primarily due to boredom, changed her mind after joining a Quality Circle. She said she couldn't leave now because, "for the first time people are listening to my ideas, and I'm having too much fun to retire.")

Toyota Experience

Toyota Motor Company was one of the first companies in the world to organize Quality Circles. Their program started in 1962 with the birth of the QC Circle movement. It is based on the premise that company — provided education and training will help the employees develop their personal capabilities. The main aim of their program is the enhancement of, 1) creativity, 2) positive attitude, and 3) sense of responsibility. Through these it is believed that "workers can improve their respective skills and develop a sense of fulfillment as members of society." This is reinforced by the company slogan: "Good Thinking, Good Products." Today, Toyota has more than 6,000 active Quality Circles that believe and work to that slogan.

Prior to starting their circle program, Toyota employed an American style suggestion system, receiving approximately one proposal or suggestion per employee in 1961. About 39% of those ideas were adopted by management. Nine years later, with the Quality Circle program under a full head of steam, the number of suggestions per employee had grown to 2.5 for 1970, with about 90% of the proposals accepted for implementation. Then, as shown in Figure 5-4, the number of proposals per employee increased dramatically. In 1985, Toyota received 2,453,105 proposals from its employees, an average of 45.6 per person per year. That's almost one idea per week for every person on the payroll! On top of that, 96% of the proposals were adopted.

Notice, however, that it took *twenty-five years* to attain this level of performance. That's a quarter of a century. Look at the progress for the first decade. It was steady improvement, for sure, but nothing like the next fifteen years. Why? I think it took that long to get Toyota's company culture and all its people turned around to the bottom round style of management. We can expect to do better than that because we can learn from the pioneers who had to work out each step by trial and error. But, it will still take a long time.

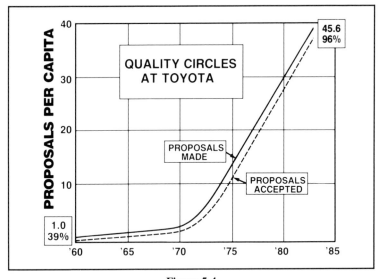

Figure 5-4

There is a second key point shown in Figure 5-4. Note that the vertical scale is measured in Proposals per Capita (not yen or dollars). The emphasis is on the number of ideas, not money. When you get more than *two million* suggestions in one year, they can't all be "home runs," but the aggregate number staggers the mind. The JUST-IN-TIME Strategy of continuous improvement needs every single idea, no matter how small, because the accumulation of all those little proposals adds up to big dollars.

Therefore, stress the number of ideas as the measure of success for your program. When computing dollar savings, do it in the aggregate, preferably for the whole program. And *never* make a "big deal" over a single, high-dollar suggestion. If you do, everybody will want that same kind of attention, but the loud and clear message will be that "it has to be a 'biggie,' so don't mess with the little ones." On the other hand, when everyone realizes that every improvement, no matter how small, is appreciated, then the stage will be set for optimum results.

SUCCESS FACTORS

The total transformation of a company culture is a long and difficult process. Much like the growth of a beautiful garden, it requires continuous nurturing and infinite patience. Management is and must be the gardener, tilling the soil of the present to prepare the way, sowing the seeds of Quality Circles to begin the new style, then caring for and feeding the growth process until it reaches maturity.

Management Participation

Without management participation, you can't expect to change your management style. More than involvement, more than approval, it means active participation on a continuing basis at all levels, including first level supervision. At Westinghouse, there were over 2000 Quality Circles in operation, under various names, at the peak a couple of years ago. Today, that number is between 1400 and 1500. The difference between the programs that are flourishing and those that died is the degree of management participation at all levels.

Voluntary Participation

The Quality Circle method of management evolution only works when there is voluntary participation. Compulsory programs may seem to start out okay, but they can actually demoralize the people involved.

Following management dictates is hardly the way to foster creativity and self-initiative. In these cases, when things go wrong the "finger pointing" starts because nobody wants to upset the boss. This is often the cause of so-called "Quality Circle Burnout." Conversely, voluntary teams develop a real "esprit-de-corps" and a "can-do" attitude, even when faced with difficult problems. They are practicing self-determination, or bottom-up management. With motivation and support, these groups grow in energy, ability and enthusiasm as time passes.

People Growth Emphasis

When people grow in ability, self-initiative and creativity, JUST-IN-TIME can become a reality. When Quality Circles are initiated with this objective, the probability of success is very high. If, on the other hand, you stress quick dollar returns, limit the subject areas to management-directed topics, exclude first line supervision from the process, ignore circle ideas that do not meet preconceived notions, or lay off employees due to productivity improvement suggestions, the probability of success is slim for the short-term and non-existent for the long run.

Integral Training

Training represents the nutrients that feed the growth of a Quality Circle program. In addition to the start-up effort, it must continue indefinitely for as long as you expect people to grow. Every year should see the introduction of more advanced techniques to the circle. Mature Quality Circles can function as expert problem solvers because they have received the equivalent of a technical education coupled with on-the-job training in the application of that knowledge. Training is expensive, and too many managers fail to see the value of the investment. It's really quite simple: *no nutrients, no garden.*

Team Building

The human relations aspects of Quality Circles are aimed at developing highly motivated, unified teams of workers and supervisors who practice bottom round management and experience great pride in their "family" and its accomplishments. Motivation and trust must have a test bed in which to develop. The intent is to substitute the words "we and us" for "I and me," first in the circles, and to extend it throughout the organization. When your facilitator tells you that topics like leadership, communication skills, feedback, and group techniques need to be included in the training material, believe it. This information, coupled with conducting meetings by the "rules," discussed earlier, is what you need to build your teams.

Problem Solving

Quality Circles undertake problem-solving activities to improve the quality of their work, work places, or work life. The identification of the problem is just the first step. Besides, most of us already have grievance committees. It is the selection of which problem to solve that starts the consensus management process working. The actual problem-solving exercise provides the mechanism for creative input and inspired thinking. Finding the answer enhances self-fulfillment (pride) and inspires further self-initiative. Problem solving is the framework upon which all the other aspects of Quality Circles are dependent.

Continuous Improvement

Many, many of the ideas generated by your Quality Circles will be of low-dollar value. This is fine. The emphasis needs to be on the number of ideas contributed. The dollars will take care of themselves in the aggregate. It is doubly important in the long run. At the beginning, you may well have a few "home runs," as there will be so much opportunity for improvement. It is much like finding the big "rocks" in the stream. Later, the big rocks will be gone and your problem solvers will be looking for smaller and smaller things to improve upon. As time goes by, and the process is really working, your circles will be looking at problems, no matter how small, as "treasures" because they represent more improvement opportunities. This will only happen if you stress many small ideas over a few big ones right from the very beginning.

SUMMARY

In a JUST-IN-TIME environment, a Quality Circle is a method to implement the people policies and practices to obtain continuous improvement at the work place level. Volunteer workers meet in small groups on company time to identify, analyze and solve local problems and present their solutions to management. Circle meetings are conducted under rules intended to promote self-initiative, open discussions, interaction, and team building by working together for common objectives. A Quality Circle can be a non-threatening "laboratory" to train supervision in holistic management methods to encourage creativity and innovation.

A Quality Circle program requires planning and organization. Team members, circle leaders (who should be first line supervisors), facilitators and the steering committee have to be thoroughly trained and have specific responsibilities to uphold. You can't shortcut this process if you expect to succeed.

Implementation should proceed at a pace within your resource capabilities, but the program should grow continuously until a critical mass have been reached which can transform the management style of the entire organization. Benefits will accrue to individuals, to the work places and to the entire company as people display self-initiative, grow in ability, and experience self-fulfillment.

Your success will be dependent on how strongly you believe in and adhere to the seven success factors described earlier and outlined in Figure 5-5. Quality Circles have worked well in American companies who followed these guidelines. Almost every failure can be traced to the omission or discontinuance of one or more of the factors.

The real beauty of Quality Circles is that they give you a mechanism to begin the transformation of your management culture in parallel with the "nuts and bolts" techniques that come next. Remember one thing, though. While you can't expect to finish your people-oriented actions before moving on to physical arrangements, processes and systems, you must *start* because many of those techniques are based on the assumption that the new working relationships *will be developed.*

SUCCESS FACTORS

- **Management participation**
- **Voluntary participation**
- **People growth emphasis**
- **Integral training**
- **Team building**
- **Problem** *solving*
- **Continuous improvement**

Figure 5-5

 FOCUSED
FACTORIES

CHAPTER 6

"A focused factory is a manufacturing layout
dedicated to a single product family
which maximizes overall productivity and quality
while minimizing space and resource requirements."

The first five chapters in this book described the "table-stakes" of JUST-IN-TIME. Starting with the basic definition that says we will continuously increase our quality and productivity simultaneously, the JIT Strategy calls for response to exact customer demand and the total elimination of waste, with no provisions for contingencies. Quality at the Source says the value adder must do the job right the first time and every time, striving to produce "perfect parts." JIT people policies and practices are established to develop a flexible, well-trained work force that is encouraged to use its brain power, and quality circles provide the mechanism to implement the necessary social environment. The next step is to examine the physical environment which, in manufacturing, is the factory floor.

There are a number of things in today's traditional plants that inhibit the implementation of JUST-IN-TIME, most of which can be traced to our emphasis on specialization. The focus on narrowly defined job descriptions, coupled with specialized equipment dedicated to volume production, has given us factories that are very *inflexible.* Perhaps we have carried Frederick Taylor's division of work concepts a step too far.

Some would say that we ought to go back to the era of the craftsman. But, craftsmen never produced every part exactly like every other part, and the costs were too high. Nevertheless, the pendulum has swung too far the other way over the years, from an emphasis on craft to excessive specialization. This has fragmented the manufacturing process and made it difficult for people to get a clear perspective of it to fully utilize their brain power. While striving for efficiency, we created complexity.

The JUST-IN-TIME approach is to find the best *balance* between craftsmanship and specialization, as shown in Figure 6-1. The best way to do this is to focus on process integration for perspective while limiting the range of production to keep it simple. A plant which is organized this way is called a *focused factory*. It's a manufacturing layout dedicated to a single product family which maximizes overall productivity and quality while minimizing space and resource requirements.

HOW WE GOT TO WHERE WE ARE TODAY

Just about every manufacturing company in America started out as a focused factory. There was only one product family, with few variations, and only one significant market channel. The company was small, people had perspective and communicated with one another. It was a very efficient operation.

As time passed, product variety increased, new products were introduced and new markets developed. More equipment was purchased and installed, usually in an available corner. Additions were made to the plant. Everything became spread out, disguising the process flow. Looking at the facility today people might well ask, "Who in the world ever designed this place?" The answer, of course, is that *nobody* did. It just sort of evolved.

More Material

Something had to be done to compensate for the greater distances between operations, so the natural thing to do was bring in more material to buffer each operation from the vagaries of the preceding and

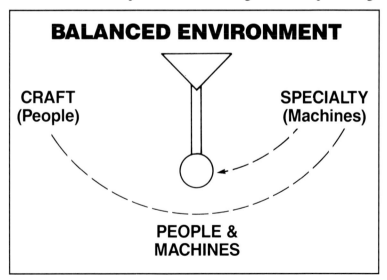

BALANCED ENVIRONMENT

CRAFT
(People)

SPECIALTY
(Machines)

PEOPLE &
MACHINES

Figure 6-1

succeeding operations. It did require more material handling, but with more material, longer production runs could be made, which improved department efficiencies. That encouraged even longer runs, requiring even more material on hand. Eventually, storage space became a major issue. So did aisle space, because it takes a twelve foot aisle to turn a fork-lift around. There was no more room on the floor for material, the fork-lifts were creating traffic jams and, worst of all, things started to get lost!

More Storage Space

When horizontal space runs out, the only place to go is up. Vertical storage racks were introduced, which doubled and even tripled storage capability. It was neat and tidy, and provided much more visibility so it was easier to find things. They also provided wonderful walls to mark departmental "territories." Of course, it did require more expensive fork-lifts to reach up to those higher rack levels, but it seemed like a reasonable trade-off to get the perceived benefits. However, storage racks introduced another problem, stock rotation. For a typical three level rack, as shown in Figure 6-2, the planned sequence would be to stock new material at level three, cycle it through level two, and then remove it from level one for consumption. Unfortunately, it seldom worked that way. New material was usually stored in the first available hole, which was typically at level one. That's why it wasn't uncommon to

Figure 6-2

see containers on the top shelf with "hot tickets" and air freight stickers attached to them that had been received six months ago!

Engineering came up with the answer to the stock rotation problem, the storage silo. Like the one shown in Figure 6-3, the silo accepted material at the top and let it work its way down to the bottom, using gravity as the mover. There was still plenty of buffer in front of the operation and the stock was rotating in the proper sequence. In fact, engineering could now tell the accountants, "We've got your inventory *turning,* as you requested!"

More Material Handling

By applying the same concept to material handling, conveyers were born. At first, they were simple roller types at ground level that used "people power" to move the material. It was just another small step to mechanize the movement with motors. Soon conveyers were everywhere, dutifully moving material from point to point. Even though they were very expensive, they eliminated the need for a lot of manual material handling. Now there was no limit to how far apart operations could be. In fact, the farther the better because all of that space could be filled with buffer stock.

Like all machinery, conveyers were a safety concern and it was hard to get around them. Sometimes bridges had to be built over them to ease personnel movement. So, the next step on the road of progress was

Figure 6-3

to hang the conveyers from the ceiling. Not only were they out of the way, but that unsightly inventory was less noticeable, especially when protective cages were built around them to prevent parts from falling on people's heads.

The ultimate "improvement" was making the conveyers recirculate to couple unbalanced operations. This had the added advantage of providing a return path for rejected parts. The trouble was, when a defective part was found there was no way to track it back to its origin to correct the problem on a timely basis. To the contrary, some parts on a recirculating conveyer seemed to develop a "life" of their own, traveling for days, weeks, or even months before the next operator actually touched them. Parts were getting lost again.

The real irony of this history can be seen in Figure 6-4. The material on the floor is there to keep the operation going when the conveyer breaks down, which is often. Material on the floor! Isn't that how it all started? We'd come "full circle."

More Specialization

Manufacturing plants have evolved to complex entities, with specialized departments surrounded by walls of inventory working independently of one another. With considerable distances between them, they are often unaware of happenings elsewhere in the facility. The people within the departments have turned inward and are motivated by local

Figure 6-4

optimums. Even within the department, there are many specialists, each doing his or her "own thing."

It isn't just manufacturing. Overspecialization seems to abound in many industries. Have you ever thought about how many different people are involved in building a house? First, there are the excavators, then cement workers and "rough" carpenters to get the building started. Next come the bricklayers, roofers, plumbers and electricians. Then, the finishing work requires plasterers, finishing carpenters and/or cabinet-makers, tile layers, interior painters and exterior painters, who are often different people. All of this work must meet local ordinances, of course, so there are inspectors of many varieties who must review and approve each step. Dozens and dozens of specialists, each limited to a narrow scope of work, most of whom have to wait for somebody else to get finished before they can do their jobs. It gets so complicated that a general contractor is usually hired to get all the right people scheduled at the right place and at the right time. No wonder it takes so long and costs so much to have a new home built.

Mercury Marine Study

You may be thinking that a construction industry example is too "far fetched" to apply to the real world of manufacturing. If so, let me tell you about a very interesting study that Mercury Marine Division, a Bruns-wick company, conducted at one of its plants as part of a company wide quality and productivity improvement effort. (They call their initiative *QUEST*, which stands for Quality by United Effort Secures Tomorrow.)

The product involved was an outboard marine driveshaft housing and the production process covered 122 separate steps in two plants. Mercury Marine discovered that only 27 of those steps added value (things like casting, drilling, trimming & painting). The majority of the steps (78%) were used to "check each other's work or move it from place to place." That happened when things went "right." There were another 28 steps involved in three repair loops when things went wrong.

Each housing traveled 20,793 feet while being manufactured, a distance of almost four miles! It took 1,496 hours, or 187 shifts to get transformed from a raw casting to a boxed, shippable product. There were 106 people who had to handle the product, most of whom did not interface with each other. The study was described by a company spokesman as "a humbling experience." But, he went on to say, "The first step toward improvement is recognizing the potential." Mercury Marine did so and is making dramatic improvements today.

FOCUSING FOR FLOW

A world-class manufacturer will not condone these kinds of "wastes." However, even if your people understand this and want to become more flexible, they can't do it when they are placed in a complicated work environment, like the one shown in Figure 6-5. With this kind of plant layout, workers have very little visibility of the overall process, are isolated from one another so it is difficult to communicate, and can't see around the mountains of work-in-process inventory. The focused factory will help overcome these drawbacks.

Defining Product Families

The first step is to examine your products to see how they naturally group themselves into "families." The chances are you are already discussing these kinds of family groups when doing business planning, sales planning or production planning. When properly defined, the product family will have (or could have) a series of similar production processes, as well as market continuity. Ask yourself how you would break up the business if you had to sell portions of it (perish the thought) or transfer portions of it, including sales and engineering support, to another plant location. For most companies, this analysis will result in less than a dozen product family categories.

The next step is to determine which equipment would have to

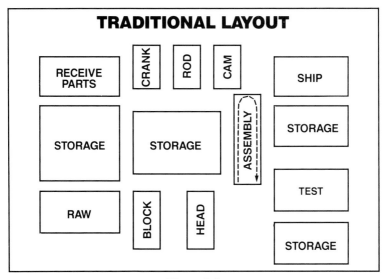

Figure 6-5

accompany each product family to its new location. The chances are you will not have enough machines to support all the families independently, as many of them now share some pieces of equipment. At this stage, that shouldn't be a major issue. You're more interested in "which ones" than you are "how many" because you'll get started with just one family anyway. That family should be one that has enough production volume to utilize dedicated equipment, is not overly complex (give yourself a chance to learn as you go), and is reasonably self-contained. You can still utilize "outside" services, but the fewer the better.

Laying Out the Focused Factory

Your focused factory layout, which could generically look like Figure 6-6, is intended to physically link all the involved manufacturing operations together to minimize the distance between them, minimize the complexity, maximize the integration and maximize the interaction between the workers. Notice that there is very little storage space, compared to the traditional layout shown in Figure 6-5. Linked operations don't require a lot of staged material. In most traditional plants today, more than 50% of the floor space is dedicated to storage and aisles. (You can verify this by analyzing a floor plan of your plant.) The small amount of material storage remaining is located adjacent to the point of use, as shown by the raw material on the left and the assembly parts in the upper right corner. (This facet is covered in detail in Chapter 13,

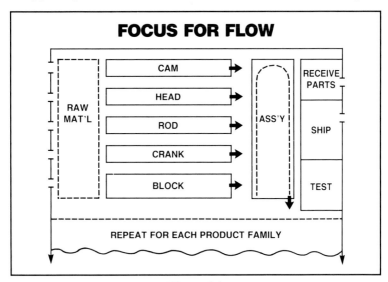

Figure 6-6

Transport Innovation.)

Wherever possible, the feeder operations are brought into the focused factory and linked to the assembly functions. This means you literally pull machines out of support departments and locate them right next to the final assembly positions. You'll discover it not only ties the process together but enhances synchronization, since you can't run production unless everybody is making the right part at the right time. If no final assemblies are needed at this moment, nobody works. When one operation in the process stops, everything stops. The physical configuration begins to approximate the idealized example described in Chapter 2. You are focusing for flow.

The example shown in Figure 6-6 is patterned after an engine plant. You'll need to replace the feeder line designations with names that apply to your business. For instance, in the motor business the machining and assembly of housings, rotors, stators, terminals and brackets would be integrated. In electronics, you would include chassis construction, cable assembly, printed circuit board insertion and soldering, power supplies and front panel assembly in your floor plan. Any product family can be built in a focused factory.

After the first focused factory is set up and running, you establish the second one, the third one, and so forth until the entire facility is a series of "mini-businesses," each concentrating on a single product family. You still have a form of specialization, but the emphasis is now on complete, salable products instead of operations and enormous benefits can be realized.

Ford Experience

Back when Ford Motor Company was designing the Escort, an addition to the Batavia, Ohio plant was planned to build the transaxle. The facility expansion was estimated at $300 million. Ford owns a portion of Mazda, in Japan, who was also invited to submit a proposal for the transaxle business. The Mazda bid included a $100 million facility, just one-third the cost of the domestic plant. Upon further investigation it was discovered that the Mazda plant was only one-third the *size* of the Batavia addition, even though it contained roughly the same complement of equipment, as shown in Figure 6-7. Mazda had proposed a focused factory dedicated to the transaxle product family which had no provisions for significant storage or aisle space. It was designed to rapidly flow material through the operation, giving them a huge advantage in terms of capital investment.

Ford also has a very fine engine plant in Valencia, Spain. It contains about 900,000 square feet and looks very similar to all their engine plants throughout the world. Conversely, the Toyota Kamigo engine plant (which is really a series of small focused factories) encompasses only 300,000 square feet, the same one to three ratio seen before. The significant item here, though, is the productivity differential. At the time this survey was taken, Valencia was producing two engines per employee per day while Kamigo was cranking out *nine engines per employee per day,* better than a four to one advantage. Toyota had minimum material handling, minimum non-value added functions in the work force, maximum integration of the feeder operations, and maximum perspective so both the interactions and the communications were simplified for the workers. The power of the plant layout cannot be overstated when evaluating these kinds of performance differentials.

Hewlett-Packard Experience

When the site for the Hewlett-Packard Greeley, Colorado Division was being planned, the intent was to build a succession of five manufacturing buildings on a large multi-acre tract. Each building was to be capable of producing an annual sales volume of approximately $200 million.

Shortly after the first building was occupied, H-P Greeley got very involved in JUST-IN-TIME, including reorganization of the shop floor into focused factories. Their success in consolidating production space

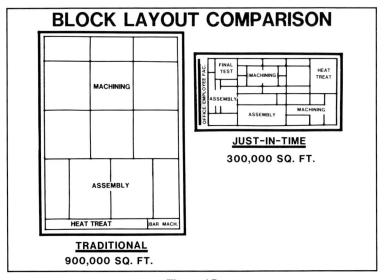

Figure 6-7

and replacing much of the storage space with even more manufacturing activities has enabled them to produce substantially more than $400 million of sales in the original building. Without the improved space utilization they would already be occupying a third structure. These are capital savings that are measurable in anybody's book.

WHERE TO START?

Most of us don't have the advantage of starting with a new piece of property or a new building, but it really isn't necessary. You can create multiple focused factories within your present facility by rearranging it over a period of time. That's exactly what H-P Greeley did.

Final Assembly Operations

You should start with the final assembly operations of your chosen product family. The trick is to find some available space to set it up if you don't already have some vacant areas. The easiest way to make space is to get rid of some inventory, especially if it is occupying premium manufacturing areas. Another opportunity is when you are closing down a product line or converting a line to build a new product.

When selecting the location, keep two things in mind:

1. The focused factory assembly layout should require considerably less space than is currently being used by the operations being consolidated.
2. The material should flow continuously through the new work area without interim storage locations.

Sometimes, the location you select will have a large piece of equipment sitting right in the middle of it and you'll be tempted to work around it to save the moving cost. Don't do it! You'll end up paying for it many times over with a sub-optimal layout which will degrade your results. Like the old Fram commercial which stated, "you can pay now or pay later," it's really more cost effective to "bite the bullet" up front.

Integrating Feeder Operations

To be the most effective, a focused factory should be as self-contained as possible. That means bringing subassembly and component fabrication operations into the new layout with direct feeds to final assembly. Depending on the process, the feeders can be spur lines or group technology cells (described in Chapter 7.) Provisions must also be made

made to provide a smooth inflow of purchased parts. Inspection stations, test stands and any final packaging should also be included.

When you run into obstacles, like "you can't have that machine because it's used for too many other requirements," try to find a different way to do that operation in your focused factory. If you still end up with some operations that must be done "outside," they can be connected to your focused factory by the "pull system," discussed in Chapter 11.

Try to incorporate every possible feeder operation into the focused factory from day one. But, if you can't integrate all the feeders at the beginning, at least have the eventual final layout on paper so you'll know where the space will be coming from when you can add them. The important thing is to get started, learn as you go and continuously improve.

Living With the Empty Space

Although space for your first focused factory may be hard to come by, it won't be long before you'll have more vacant areas than you'll know what to do with. When this happens, there are two important things to keep in mind:

1. The vacant areas are opportunities for growth. Keep them empty (rope them off, if necessary) as visual reminders to management that space for new business is available here and now.

2. Don't penalize the new focused factories with over-head costs that relate to the empty space. Cost the products based on actual resources applied and treat the empty space cost as a separate category, like the "super burden" discussed in Chapter 15.

HOW FERRO DID IT

Ferro Manufacturing Company has been a supplier to the automotive industry since 1915. Its Pikeville, Tennessee plant makes door mechanisms and latching systems. The company's operating philosophy is: "Our obligation is to continually improve each of our products, constantly making them better and manufacturing them to increasingly higher standards." This is very compatible with the JIT strategy.

The Pikeville plant manager was a veteran of 35 years in manufacturing. Although skeptical about JIT and the focused factory concepts at first, he recognized the order of magnitude improvement potential if everything worked out as planned. A decision was made to create nine "mini" focused factories in the window regulator product family. Project objectives established for the first pilot line included:

1. Smooth the production flow and establish **hourly targets.**
2. Eliminate material handling labor by **integrating support operations** with final assembly.
3. Drive changeover times toward **ZERO.**
4. Force work-in-process inventory **down** by putting the operations close together.

The First Pilot

The first three months were spent getting educated about the things that had to be done, planning the project and developing a preliminary layout for the first line. The operators were brought together and the pilot project was discussed with them. This was to be a total involvement program and their ideas were earnestly solicited. After several revisions, the equipment for the first line was moved into place over a weekend. Within days they were adjusting the layout even further as improvement potential became visible.

A layout for one of the lines is shown in Figure 6-8. A window regulator is a mechanism that enables a car window to be raised or lowered. It is formed into a hollow "T" configuration from a strip of steel (roll former), which is bent into an oval shape (bender), pierced

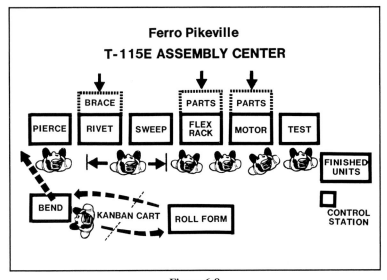

Figure 6-8

(press), welded (welder) and profiled ("sweep" machine). Plastic gear teeth (called a flex rack) and various brackets are assembled to it to make the final product. Electric motors are added for the automatic versions, which is the case in this example. Final operations entail testing and packing the product for shipment. It should be noted that the bender, press, welder, sweep machine and motor subassembly were all moved into the focused factory from secondary departments.

Material handling between operations in the new layout was accomplished by hanging the parts on a piece of pipe, angled downward, and letting gravity move the part from one station to the next. (See Figure 6-9.) As the stations got closer to one another the pipes were shortened, reducing the inventory between operations. What used to be thousands was now a few dozen.

Component parts, previously brought to the line in large tubs via fork-lifts, were now supplied in small, person movable plastic containers by two roving material handlers. This job used to require nine fork-lift drivers, one for each line.

Making Improvements

Each operator was trained to perform every function in the line, including final test and hourly progress reporting at the control station. They rotated jobs at each break to maintain their skill levels. The operators maintained their own P-Charts for rejects and were given the

Figure 6-9

authority to stop the operation if things went wrong. As the integrated process began to eliminate WIP, the problems began to surface. The operators addressed each problem, which ranged from faulty equipment to improperly fitting parts, by asking "Why?" Improvement ideas began to pour forth.

In addition, of course, they now had a perspective that was never available to them in the past. For example, the sweep machine is not really a machine at all. It is a pair of die sets that used to be installed in a 250-ton press for this operation. It was an operator who asked the question, "Why do we even need a press to form these light weight pieces of material?" Instead, they decided to actuate the dies with compressed air, making "machines" out of tools. Not only did they now have a dedicated station for this operation, but it also could be changed from right-hand to left-hand parts by switching the air hose.

Handling Exceptions

The roll former, on the other hand, had to serve all nine lines so it could not be incorporated into any one of them. The solution was to connect it to the lines with "pull signals," or "Kanban" carts. (See Chapter 11 for a full explanation of this concept.) Each line was assigned two wheeled carts, each holding enough formed material to support one assembly shift, as defined by the height of vertical stanchions on the carts. As operators were using parts from one cart, an empty one was

Figure 6-10

waiting in line at the roll former to be filled, as shown in Figure 6-10. In order to get more material from the roll former, an empty cart had to be exchanged for a full one. This kept the reordering sequence properly prioritized for all the assembly activities.

Implementation Time

The timetable for the whole project is shown in Figure 6-11. Six weeks after launch, most of the major moving and fixing was completed for the first line. Four weeks after that the new process had been time studied, documented and was producing the best window regulators in the plant's history.

The second and third lines were started together as the first line was being finalized, with similar results. The conversion time dropped for each successive line as knowledge and experience were gained. Ten months after the initial decision to proceed, all nine assembly lines had been converted to "mini" focused factories.

Measurable Results

Ferro Pikeville reaped substantial benefits from its focused factories in a relatively short time. Measurements taken fifteen months after the project launch showed some eye-opening results:

Productivity up by 46% This was accomplished by a 20% increase in shipments coupled with a 17% reduction in the work-

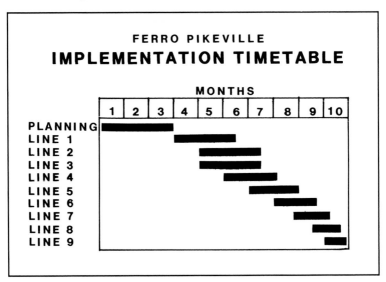

Figure 6-11

force, all by attrition. There were no layoffs.

Scrap rate reduced by 67% Smaller amounts of material between operations meant less to scrap when a major problem did occur.

Rework hours reduced by 93% Authority to stop the operation prevented production of marginal parts while somebody was "making up their mind."

Total cost of quality reduced by 47% Detection and correction were replaced by prevention.

Assembly floor space reduced by 15% Even with the extra feeder operations brought in from other areas, the total floor space for this product family was reduced.

In addition to the numbers, a significant increase in operator self-reliance, positive attitudes and improvement ideas was seen, as workers pursued schedule goals, efficiency targets and quality standards which they had a hand in establishing.

SUMMARY

Over the years, our emphasis on specialization and measuring the efficiency of discrete operations in manufacturing plants has created enormous wastes. We have many times more material, storage space, material handling and job descriptions than we need, which complicates our business and places us at a competitive disadvantage. By subdividing our plants into "mini" plants which focus on integrating the entire manufacturing process for specific product families, we can simplify the process, eliminate the waste, enhance communications and give our people a better perspective to generate improvement ideas.

Companies who have converted to the focused factory concept have experienced substantial, measurable benefits, as shown in Figure 6-12. Productivity improves greatly because non-value adders are no longer needed to produce the same or higher levels of output. Process control is easier when subsequent operations are adjacent to one another due to better visibility. With little or no material between operations, quality goes up because problems surface immediately, are communicated between nearby workers, and don't require massive rework efforts when the problem is fixed. All of these lead to greater output for less input which translates to more profit dollars for the business.

When a large plant transforms to a group of pseudo small businesses operating under the same roof, each one can run "lean and mean," just like real small businesses. This means fewer layers of management, and commensurate bureaucracy, are required to function effectively. Less complex businesses are simply easier to run. Integrated processes require less floor space and almost no storage space, providing opportunities to produce at least one-third more (and up to three times as much) output without adding a single brick. With no inventory queues to work through, the actual production leadtime begins to approach the value-added time, which dramatically improves customer response.

The opposite is also true. I know of a small farm implement company in Illinois that used to operate like a focused factory. Then, two plants were merged and a decision was made to become "scientific" by converting to operations standards and specialized departments in the new layout. The results? Productivity dropped by five to seven points, the scrap rate tripled, inventory turnover fell to half of what it used to be, and labor relations problems went up by an order of magnitude. Profitable simplicity gave way to costly sophistication.

In a focused factory, greater manufacturing productivity can be achieved with fewer resources expended. It is a proven, practical way to go "head-to-head" with world class competition.

FOCUSED FACTORY BENEFITS

IMPROVED
- **Productivity**
- **Quality**
- **Process Control**
- **Profitability**
- **Communication**

REDUCED
- **Mgmt Layers**
- **Complexity**
- **Leadtime**
- **Space**
- **Inventory**

**"Fewer Resources Required
For Greater Productivity"**

Figure 6-12

GROUP TECHNOLOGY

CHAPTER 7

*"Group Technology is an equipment layout
dedicated to the complete production of a family
of similar parts, one-at-a-time, by linking together
all possible operations in the process."*

In the last chapter, we discussed the focused factory as a macro approach to arrange our plants for better productivity and quality. Not every focused factory, however, can have every single operation in the process physically linked together as was shown in the examples. Sometimes it must be subdivided into smaller segments which are even more focused, such as component part manufacturing, subassembly work or fabricating common modules which will be used in more than one final assembly area. (Remember, the Ferro example had nine separate lines in its focused factory.)

The same principles that apply to a focused factory can also be employed at the micro, or detail, level to lay out and operate these subdivisions. The name given to this element is Group Technology, or GT. Group Technology is an equipment layout dedicated to the complete production of a family of parts, one at a time, by physically linking all possible operations in the process.

In this case, the family is a group of parts that have similar physical and/or chemical characteristics and roughly follow the same steps, or operations, during the manufacturing process. To link the operations, we have to physically link all the equipment needed to produce the parts together in one geographic area. We want every operation in the process to be included in this arrangement, even things like washing, testing and packaging. In effect, we are creating integrated, self-contained parts factories within our focused factory.

With this kind of equipment arrangement, we can apply the principles of Henry Ford's assembly line to parts manufacturing, as shown in Figure 7-1, and gain the same benefits. In this case, instead of people passing single pieces to one another as they do in assembly, we envision machine tools doing it in manufacturing. There's nothing new about that idea when we think about automatic transfer lines for high volume production of one part number, but the thought of making a whole series of part numbers this way in *low volumes* is a very new concept to many people.

WHY DEPARTMENTAL SPECIALTY?

You might well ask, "If group technology is such a great idea, why hasn't everybody already done it?" I believe the reason is that it is so radically different from our historical perception of the mission of manufacturing and our traditional means to accomplish it. The fundamental premise has been that customer demand is so varied and unpredictable that manufacturing must be organized to respond to an infinite variety of requirements in a "cost-effective" manner.

The answer to the first part of the mission statement was to organize into departments by operation specialty. This way every demand could be treated as a unique requirement and routed to the proper departments to be made. The motto was, "We are a job shop, not a production house." The fact that most companies tended to do a lot of repeat business, making products to standard or "almost standard" drawings, never changed this job shop perception. Consequently, over the years this organization was never challenged. Instead, it was a "given."

The issue of cost effectiveness was addressed by insuring that every person and every machine was kept busy. Longer runs made the operator efficiency and machine utilization numbers look better, so

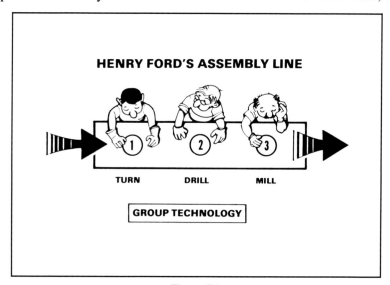

HENRY FORD'S ASSEMBLY LINE

TURN   DRILL   MILL

GROUP TECHNOLOGY

Figure 7-1

minimum lot sizes were defined. The fact that all of those parts weren't needed at that time, or in some cases would never be needed, didn't enter into the equation. In fact, parts were often manufactured on speculation rather than have an idle worker or machine. Schedulers and dispatchers were needed to try to balance the work loads between the departments while still meeting customer demands. The resulting confusion, priority conflicts, lengthy production cycles and excess inventory reaffirmed what everybody already knew, that manufacturing was, indeed, a very complicated business.

Traditional Layout

The built-in problems are easier to visualize if we look at a hypothetical shop, like the one shown in Figure 7-2. It has five departments: saws, lathes, mills, presses, and heat treat. The lines with the arrows show the routing, or the path a part has to travel to get transformed into a finished unit. The circled numbers are the operators who work on the part at each operation in the routing. Operator #1 cuts bar stock into segments with the saw. In the lathe department, Operator #2 turns the outer diameter of the piece to a "rough" dimension. At the mill, Operator #3 adds a key way before the part is heat treated by Operator #4. Then it goes back to the lathe department, where Operator #5 does the finish turning. Finally it goes to the press department, where Operator #6 presses a key in the key way.

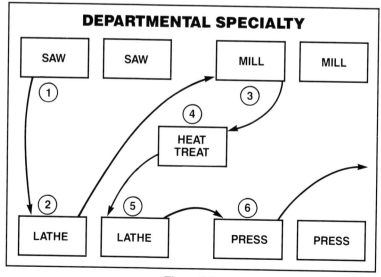

Figure 7-2

The resultant travel path is convoluted, at the very least. Yet, this example is relatively clean compared to most real shops. You can check this out for yourself. Take a routing sheet for one of your popular manufactured parts and, using a magic marker, trace the path traveled by the part on a copy of your plant layout. The result may very well look like spaghetti! And the shop floor is just as confusing as that picture demonstrates.

The Cost of Queues

Each of the operators in Figure 7-2 has a queue of work in front of him or her. Sometimes it's a result of the "system," but more often it's there because "everybody knows" that people will work faster when they see a large backlog in front of them. What everybody doesn't know, though, is that the large backlog in queue is almost guaranteed to subvert the priority system.

Think about it. If you were an operator being measured by how fast you produce, and you had your choice of ten jobs to work on, would you pick a difficult one, even if it had top priority? Not likely. Instead, you would "cherry pick" the easiest job, hoping that the person on the next shift would get stuck with the "dog" when the expeditor came by with the "hot list." This happens daily in most operations, despite the dispatch lists that are so carefully developed by production control.

Distorting queue priorities also impacts the work loads for downstream operations in a traditional shop. When Operator #2 takes liberties with the job assignments, it can result in Operator #6 running out of work, even though the schedule says otherwise. Then you have the worst of both worlds, hot jobs not being worked on in some areas with people out of work in others.

Queues at each operation also cost us time. The bigger the queue, the longer it takes to get a job through the workcenter. The more operations you have in the process, the longer the manufacturing time. Yet, the real value added time is quite short by comparison. In most companies, it is less than five percent of the total leadtime. Check it out for yourself. Add up the standard process times on the routing sheet you used earlier and divide that number by the leadtime in your MRP system or the customer quoted leadtime for that part. I know of cases where it turned out to be less than one percent! That's why it takes 20 to 100 times longer to get a normal job through the shop than it does when it is "hand carried."

By employing queues to maximize the efficiency of each operation in the process, we unwittingly sub-optimize the total process, paying a price in terms of schedule adherence, work load balance and longer manufacturing leadtimes. When you consider the dollar investment in WIP inventory that is made, it begins to look like a bad bargain. On the other hand, when all the operations are linked together these problems almost totally disappear.

The Distance Penalty

It costs more to transport material 100 feet between operations than it does 10 feet. The greater the distance the greater the cost, all of which is unnecessary if the operations are next to each other. A good way to get your hands around the size of your distance problem is to measure how far a part travels on its journey through the shop today. You can scale it from the plant layout "spaghetti diagram" you made earlier. As improvements are made, distance reductions will be a good indicator of progress.

Distance directly affects manufacturing leadtimes, as the "move time" component, and also because production in a job shop tends to be transferred in complete lots. When a lot has to be finished before it can be moved, even value added time has to stack up in series. Suppose, for example, that each operation in Figure 7-2 required one week for completion. Since there are six operations, it would take six weeks to complete the part, as shown by the shaded bars in Figure 7-3. But,

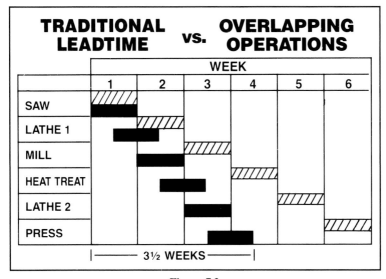

Figure 7-3

if we could send half a lot to the next operation just as soon as it was completed, the individual operations in the process would overlap, as shown by the solid bars, cutting the total process leadtime almost in half. If we were to transfer material in quarter lot batches, the process time would be just over two weeks long.

It looks good on paper, but there are some practical limits to how far we can go. For one thing, we'd soon reach a point where material handling costs would be "out of sight." Also, the smaller the transfer quantity, the tighter the schedule would have to be in subsequent operations. In fact, it could turn into a scheduling "nightmare," which is probably why few people have tried it. An easier solution is to build a group technology cell.

BUILDING GROUP TECHNOLOGY CELLS

The starting point is to select a family of parts, much like product families were selected for focused factories. In this case, however, we are talking about component parts or subassemblies within the focused factory. For example, the layout in Figure 7-4 is an automotive seat track focused factory of Johnson Controls Inc. (JCI) in Linden, Tennessee. Notice that it is subdivided into seven interacting GT cells — two for components, three for subassemblies and two for final assembly, which include the test rooms. (We will return to this example later.)

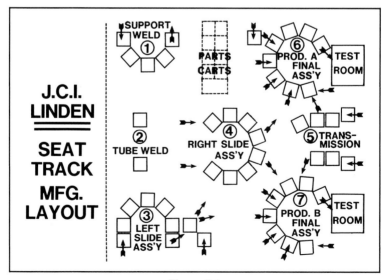

Figure 7-4

There are some very sophisticated software systems available today that can help you sort your current manufactured part numbers into logical family groupings, based on their physical characteristics and the associated production operations. They are helpful but can also be very expensive and time consuming if you have a large data base. It is not a prerequisite to getting started on your first GT cell. The initial families will be almost self-evident to the production people who work with them every day. Select one with enough production volume in the combined family to reasonably justify dedicating equipment to it.

Basic GT Cell Layout

The equipment complement should be taken from existing departments and grouped closely together in the assigned location in the focused factory. For instance, if we created a GT cell for the product discussed in Figure 7-2, it would look like the layout shown in Figure 7-5. The saw, two lathes, a mill and a press have been moved from their previous locations to this cell. (Heat treat is a shared resource which cannot be duplicated, so it is handled as an exception, as will be shown.) There is a place for raw material at the lead-off operation and a spot for finished units at the end of the process. Otherwise, no provisions are made for WIP storage.

In a GT cell, a single worker performs every operation, in the proper sequence, to make one finished unit at a time. In our example,

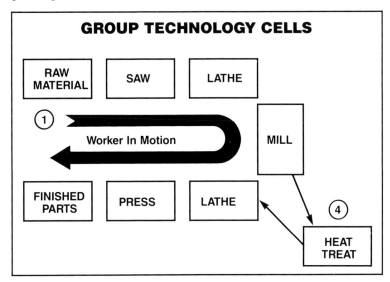

Figure 7-5

he or she takes a piece of raw material, cuts it off at the saw, walks over to the lathe to do the rough turning, then mills in a slot at the next position. At this point, the part must be heat treated at a remote location, so the worker places it in a small container which will be delivered to heat treat and returned, when finished. (More on this later.) The worker then picks up a heat-treated piece from a container next to the lathe, does the finish turning operation, presses a key in the slot, and places the finished unit in a container, thus completing one work cycle. The manufacturing leadtime for that part is very close to the value added time in the process.

GT Cell Advantages

There are a number of other advantages to using GT cells for manufacturing and fabrication besides space savings, leadtime reduction and less WIP inventory. Since the operator is moving a part from one operation to another by hand, a lot of mechanized material handling can be eliminated. While carrying the part, the operator can perform a visual inspection after *every operation on every part made.* If specific measurements need to be taken, a test position is added to the sequence for the operator to use. This provides immediate feedback and, coupled with the visual inspection, enhances process control and improvement.

There are other less obvious advantages to the GT cell. A worker in motion has much more capability than one who is sitting down. The reach is better, more movements can be executed and even thinking is improved. Studies have shown that people in motion think more clearly than those standing still, and that they, in turn, think better than those sitting down. It probably has something to do with blood circulation.

Of course, people who are used to sitting may object to the idea of being on their feet all day, especially at the beginning. This requires that management be able to explain the value of the new arrangement to the employees, both in company terms and in personal gains. For example, I was visiting a plant some years ago that had one of the largest GT cells I had ever seen, encompassing about 65 operations. It must have been forty feet long. When I asked my host how he had sold his employees on that long walk, he replied, "Well, our people are very health conscious, aren't yours?" I agreed that a lot of our personnel exercised and jogged but still didn't see the connection. He continued, "I got my hands on a government pamphlet that recommended walking five miles a day to feel and look better. I showed it to the employees and explained that this group technology cell took care of three of those miles, but for the other two they were on their own!" That was a pretty creative solution to what could have been a very "sticky" problem.

Tight U-Line Configuration

The shape of the GT cell is very important. It should approximate a "U" or a "C" in its configuration so the starting and ending points are near each other. This allows the worker to maximize the amount of value added time in the work cycle. When straight lines are employed, it builds in idle walk time. The inside of the U-Line should be free of tables, fixtures and other encumbrances that would interfere with the operator's walk path.

The equipment should be placed as close together as is possible, to minimize the walking distance. Since we've historically tended to have lots of space between equipment for maintenance access, this is a hard transition for some people to make. But, remember that the operator will have to walk the work path every time a part is made while maintenance will only be done at specific intervals. You may end up having to slide a machine out of the GT cell to maintain it, but it is a worthwhile trade off for production effectiveness.

Despite all that's been said about tight spacing, most companies who try GT cells for the first time still spread them too far apart. It's only after the first experience that the understanding of what I've been saying here begins to sink in. Subsequent cells are usually much better.

Fisher Guide's First GT Cell

This happened with Fisher Guide's first GT cell. They were making windshield wiper cowls from expensive bimetal in the traditional departmentalized fashion, and it was costing them money because of a high scrap rate. A major reason was that even a minor misadjustment at the first operation, a rolling mill, could distort the pieces so they could not be formed in the next operation. Unfortunately, when the problem was discovered an entire basket of parts had to be scrapped.

The solution was to link the rolling mill, a forming press and two punch presses together in a GT cell. With all the operations adjacent to one another, pieces were fed directly between operations, misadjustments showed up immediately, and only a few parts had to be scrapped when that happened. The good news is that scrap was reduced by more than 90% and productivity went up significantly. The bad news is that the cell was built along a straight line conveyer with the equipment spaced far apart on both sides of it, which limited the flexibility of the operation and , of course, occupied much more space than was necessary.

Even so, this first effort was a major improvement over the previous situation. It may give you some inkling of how powerful GT can be, even when some of "rules" are not precisely followed.

How Tight Can It Be?

I did have one client who really surprised me, though. The first GT cells at Ferro Pikeville were as good as any I had seen. One of them is shown in Figure 7-6. When I told the plant manager how impressed I was with his initial effort, he said, "That's nothing. We've got some ideas to compress them even further." On my next visit to the plant he showed me the cell shown in Figure 7-7. Now, that was *tight!* Some people were almost touching one other. I asked, "Bob, don't the people object to those close quarters?" He replied, "No, they say it's like an efficiency kitchen in a house trailer, where everything is within easy reach.

However far you're willing to go, remember these three basic rules when you build your GT cell:

1. Bend it around into a U-Line.
2. Keep the equipment close together.
3. Keep obstacles out of the travel path.

Figure 7-6

OPERATING GROUP TECHNOLOGY CELLS

Sooner or later, you're likely to wonder how GT cells can be cost justified if all the equipment in the cell is going to be idle except for the one the operator is working with at the time. It rarely happens in actual practice because there are a number of things done to minimize those occurrences.

Presetting the Equipment

When a given part number is being set up in a GT cell, pieces are indexed through the cell until every machine has one unit in it at its respective step in the production sequence. For example, referring again to Figure 7-5, a piece of raw material would be processed up to the press and left there. Then another piece would be processed up to the finishing lathe and left there. These steps would be repeated until each machine in the cell had a piece of work in it. This would all be part of the setup activity.

The operator's role then becomes one of "remove and replace." He or she takes a piece of raw material to the saw, removes the piece already there, replaces it with the raw stock and hits the start button. While the saw is operating, the previously sawed piece is carried to the rough turning lathe, where a similar exchange takes place. This is repeated as the worker walks through every operation in the cell.

Figure 7-7

In this scenario, the operator is busy all the time and the machines are cycling in parallel with him or her. However, there may still be more machine downtime than you wish to see.

Each Operator Doing the Entire Process

To maximize the utilization of both people and machines, additional workers can be placed in the cell. You can get up to one less person than there are positions in the GT cell if the operations are reasonably balanced. Otherwise, the maximum number will be paced by the bottleneck operation in the cell.

Everybody performs every operation so, in effect, they "chase each other around in a circle." Strange as it may seem when you first hear about it, it works like a charm. Moderate imbalances between operations are not a big problem because the work cycle is the entire process.

When a worker is absent, it will reduce the output rate of the cell but won't shut it down because the remaining workers can and do perform every operation. Output can be increased by adding workers to the cell or decreased by transferring them out of the cell to other jobs. It is a very flexible workcenter, requiring absolutely no reprocessing when volume demands change.

The utilization of the non-bottleneck operations in the cell will be dependent on the bottleneck, so there's no need to worry about trying to maximize the utilization of every machine in the cell. In a way this makes life easier and much more rational for the industrial engineers. After all, why try to maximize the utilization of a machine for which there is less than maximum demand? On the other hand, real bottlenecks become obvious (the operators will actually queue up behind them), so everybody knows what needs to be improved to increase the real production of component parts and subassemblies when the demand goes up.

Multiple Operators Sharing the Process

There will be times when a high production rate or the nature of the process itself dictates that the operations be split among a number of workers in a GT cell. This can be handled, but there are a couple of important things to keep in mind.

First, to ensure flexibility every person in the cell should be trained to perform every operation. People should then rotate jobs during the work day to maintain their skills. A natural time to do this is at break time, which could have a person doing four different work cycles during a given day. When you do this, you'll learn a lot about flaws in the process that have been compensated for by the acquired skills or dexterity of a seasoned worker. However, until everybody on the team can do an operation with ease, it probably needs more refinement.

The layout should still take the shape of a "U" or a "C," and the workers should be on the *inside* of the cell, not the outside. If they can't easily communicate, it cuts down on the effectiveness of the cell. Also, as shown in Figure 7-8, parts can be delivered to the cell without disrupting the work going on inside it. Here, again, the operations should be as close together as possible. A good way to insure this is to provide little or no staging space between work positions. Even if no operator walking is planned at the beginning, it may become necessary if the production rate changes, so travel distance will still be an important issue. This is shown in Figure 7-9.

Suppose that this was a 12 operation process, with each worker performing two operations, and a drastic schedule change required that the output be cut in half. Traditionally, the cell might have been re-scheduled to run at full speed for half the time, but this is not cost effective nor is it producing to "exact customer demand" as required by the JUST-IN-TIME Strategy. To balance supply with demand, the cell would have to run at half speed, which means reducing the number of workers in the cell from six to three.

The typical approach would be to assign four sequential operations

Figure 7-8

(i.e., 1-4, 5-8 and 9-12) to each of the remaining workers, which would require walking. The problem is that the return trip from the last operation in the sequence to the first would be idle time, with no value being added. That's a waste. A much better way would be to have the first operator do a 1-2-11-12 sequence, the second one do 3-4-9-10, and the third worker do 5-6-7-8. Since every operator should know every operation, this would be an easy adjustment. The value is that the walk time across the aisle is usually much shorter than the return walk time for the sequential cycle, *if* the cell is configured tightly.

Miller Electric Experience

Both types of GT cells, single operator/entire process and multiple operators/shared process, were successfully employed by Miller Electric Manufacturing Company in Appleton, Wisconsin. A leading supplier of arc welding equipment since 1929, Miller saw JIT as a way to increase its competitiveness and GT cells as essential elements of that effort.

The first GT cell, shown in Figure 7-10, had two workers machining aluminum die cast housings. The first operator picked up a raw casting from a cart, ran it through a four-axis, semiautomatic drilling machine and bored a hole in it with a chucker. The part was then "handed off" to the second operator, who milled a slot in the casting, carried it over to a table holding six single spindle drills for drilling and tapping

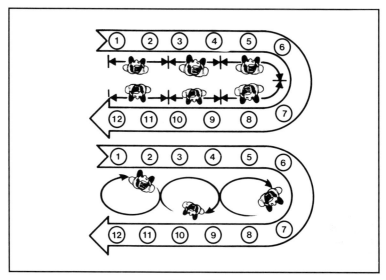

Figure 7-9

operations, washed the part in mineral spirits, air-dried it and placed it in a container for delivery to the assembly department. The raw casting was converted to a finished machined part in 14 minutes.

Previously, the part had to be moved through four different departments to be machined, which took three weeks. Lot sizes in the GT cell were cut to a one week supply of castings, which reduced WIP by two-thirds. Scheduling was easier, too, because there was only one "operation" to worry about.

Miller's second GT cell, shown in Figure 7-11, had one worker perform all the operations required to machine and gauge engine drive armature shafts. In this case, moving a saw into the cell for the first operation could not be economically justified, so a one week supply of pre-cut bar stock segments was delivered to the GT cell in person movable carts to start the process. The operator removed a segment from the cart, centered it in a dedicated machine, turned the outer diameter on a Monarch lathe, gauged the part (and used the information to adjust the lathe when needed), milled in a keyway on a Bridgeport and staked a key in the shaft at the final operation. A complete part was processed in seven minutes.

This part used to be manufactured in 1500-piece lots. It traveled over 1500 feet on its routing, required four machine setups, involved six different people to handle it and took more than a month to be completed. The staking operation was done on a 750-ton press which

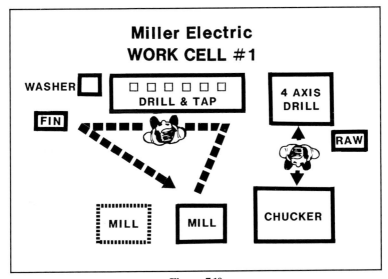

Figure 7-10

was in high demand, so the 1500-piece lot could seldom be run without breaking into it for other priority requirements. There was no way the press could be assigned to the GT cell, so the Miller people rethought the process and built an inexpensive staking machine that could be dedicated to the GT cell. Not only did it provide relief to the 750-ton press, it paid for itself in less than two months.

Miller's second GT cell was ready for operation five months before it could be activated because there was that much work-in-process on the shop floor that had to be "worked off." Little wonder, then, that WIP was reduced by 93% after the cell was operational. By the way, this is a very "normal" discovery when people first get into Group Technology. The sheer simplicity of the process when operations are linked together in a GT cell makes it easier to do a better job with far less inventory.

OTHER GT CONSIDERATIONS

When you start to apply group technology concepts to your plant, many kinds of situations will arise which will seem to be constraints. Let's face it, the "real world" is seldom as tidy as a "book explanation" describes it. However, when you understand the fundamentals, they can be varied to adapt them to almost any peculiarity you may encounter. The important thing is to view the constraint as a challenge to your "creative juices" instead of a discouraging road block.

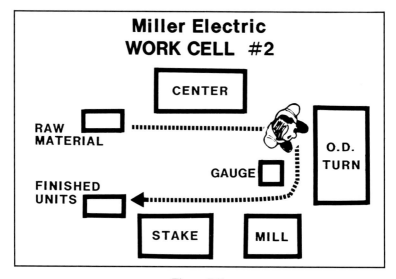

Figure 7-11

Worker Flexibility

Group technology requires flexible workers who can and will do a variety of operations in the process, including many which have been previously classified as "indirect" functions. There is always a concern that they won't want to do that, that the union will oppose it, or that the required cross-training will be unaffordable. It's one of the reasons the creation of the right people environment was stressed so strongly in Chapters 4 and 5. The interesting thing, though, is that once the "ice" is broken by the first GT cell in a plant it usually sells itself to those who work in it and others who just see it in operation.

A major reason is that the work in a GT cell is much more enjoyable than repetitively doing a single operation. There is nothing more boring than standing around watching a machine go through its work cycle. The variety of functions in a GT cell is simply more interesting and has the added advantage of letting people identify themselves with a finished part or product, which is much more fulfilling than "drilling holes" for a living. After countless interviews with workers in GT cells, I have yet to find one who would prefer going back to the "old way."

With the variety, there is less depth of skills required. A journeyman machinist must be able to convert a designer's sketch into a finished part, yet is seldom called upon to exercise that capability in a manufacturing plant. A GT cell operator is working on a limited family of parts, following a predetermined process, and only needs to know how to setup and operate the equipment for this limited range of activities. It's really the best of both worlds — more interesting and less taxing.

Operator Fine Tuning

Adjusting the output to meet "exact customer demand" is easy in single operator/entire process GT cells; you just modify the number of personnel. In a multiple operator/shared process cell, work segments must also be changed. I don't know of any company that has enough industrial engineers to reprocess an entire shop floor when demands change, so the only practical way to do it is to enlist the aid of the operators in the cells.

For example, the worker in Figure 7-12 was one of four people in a cell making vacuum-assist devices for automobiles. The original work segment was to take a drawn shell from a container, weld three studs to it on a series of projection welders, hang it on an automatic paint line conveyer, remove a painted unit from the conveyer, and hang it on a rack for the next worker to continue the process. At this point in time, the demand for the product was reduced, requiring only three operators to meet the target output rate.

The problem was presented to the GT team and they were asked to suggest the necessary modifications. Since each operator knew and performed every operation due to job rotation, they were able to come up with new allocations of work that not only met the target rate but were also very evenly distributed. (After all, each operator was going to end up doing every work segment so the motivation to achieve balance was strong.) The change developed for the operator in our example was to extend the work cycle to include pressing insulators in the shell before passing it on to the next worker.

That's a pretty simple change, but they usually turn out that way. The problem isn't complexity; it's the sheer number of operations that have to be studied. With GT cells, you can change the output every month by marshaling the expertise of hundreds of "industrial engineers" who know their processes intimately.

Families of Parts

Although it's been said before, it's worth repeating: a group technology cell is not intended to be a high-volume, single-part workcenter. Quite the contrary, it is a low-volume, high-mix center to achieve manufacturing effectiveness for an entire family of similar parts. This flexibility calls for a wide variety of activities to be performed

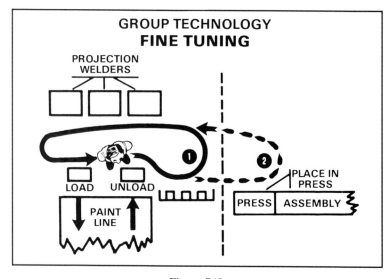

Figure 7-12

within a GT cell, linkage to those that cannot, and the combining of cells into a focused factory.

Take another look at the JCI layout in Figure 7-4. Cells #1 and #2 are welding piece parts. They receive material from the press department and outside suppliers, then send completed parts to the plating department. Cell #5 is assembling transmissions, using material from inside and outside suppliers. All three of these activities used to be done in specialized secondary departments. Each is making a variety of part numbers but the physical proximity to the other cells makes it much easier to control the schedule to support the assembly cells, even without the advantages of the pull system, which will be discussed in Chapter 11. In addition, tracking is easier because every part that leaves the area to go to plating is coming right back to the same focused factory.

Cells #3 and #4 are making subassemblies for both assembly cells, using different techniques to fit the processes. Cell #3 has a U-Line assembling a base part, with the variations being added at the last operation. In Cell #4, however, it was necessary to dedicate each half of the C-Line to a separate sub-family and switch the personnel back and forth between them. In Cell #5 the flow can be straight or zigzag, depending on the part. All of these cells were tailored to meet the specific requirements and limitations of their respective processes.

The assembly cells, #6 and #7, are also making multiple part numbers within a given family. Changeovers are quick and all internal sources of supply are within easy reach. Parts are packaged right at the final test operation and moved to shipping. In a way, you could say that each cell in this focused factory is comparable to an operation in a GT cell.

All Possible Processes

Although we've spent some time discussing ways to interface with operations that could not be incorporated into GT cells, don't accept a limitation without trying to figure out a way to overcome it. I've seen a lot of things incorporated into GT cells that might have seemed impossible at first glance. You've already seen examples of washing and packaging in cells. I've also seen such exotic things as induction heat treating, vacuum impregnation and even painting done in a GT cell.

At Jidosha Kiki Corporation (JKC), a Japanese licensee of the Bendix Corporation that I was studying in the early 1980's, painting was incorporated into an alternator assembly cell. The first attempt had a spray booth and a drying oven installed after the last assembly operation. It worked, but the doors on the oven turned out to be a bottleneck because the worker really needed three hands to open the door, remove a dry alternator, deposit a freshly painted one, and close the door.

The second version is shown in Figure 7-13. The operator is applying masking tape to a unit which will be spray painted in the small booth to his immediate right. To remove the oven door bottleneck, the door was eliminated. Crisscross vertical dividers were attached to a rotating table in the base of the oven so three sections would be inside while the fourth one was accessible to the worker from the front. He can now remove a dry unit with one hand while depositing a wet one with the other hand, an easier and faster sequence.

This was obviously a home-made device; and when I expressed my admiration for the ingenuity shown, my host took me around to the rear of the oven for a look at the heating elements. I was amazed to see *hair dryers* being used, as shown in Figure 7-14. I asked why industrial drying elements weren't being used and he replied, "Because they cost twice as much and last half as long. Besides," he continued, "we have an all night-drug store across the street so I don't even have to stock spare parts."

Balancing and Simplifying Work

While the JKC example may be a bit unusual, it demonstrates the power of GT cells to enhance work simplification by highlighting the

Figure 7-13

imbalances. The visibility of each operation in the process and *how the pieces fit together* gives workers and engineers alike a far better perspective than was ever available before.

When GT cells are installed it seems as though the workers suddenly become "smarter," because the number of improvement suggestions increases dramatically. The truth of the matter is that it's pretty hard to come up with a lot of brilliant ideas when your work cycle is limited to doing a simple function over and over again. A worker in a GT cell not only performs every operation in the process but also sees how they relate to one another. This visibility triggers the thinking process and leads to a whole new world of improvement ideas.

Sometimes those ideas mean going back to the basics. At a company named U.S. Graphite, in Saginaw, Michigan a GT cell was being designed to manufacture small lots to get these "nuisance" jobs out of the main production flow. The bottleneck operation turned out to be a multi-spindle drill, which worked just fine in a specialized department but stopped the flow in the GT cell. The answer was to replace it with a series of single-spindle drills (which were available and mostly unused) which balanced the cell and smoothed the flow within it. As a side note, the cell worked so well and leadtimes were so short the biggest problem was that production control kept trying to run larger lots through it to meet priority requirements.

Equally important is the perspective that can now be given to the

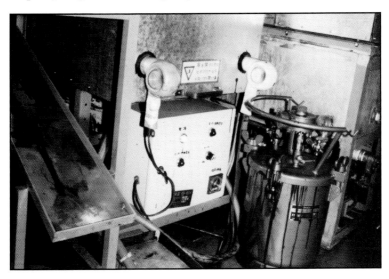

Figure 7-14

design engineer. How many times have we complained that our designers don't understand our processes when they develop new products? Yet, in the past if one ever did show up to see how our process worked, he or she was guided through a maze that probably created more confusion than enlightenment. On the other hand, a GT cell provides a visible picture of the entire process flow, including its limitations, that can be seen in *minutes!* It is the first step toward building the needed understanding that makes it possible for the product and the process to be designed together, the ultimate competitive weapon for manufacturing companies.

GT IMPLEMENTATION AT DAYCO

Dayco Corporation, headquartered in Dayton, Ohio, started its first GT cell at the Rock Island, Illinois plant. They began with a simple product line, coolant hose assemblies, to test the concept. In addition, the initial cell only included four of the eight process steps required to manufacture the product. In other words, they "played it safe" until they fully understood how to make GT work in a microcosm. It was a smart approach for them because their first GT cell was a resounding success.

The Old Way

Each operation used to be performed in separate locations. First, hose was cut to length in the Cutting Department in 1000-piece lots. The pieces were placed in a laundry hamper and moved to the skiving operation, where the ends were prepared to accept fittings. They went back in the laundry cart and were moved to the next department, where the proper fittings were "pushed-on" the hose. The cart full of assemblies was then moved to the crimpers, where the fittings were secured on the hoses. From there, they were moved again to the "clean up" and inspection area, after which they were sent to final test and, finally, sent on to be packaged for shipment. Does this sound familiar? This product family required 6900 square feet of production space. There were 17 people involved to produce 54,400 units a month, or about 20 units per hour. It took five days to manufacture a lot of hoses and there was $72,800 of work-in-process (WIP). In fact, WIP was actually "choking the flow of product," according to Bob Weibel, Corporate Packaging Manager at Dayco. When problems were found, either at a subsequent operation or at inspection/test, 1000 pieces had to be sorted, reworked or replaced. When inspection rejected part of a lot, a rush order for the "make up" quantity had to be ushered through the shop, interrupting the other jobs and reducing efficiency.

The New Way

The first step was to combine the four assembly steps into a GT cell, as shown in Figure 7-15. Note that it is designed for two operators to work as a team, using a small table between them to transfer work. One person could easily run the entire cell at a lower volume, if needed, by removing the table since the machines are very close together.

Lot sizes were reduced to exact customer orders, wherever possible, which cut the average lot size to around 100 pieces. Any problems found in the GT cell only affected a few pieces, which were handled on the spot. Thus, when an order left the cell it was complete, deemed "good" by the operators, and seldom had to be sorted or reworked. The cell reduced the manufacturing leadtime to one day and cut WIP by 95% to a mere $3700, while still producing 54,080 units a month. Even though this GT cell only included the first four process steps, the total number of people required was reduced by 24% and the units per hour went up to 26%, a 30% improvement. Space was reduced by 26%, to 5100 square feet, and the company ended up with more surplus laundry baskets than they knew what to do with.

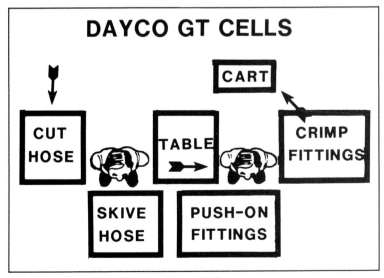

Figure 7-15

Continuous Improvement

Dayco has recognized that their success to date is just the beginning. With the increased visibility of connected operations in the GT cell, opportunities for automation are being explored. In addition, incorporating clean-up, inspection, test and packaging are next on the agenda to make the workcenter a complete "mini" focused factory. Beyond that, of course, will be the expansion of the concept to other product lines. There is much more to be done.

SUMMARY

Group Technology cells are the building blocks of focused factories and a "low-tech" way to produce families of complete parts and subassemblies in highly effective, low-volume high-mix workcenters. They eliminate many of the "wastes" that occur in departmentalized manufacturing operations. Their adoption is dependent on viewing current practices through a "new set of eyes."

The techniques involved are straightforward. Simplicity and visibility should be the guiding principles for their design, even though each GT cell must be tailored to perform specific processes. Layouts should be tightly spaced in "U" or "C" configurations, every possible operation in the process should be included and every worker should perform every operation in the cell, whether it is a single worker/entire process or a multiple worker/shared process arrangement.

The goal of a GT cell is to build to exact customer demand. The only machine in the cell that will be fully utilized is the bottleneck operation. Although worker generated improvement ideas over time will enhance the balance between operations, it is more important to have a fully utilized person than to have a fully utilized machine.

The bottom line for Group Technology is that it takes the guesswork out of manufacturing and gives us the best opportunity to maximize both operator and equipment effectiveness. It provides visibility for continuous improvement on the shop floor so the product and the process can be designed together.

DESIGN FOR AUTOMATION

CHAPTER 8

*"Design for automation is a systematic way
to simplify and understand production operations
so products and processes can be designed together."*

Automation is the "high-tech" answer to competitive survival. It is scientific, exciting and even "romantic." It is also very expensive and can be "downright scary" to those who are responsible for the purse strings. Automation proponents tell us how good things can be in the future, using catch phrases like "quantum steps" and "leapfrog the competition," which reflect the "home run" attitude discussed in Chapter 2. Although American companies have spent untold billions of dollars chasing this elusive goal, it remains an unfulfilled promise for most of them.

There are many reasons for this, but three major ones stand out. First, you can't buy your way out of a problem just by "throwing money at it" for state-of-the-art technology. General Motors learned this the hard way by investing over $40 billion in advanced automation in the 1980's, only to end up with "robots painting each other," according to The Wall Street Journal. GM concluded that it had tried to do "too much, too soon," which is symptomatic of the second key issue: when you automate complexity, you get faster confusion. Finally, the JUST-IN-TIME strategy calls for continuous improvement, in small steps, which means we should learn how to walk before trying to run.

Worst of all, nobody seems to agree on what automation is in the first place. Webster's definition, "The technique of making an industrial machine, process or system operate without human control or regulation," seems straightforward enough, but the translation to factory applications is something else. Automation can encompass everything from numeric control machines to transfer lines to flexible manufacturing cells to computer integrated manufacturing, depending on who you talk to. But, no matter how sophisticated the end result may be in your mind, it must be carefully designed and must include both end product and manufacturing process considerations.

Automation can and should be a good way to help improve both productivity and quality. In fact, it can be the ultimate elimination of waste when properly installed. First, however, we need to understand our current manufacturing processes and then simplify them to make automation easier. At the same time, we must examine our product designs with the idea of making them easily and consistently reproducible when using those processes. Only then will we be in a position to prudently invest the large sums of capital that are needed to migrate to full-scale automation or the factory of the future.

This approach is consistent with the JUST-IN-TIME strategy. We call it Design for Automation and define it as a *systematic way to simplify and understand production operations so products and processes can be designed together.* The idea is to proceed in a controlled fashion, step by step, and to continuously improve.

AUTOMATION STAGES

In reality, automation has no single definition. There are four stages, or phases, that follow one another as less and less human control and regulation is involved. It helps to understand how each stage works and how it progresses to the next one.

Manual Simulation

Group technology, as discussed in Chapter 7, is really the first stage of the automation process, called *manual simulation.* At this phase of development, existing equipment is grouped together in work cells

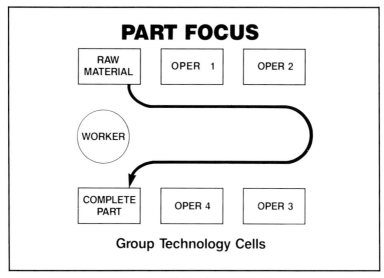

Figure 8-1

to build a family of parts in the normal sequence of operations. The emphasis has shifted from a focus on operation specialities to a focus on completed parts, as shown in Figure 8-1. While operators are still required to manufacture the parts and move them from station to station, this arrangement provides outstanding visibility of the interactions between process steps, equipment imbalances, bottlenecks and problems.

Beyond that, though, it provides an opportunity to simulate automation improvements without spending much money. When I was visiting JKC, I saw an excellent example of that. They had just put together a GT cell to manufacture metal rings, which had to be broached, drilled and tapped. A wash tank was placed between the broaching and drilling operations, which turned out to be a bottleneck. Their low-cost solution is shown in Figure 8-2.

The feet at the upper left belong to the first operator who broaches the part and drops it into the angle iron trough in the lower left. Powered by gravity, the ring reaches a stop at the end of the trough (A), which is on the left edge of the wash tank (B). A small basket (C), fashioned from expanded metal, is connected to the right side of the wash tank with a hinge so it can dip into the tank. A second expanded metal basket (D), seen at the right of the tank, serves as a drain board. A piece of wire is connected to the hinged basket and runs upward, around a pulley (E) near the top of the picture, and then leftward (F) to the broach arm, which serves as a "free" power source.

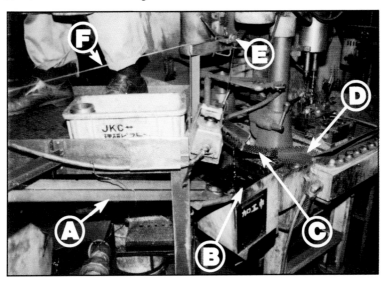

Figure 8-2

When the broach cycles, tension on the wire is relaxed and the hinged basket dips into the tank. On the way down, it trips the stop at the end of the trough and the waiting ring falls in the basket. On the upstroke of the broach, the wire pulls the basket out of the tank, resetting the stop on the way up. When the left side of the hinged basket gets higher than the right side, the ring slides onto the drain board, where the next operator can pick it up and proceed with the drilling operation.

JKC couldn't have spent more than a few dollars on that "contraption," but look at the improvement. What had been a bottleneck that slowed the operation was now an automated process step, perfectly synchronized with the preceding step, and achieved at very little cost. That's why this stage is often referred to as "poor man's automation."

Mechanization

When all of the low-cost automation options have been wrung out of the GT cell through manual simulation, the next step is to find ways to do the same work with fewer operators. Since the primary operator role in the cell is to load/unload stations and move the material between stations, much can be accomplished by adding simple automatic transfer devices between the stations. This stage is called *mechanization* and is shown in Figure 8-3. Note that a worker is still in the area because a monitoring function must still be performed to insure that all stations are working properly and that quality parts are being made.

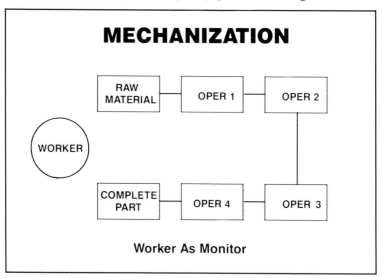

Figure 8-3

Here, again, the emphasis should be on low-cost approaches. You can get pretty fancy in this stage if you get carried away. In fact, transfer lines, like the one shown in Figure 8-4, can cost millions of dollars. Many people think of transfer lines as full automation and they can be very imposing. The problem is they are usually designed for high volume production and are very inflexible. When volume demands drop off, they can become a drag instead of an asset. For all of that, transfer lines are simply dedicated stations connected by transfer devices, which is the definition of mechanization.

Pre-Automation

To proceed beyond the mechanization stage, a means must be found to allow the work cell to consistently produce good parts without the continuous presence of any operators. It requires the addition of inspection stations to verify that the process is in control, as shown in Figure 8-5. This stage is called *pre-automation*. In it, the machines monitor themselves and shut down when an out-of-control condition is reached or a condition is sensed that might damage the machine. A signal is then activated so a maintenance person can respond to "trouble-shoot" the problem, fix it and restart the process. Operators no longer have to be on-site and each one can be responsible for a number of workcenters, so the total work force required is reduced.

Figure 8-4

It should be understood that automated test equipment which *sorts* good pieces from bad does not qualify as pre-automation. That is nothing more than a mechanized version of the archaic quality attitudes which were addressed in Chapter 3. Pre-automation, on the other hand, is a mechanized version of Q@S Principle #5, which is "Stop and Fix the Problem."

Improvements made during this stage are usually focused on upgrading the monitoring functions so they can become self-correction feedback loops. For example, if the inspection station in Figure 8-5 was measuring the output from a lathe operation which began to drift outside the control limits, this could be translated to cutting head adjustments which would bring the process back in control, without the necessity of shutting down the equipment or calling for an operator. As these improvements accumulate, even fewer roving maintenance operators are needed to support the machines. The capital investments required are larger than those for Stage 2, but are still much smaller than the "megabucks" needed to go "all the way."

Full Automation

Even when 100% feedback control at every station has been accomplished, worn or damaged tools will have to be replaced from time to time and the equipment will have to be changed over for different part numbers in the family being produced by the workcenter. This

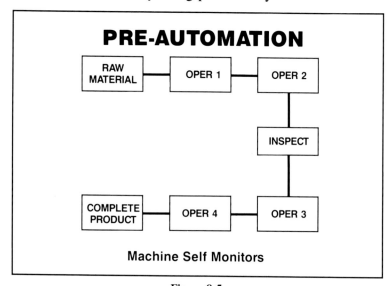

Figure 8-5

must be achieved without human intervention before *full automation,* the ultimate stage, can be attained.

This level requires that central computers be introduced to the system. All the activities in the workcenter — individual operations, in-process material movement, setup, self-inspection, tool adjustments, raw material input, finished unit handling, and scheduling/dispatching — must be under precise computer control.

The name most commonly given to this stage of automation is "flexible manufacturing systems." A schematic diagram of such a workcenter is shown in Figure 8-6. Note that all the operations are linked together, controlled by a computer, and produce multiple products, represented by the parallel lines between stations. Without this flexibility, the work center becomes just another high volume transfer line with fancier controls.

Ramchandran Jaikkumar, a professor at Harvard University, conducted a study of 95 flexible manufacturing systems (35 in the United States and 60 in Japan) which clearly demonstrated that without this flexibility the payback for such investments in the U.S. is highly suspect. He found that the American systems took 2.5 to 3 years to develop, produced an average of 10 part numbers (20% of them made only 3 parts), were utilized only 52% of the time and, once put in place, were seldom modified (an average of one new part number per year was added). By contrast, the Japanese systems took less than 21 months

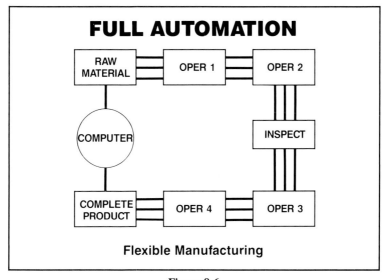

Figure 8-6

to develop, averaged 93 part numbers, with 22 new ones introduced each year, and were utilized 84% of the time. His conclusion was, "Making automation work means a whole new level of process mastery."

Full automation can be an extremely complex, costly and disappointing experience if you try to jump directly into it before progressing through Steps 1, 2, and 3. On the other hand, the step-by-step approach will enhance your probability of success while minimizing total investment because you will be automating simplified, thoroughly understood elements which are already flexibly producing families of parts.

ROLE OF ROBOTICS

Factory automation cannot be fully covered without including robots. Indeed, that's what many people equate to automation. Robots literally personify the high-tech glamour that people equate to the "future." We see them in "Star Wars" movies and at Disney World. Not long ago, Fiat ran a television commercial, featuring its robotized plant, which ended with the tag line, "Hand-built by robots." They can be wonderful tools when effectively employed, but like all equipment requiring capital investment, they should be selectively applied to the areas where it makes good sense.

New Dimensions

The thing that differentiates robots from hard automation is that they are *flexible,* due to their programming capability and a wide range of motions. In other words, they can be "taught" how to perform many tasks involving complex motions that only humans could perform in the past.

You could find a robot in Stage 1 of the automation process if one of the machines in the GT cell happened to be numerically controlled. That was one of the earliest forms of robotics, in which both the geometric positions of the component and the machine feeds/speeds were programmed directly into the machine console. The first robotic application to a complete process is usually at Stage 2. That's when the mechanization of adjacent operations is initiated, especially for material transfer or material handling, and when process improvements for value adding activities are introduced.

The simplest kind of a programmable robot is a point-to-point machine that travels along a track from one x-y position to another. The vast majority of your applications could be this simple. (In fact, 70% of Japan's 50,000 plus robots are of this basic variety.) Each additional motion dimension, called a "degree of freedom," adds to the robot's capability and also to its complexity. The most elaborate robots, offering six degrees of freedom like the one shown in Figure 8-7, have shoulder, elbow and wrist joints, much like those of a human being. They also inherit the same limitations. They can move no faster than humans, are not precisely accurate, have load limitations and are unable to compensate for mislocated work. These constraints need to be recognized when applying robotics to the workplace.

The New Elitists

The problem with any emerging technology is the tendency to get caught up in the enthusiasm of what it might do, coupled with the fear that a competitor might use it first to obtain a competitive edge. Sometimes, there is almost a compulsion to "get one," even if we're not sure what to do with it. Remember how it was when computers first came out? Everybody had to have one — almost like "keeping up with the Joneses." We even built glass walls around our computer so we could show it off to company visitors.

It's happening all over again with robots. I've visited many plants where I was ushered out to the plant floor to see the new robot, which was standing there *motionless* because a use for it had yet to be determined. I'm well aware that this may have been a motivational attempt by management to spur the introduction of new technology to the shop,

Figure 8-7

but it sure seems like a "brute force" approach and it certainly doesn't conform to the JIT principle of continuous improvement.

Then, there is the issue of sophistication. There are those who will argue that "it isn't a robot if it doesn't have six degrees of freedom." Laboratory research is now underway at major universities to build robot hands that have the flexibility and dexterity of human hands, to create devices that can see well enough to differentiate between complex objects and their relative orientations, and to create "artificial intelligence" which can be "taught" to make simple, "logical" decisions in special fields of expertise. There are even projects underway to build a computer that will mimic the human brain, using microscopic transistors that behave like the brain's neurons, which may someday be able to learn from experience as well as programmed instructions. Granted that these are exciting possibilities for the future, the track record to date has been more promise than payoff. In addition, any degree of sophistication beyond that which is needed to the job at hand is a *waste* in a JUST-IN-TIME enterprise. Thus, the use of a complex robot like the one in Figure 8-7 to do a simple pick and place function would be a misapplication of resources. The goal, then, should be to utilize this new dimension of automation where it gives us real productivity and quality advantages and to do it in the simplest possible form.

Beneficial Use of Robots

Where do robots make the most sense in a JIT shop? First, in those job areas that are dull and monotonous but have defied hard automation attempts in the past. One real advantage of having a machine do this kind of a job is that it doesn't get tired or lose interest like a person does. Figure 8-8 shows a robot mounting wheels on an automobile. The device picks up a wheel and tire assembly from a magazine, matches the mounting holes in it to those on the car while the assembly line is moving, inserts five lug bolts and tightens them down. This is a back-breaking job for a human being, but one that couldn't be automated until robotics were developed.

Hazardous environments present many opportunities to employ robots to protect human beings. Welding and painting are areas in which the flexibility of robotics has opened up new ways to automate functions that used to demand a person yet placed him or her in jeopardy from things like toxic fumes, or significant discomfort from heat or confinement. With robots taking on jobs like these, people can be redeployed to roles which can utilize their strength — brainpower.

Robots can and should be applied at any stage in the automation process that can result in cost-effective flexibility. With their capacity to be programmed and reprogrammed, they should be able to repetitively perform many mundane tasks that would lull people into making mistakes. With their range of motion, they can perform hazardous tasks that we would prefer that people not have to do. In each case, however, the simplest form of robotics possible should be employed to minimize the initial cost, minimize the maintenance requirements, and to keep the production process as straightforward as possible.

COMPUTER INTEGRATED MANUFACTURING (CIM)

Full automation, even coupled with robotics, is nowhere near the end of the road to the "factory of the future." It only gives us "islands" of automation. In most companies today those islands must be connected by people - from clerks to managers — doing reams of paperwork to keep the factory running. In fact, the more we automate, the larger this cost becomes as a proportion of the total manufacturing cost. Yet, as we begin to see how effectively the integration of all the functions in an automated workcenter, under the control of a central computer, improves quality and productivity, it is only natural to want to expand the concept to the entire factory. At that level, however, there are many, many more elements which must be understood and integrated.

Figure 8-8

Elements To Be Integrated

Manufacturing, even with JIT, is a comprehensive process requiring the inputs from and interactions among a whole series of diverse functions. Products must be designed, engineered and tested. Processes must be developed and equipment marshaled to manufacture components and assemble them into finished units. Schedules must be created to coordinate the related activities. Material must be acquired, stored, and delivered to the right place at the right time. Quality must be maintained, costs must be known and status must be reported. There are a lot of pieces to this pie.

Islands of automation have already appeared in many of these functional elements. For example, there are:

CAD - *Computer Aided Design,* with which a designer can access and manipulate data in a computer to create a new product and generate drawings, bills of material and specifications in a fraction of the time required to do it manually;

CAE - *Computer Aided Engineering,* whereby an engineer can simulate operating conditions, analyze structural stresses, and "wring a new product out" before the first piece is manufactured;

CAM - *Computer Aided Manufacturing,* by which design data stored in the computer can be translated to geometric positions for manufacturing equipment and "down loaded" to their control computers to produce parts;

FMS - *Flexible Manufacturing Systems,* already discussed, which can accept computer commands to make an entire family of parts, in any sequence or quantity;

ROB - *Robotics,* also reviewed earlier, which adds new dimensions to automation potential in terms of motion and programming flexibility for material movement and value added processing;

AAS - *Automated Assembly Systems,* which are the assembly equivalent of Flexible Manufacturing Systems;

ATE - *Automated Test Equipment,* whereby a wide range of parameters for every product produced can be monitored, recorded and used to adjust the manufacturing process;

AMH - *Automated Material Handling,* systems which can store, retrieve and deliver upon computer command; and

MIS - *Management Information Systems,* which are required to tie the pieces together and report status.

We have a veritable "alphabet soup" of things already in existence or on drawing boards, but most of them are still independent of one another. How do we make some semblance of order out of this assortment of possibilities to even think about CIM?

The Steps to CIM

The first step, I believe, is to recognize that the islands of automation, which are insulated from one another today, can be the building blocks of an automated factory if we can get them to "talk" to each other. This is certainly no easy task, especially if each island is complex. If you are familiar with MRP systems, you know how difficult it is to integrate the applications modules, and that's "child's play" compared to this job. On the other hand, by first simplifying the islands, the integration job will be much easier and more effective. For those who have followed the step-by-step approach to full automation, this is just an extension of the same concepts to a broader scope of activity, which can lead to an automated factory.

Some people call this a "lights out" factory because it can literally run unattended during the night shift. Mazak has such a plant in Lexington, Kentucky. There, second shift operators end the day by loading pallets of work which will be processed during the night by the automated factory. The last person out the door at the end of the second shift *turns off the lights* because the robots and flexible manufacturing cells don't need to "see" in order to perform their tasks.

As awesome as the Mazak plant might be, it still isn't CIM. To complete the integration, all links to management planning and the outside world, including customers and suppliers, must also be incorporated. What CIM really becomes, then, is an integrated business, as shown by the capstone in Figure 8-9. The first and second levels in the pyramid represent the steps to get there. While CIM technology is still being developed, including a universally accepted communications protocol, we can suggest a definition which captures the essence of the goal:

CIM is an interactive (people-computers) automation network
to design and produce products to meet
the strategic objectives of a manufacturing business.

The key word in that definition is strategic. By the time you reach this level of automation, you are talking about "megabuck" investments. It is not the thing one rushes into without a very carefully conceived plan that supports long term company objectives. Although it embraces many new ideas and technologies, it is an evolutionary process, not a "revolution in manufacturing," as some would suggest. (Remember, revolutions can get "bloody.")

Above all, CIM is unique in its approach to automation because the focus is on flexibility. It is intended to manufacture lot sizes as small as *one* for a wide variety of end products and will accommodate changes to the product family as time goes by. Thus, a CIM investment cannot be evaluated in terms of product life since it should outlive any product it is making. It's a long climb to the top of this pyramid but well worth the effort when properly done.

CIM At Allen-Bradley

There are a few very good examples of CIM implementations in America. One of the best can be found at the Allen-Bradley World Contactor Plant in Milwaukee, Wisconsin. This 45,000 square foot focused factory was installed on the eighth floor of an existing manufacturing building to produce electrical contactors that meet standards set by the International Electrotechnical Commission at world-wide competitive prices. The strategic objectives were to protect a core business from foreign competition and to allow Allen-Bradley to expand its market to the entire world. Initially designed to produce 125 varieties of two sizes of contactors in lot sizes as small as one, it now produces 770 varieties and delivers them *one day after receipt of the order.*

As shown in Figure 8-10, it doesn't look like the usual factory. It

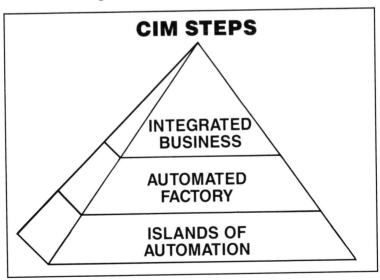

Figure 8-9

has 26 integrated workcenters, including component manufacturing, assembly, testing and packaging, which produce contactors at the rate of 600 per hour, untouched by human hands. The facility has only two doors. Materials such as brass, steel, silver, molding powder, coils and springs enter through one door and finished, packaged products exit through the other. Only six attendants are needed to maintain the facility. Setups and changeovers are automatic. Cost advantages over traditional manufacturing methods as high as 60% have been reported. Automated statistical process control, involving 3,500 data collection points, has been incorporated, resulting in a *reject rate of only 20 parts per million.*

The system has five operating levels. At the top, a mainframe computer is used for overall planning and execution, for communication with the customer network and for interfacing with lower levels in the hierarchy. Distributors enter orders from their terminals directly to this computer. The second level accepts customer orders from above, schedules daily production and provides status information. At the third level, orders are sequenced for production. The fourth level translates product requirements to workcenter tasks, and the fifth level directs each machine to execute its assigned job. Status information is collected and sifted at each level, with appropriate summary data transmitted upward. The system is integrated and interactive.

It didn't get that way by accident. According to C. Tracy O'Rourke,

Figure 8-10

Allen-Bradley's CEO, CIM requires "a new way of thinking." His recommendations to help make it possible include:
- "Don't start the trip without a road map. You must have long term objectives and these should be supported by long term plans.
- For new products, design the product and the process together. Don't make one a slave to the other.
- Set your sights high — make zero defects and a lot size of one your goal.
- Seek the flexibility to give your facility a longer life than the product it's producing and remember, CIM's *economies of scope* make economies of scale possible.
- Make your system great, *then* automate. Automating a system that's out of whack can only give you automated confusion.
- Only automate things that add value.
- Don't focus only on reducing direct labor. You can achieve bigger savings by reducing indirect labor, trimming inventory and lowering the cost of quality.
- Plan from the top down. Implement from the bottom up. Don't buy hardware until you have a blueprint.
- Eat the elephant one bite at a time but remember, there's a difference between step-by-step automation and piecemeal automation.
- Don't implement without trained people. Each employee is a critical link in the system. These individuals must be properly trained, motivated and rewarded."

THE DESIGN PROCESS

Allen-Bradley created its CIM factory in just over two years. During that time, a new product line and a new facility were developed *simultaneously.* This bold new venture demanded that the products and the manufacturing processes be designed together. In A-B's case, the motivation was strong, management provided the leadership and the excitement of creating a totally new technological breakthrough spurred a high level of cooperation among all the functional groups who contributed to the project. What emerged from this experience was the realization that the traditional design process was inadequate for an undertaking of this magnitude. What we can learn from A-B's success is that their design approach is applicable to all product development, regardless of how far we may be along the path to computer integrated manufacturing.

Traditional Design Approach

Over the years, the product design process in most manufacturing companies has followed the same pattern as the shop floor; operations specialization. Each contributor to the development process concentrated on a narrow field of expertise, accepting input from the preceding function and "handing off" to the next function in series. Schematically, it looked something like the sequence shown in Figure 8-11.

Marketing started the process by surveying customers and the competition to develop a "wish list" of features and target prices. These were presented to design engineering which spent months and sometimes years trying to develop a product to meet the objectives. Compromises had to be made, due to technology and cost constraints, so the final model seldom met marketing's original goals. Oftentimes trade-off decisions were made without any input from marketing. The resultant product was then given to manufacturing engineering to figure out how to build it. They had to develop production processes which often had to compensate for incredibly complex configurations, inherent in the product design. As tooling needs were developed and make or buy decisions were made, purchasing entered the process to establish sources of supply. To their chagrin, they found that many sourcing decisions had already been made by design engineering much earlier in the development process. The "rub" was that those decisions were usually based on supplier technical competence and promises of production

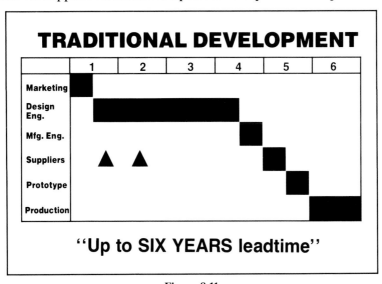

Figure 8-11

capability, which weren't always met, resulting in friction between purchasing and engineering.

Eventually, everybody tried to pull together to align all the elements necessary to produce a prototype run of the product with production tooling. While the objective was to use that experience to make any needed modifications to the product design or the production process, the accumulation of earlier problems and delays often forced the prototype run to blend right in with full production. Sometimes it took a full year to work out all the "bugs" in manufacturing.

Does any of the foregoing sound familiar to you? The time table in Figure 8-11 is based on the traditional design cycle for the American automobile industry, which took between five and six years to complete. Those "in the know" in that industry always cautioned against buying a new car during its first year of production, and you can see why. Your design cycle may be shorter, so you can assign months or quarters to the time line to make it fit. The sequence, however, is almost universal, no matter what the industry.

The price we have paid for the traditional approach is long leadtimes and excessive development costs due to inadequate communication and coordination between the contributing functions. The lessons learned in going from specialized operations in manufacturing to focused factories and group technology cells can also be applied to product development. By creating teams from all the needed functions which work together from "day one" and focus their entire effort on designing both the product and the manufacturing process at the same time, we can develop better products faster and at a much lower cost.

Simultaneous Engineering

I was amazed when I heard that Allen-Bradley had designed an entire product line and a CIM factory in only two years time. The American automobile industry was also surprised when it learned that its Japanese competitors were designing new cars in half the time and at lower costs than had been accepted as "normal." What each had done was to overlap the functions in the design process, as shown in Figure 8-12, and take a team approach to accomplish the mission. While there have been many names given to this process, a very descriptive one is *Simultaneous Engineering*.

In this scenario, marketing not only brings its survey input to the project but stays with the team as the designers try to rationalize the wants, needs and technology constraints. When compromises have to be made, the voice of the customer is represented and marketing both understands and "buys into" the needed compromises.

Similarly, with the early involvement of manufacturing engineering, process limitations and production considerations become an integral part of the design criteria. A quality plan can be conceived right from the beginning and integrated with simplification procedures and value analysis techniques. When these issues are added to the classical "form, fit, function and cost" design objectives, the resulting product is one that meets customer expectations yet is simplified for easy, high-quality production by automated processes. The interesting thing about it is that it also results in products that are easier to make using manual processes.

The early involvement of purchasing eases the interface with outside organizations, helps insure that supplier expertise is also incorporated in the design process, and assures that the issues of quality production capability, delivery reliability and competitive pricing will be addressed before any costly commitments are made.

There is no doubt that this approach to product design may appear to be more "inefficient" and time consuming to the participants than the traditional, "everybody does their own thing" sequence. That's because the team is practicing consensus decision making, as was described in Chapter 4, to synthesize the inputs from all the contributors. Indeed, each function, except design engineering, will *spend more time* on product design activities than ever before.

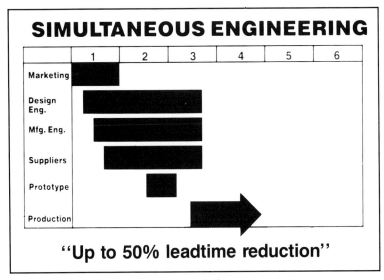

Figure 8-12

However, because the tasks overlap, the total design time is sub-antially reduced. A better product design ensues, largely because of the elimination of many "blind alleys," emergency compromises and redesigns caused by inadequate "up front" planning for production in the traditional serial approach to design or by arbitrary executive decisions made in a "vacuum." The process is one of engineering rather than "opinioneering."

The time saved also means that a prototype run, using production tooling, can actually be scheduled and executed before full production begins, providing the needed feedback for corrective actions and fine tuning to insure the delivery of high-quality, cost-effective production products to the customer. The time spent here will result in much *less* time required to "debug" and "fight fires" after production is underway.

This is the process that was used by Xerox to cut its copier design cycle from five years to two years. Honeywell used a similar approach to reduce thermostat design times from four years to one year. It was also the method used by Ford for the development of the Taurus and Sable automobiles, which were the recipients of many awards when introduced. If a new car, containing more than 4,000 parts, can reach the market in less than three years, how long should your design cycle be?

Technology and People

The simultaneous engineering process, coupled with the journey through the four steps of automation to CIM and the factory of the future, must also include provisions for the technological evolution of the work force. The more we automate, the greater the emphasis will be on the intellectual capabilities of people. This means that a carefully planned program to re-educate and retrain the existing work force must be incorporated in the design process. It should not be "thrown in" as an afterthought.

When Mazda opened its new plant in Flat Rock, Michigan in 1988, its president, Kenichi Yamamoto, flatly stated, "Without the right people, our highly automated $550 million plant wouldn't be worth a dime." He went on to say, "When we invest very large sums to introduce the best in factory design and automation, we also invest in showing our employees how to get the most out of the man-machine equation." In Mazda's case that meant a ten-week (400-hour) training course, followed by off-line training with a team leader, for every new hire.

You might be thinking, "That's fine for a new facility and a brand new work force, but what about our existing plant and the present employees?" Here, too, the same principle applies. IBM recently constructed one of the most modern, automated typewriter manufacturing plants in the world in Lexington, Kentucky at a cost of $350 million. They spent another $100 million to retrain their existing work force to operate that facility. That expense was just as necessary as the new equipment and had to be planned just as carefully. Allen-Bradley took the same position during the design of its CIM factory. Extensive training is essential and the needed funding must be planned for.

The advantage we have, if we follow the step-by-step process described in this Chapter, is that *we don't have to do it all at once.* We can migrate toward the goal of a totally intellectual people resource as we displace manual functions with automated ones. Given a stable work environment and carefully developed training, the employees' fears of job loss can be replaced by the stimulation of higher-level mental challenges in a technological environment that rewards continuous improvement. The "secret" is that the training must be a continuous part of the process, not something we only do when profits are up. It is a major investment; but if you think this level of education is expensive, consider the cost of ignorance.

SUMMARY

Automation can be the ultimate elimination of waste if it is implemented as a systematic way to simplify and understand production operations so products and processes can be designed together. Money alone, cannot create a world-class business. Taking giant strides forward to leapfrog the competition is impractical for most companies. Continuous improvement, with step-by-step migration toward the factory of the future, is practical and achievable for everybody.

The four stages of automation: manual simulation, mechanization, pre-automation and full automation, provide the framework for understanding and continuous improvement. At each stage, the objective is to simplify and enhance at the lowest possible cost. The end goal is to replace expensive complexity with low cost simplicity.

Full automation on the factory floor, even with the addition of robotics, only represents one island in the manufacturing archipelago. Many other islands of automation, from product design to customer interface, are also vital elements. The integration of all those pieces into an interactive computer network to help people achieve the strategic objectives of the business can lead to CIM, Computer Integrated Manufacturing, and the factory of the future.

The road to automation and CIM requires that simultaneous engineering be employed to design products and processes together so customer expectations can be met faster with better, lower cost solutions. For some, designing for both efficient function *and* simple manufacturing will represent a radical departure from traditional practices. On the other hand, the simultaneous engineering team will be listening to the voice of the customer and responding to "exact customer demand" in less than half the time than traditional practices have achieved.

The evolution to automation must also include a training process for the technological migration of the people, who are the intellectual resource needed for process improvements. The first factory that employs no people at all will be a factory that never sees another improvement.

Above all, the byword must be *flexibility.* All the steps in the process are pointed toward the development of a highly automated facility that can respond rapidly to a wide variety of end item demands for small quantities in a cost effective manner.

Design for Automation is a strategic approach to the factory of the future which employs JUST-IN-TIME as the bridge to get there from where we are now. That's why JIT is the centerstone of the management process pyramid, shown in Figure 8-13, and will be with us for many years to come.

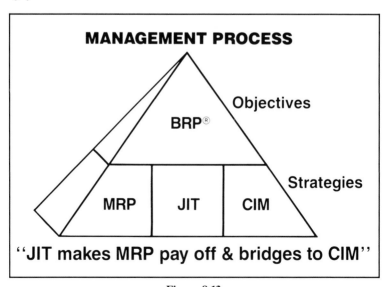

Figure 8-13

SETUP REDUCTION

CHAPTER 9

*"Setup reduction is a systematic process
of minimizing equipment downtime
between part number changeovers
to facilitate small lot production."*

A flexible manufacturing business can produce many varieties of products in small quantities on short notice. It is natural to reflect on the progress made by some companies and rationalize that we can't do any of those things because we don't have the money to automate, even if we follow the step-by-step approach described in Design for Automation. There is, however, much that can be done at very little cost to begin the journey toward more flexibility. The first step is to begin reducing manufacturing lot sizes.

The biggest obstacle to lot size reduction is the time and cost associated with product setup or changeover. Overcoming that "rock" or problem is the key to making JUST-IN-TIME a reality at most plants. It turns out that there is a straightforward way to accomplish this in a relatively short period of time with minimal cost outlays, provided that it is approached in a systematic, logical fashion. Setup can and should be a process. As such, it needs to be carefully designed and followed to achieve the maximum benefits.

SETUP REDUCTION OBJECTIVES

While the obvious overall objective of a setup reduction effort is to reduce setup times, there are some corollary objectives which need to be stressed. First, and foremost, the "name of the game" is to *facilitate small lot production,* which will require some rethinking about and even the *rejection of the Economic Order Quantity (EOQ) formula.* The first plateau is to be able to *run every part every day.* Eventually, you want to be able to *evolve to lot sizes of ONE,* in which case *the first piece must be good every time.* In a nutshell, this means that you will have to achieve *single minute setups* throughout your plant on a routine basis. Each of these corollary objectives will be explored in more detail in this section.

Facilitate Small Lot Production

Once you have tasted success with a setup reduction program, it is important to keep in mind that the objective is to reduce lot sizes to enhance manufacturing flexibility, **not** to cut setup costs for a short term labor savings. There will be pressures from many quarters to reduce the setup personnel headcount to make the "numbers" look good, but to do so would be self defeating. When you hold total setup costs constant while continuously increasing the number of setups performed for that cost, the benefits will come from faster response to customer demands, lower inventories, higher productivity and better quality, as well as manufacturing flexibility. Those are the measures that really count in the long run.

Reject the EOQ Formula

Another major obstacle is the Economic Order Quantity (EOQ) Formula, the hallowed algorithm in most of our computer systems that balances setup costs against inventory carrying costs to determine the optimum run size. While nobody can dispute the mathematics involved, there are three major reasons why EOQ fails to give us the proper guidance in determining lot sizes:

1. While the output number is precise to the unit, the cost inputs are, at best, estimates that can be 10% to 50% in error.

2. When you take a look at a graph of all possible lot sizes for the input estimates, it resembles a "bathtub," as shown in Figure 9-1. It is easy to see that a wide swing in lot sizes has very little impact on total cost near the so-called optimum point.

3. Dependence on a "magic formula" focuses attention on the answer instead of the inputs that produced the answer.

The issue with EOQ, then, is that it clouds our vision of the real objective, which is to concentrate on setup reduction to make smaller lots without increasing the total setup cost budget.

Run Every Part Every Day

Setup reduction is a continuing process. You won't reach the ultimate the first time. But, as setups are reduced and the lot sizes are reduced proportionately, a major milestone is to reach the point where you can run every part every day. Your first reaction to such a goal might be disbelief that anybody could do that. Or, you might rationalize that while a "simple" business might "pull it off," your data base is too large. Yet, I have visited numerous companies who are doing this, including one that manufactures over 11,000 different part numbers every single working day. Obviously, they didn't get there over night, but making every part every day is both achievable and practical.

Evolve to Lot Sizes of ONE

As difficult as making every part every day might seem, it is only one milestone in the continuous journey to making every part every hour and eventually evolving to lot sizes of one. When trying to achieve a manufacturing process that flows instead of moving "lumps" around, the ideal lot size is one piece.

To make this happen, setup literally has to become a *non-event.* This is not as far-fetched as you might think. Consider, for example a key-making press. With every upstroke of the machine, the cutters index to produce a different key on the next downstroke. I have also seen this done manually on a riveting machine that alternated between right and left handed parts. It isn't as monumental a task as it might first seem to be.

First Piece Good Every Time

When every part manufactured is different from the ones before and after it, that part has to be a good one. With this as the ultimate goal, it means we have to set our sights on making the first piece of

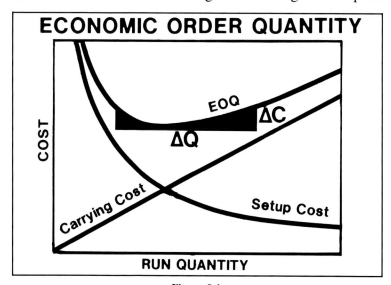

Figure 9-1

any lot a good piece, right from the beginning. This may require a major mindset change because many of today's setups include running parts and making adjustments on a "cut and try" basis as the standard operating procedure. Making the first piece good every time is, however, entirely consistent with the First Principle of Quality at the Source, which calls for "perfect parts every time." It just means that every *time* includes the first piece.

Single Minute Setups

All of the foregoing objectives can be translated into one very visible goal, which is to accomplish any setup in single minutes; i.e., less than ten minutes. If you've done any reading in this area, you already know it is being accomplished every day by many American companies. If not, your thoughts may be like mine were at the beginning.

When I was first learning about JUST-IN-TIME, I ran across an article published by some Toyota engineers that claimed they were achieving single minute setups on an 800 ton press. A chart from that article is shown in Figure 9-2. I was stunned because a similar setup at my company took between one and two shifts to complete (not the six hours shown) and we ran parts for many days before changing again. The idea of running three setups in one day or producing a lot of 250 pieces or less on that size of equipment was inconceivable to me. When I finally got to see that setup with my own eyes, I was surprised again. It wasn't

HOOD & FENDER SETUP COMPARISON
(800 Ton Press)

	Toyota	U.S.A.	Sweden	W. Germany
Setup Time	10 min.	6 hr.	4 hr.	4 hr.
Setups/Day	3	1	—	1/2
Lot Size	1 day*	10 days	1 month	—

* For low demand items (less than 1000/month)
  Up to 7 days

Figure 9-2

one press, like we had, it was a line of five presses including material handling devices between them, and the whole combination was changed over in less than ten minutes.

The best surprise of all was that no fancy automation was involved in the setup. They weren't using anything we didn't already have in our plant. That's when I realized that the setup time obstacle could be overcome without the necessity of making large capital investments. All it takes is a systematic process, rigorously applied, and some good old Yankee ingenuity. That's the reason why many companies start their JUST-IN-TIME efforts with setup reduction. It turns out to be one of the easiest JIT elements to implement.

THE 3-STEP APPROACH TO SETUP REDUCTION

What does setup time mean to you? In most plants there is a tendency to think of it as a number of isolated pieces. For example, teardown time, tool-exchange time, run-in time, first-piece inspection time, and even cleanup time are commonly used. Often, different people are responsible for the pieces of the process. The JUST-IN-TIME definition of setup time includes all of the above and anything else that might have to be done before a machine can run the next part number. In other words, it's the *total length of time a piece of equipment is shut down (downtime) from the moment the last good piece of a prior run is completed until the first good piece of the next run is produced.* That's the period of time we want to reduce to less than ten minutes!

Outlining the Steps

Any traditional machine setup can be reduced by 90% or more by following a simple 3-step process. The steps will be outlined here and will be followed by more detailed explanations and examples later.

The baseline definition of setup time can be subdivided into two parts, as shown by the top bar in Figure 9-3. The *internal* portion is comprised of those things which *must* be done while the machine is stopped, such as changing tools. The *external* portion includes those things that are currently done while the machine is stopped but *could* be done while the machine is still operating, like prestaging the tools for the next setup.

The first step is to *eliminate external downtime.* When we apply some very common sense approaches to this portion, it is not unusual to cut existing setup times by 50%, as shown by the second bar in

Figure 9-3. These gains are achieved at very low cost and, in some cases, at no cost.

The second step is to study the remaining internal setup time, develop the best *methods* to achieve the setup and, as the resulting process may require more than one person, *practice* the setups until the team gets skilled at them. As shown by the third bar in Figure 9-3, these things can cut internal time by half, bringing the total reduction to 75%. Some machine modifications may be required for this step, but most of them are low-cost enhancements.

The third step is to *eliminate adjustments.* The idea here is to eliminate as many variables as possible, not only to reduce the setup time but also to insure that the first piece is a good piece. It brings the total setup reduction from the original time to 90% or more, as shown by the bottom bar in Figure 9-3. It is also the most expensive step, but the only way to make the first piece good every time.

Housekeeping

A properly executed setup will be very similar to the Indianapolis Pit Stop analogy introduced in Chapter 3. The only way to do in minutes what used to take hours is for each person involved to have a specific job, to know it well and to have the wherewithal to execute it effectively. Thus, the Five Steps of Housekeeping are particularly applicable to this JIT element.

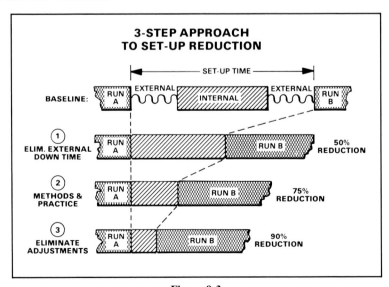

Figure 9-3

1. *Simplification.* Only the steps that are absolutely necessary to the setup should be included in the process and all extraneous physical items should be removed from the setup area.

2. *Organization.* There needs to be a proper place for every person, tool, die, container, etc., at every step in the setup process.

3. *Discipline.* The team has to follow the same process every time to become consistently effective.

4. *Cleanliness.* The cleaner and tidier the area, the more likely the setup will be executed as planned. Unexpected clutter will cause unplanned delays.

5. *Participation.* Everyone has to work together to make it happen, including management, as setup reduction is the key element to make flow manufacturing possible.

The Housekeeping Steps should be used as guidelines when applying the 3-step approach to setup reduction to your plant. They will help insure your resulting setup process is executed the way it was intended.

STEP 1: ELIMINATE EXTERNAL DOWNTIME

An incredible amount of time is spent in traditional setups just figuring out what to do next. Very often nothing starts until a machine is shut down. **Planning and staging** the next setup ahead of time, shifts preparation activities from external *time* to external *functions* that can take place while the machine is still making parts. This makes a big dent in traditional setup time. Putting everything possible on **wheels and rollers,** which can be manually actuated by the setup team members, takes another major chunk of time out of the setup activity by reducing waiting time for material handlers and special equipment. Let's take a look at these two areas in more detail.

Planning and Staging

Effective setup planning entails knowing what part number is coming up next, when the change will take place, what tools and equipment will be needed and who will be involved in the process. A simple schedule, preferably posted on each machine, can be used to tell everyone what and when the next setup will be. Each person who will be involved in the setup should be aware of the approximate time the setup is to take place, via the schedule, but there should also be a signaling system to assemble them when the actual moment arrives. This can range from telephone calls to lights, bells or pagers.

A setup card or sheet, describing each die, tool, fastener, insert, etc., needed should be prepared to ensure that nothing is forgotten. Preparation work should be done before the actual setup begins and all required items on the setup card should be staged near the machine ahead of time. Some companies organize these items into kits — in containers, on carts, or in reserved floor space if they happen to be large things. A small setup kit with its setup card is shown in Figure 9-4. All of the gauges and instruments for first piece inspection should be included in the setup kit. If your first piece inspection must be done in a separate test area, the people and equipment required should be ready to inspect the first piece the moment it arrives. Raw material should also be located and staged near the machine.

Good setup planning also includes postponing any activities that don't have to be done during the time the machine is shut down until the time when parts are running again. Many cleanup functions and area rearrangements can be deferred until then. The guiding question should always be, "MUST I do this function while the machine is shutdown?" If the answer is, "No," then it should be an external function. These preparations are the foundation for transforming a setup from a random event to a systematic process.

Wheels and Rollers

As you begin working on setup reduction at your facility, wheels and

Figure 9-4

rollers will fast become your best friends. The amount of time we have traditionally spent waiting for a die truck or a forklift to show up is embarrassing. It not only lengthens the setup but it creates idle time, which is a waste in anybody's system. In addition, the time it takes to maneuver some of these ungainly pieces of equipment around during the actual setup is also a waste. When we decouple the setup team from dependency on outside parties and equipment, these wastes can be eliminated.

First, put wheels on every container that can't be lifted by a person. Even large 4X4 raw material and scrap bins can be moved around by a person if the wheels are large and the floor is clean. (Remember the housekeeping points.) You can construct wheeled frames from angle iron and place your existing containers on them, as some of our clients have done. Many times a wheeled cart is used to handle things like setup kits. Material handling equipment may still be required to move items from remote storage locations to the machine, but this can be accomplished outside of the setup shutdown time as an external function.

Next, put rollers on every horizontal surface within the setup area that will have to bear more weight than a person can lift. Preferably, the rollers should be spherical, rather than cylindrical, because movement will be required in more than one direction. When applied to a machine bed, they need to be spring loaded so the tools being moved in can be clamped in place. (For machines with T-slot beds, like press bolsters, roller inserts are commercially available.) Work tables and roller platforms that serve as staging areas should be similarly equipped. The main idea here is to make all movement during the setup manually controllable by the team members.

Overcoming Constraints

Sometimes there just isn't room around the machine to place a stationary staging area. In many cases, folding brackets, with rollers in the top surface, can be attached to the machine for use during the setup but which will swing out of the way during production operations. Portable brackets, which can be attached during the setup and removed after the tool exchange, are also commercially available.

Wheeled carts can be fitted with rollers on the load surface to serve as mobile staging areas, as shown in Figure 9-5. In this case, using a fixed roller platform required a four-step process to exchange dies in a press:

1. The die was disconnected and rolled out onto the platform.

2. A crane lifted the die and moved it to a staging area near the press.

3. The crane picked up the new die from the staging area and deposited it on the platform.

4. The die was rolled into the press and reconnected.

By using wheeled roller carts as the die carriers, the dependency on the crane operator during the setup was eliminated. The new die on its cart plus an empty cart for the old die were staged next to the press as external functions and the setup process was reduced to two steps:

1. The old die was disconnected and rolled onto the empty cart.

2. The new die was rolled into the press and connected.

After the press was making good parts, the old die and the empty cart were removed as external functions.

Constraints are really just opportunities for improvement. The Vollrath Company, a Wisconsin manufacturer of commercial cooking vessels, uses deep draw dies in its process that weigh up to 20,000 pounds. There was no way they could manually push them around on spring-loaded rollers. Rather than give up in despair, though, they devised an ingenious method to accomplish the same objective. They milled a half-round groove in the bottom of each die set, which formed a circular trench close to the outside perimeter of the die. Next they fitted an inflatable "sausage" into the trench. The sausage had holes punched in the portion that extended beyond the bottom surface of the die set. When the sausage was inflated with compressed air (which was avail-

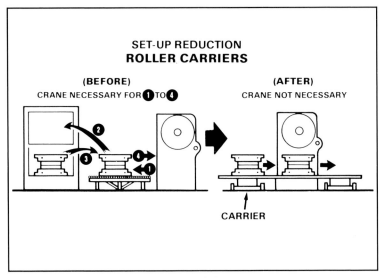

Figure 9-5

able at the work center), some of it escaped through the holes, lifting the die slightly on an air cushion. One person was then able to move this huge die set by hand to position it. When the air pressure was released, the sausage collapsed into the trench and the die could be secured to the press. Like the old proverb says, "Where there's a will, there's a way."

STEP 2: IMPROVE METHODS AND PRACTICE THEM

Having moved all the external time to external functions, the second step in the setup reduction process is to perform a *time and motion study* of the remaining internal time to find a better, faster way to do it. The study will show that a lot of time is taken to unfasten and resecure nuts and bolts, so the *elimination of threads* becomes a major thrust. The study will also show that many tools and fixtures are laboriously exchanged in cumbersome bits and pieces, so techniques must be developed to effect *unit tool changes,* which may involve tool assemblies. Finally, the new process will often require a coordinated group of people for effective execution, so *team practice sessions* will be required. Let's explore each of these in more detail.

Time and Motion Study

To improve our setup method, we first have to have one. In most traditional manufacturing companies every setup is a totally new experience. I once observed the same tools being exchanged on the same machine three different times, and never once was the same procedure repeated. They were random events.

In the past, we didn't tend to think of setup as a process. Rather, it was a skilled trade job to be creatively completed in a target amount of time. The same setup was done so seldom it didn't seem cost effective to develop a process for it like we did for production work. When setup was addressed, the usual objective was to save labor hours, with no thought given to changing lot sizes. Even then, the typical solutions required significant capital investment and were often rejected by management. Of course that's all changed now, especially for companies who are moving to JUST-IN-TIME.

There is a best way to perform a given setup which can only be determined by study. It will require some changes in tooling and equipment. The same techniques that have been previously applied to production jobs can be applied here, with comparable results. There is an even simpler method, using videotape, which will be described later in this Chapter. The important point is that we must have a consistent process, however it may be developed, which will be precisely followed every time. That way, not only can we set up faster and more predictably, but any improvement will benefit everyone, not just the inventor.

Eliminate Threads

Earlier, I suggested that wheels and rollers would be your biggest friends in a setup reduction project. Now I must warn you that *threads are your biggest enemy.* Nuts and bolts consume more time and cause more trouble than most people can imagine. A bolt must have a mate that fits, either a nut or a threaded insert. It requires a compatible hand tool to secure it. That's complexity. Different lengths are often required. In fact, most bolts are usually much longer than necessary to do the job, which requires many turns to secure them. One setup can involve 16 to 32 bolts, or more. That's *time.* If it only takes 30 seconds to fasten a bolt, this activity, alone, can easily exceed the under 10-minute target we're trying to achieve. Bolts get dirty and may have to be cleaned during the setup, or get lost, or fall on the floor and roll under machines. That's *waste.* When you study a setup, try to eliminate all threads.

There are many other forms of clamping devices which can do the job as well and are faster than bolts. The one most people think

Figure 9-6

of immediately is a hydraulic clamping system built right into a machine. It will work well and is very fast but costs a lot of money. Portable hydraulic clamps that slide into T-slots are a less expensive way to go, but ratchet clamps, like the one shown in Figure 9-6, are even less costly and just as effective. Camlock mechanisms are also excellent, and they have the added advantage of built-in leverage, so no hand tools are required.

If bolts must be used, try to standardize on one size and length. This will require uniform mounting flange thicknesses on all the tooling for a given machine. You can accomplish this by machining the flanges down to match the thinnest one, building them up with shim stock to equal the thickest one, or some combination of the two. As a further improvement, put slots in the flanges instead of holes so the bolt can be secured to the machine at one end with a hinge pin, as shown in Figure 9-7. With this arrangement, unfastening takes only a few seconds as the bolt need only be loosened a half-turn or so and swung out of the way. Resecuring is just as fast as the bolt is swung into the slot on the tool mounting flange and tightened with less than a full turn. It's fast and it works.

Try to build any needed leverage into the clamping device. It could be something as simple as welding a bar to the nut shown in the last example. When you don't have to look for a hand tool, you've simplified the job and eliminated a potential delay.

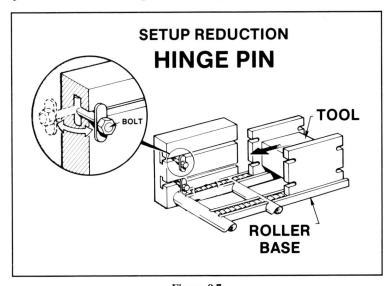

SETUP REDUCTION
HINGE PIN

BOLT

TOOL

ROLLER BASE

Figure 9-7

Unit Tool Change

Getting the old tool(s) out and the new one(s) in can be the trickiest part of a setup. The preparation, staging, methods and simplification activities should culminate in the rapid exchange of *tool units.* In truth, however, many of our tradition setups involve changing a lot of complex bits and pieces.

I've seen setup men spend hours assembling fixtures on a rotary machining table from modular segments. The price paid for a little tooling savings was a lot of machine downtime. That is not to say that modular fixtures are bad. What is needed is to duplicate the common pieces so a set of fixtures can be assembled as an external function while the machine is still running parts. Then, complete fixtures can be exchanged quickly. This is *transferring internal time to external work.*

Many setups require compressed air connections. If only a couple are needed, quick disconnects will suffice. But, if many connections are involved it is much more effective to assemble a manifold so all the connections can be made at once, as a unit.

Even clamping can be set up as a unit. Plasti-Line, Inc., in Knoxville, Tennessee, had hydraulic clamps on their vacuum forming presses, but there were more than a dozen of them. Each one had to be manually set for a different panel size. Their solution was to mount the clamps to movable extrusions which formed four sides of an adjustable box. This reduced the number of setup elements to four. It wasn't a single unit but was a substantial improvement from the previous setup procedure.

Many die sets are built with replaceable inserts to handle minor part variations with on-line replacements. Yet, I have seen this carried to such an extreme that the die was practically rebuilt while still in the press, a process that took hours to accomplish. Changing one insert is a unit change, but multiple insert changes should be done in the tool room as external work.

Sometimes a unit change ends up being a mass replacement. One company had unit fixtures for its rotary machining table, but there were eight of them and eight mating machining heads for drilling and tapping motor castings. Their best setup took more than two hours to complete. Their solution was to purchase a second table and eight additional heads (including the gearboxes) so the entire set could be prepared in the tool room as external work. The resulting setup involved a team of two men replacing the nine pieces, using a chain hoist to lift the table. This setup is now being done in five minutes!

Team Practice Sessions

The most effective setups usually require a team of people. The good news is that two people can perform a setup is less than half the time it takes for one to do it, due to the logistics. For example, control panels are often located remotely from the "business" side of a machine, requiring walking back and forth during the setup. Properly positioned people who communicate with one another can eliminate the walking time. Two or more people can easily handle cumbersome tools, guards and material that one person would struggle with alone.

The bad news is that teams aren't very effective without practice. A coach can't expect his football team to execute well on game day by just drawing X's and O's on a blackboard. They have to practice those plays. Even a great setup process won't become a reality until the team has had an opportunity to rehearse it, to smooth out the "wrinkles."

Since the team will be learning to perform specific steps in a formal setup process, you won't need as many highly skilled setup specialists. The teams can and should include the equipment operators, who will be helping with the setup during what might otherwise be idle time for them. The operators can also learn how to do some of the external work while still monitoring the machines during production, which will improve productivity. It does, however, require that they be trained to do so.

Most companies don't believe they have the machine capacity or may not wish to interrupt production operations to practice setups during normal working hours. In such cases, the only solution is to practice on overtime, like on a Saturday morning. In a half day, the team can set up and tear down numerous times to optimize the timing and coordination. The long-term value of this training will far exceed the short-term cost of the overtime premiums.

STEP 3: ELIMINATE ADJUSTMENTS

Exchanging tools quickly is only part of the job to make a setup a non-event. After all, precise tool positions and settings are required to make a good part. The more adjustments that must be made the longer it will take and the more uncertain will be the outcome. The best adjustments are no adjustments, so creating predetermined locations or settings at *fixed positions* can eliminate some of them. Transferring mandatory adjustments to external work through *preset tooling* will help even further. Finally, even the basic operations of the machines must be examined to eliminate adjustments, like establishing a *standard enclosure space* for each one. Each of these reduces the setup time, reduces the variation between parts from different runs, and makes it possible to make the first piece a good piece.

Fixed Positions

When you stop to think about it, a setup is an attempt to recreate the exact same set of circumstances that existed the last time the part was produced. But, that isn't so easy when we have to eyeball locations or make adjustments with a crowbar or even a fork-lift. If the name of the game is to put a tool in a precise spot, then the job is to mechanically establish that position in a cost-effective manner. Then, when a tool is slid into a machine, it has to end up in the right location.

A very cost-effective way to do that when tools are lowered onto the machine is shown in Figure 9-8. I ran across this one when I was working on a setup reduction project that the plant manager wanted essentially "for free." Our problem was that the footprint of every die we were using on a 150-ton C-frame press was different. This solution handled that situation nicely and required only a little toolroom expense.

First, an "X" pattern of holes, about four inches apart, was drilled in the bolster and the ram plate of the press. Two holes were drilled in the top and bottom of each die set which corresponded to two of the holes along one leg in the X pattern. Then, four pins were machined, as shown in the lower portion of Figure 9-8. When a changeover

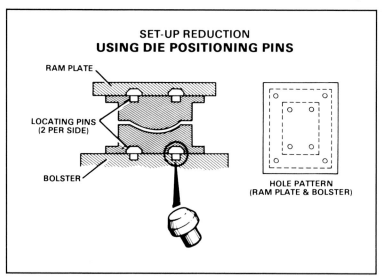

Figure 9-8

was required, say from a large die to a small die, the two pins in the bolster were simply moved closer to the center to accommodate the mating holes in the new die. Two more pins were dropped in the top of the die along the opposite leg of the X and the ram was lowered. The chamfer on the pins helped guide the die to the bolster and to the ram so the collar could seat and establish the exact position desired.

On many machines the tools are slid into position instead of lowered. Figure 9-9 shows an even less expensive way to handle that condition. In this case, plate stock is machined to form matching V-blocks. The piece with the projecting V is secured to the machine bed with the point along one center line. The block with the indented V is fastened to one side of the tool, as shown in the Figure. The distance from the edge of the tool to the block edge containing the indented V is selected to match the other center line of the tool with the mating center line of the machine. For large tools the block will be short and for smaller tools the block will be longer. When the tool is inserted and the two V's nest it is perfectly centered in the machine.

What about vernier dial adjustments? Each person will make a setting slightly different, requiring a cut-and-try approach using up "run-in stock" until a good part is made. Those settings can be predetermined and connected to a detent switch so they can be set by "clicking" to the right position. Sometimes, this is called the ***one touch method.*** With one-touch, you can recreate the exact same situation that worked

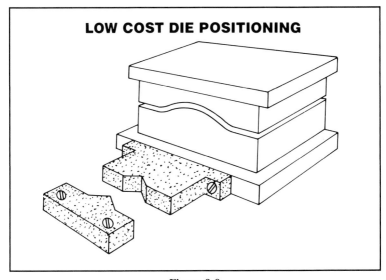

LOW COST DIE POSITIONING

Figure 9-9

the last time good parts were produced.

Even something that, at first glance, seems to require infinite variations can be improved. For example, a lathe typically has a movable headstock and a movable tailstock but why move both of them? At least fix the headstock in place. Then, take a look at the parts being made on the lathe. The chances are, for production pieces, that a manageable number of finite part lengths are being produced. Why not put spring loaded fixed stops along the base which correspond to each part length? When a new part is introduced a new stop can be added. The emphasis should be to eliminate every possible adjustment, no matter how small it may seem, step by step.

These are just a few examples to give you the sense of what needs to be done. The exact solution for each type of machine will vary. Not every one will work out as easily as you would hope and you may have to settle for "half a loaf" at times. However, the principle of predetermined, fixed positions can be applied to almost any situation.

Preset Tooling

Many adjustments can be transferred to external work. Cutting tools are a good example of this category. In a traditional setup, a drill or a tap would be removed from the machine, a new one inserted, and then several trials would be needed to adjust it to the correct depth (typically by using a sample piece). All this while the clock would be "ticking," consuming valuable machine time.

Wouldn't it be simpler to remove the tool and tool holder combination and replace it with one that had been preset in the tool room? The change would be quicker and the setting would be assured. In addition, if the one being removed was still sharp the tool/tool holder combination could be stored for the next setup and *nobody* would have to make an adjustment. It does mean that you'd have to purchase extra tool holders. Some managers would object to that, even though the same people would readily accept duplicate tool holders as a "given" for a magazine loading automatic machining center. This approach is a lot less expensive, and the investment will be repaid many times over.

The other end of the spectrum is represented by the mass replacement example used in the Step 2 discussion. Not only did those people mount the eight fixtures to the spare rotary machining table as external work, they also replaced all the cutting tools in the eight machining heads and preset them. Then, they matched the heads to the fixtures in a jig so they knew everything was right before sending the machining heads to the workcenter.

Preset tooling not only reduces setup time and variability, it actually costs less. Most people understand that production work done in an engineered workcenter can be done better and for less cost than when it is done by a service person in the field. The same thing applies here. Cut-and-try adjustments made at a machine are like work done in the field. Presetting in the tool room or a dedicated area, using proper jigs and fixtures, gets the job done correctly the first time and therefore in much less time.

Standard Closure Space

Many machines, like presses, die casters, and injection molders, require a closure space adjustment to accommodate different die sizes. When this adjustment is made, it not only takes time, but introduces one more variable to the setup. This step can be completely eliminated if the dies are modified to make them all the same height.

Like the flange modifications discussed earlier, this will involve removing material from some dies and/or adding to others. Usually, the easiest and least expensive way is to add parallels to the dies. However, it should be remembered that parallels don't work very well on roller surfaces, so a flat plate may have to be added. The job can be simplified if you group similar size dies together and assign them to a specific machine, so only minor modifications have to be made. This also lets you start with one machine and gradually work your way through the whole complement of equipment as funding permits.

Some companies, however, recognize the importance of this move and expedite its implementation. In Flint, Michigan, an automobile company press shop undertook just such a project which not only reduced setup time but also resulted in better machine performance. In this 128 press facility, they had been experiencing a crank breakage rate of about one press per month. After completion of the standard closure space project, they only broke one crank in the next eighteen months! The message here is loud and clear. Not only does the closure space adjustment introduce a variable that can impact the quality of the parts, a gross misadjustment can shorten the life of the equipment itself.

DESIGN CONSIDERATIONS

The 3-Step approach to setup reduction provides the basic framework to guide a setup reduction effort. By eliminating external downtime, establishing an improved setup process and practicing it, and eliminating adjustments, machine setup time can be reduced by 90% or more. As you get into the details of your project, many questions will arise about specific machines that were not covered in this Chapter. While there is no reference book that covers everything, I recommend Shigeo Shingo's, *A Revolution in Manufacturing: the SMED System,* published by The Productivity Press, Cambridge, Massachusetts. It contains more than 200 detailed examples for a wide range of equipment.

There are some additional design considerations that may help facilitate your setup reduction program. Some of them are just common sense items that we don't always think about, some are nuances about topics already covered and some address the impact of setup reduction on new product design and vice-versa.

Classify Parts

When a setup truly becomes a non-event, the sequence of parts manufactured will be irrelevant. In the meantime, however, some of today's setups are more difficult than others. The easy ones happen when the change is small, like changing one parameter or making a single tool change. These are minor setups. Major setups are those requiring wholesale changes. Careful management of the parts manufacturing schedule can reduce the number of major setups required, even before reduced setup times are achieved.

Since most minor setups are variations in the same family, they can be scheduled as a group before shifting to another family. Shop supervisors already know this and try to do some grouping on their own, where they have some latitude. But, somebody has to tell production control what those family groupings are if you want their help. With this input and some organization, they will be able to build this rationale into the schedule right from the start.

Standardize Everything

When every tool, die or fixture going into a machine looks the same, setups will be faster and it will be easier to produce good parts with the first stroke. With all the work that will be required to modify existing tools, etc., start thinking now about establishing standards for all future ones. As each improvement is made, keep a record in a log book as a basis for developing design standards. There's nothing more frustrating than seeing new tools that are out of step with the improved old ones, so get your tool engineers and manufacturing engineers into the loop as soon as possible.

Setup reduction will even help you with parts standardization, as your studies will often expose parts varieties that aren't even needed. A midwestern capital equipment manufacturer was working on setup reduction for a machining center. The only significant change required between two particular parts was the size and drill angle for an oil port — one was 37½ degrees and the other was 42 degrees. Since the easiest change is no change, the team asked product engineering why the two different angles and sizes were necessary. It turned out that they weren't. The two parts had just been designed by two different engineers in different years. Needless to say, they quickly settled on one size and angle, simplifying both the setup and the parts.

Assign Specific Machines

Sometimes machines seem to have personalities, almost like people, in that they seem to show a preference for some tools. (I can remember cases where a die set would work like a charm in one press yet it was almost impossible to get it to work in another one, even though it was the same make and model.) Maybe it's because those machines are usually hand-built and hand-fitted so they aren't really identical, no matter what the nameplate says. Some might say we should *make* them identical, what ever the cost. Maybe, but I'm a firm believer in taking advantage of something that works well; and if marrying certain tools to certain machines will reduce my setup problems and make it easier to produce parts, then I'm for it.

Here, again, somebody has to tell production control about those combinations or they will continue to schedule production as though any tool will work equally well in any machine. Someday, when people start making machines as consistently as we're trying to make products in JUST-IN-TIME, it might actually work that way. For the interim, however, the smart manufacturers are recognizing the realities of the situation and acting accordingly.

Simplify Material Handling

During the discussion about wheels and rollers as a means to decouple the setup team from dependence on material handlers, no mention was made of where everything was coming from. In traditional shops it's coming from *everywhere*. In a JUST-IN-TIME shop you want everything possible as close to the point of action as it can be. This means moving the tool room as close as you can to the machines it is supporting — right across the aisle, if possible. Similarly, when tools are assigned to specific machines, they can be stored next to them, or at least near them. Besides simplified material handling, this will give everyone better visibility and make communications easier.

Don't Fasten If Not Required

The discussion about eliminating threads concentrated on replacing them with faster alternatives. There may be situations where you don't have to fasten at all, especially if the force in the machine is straight down. At Fisher Guide, in Detroit, Michigan, that idea changed a setup into a real non-event.

Fisher had a group of six small rivet presses that took about ten minutes each to change over from a right-hand to a left-hand part. Each press required the removal of one fixture, replacing it with another and bolting it in place. Two setup men were able to complete the job in 30 minutes, but six operators were displaced for that period of time. After studying the setup, Fisher discovered that both right and left-hand parts could be riveted on a common fixture except for one set of locating pins. They mounted the pins on both sides of a movable center section, as shown in Figure 9-10, which could be reversed in the common fixture to make either part. There was no need to fasten the center section because there was no sideways force. Setup time was reduced to less than ten *seconds.*

Figure 9-10

There was no longer any need for special setup help as each operator could literally change parts with every stroke of the machine. Counting both setup hours and idle operator time, four person hours were saved as well. One setup per day the old way translated to thousands of possible setups per day the new way!

Design Parts for Fast Changeover

In the Chapter on Design for Automation, I stressed the importance of designing parts for manufacturability, which required integrating the design of the part and the process. Here, we have to insert another item in the designer's criteria list. The need to quickly change from one part to another adds a new dimension to product design. It means that product designers need to understand the setup process, just as they do the production process, to fully engineer a new product for a JUST-IN-TIME company. They will quickly recognize that the best change is no change, which should help lead to product simplification. The fewer part numbers in the system, the easier it will be to run the business.

VIDEOTAPE SETUP ANALYSIS

In concept, a setup should be very similar to changing cassettes in a videotape machine. When you push the right button the cassette is ejected in one motion. When you insert a replacement, there is only one orientation that the machine will accept. Once inserted, it self-adjusts into a fixed position for operation. It is a good mental model to use for the setups you will be working to improve.

Video is also a wonderful way to analyze your current setups for improvement ideas. Not only is the videotape easy to make, it can be viewed and reviewed many times from many perspectives when going through the analysis. It is the most successful technique I have found for setup reduction and, if you follow *all* the steps I am about to outline, the results are almost "automatic."

Establishing the Team

A setup reduction team should have representatives from the various functions that are normally involved with performing or supporting a setup. The representatives should be the "doers," who are the real experts in this field. Typical teams include:
- Setup people, who do it today.
- Operators, who may be team members tomorrow.

- Toolroom people, for tooling modifications.
- Maintenance people, for equipment improvements.
- Material handlers, for movement coordination.
- Quality people, to focus on first piece approval.
- Department supervision, for resource allocation.

The individuals should be familiar with the machine you select for your first project. While you will start with one machine, remember that the objective is to reduce the setup times for all the parts that are produced on that machine, not just for one set of tooling.

The team should meet in a conference area and be thoroughly briefed on the goals of the program and the 3-step process for setup reduction. The next step is to videotape what you do now, so a volunteer will be needed to "star" in the show. It should be made very clear that the videotaping is not intended to "make fun" of anybody and that the improvements will be developed by the team, not sent down from "on high."

Equipment Required

You may already have a video camera, but there are some features that are necessary to produce an effective tape. First, it should be capable of recording images in low light areas, as it turns out there are a lot of deep shadows in machine shops. You should try to avoid using supplemental lighting as it turns the whole process into a circus-like affair. A camera using available light is soon forgotten during a long, involved setup.

The camera should have an elapsed time clock generator that will record on the videotape, usually in one of the lower corners. The clock should display hours, minutes and seconds. Even though your first tapes may be hours long, it's incredible how quickly nearest-minute data becomes too crude to meet your needs. For many video cameras you can order plug-in boards as options to obtain this feature. Don't scrimp on this one. Timing a videotape with a stop-watch is just as big a pain as it is doing it live. It doesn't help the attitude of the team members either. Having the elapsed time recorded on the tape will simplify the analysis immensely and let the team concentrate on process improvements.

Make sure you have a tripod for the camera. Typically, first setups are long ones and nobody needs to hold a heavy camera for that period. An unattended camera gets less attention than does a roving cameraman. There is also less chance of missing an important step because the camera operator was concentrating elsewhere.

Videotaping the Setup

You should ask everyone involved to follow their normal procedure because you're trying to record a "typical" setup. However, don't be surprised if what you get on tape turns out to be a new record! It's partly the Hawthorne Effect and partly that the adrenalin is flowing a little faster for the participants. It doesn't really matter since any improvements made for the test run will be on the tape and can be permanently incorporated in the new setup process.

Position the camera and tripod on the same side of the machine where tooling will be exchanged. Make sure it will be out of the way of all material handling equipment that will be involved in the setup. The camera viewfinder should show the area where the change will occur plus enough peripheral vision to capture happenings to the right and left of the target area. Close-up detail isn't necessary because the setup people will describe their activities during the videotape analysis.

Begin taping with the clock generator *off* while the machine is still producing parts. When the operator hits the machine stop button, *turn the clock generator on.* Once you're sure you have the scene in focus and the clock time is recording, let the camera run by itself. You just have to be sure nobody blocks the view or tips the video camera over by accident.

You should know the estimated length of the setup, based on history, to assure having sufficient blank tape on hand. It is better to get the whole thing on one tape, even if you have to record at a slower speed. If you have to change tapes during the setup, leave the clock generator on so the pick up time on the next tape will be correct, even though you'll miss a little of the action during the exchange.

Analyzing the Videotape

Once you have the videotape, schedule a team meeting to begin analyzing it. Use a large flip chart on an easel to record the information, as shown in Figure 9-11. Note that the chart is divided into four columns under the headings: Elapsed Clock Time, Setup Activity, Internal Time and External Time.

Starting when the clock reading is 0:00, look for a natural break in the setup activity to stop the tape and define a meaningful segment. Write the time in the first column. Then, place a short description of that segment under the Activity column. If there is any doubt about what is happening on the tape, ask the person who did it to give details about the segment. Finally, decide whether that activity segment was internal time or external time (could have been done as an external function) and enter the segment time in the third or fourth column, as appropriate. Proceed to the next segment and repeat the process until you've gone through the entire setup.

In the setup shown in Figure 9-11, as soon as the operator hit the stop button on the machine, he left the camera view and we were looking at a deserted machine. We immediately pushed the "fast forward" button on the video player until the operator reappeared. This occurred at 05:30 on the clock and defined a natural segment. When we asked the operator where he had gone, he replied that he was checking the schedule to find out what to run next and calling the tool room for the required die set. When the team agreed that those things could have been done as external functions, the activity time of five and a half minutes was assigned to the External column.

By contrast, the next natural segment was internal time because it covered the removal of a cumbersome wood and expanded metal guard which had to be kept in place while the machine was running. Since the segment ended at 15:00 on the clock, the interval of nine and a half minutes (15:00 - 05:30) was placed in the Internal column.

As you proceed through the videotape analysis, many flip chart pages will be required. However, upon completion you will have the entire setup procedure subdivided into manageable pieces which can easily be improved, one by one. It will also prove useful to group the segments

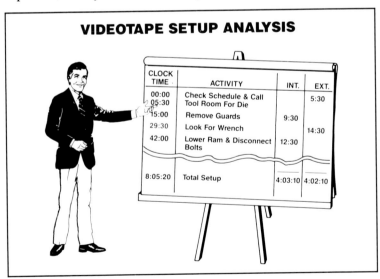

VIDEOTAPE SETUP ANALYSIS

CLOCK TIME	ACTIVITY	INT.	EXT.
00:00 05:30	Check Schedule & Call Tool Room For Die		5:30
15:00	Remove Guards	9:30	
29:30	Look For Wrench		14:30
42:00	Lower Ram & Disconnect Bolts	12:30	
8:05:20	Total Setup	4:03:10	4:02:10

Figure 9-11

together by major category, like clamping, tool exchange, clean up, inspection, etc., to see where the bulk of the setup time is being spent. You'll then be able to see where an improvement in one segment will benefit another and how much time will be saved by doing so.

A "real world" setup analysis looks like the two-page one shown in Figures 9-12 and 9-13. The format is one my firm uses when working with clients (Johnson Control's Lexington, Tennessee plant in this case). The example was picked for its brevity, which was made possible by the fact that this was the third iteration for this machine, a 750-ton press, so the setup time had previously been reduced to 42 minutes. As a result, external time (except for the coil reset button problem) had long ago been eliminated.

The circled numbers on the form identify each segment so it can be referenced later without duplicating all the words. The summary on page 2 (Figure 9-13) uses those numbers and their associated times to provide visibility of major setup categories.

Improving the Segments

The first column the team should examine to make improvements is External Time. Asking, "Why was it done this way?" and "How can it be transferred to external work?" will stimulate the answers needed to eliminate these activities from the elapsed setup time. For a machine which has not previously been studied for setup reduction, this should cut the time in half. (A client once called me to say he only got a 47% reduction in this step, but it was achieved in only one analysis session.)

When an improvement decision is made, the necessary action required should be listed on an Action Item Sheet for later incorporation in the new setup process. It should reference the segment steps and setup time saved. The sheet can also serve as a check-off list for follow-up. A sample, which came from the JCI Lexington setup described earlier, is shown in Figure 9-14.

Most of the improvements to the JCI setup addressed internal time as it constituted almost 90% of the setup time at that stage of development. A closer look at the action items in the list will help illustrate some typical improvements.

During Step 1, one man cut the steel strip, indexed it out of the die by activating the press and pulled the coil end out of the other side. By placing spacers between the die halves and leaving the strip in the die, the strip removal was transferred to external work. The work in Step 8 was also moved to an external function for the material handler.

SETUP ANALYSIS

COMPANY JCI	DEPARTMENT R-1	MACHINE PRESS #8
DIVISION PLANT LEXINGTON	TOOL OUT 85002-9	TOOL IN 87005

CLOCK TIME	ACTIVITY	INTERNAL TIME	EXTERNAL TIME
0:00 2:20	① STOP PRESS, CUT COIL, PULL OUT END, INDEX THRU DIE BY HAND (~8 HITS)	2:20	
3:40	② LOWER RAM TO CLOSED POSITION & REMOVE 2 AIR BLAST CONNECTIONS	1:20	
4:40	③ REMOVE 2 DIE CLAMPS (BOTTOM) & 3 CLAMPS (TOP) FROM EACH SIDE (2 MEN)	1:00	
5:10	④ CLEAR SLUGS, RAISE RAM, REMOVE TOOLS FROM BOLSTER SURFACE	:30	
5:40	⑤ REMOVE DIE SET WITH FORK-LIFT (MAT'L HANDLER)	:30	
8:10	⑥ DOUSE BOLSTER W/WATER, CLEAR SLUGS FROM T-SLOTS, WIPE DOWN BOLSTER SURFACE	2:30	
9:10	⑦ ROUGH RAM HGT. ADJ. W/TAPE MEAS (MAN 1) REMOVE DIVIDER BETW. PARTS BINS (MAN 2)	1:00	
9:40	⑧ CLEAN BOTTOM OF DIE ON FORK-LIFT (MAN 2) FINE ADJ. RAM HEIGHT (MAN 1)	:30	
10:10	⑨ DISCONNECT PARTS CHUTE (1 CLAMP) & REMOVE FROM PRESS	:30	
12:20	⑩ SET & POSITION DIE W/FORK-LIFT USING POSITION PINS (MAN 1 + MH)	2:10	
13:05	⑪ FINE ADJUST DIE POS. W/CROWBAR & FINE ADJ. RAM HGT. (2ND TIME)	:45	
13:35	⑫ DOUBLE CHECK DIE POSITION WITH TAPE MEASURE	:30	
16:35	⑬ INSERT & TIGHTEN 2 CLAMPS (TOP) & 3 CLAMPS (BOTTOM) ON EACH SIDE (2 MEN)	3:00	
18:10	⑭ CONNECT PARTS CHUTE TO DIE & PRESS (MAN 1), FEED COIL TO PRESS (MAN 2)	1:35	
19:30	⑮ RECONNECT 2 AIR BLASTS & CYCLE PRESS (MAN 1), BRING IN BIN FOR NEW PARTS (MH)	1:20	

Date 12/10/87   Page 1 of 2

Figure 9-12

SETUP ANALYSIS

COMPANY JCI	DEPARTMENT R-1	MACHINE PRESS #8
DIVISION/PLANT LEXINGTON	TOOL OUT 85002-9	TOOL IN 87005

CLOCK TIME	ACTIVITY	INTERNAL TIME	EXTERNAL TIME
24:00	⑯ DELAY - PROBLEM WITH COIL RESET BUTTON		4:30
25:30	⑰ FEED IN COIL, ADJ. WITH BAR TO GET INTO DIE, MAKE 1ˢᵀ HIT	1:30	
28:45	⑱ THREAD COIL THRU DIE (HIT BY HIT) & ADJ. STEEL FOR PROPER FEED UNTIL 1ˢᵀ GOOD PART	3:15	
30:45	⑲ VISUAL 1ˢᵀ PART, GET STEEL TAG, TAKE TAG & PART TO INSPECTION, RETURN TO PRESS	2:00	
40:10	⑳ WAIT FOR INSP. APP'L, MAKE MINOR ADJ., CLAMP DOWN PARTS CHUTE, POS. TROUBLE LIGHT	9:25	
42:00	㉑ 1ˢᵀ PIECE OK'D, GET SET TO RUN, CYCLE PRESS ONE TIME, HIT AUTOMATIC	1:50	
		37:30	4:30
	SUMMARY		

COIL ADJ.	CLAMPS	CLEAN UP	DIE EXCHANGE	RAM ADJUST	INSP.
① 2:20	② 1:20	④ :30	⑤ :30	⑦ 1:00	⑲ 2:00
⑯ 4:30	③ 1:00	⑥ 2:30	⑩ 2:10	⑫ :30	⑳ 9:25
⑰ 1:30	⑨ :30	⑧ :30	⑪ :45		
18 3:15	⑬ 3:00	㉑ 1:50			
	⑭ 1:35				
	⑮ 1:20				
11:35	8:45	5:20	3:25	1:30	11:25

 **Ken Wantuck Associates**
24655 Southfield Road, Suite 207, Southfield, MI 48075

Date 12/10/87 Page 2 of 2

Figure 9-13

JCI LEXINGTON

SETUP REDUCTION ACTION ITEMS
(Press #8, 85002-9 to 87005)

STEP	DESCRIPTION	SAVINGS
1	Cut strip at die. Leave strip in die set and block with coil steel spacers. Have Operator #2 remove coil end.	2:00
4	Have Operator #2 do this in parallel with Operator #1 doing step 2B.	:30
6	Get stiff bristle brush with handle to agitate water on bolster and ease wipe down.	1:00
7	Fix ram shut height meter.	1:00
8	Assign to material handler as prework.	:30
9	Have Operator #2 do this in parallel with Operator #1 doing step 2B.	:30
10	Fix rollers in bolster if they are sticking. Limit material handler to **one** adjustment.	1:10
11	Eliminate per Step 7, above.	:15
12	Fix any inaccurate locator slots on die set bottom plates (87002, 87003 and 87005 are suspect).	:30
13	Know correct clamp location ahead of time. (Allow :30 per clamp)	:30
14/15	Know which air blast goes where ahead of time (label them).	:55
16	Assure coil dereeler working earlier in setup.	4:30
17	Do this in parallel with Steps 14 & 15.	1:30
21	Do this in parallel with Inspection.	1:50
	TOTAL	16:10

Figure 9-14

By having a second man pull out the coil end during Step 1, this work element was moved in parallel to the spacer insertion, instead of in series, which saved elapsed time. Rearrangement of work assignments to achieve parallel activities also produced the savings shown for Steps 4, 9, 17 and 21.

During Step 6, a lot of time was spent cleaning the bolster because slugs were adhering to it due to the viscosity of the lubricant. The addition of a long-handled, stiff-bristled brush to the setup kit gave the operator an effective agitator which eliminated 40% of that time. Very often, simple low-cost tools will produce significant time savings.

Most of the time spent on Steps 7 and 11 should have been unnecessary. The press had a digital shut height control, which had been added as the result of a previous setup analysis, but it was not functioning. The same thing held true for the sticking rollers in Step 10. Similarly, the hand positioning in Step 12 was caused by slight inaccuracies in the locator slots on the die set used for that setup. In those cases, previous improvements had stopped contributing because of insufficient maintenance or communication. This can happen a lot because shop people are so accustomed to "working around" equipment shortcomings that they often don't even tell anyone about them. It takes a lot of time to change this practice to one which says, "Everything must be and will be right."

Steps 13 and 15 included some "cut-and-try" time as the men tried to find the right clamping locations and match compressed air fittings. This was remedied by clearly labeling mating items and insuring that the team knew how they went together.

The reset button problem on the coil dereeler in Step 16 was fixed quickly during the setup but wasn't discovered until late in the process. The answer to this one was to move this step to an earlier point in the process to allow for recovery time in parallel with other steps. In general, all items used in the setup should be preset or pretested as external work or, if that's not possible, slotted at an early point in the process.

The estimated time savings for all the action items was 16 minutes and 10 seconds, reducing the total setup by 39% to 25 minutes and 50 seconds. You've probably noticed that there was no action item for first article inspection, which constituted almost 45% of the remaining time. This was because the issue of operator self-inspection, while embraced conceptually at this plant, had not yet been worked through for all parts in the system. As a parallel program, the quality department was figuring out which parts could be inspected on-site and what items had to be added to the setup kits to make it possible. For those parts requiring a more sophisticated layout in the quality lab, procedures for prework, notification and fast turnaround were being developed. You may well have a similar situation at your company. That's why it is so important to have a quality representative on your setup team.

When you have addressed every segment on your analysis charts and squeezed out all the excess time you could by applying the 3-step process, you're ready to assemble the segments into a setup procedure.

Designing the New Setup Procedure

The easiest way to design your new setup procedure is to mark up the video analysis sheets to reflect the improvements and to transfer the modified segments to a multi-column process sheet like the JCI Lexington example shown in Figures 9-15 and 9-16. The Clock Time column shows the elapsed time during the setup by which all of the activities shown to that point should have been completed. Personally, I like to draw a heavy line below those clock times to keep all the related activities lined up.

The first activity column usually establishes the critical path for the setup as that person is typically the key one in the process. Insert those activities and their associated elapsed times to get a first cut at the minimum length setup process.

In the additional activity columns, the first priority is to assign those work segments that are necessary to assist the key person to meet the minimum total time goal. It may require one, two or more helpers to achieve it so this step will determine the probable team size needed to meet the goal time. There will usually be some latitude on the timing of the remaining work segments, so they can be slotted in the available spaces for the other team members. Always try to load the left most column to full capacity before assigning work to another person.

The ideal procedure will have a minimum critical-path-time and the smallest possible team, all fully loaded for the entire setup. It doesn't always work out that nicely. When imbalances do arise, try to fully load all team members at the front end of the setup period, letting them leave as their work assignments are completed. This enables everyone to be notified of one starting time, which simplifies communications. When a team member has to come in late in the process, like an inspector would, the offset time; e.g., 15 minutes after start time, should be known and rigorously met.

SETUP PROCEDURE

COMPANY JCI	DEPARTMENT R-1	MACHINE PRESS #8
DIVISION/PLANT LEXINGTON	TOOL OUT 85002-9	TOOL IN 87005

CLOCK TIME	OPER. #1 ACTIVITY	OPER. #2 ACTIVITY	MAT'L HANDLER ACTIVITY
PRE-WORK	PRECLEAN SLUG FROM BOLSTER AS SETUP TIME NEARS	PRESTAGE BRUSH & WATER BUCKET	SET NEXT DIE SET, CLEAN BOTTOM & STAGE NEAR PRESS
0:00	① STOP PRESS, CUT COIL AT DIE (LEAVE IN) & BLOCK DIE WITH COIL	PULL COIL END FROM PRESS	POSITION FORK-LIFT TO REMOVE DIE FROM PRESS
0:20	STEEL SPACERS		
0:40	② LOWER RAM TO CLOSED POSITION	WAIT	
1:40	③ REMOVE 2 AIR BLAST CONNECTIONS, RAISE RAM	DISCONNECT PARTS CHUTE & CLEAR BOLSTER OF SLUGS	
2:40	④ REMOVE TOP (3) AND BOTTOM (2) DIE CLAMPS FROM FRONT SIDE	REMOVE TOP (3) AND BOTTOM (2) DIE CLAMPS FROM BACK SIDE	
3:10	⑤ GUIDE FORK-LIFT DRIVER	GUIDE FORK-LIFT DRIVER	REMOVE DIE SET WITH FORK-LIFT
4:40	⑥ CLEAR SLUGS FROM T-SLOTS, WIPE BOLSTER	DOUSE BOLSTER WITH WATER, AGITATE WITH BRUSH & WIPE DOWN	PUT DOWN OLD DIE & PICK UP PRESTAGED NEW DIE
5:40	⑦ GUIDE FORK-LIFT DRIVER	GUIDE FORK-LIFT DRIVER	SET NEW DIE WITH 1 ADJ. (MAX)
6:10	⑧ FINAL POSITION DIE BY HAND & LOWER RAM TO PREDETERMINED HGT. READING	GUIDE OPER. #1	LEAVE TRUCK & ASSIST STEEL CLERK FEED COIL TO PRESS
8:40	⑨ INSERT & TIGHTEN 5 CLAMPS (FRONT)	INSERT & TIGHTEN 5 CLAMPS (BACK)	
11:10	⑩ FEED COIL IN DIE, ADJUST AS NEEDED, MAKE 1ST HIT	RECONNECT 2 AIR BLASTS, CONNECT PARTS CHUTE TO DIE & PRESS	TAKE OLD DIE BACK TO RACK

Ken Wantuck Associates
24655 Southfield Road, Suite 207, Southfield, MI 48075

Figure 9-15

SETUP PROCEDURE

COMPANY JCI	DEPARTMENT R-1	MACHINE PRESS #8
DIVISION·PLANT LEXINGTON	TOOL OUT 85002-9	TOOL IN 87005

CLOCK TIME	OPER. #1 ACTIVITY	OPER. #2 ACTIVITY	MAT'L HANDLER ACTIVITY
11:10	⑪ THREAD COIL THRU DIE (HIT BY HIT) & ADJ. STEEL FOR PROPER FEED	ACTIVITY COMPLETED	POSITION BINS FOR NEW PART
14:25	UNTIL 1ST GOOD PART		ACTIVITY COMPLETED
	⑫ VISUAL 1ST PART, GET STEEL TAG, TAKE TO		
16:25	INSPECTION. RETURN	INSPECTOR	
	⑬ MAKE FINAL ADJ., POSITION TROUBLE LITE, GET READY TO RUN ...	1ST PIECE APPROVAL	
25:50	(WAIT FOR INSP.)	↓	
	⑭ HIT AUTOMATIC		

Ken Wantuck Associates
24655 Southfield Road, Suite 207, Southfield, MI 48075

Date 12/18/87   Page 2 of 2

Figure 9-16

Refining the Setup Procedure

The final step is to try out your new setup procedure. As you go through practice sessions, the team will become coordinated and some work segments may go even faster than planned. In addition, ideas to make even further improvements will arise. These should all be incorporated in the standard procedure and universally practiced, at least until you do the next videotape analysis to make further improvements.

Many of the ideas you come up with during your first project can lead to plant wide activities that will impact other setups even before they've been studied. Equipment and tooling modifications can be made "across the board" on a programmed basis as money, schedules and capacity permit. Incorporating those improvements into machine and tooling standards will help assure that future products will start their life cycle with the advantage of faster changeover times.

The JIT principle of continuous improvement is especially applicable to setup reduction. Most of us aren't smart enough to figure out every possible improvement at the beginning. Study and restudy, paying strict attention to details, is the only way I know to turn setups into non-events.

For example, consider the injection molding machine project shown in Figure 9-17. It took that team four months to get organized and educated, to complete the first videotape analysis, and to implement its first setup procedure. While they did cut the original setup time by

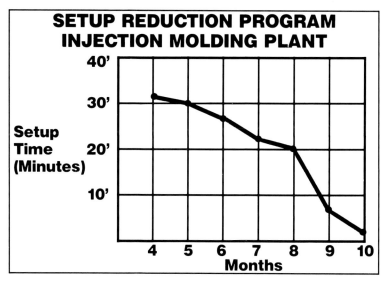

Figure 9-17

more than half, they were nowhere near the under 10-minute target. Subsequent study made further improvements in small steps until they were down to a 20-minute changeover. It still wasn't good enough. Then, one of the team members got a brainstorm. He noted that the old molds were hot when removed from the molding machine, requiring the use of insulated gloves. The new mold was cold and required heating time before the proper molding temperature was reached. Why not preheat the mold as external work? This idea saved 13 minutes in the setup time, a real "home run." But they didn't stop there, even though they were now under 10 minutes. Further improvements reduced that setup to *three minutes,* a true non-event for that business.

MAKING SETUP REDUCTION PAY OFF

The true benefit of setup reduction comes with its widespread use in manufacturing to reduce lot sizes. While that may seem obvious, and has certainly been emphasized in this Chapter, it's amazing how many teams "rest on their laurels" after the initial flush of success. I know of one project that reduced the setup time on a complex machine from two hours to just six minutes but, after the success story was published in the company newspaper, the effort just died! The tooling developed for the quick setup was put on the shelf and resurrected only when a visiting dignitary needed to be impressed.

Alan King, the comedian, used to do a routine he called "Once is Always." In it he complained that if he ever did something his wife objected to just once, she would forevermore chide him with the accusation, "you always do that." Once sure isn't always in setup reduction. Until you can demonstrate the widespread application and benefits of the effort, it's just an interesting exercise.

Tracking Average Setup Time

Knowing the best setup time ever accomplished for a given machine is worthwhile, as it gives us a record to try to better. That alone, though, won't tell you how well the real objectives are being met. A much more effective way is to monitor the average setup times for all the equipment in your shop and tabulate them as shown in Figure 9-18.

The data shown is for a real shop containing over 5000 pieces of equipment. When this company started its setup reduction program, more than 1500 machines took longer than an hour per setup and not one was accomplished in less than five minutes. Aggressive implementation across the board enabled them to get every setup in the place to under 30 minutes in only one year. Even more incredible was the fact that 58%, some 3000 machines, were being set up in *less than five minutes.* That was the "gravy" year. It took three more years of hard work to achieve the levels shown in the last column, wherein setups for 62% of the machines were a real non-event, consuming less than two minutes each. Still another three years were required before every machine in the plant could claim single minute setups.

More Setups for the Same Money

Tracking plant-wide setup times will tell you how well the program is doing technically. The missing link is whether the plant is taking advantage of those improvements to reduce lot sizes and, if so, at what cost. For this information, I recommend a chart that compares total setup costs for workcenters, departments and the whole plant against the number of setups made, as shown in Figure 9-19.

The dollar portion of the chart tracks total charges against the setup category. The objective is to hold that line on an even level. That way no more setup dollars are being spent than before (which is comforting to the financial people) even though the mix and type of "spenders" may have changed dramatically. Rather than get bogged down in excess detail, this macro number covers everything. The figures are usually easy to obtain because most companies report setup as a

SETUP REDUCTION RESULTS

Setup Time	START %	1 YR %	4 YR %
>60 min.	30	0	0
30 - 60 min.	19	0	0
20 - 30 min.	26	10	3
10 - 20 min.	20	12	7
5 - 10 min.	5	20	12
100 sec. - 5 min.	0	17	16
<100 sec.	0	41	62

Figure 9-18

separate cost category today and the numbers are already in the system. The number of setups made per period (it could be daily, weekly or monthly) tells you what's happening to your lot sizes without the necessity of collecting detailed job order data or going through any calculations. All you have to do is count the setups each day or take the number from the labor tickets turned in for setup cost.

The combination of the two lines on Figure 9-19 is a vivid graphic representation of how well your setup reduction process is facilitating small lot production at your plant. If the number of setups stays level and the cost line comes down, somebody is mortgaging your future for short-term profit gains. Don't let that happen at your facility.

SUMMARY

Setup reduction is the key to making JUST-IN-TIME a reality in manufacturing. By breaking the barrier to small lot production, it is the catalyst which, coupled with continuous improvement, can convert "lumpy" manufacturing to a true flow process. It is also the easiest of all the JIT elements to implement.

Any unimproved setup time can be reduced by 90% or more by following the 3-Step setup reduction process. When external downtime is eliminated, practiced teams follow a well-designed, structured process and adjustments are no longer required, single-minute setups can

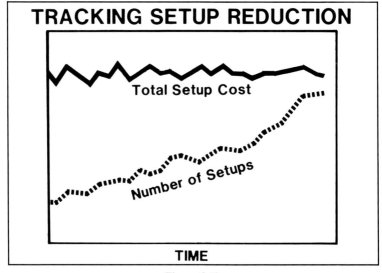

Figure 9-19

be achieved and the first part made will be a good part. Interim success will be reflected by the ability to run every part every day. The ultimate goal is to make setups *non-events* leading to lot sizes of one, even for component manufacturing.

Major strides in setup reduction can be made without vast expenditures for capital equipment. Most of the investment at the beginning will be for people's time, tooling modifications and items which can be expensed. The ingenuity of the "experts," using videotape analysis as the mechanism, can take you a long way before "big ticket" items have to be considered. This is important because the many types of equipment in your shop will require varied solutions which can only be determined by applying the principles which have been discussed in this Chapter.

Benefits

Setup reduction is also the first step toward the realization of JUST-IN-TIME benefits. They won't come from reduced setup costs. Instead, without increasing total setup costs the benefits will come from reduced lot sizes.

For example, the plant will be more flexible and more responsive to customer demand because the entire variety of products can be made more frequently. Quality will increase with the closer tie-in between the operator and the setup. In fact, the operator will qualify the first piece and assure the quality during the manufacturing process. Productivity and profitability will increase because many of the non-value added activities associated with moving, storing, inspecting, reworking and accounting for large quantities of material will be eliminated. There will even be potential extra capacity for emergency situations.

With those improvements will come many decreases. Smaller lot sizes will be accompanied by a proportional reduction in manufacturing leadtime. Inventory will shrink and less space will be required to store it. That space can be used to bring in more business and to get more production out of the existing facility. Even scrap will be reduced, lowering unit costs.

It is these benefits that will make an enlightened management eager to invest the time and resources needed to initiate setup reduction programs. When the profit power of this undertaking is fully appreciated, even capital expenditures will be authorized. I know of one company that reduced setup times on a very complex machine to under 30 minutes using the standard approach. A major machine modification was required to take that number down to about three minutes. Not only was the commitment made to move ahead on the first machine, but the organization also bought an overhaul specialty company to modify every one of the hundreds of machines they owned. The company prefers to remain anonymous because they expect to achieve a significant economic advantage over their competitors.

Setup reduction is not a "magic pill." It is not even the final answer. It is, however, the *key* to JUST-IN-TIME production.

UNIFORM
SCHEDULING

CHAPTER 10

*"Uniform scheduling is a planning method
for resource allocation based on
smooth, homogenized production flow (level load) and
fast communication of support requirements (cycle time)."*

By breaking the barrier of large lot production through setup reduction, a JUST-IN-TIME company is capable of manufacturing smaller and smaller lot sizes, eventually making every part every day and even every hour. In this situation, manufacturing schedules can be developed using a *variable flow* management concept instead of trying to coordinate "lumps" of production. This not only makes it easier to establish and maintain a plan, but the plan can also be communicated to all the supporting activities more quickly.

Called uniform scheduling, it separates planning function from the authorization to execute the plan. Traditionally, people have tended to blend the two together. A schedule has always been an authorization to initiate action. Uniform scheduling, however, concentrates only on *marshaling the necessary resources* to meet planned production. The *action is delayed* until the last possible moment to account for last-minute changes. Execution authorization is initiated by a final assembly schedule, to be introduced at the end of this chapter, and by the Pull System, which will be covered in Chapter 11. Since the separation of planning and execution authorization is a radical departure from past practices for many people, it may take some time to get this thought implanted in your company.

Uniform scheduling can be thought of as *getting ready for production*. It has two major component parts. The first one is to develop a **level load** for the entire manufacturing network. This provides a smooth demand for manufacturing and makes it easier to determine resource requirements, since everything is based on average needs and average capacity. Then, **cycle times** are computed to quickly communicate that plan to all the support functions in the network, without the need for elaborate software systems or complicated calculations. Together, level loading and cycle time communication will tell everyone what has to be done to get ready to meet the planned demand.

LOAD LEVELING

Level loading, in a nutshell, is planning to build the same product mix every single day during a given month. Levels may change from month to month, but each day within that month will be exactly the same. That's where the term, variable flow, comes from. The production level and product mix can vary from month to month to meet changing customer demands, but will flow smoothly and evenly each day within the month. In a way, it's a compromise between unbridled flexibility, which is the ultimate ideal of JUST-IN-TIME, and the long-term, "frozen" schedules that most manufacturing people have dreamed about for years.

Traditional Scheduling

The classic approach to production scheduling has been to minimize change. Master schedules were "locked in" for months at a time. Manufacturing schedules for component parts were set up to produce several months of requirements in one run. Even high volume parts were run only once a month. In fact, I once had a boss who said he would hold me personally responsible if he ever learned that a part was run more than once a month. The entire scheduling process was governed by a "monthly mentality."

A typical schedule looked like the one in Figure 10-1. The four parts, A, B, C and D, were usually sequenced with the longest job first

PRODUCTION PLANNING
TRADITIONAL

DAY / PROD	SCHEDULE				
	1 2 3	. . . .		30	
A	████████				
B		███			
C			███		
D				██	

"Produce Monthly Quantities"

Figure 10-1

to make the "numbers" look good. Early in the month we seemed to be preoccupied with efficiency and utilization figures because this kept the financial people happy. As the month progressed, however, the emphasis shifted to "getting parts out the door" so short runs and split lots were tolerated to make the billing target. The pandemonium at month end usually got the job done, but at a high price. Not only did the accumulated shipments chart look like a "hockey stick," but the high cost variances also refocused everybody's attention on efficiencies and utilization again, so the cycle repeated itself the next month.

To make matters worse, the schedule worked against providing good customer service. A customer who wanted Part D early in the month would have to wait until late in the month to get it or the schedule would have to be changed, raising havoc with the costs. We knew how to minimize that problem. Short order scheduling techniques told us to run the shortest job first, then the next shortest, etc., so we would have a mix of all products at the earliest possible point in the month. Very few people took advantage of that approach, however, because it conflicted with the "numbers game." Until JUST-IN-TIME came along it was taken for granted that those conflicts were just "real-world constraints" that we had to work our way around.

Uniform Daily Scheduling

Resolving the conflict between productivity and customer demand is a major reason why JIT emphasizes the ability to reduce lot sizes to the point where every part can be economically produced every day. It is the only way to respond to exact customer demand while still maximizing productivity.

The idea is to establish a firm monthly production plan for all the parts you intend to build and to subdivide it into daily slices. That way, every working day in the month looks like every other day, so far as the schedule is concerned. For planning purposes, it is much easier to work with averages than to have to consider time-phased events. When the average capacity for the period equals the average demand you know you have a "do-able" plan because each day will be the same.

When you make some of everything every day, a customer can be furnished with at least a partial quantity of any product. Most "urgent" customer orders ask for more pieces than are needed immediately. Often, the order is for a minimum quantity that we establish. But, when you can offer a small quantity today, some more tomorrow and more every day after that (as opposed to nothing until the end of the month), like the schedule shown in Figure 10-2, the chances of satisfying that customer's actual needs are very high. And you can do it without the high costs associated with rescheduling the shop, breaking into jobs or splitting lots to meet that customer demand.

Remember, though, this is just a plan so far. Nobody is going to *do* anything except marshal the necessary average resources to achieve the daily plan when, and if, the authorization to proceed is issued. The only thing that will be held firmly is the *"envelope" of production requirements for an entire family of similar parts or products during the first month of the plan.* That is necessary to fully utilize the resources being assembled to support the plan.

Traditional production planning refers to the amount of a product family to be made each month as the *production rate,* since it is a quantity per period. Efforts are made to keep that rate as level as possible. However, under uniform scheduling each month in the plan may call for a different production level than the previous one, depending on the forecast of gross customer demand. Since supply and demand are equated in JUST-IN-TIME, the production quantities must change as demand changes. I've chosen to call the monthly product family amount a *production envelope* to emphasize the difference.

Uniform scheduling is also quite different from traditional master scheduling, where so much work is done to stabilize the product mix (the relative quantities of the end products in the family). As a result, the

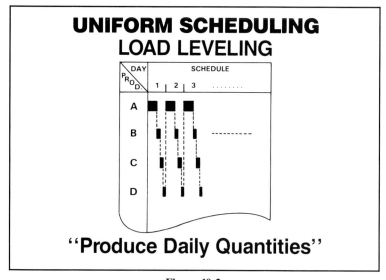

Figure 10-2

typical master schedule is leveled *by end product part number for many months in a row.* The difference between the master schedule and real customer demand is absorbed by finished goods. Under uniform scheduling, the aggregate production envelope is only fixed for a *family of products in the first month* and often changes in subsequent months to meet changing customer demand. Ideally, there won't be any need for finished goods.

With different production envelopes each month, the level loading part of uniform scheduling only applies to the daily slices of the envelope within a given planning month. You are *planning* to have the same product mix every working day in that month. (You may be thinking that real-world customer demand is surely going to change from what you thought it was going to be when the plan was generated. It will, and that change will be accommodated by the Pull System, to be covered later. For now, though, let's just concentrate on building the uniform plan and communicating it to everyone who has a need to know about it.)

CYCLE TIME

When the planned production level for each day in the month is the same, you can express the output as a rate per period of time or an interval of time between units. For example, 60 units per hour means the same thing as one minute between units. Under uniform scheduling the *interval*

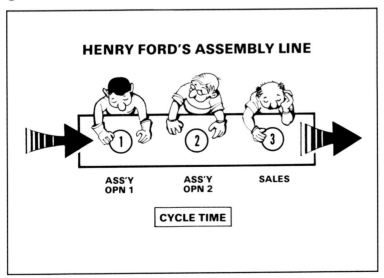

Figure 10-3

between like units is called *cycle time*. Since we want the production rate to equal the sales rate, it would be like putting a cash register at the end of the production line, as shown in Figure 10-3. If we rang the cash register each time a customer accepted a product, the average time interval between those sales during the month would be the cycle time for that product. You can also compute a cycle time for the whole product family. Cycle time is an easy way to tell everyone in the supply network what resources must be marshaled to support the monthly production plans.

Unfortunately, the term "cycle time" has had many other applications in manufacturing. To some it means a machine rate. To others, it is the production capacity, regardless of demand. In almost every case it has meant a fixed number. When we use cycle time under uniform scheduling, however, it means *the desired production interval during a month, which will be equal to the sales interval for the same month.*

Computing Cycle Times

Cycle times are easy to compute. Suppose we had a monthly production plan for a family of products like the one shown in Figure 10-4. The sum of all the products in the family is 32,000 pieces. Dividing the monthly total by the number of working days in the month, then by the number of working hours in a day and, finally, dividing that answer into 3600 seconds per hour results in a cycle time of 18 seconds for the family. That means one product in that family will be completed every 18

ASSEMBLY LINE CYCLE TIME

MODEL	SALES
A	16,000
B	10,000
C	4,000
D	2,000

TOTAL 32,000/Month
20 Days = 1600/Day
8 Hours =   200/Hour
Or 1 Every 18 Seconds

Note: Sales Rates will be different from current Production Rates

Figure 10-4

seconds. Using the same method, the cycle time for individual products in the family will be: A = 36 seconds, B = 57.6 seconds, C =
144 seconds (or 2 minutes, 24 seconds), and D = 288 seconds (or
4 minutes, 48 seconds).

The shorter the cycle time, the faster the parts will be made. You can
quickly see the relative production rates for individual part numbers.
For example, Part A (36 sec.) will be produced four times as fast as
Part C (144 sec.) and eight times as fast as Part D (288 sec.). When
planning resource allocations, however, the *family cycle time (18 sec.)
is the driver for the system.*

Computing Crew Sizes

When planning resources to meet the computed cycle times, you can
be sure that adjustments will have to be made. Rarely does today's production rate equal today's sales rate. On top of that the figures will change
from month to month under uniform scheduling. Happily, it turns out
to be a fairly simple job.

The first step is to compute the labor content of the product being
scheduled and to store it for future use. Labor content is what you are
paying per piece today. Although you may have labor standards in your
system, the best way to develop this number is to use actual data as
it will include all the efficiency and lost time variables. Dividing the
total labor cost for a product family in a production period by the total
number of units made during that period will give you a real-world cost
per unit.

Suppose, for the example used in Figure 10-4, that we had a crew
of 10 people in a workcenter producing 400 units per hour. The labor
content would be the output cost divided by the number produced. In
this case, it would be 10 people times 3600 seconds per hour divided
by 400 units per hour, or 90 seconds per unit. This cost figure will be
constant for that product until the manufacturing process is changed,
so we can store it away for future use. Then, any time we want to compute the needed crew size for a given month, we just divide the labor
content by the desired cycle time. For our example,

$$\text{CREW SIZE} = \frac{\text{LABOR CONTENT}}{\text{CYCLE TIME}} = \frac{90 \text{ SEC/PC}}{18 \text{ SEC/PC}} = 5$$

Crew sizes for different sales forecasts are shown in Figure 10-5.
Note that the labor column is constant and the only variable is the

desired cycle time. It really has to be that easy or we'd never be able to recompute the crew sizes every month to meet varying customer demand. (By the way, this is how we arrived at the crew size target figure when we asked the personnel in the group technology cell in Chapter 7 to rearrange their own work segments.)

Communicating With Feeders

Typically, feeder operations and outside suppliers can compute their own crew sizes once they know the desired cycle times for their customer's products. When the customer generates a monthly production plan and its associated cycle times, that information can be sent to everyone in the supply network at the same time. There is no need for bill of material explosions, leadtime off-setting, or level-by-level netting of dependent requirements. The transmitted "schedule" consists of just two columns of data, the customer final assembly numbers and the cycle time for each, as shown in the left side of Figure 10-6.

The feeder operation has a "used-on" cross reference which can be stored in a computer or just printed on paper. Some people call it a "goes-into" list. It tells the feeder which components and how many of each are required to support the customer's final assembly. As shown in the middle section of Figure 10-6, for each customer final assembly A1, the feeder must produce two P1 components.

The feeder will compute the required component cycle time by

CYCLE TIME/CREW SIZE MATRIX

SALES PER MO.	LABOR CONTENT	÷ CYCLE TIME	= CREW SIZE
64,000	90	9.0	10
38,400	90	15.0	6
32,000	90	18.0	5
25,600	90	22.5	4

Figure 10-5

dividing the customer's final assembly cycle time by the component "quantity per." Referring again to Figure 10-6, the cycle time for component P1 would be:

$$\text{P1 C.T.} = \frac{\text{A1 C.T.}}{\text{P1 QTY.}} = \frac{18 \text{ SEC}}{2} = 9 \text{ SEC}$$

Take a look at the second line on the figure and see if you can compute the cycle time for component P2.

The beauty of cycle time as a communication tool is that it is so fast and yet so simple. When a classic MRP system is used for production planning, a fifth level supplier might have to wait five weeks to receive specific planning information. With cycle time all levels can be notified *at the same time.*

Improving Productivity

When cycle time communication is firmly implanted in everybody's mind it can even serve as a tool for productivity improvement. It helps people look at old problems in a new way.

Consider again the example used during the discussion on crew size calculations. We determined that, for a cycle time of 18 seconds, a crew of five people would be required and that the labor content would be 90 seconds for each piece produced.

If we were to look closely at the amount of value added time in the

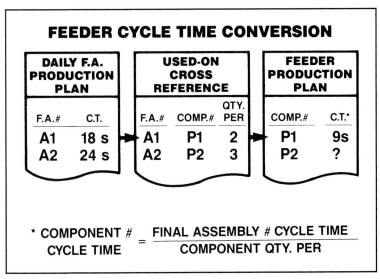

FEEDER CYCLE TIME CONVERSION

DAILY F.A. PRODUCTION PLAN		USED-ON CROSS REFERENCE			FEEDER PRODUCTION PLAN	
F.A.#	C.T.	F.A.#	COMP.#	QTY. PER	COMP.#	C.T.*
A1	18 s	A1	P1	2	P1	9s
A2	24 s	A2	P2	3	P2	?

$$* \frac{\text{COMPONENT \# }}{\text{CYCLE TIME}} = \frac{\text{FINAL ASSEMBLY \# CYCLE TIME}}{\text{COMPONENT QTY. PER}}$$

Figure 10-6

work cycles for those five people, it might look like the bars shown in Figure 10-7. Here, only one of the five workers (#2) is adding value for the entire 18 seconds. The other four have a lot of idle time in their work assignments. This is not an unusual situation in manufacturing, since work load balancing is a perpetual challenge for the industrial engineers. In this case, although the total cost of the product is 90 seconds of labor, the actual value added content is only 74 seconds.

Given this problem in a traditional plant, good industrial engineers would *attack the bottleneck operation,* since that's the way they were trained. Through clever fixture design, motion improvements or other refinements, an engineer could trim several seconds from the bottleneck operation, as shown in Figure 10-8. With this improvement, both worker #2 and worker #3 would be adding value for the entire work cycle and only four seconds of idle time would remain for all the other workers.

The good news is that this solution would represent a productivity improvement of 16.7%. It would also increase the output of the work center by 40 pieces per hour which would be praised in a traditional shop. However, those extra pieces would result in a buildup of inventory, which is unacceptable in a JUST-IN-TIME shop. Even if prudent inventory control was being practiced in the traditional shop, the only alternative would be to shut down the workcenter earlier in the month and find something else for the people to do.

In truth, the relationship between the process improvement and the

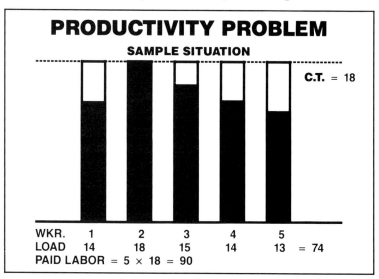

Figure 10-7

output change often went unnoticed in the past. Under uniform scheduling, however, the change in cycle time would be picked up immediately, as shown by the 15-second line in Figure 10-8. Since this output rate would not balance the demand rate, the solution would be unacceptable.

What, then, would be a good JIT solution? First, the 18-second cycle time would be treated as "gospel." Any solution would have to conform to that number. Second, instead of attacking the bottleneck operation, the *entire process would be studied.* Work would be shifted between workers as shown in Figure 10-9. (Remember, in a JIT workcenter, every worker can perform every operation, so rebalancing is much easier.) In this case, four seconds of work was shifted from #2 to #1, four seconds was shifted from #3 to #2, seven seconds was moved from #4 to #3, and eleven seconds was shifted from #5 to #4, leaving only two seconds of work for #5 to perform. If our JIT industrial engineer is almost as clever as the traditional one was, the remaining two seconds can be eliminated along with the need for the fifth worker who can be transferred to an area where the resource is needed. This solution gives better productivity improvement without compromising the desired output rate.

This was not a "made up" example. I saw it working at a Toyota plant. The workers themselves had constructed a display board describing every step that was taken during the manufacturing process and showing the exact location for each process step. (It looked like an Arthur

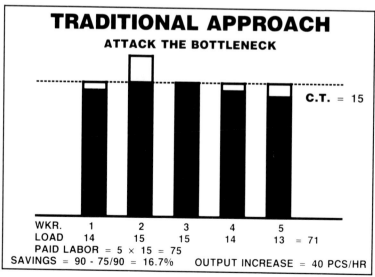

Figure 10-8

Murray dance chart.) Their bar charts showed value added time, non-value added time ("busy work," like fetching parts from off-line, that shouldn't be required) and idle time. They were constantly trying to figure out ways to eliminate the latter two categories and to shift the value added work so two people could do the jobs now requiring three people. If it seems extreme to you, remember it's also your competition.

MIXED MODEL SCHEDULING

Most people start uniform scheduling with the idea of just getting to the point where they can run every part every day. It's a good milestone but hardly the ultimate objective. True flow production won't be achieved until the daily schedule is completely homogenized, so every hour looks like every other hour. This is not a "pipe dream" either. More and more companies are graduating to this level. Eventually, so will you. Therefore, it important to know how to implement this advanced phase of uniform scheduling in anticipation of that achievement.

Why It Is Important

If you've ever toured an automotive assembly plant, you've seen mixed model scheduling in action. Every car coming down that line is a different product in the same generic family. Each one is a different color and has different options or accessories, such as air-conditioning,

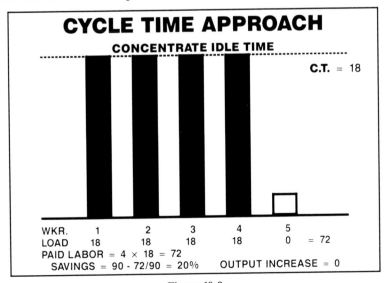

Figure 10-9

power devices or radios. Each one is being built to a specific customer order. To handle such a wide variety of products on a moving assembly line, it is necessary to balance the labor required for these variables during the course of a working day. For example, if one-third of the cars were air conditioned, every third car on the line would call for this accessory. Sending two or three air conditioned cars in a row down the line would jam up that work station and bring the line to a halt.

For the automobile business, mixed model scheduling has been a necessity. For the rest of us, there is a valuable lesson to be learned from that industry. Blending all the variables into the smoothest possible flow of product **maximizes the productivity** of the assembly work force. Even more importantly, it generates the **smoothest possible set of demands** for all the supply operations in the support network. This is the strategic rationale behind mixed model scheduling and the reason why it is needed to achieve the maximum benefits from JUST-IN-TIME.

Determining the Minimum Sequence
Mixed model scheduling in final assembly starts with a daily slice of the monthly production plan. The next step is to determine from that slice the minimum sequence of end product numbers within the product family that can repeated throughout the day. This will provide the most homogeneous possible plan for that particular product mix.

Like every thing else in uniform scheduling, the sequence will have to be recomputed each time the plan changes so the technique must be simple and easy to use. Here, again, cycle time is used to make the determination. First, let's develop a simple sequence empirically, then we will discuss the formula to be used for the more complex situations.

Suppose we had a product family comprised of three product numbers — A, B and C. The production plan, daily quantities and cycle times (based on a single 8 hour shift and 20 day month) would be as follows:

Product Number	Monthly Quantity	Daily Quantity	Cycle Time
A	5000	250	2 MIN
B	2500	125	4 MIN
C	2500	125	4 MIN

The relative cycle times tell us that Product A will be built twice as fast as Products B or C, which are equal to each other. Therefore, the minimum repeatable sequence will include two A's, one B and one C.

When we homogenize that sequence to make the flow of production as smooth as possible, it becomes: A - B - A - C. That sequence will be repeated over and over again during the day and each day during the month.

Your schedule will undoubtedly be more complex. Seldom will you have such tidy ratios as two to one. Therefore, you'll need to use a formula to handle the "odd-ball" situations, but it's not a difficult one. When you add the reciprocals of the cycle times for all the product numbers in the sequence, the resulting ratio will give you the total number of units in the minimum sequence and the total sequence time, as follows:

$$\frac{1}{CT_a} + \frac{1}{CT_b} + \cdots \frac{1}{CT_n} = \frac{\text{UNITS IN SEQUENCE}}{\text{SEQUENCE TIME}}$$

For the previous example, Products A (2 min.), B (4 min.), and C (4 min.) would be plugged into the formula as follows:

$$\frac{1}{2 \text{ MIN}} + \frac{1}{4 \text{ MIN}} + \frac{1}{4 \text{ MIN}} = \frac{2}{4} + \frac{1}{4} + \frac{1}{4} = \frac{4 \text{ UNITS}}{4 \text{ MINUTES}}$$

In other words, there are four units in the minimum repeatable sequence and that sequence will take four minutes to complete.

The formula will work for any combination of cycle times. Suppose the cycle times for Products A, B, and C were 1, 3 and 5 minutes, respectively. In that case the calculation would be:

$$\frac{1}{1 \text{ MIN}} + \frac{1}{3 \text{ MIN}} + \frac{1}{5 \text{ MIN}} = \frac{15}{15} + \frac{5}{15} + \frac{3}{15} = \frac{23 \text{ UNITS}}{15 \text{ MINUTES}}$$

The minimum sequence would contain 23 units and would take 15 minutes to complete. This equates to a line speed of 1.53 units per minute (23/15) or a cycle time of 39 seconds (15/23 X 60) between any two units in the entire family of parts.

Laying Out The Sequence

I don't have a formula to cover the distribution of products within the minimum sequence. The easiest way to lay out the minimum sequence by product number is to "drop them in," based on the percentage of the total they represent. In the last example, the high volume item was Product A (15 units out of a 23 unit sequence). That's almost two out of three. The first step, then, would be to place Product A in the 23 bucket sequence as smoothly as possible, which might look like:

A A __ A A __ A A __ A A __ A A __ A A __ A A __ A __

The next largest quantity is Product B, so those five units would be dropped in the open spaces as uniformly as possible:

A A B A A __ A A B A A B A A __ A A B A A __ A B

Finally, the remaining spaces would be filled by the three Product C's, producing this final sequence:

A A B A A C A A B A A B A A C A A B A A C A B

As you can see, there is some room for minor variations to the sequence. Just don't make a "career" out of the exercise.

Mixed Models at AT&T

The AT&T plant in Shreveport, Louisiana is a recent convert to mixed model scheduling. (The entire operation was transformed to JUST-IN-TIME in less than three years.) The Merlin® family of telephone handsets is integrated on a single assembly line. The mix is based on the production plan. As shown in Figure 10-10, there are significant differences

Figure 10-10

between the models, including case sizes, color and internal configurations. The smooth flow of these products is also reflected in the feeder operations. Even printed circuit board assembly is intermixed on a single line to support the final assembly flow.

As a result, AT&T Shreveport has reduced its manufacturing lead-time by more than 98 %. What used to take weeks is now done in hours. Only a few years ago this plant faced the prospect of losing business to foreign competition. Today, they are selling products *into* the Asian market.

UNIFORM SCHEDULING BENEFITS

Uniform scheduling is an easier way to match resources with demands and to schedule those resources to maximize both customer response and productivity. If it sounds too simple, remember that one of the basic thrusts of JUST-IN-TIME is to simplify everything, including scheduling. When production flows smoothly you can work with averages, which are much easier to handle than discrete, time- phased increments.

Uniform scheduling won't work very well in a start-stop environment. That's why the first nine chapters of this book were devoted to showing you how to convert to flow production. Although your business may have always been run like a job-shop, you should be able to run a significant portion of it in a flow mode. Even make-to-order businesses utilize some standard components and subassemblies. They don't have to be high- volume parts, either. Low-volume items can be built in a repetitive fashion and uniform scheduling will be applicable to them.

Marketing Advantage

The sales and marketing people are major beneficiaries of uniform scheduling. For years we have been telling them to forecast exact customer requirements by specific product number far into the future, due to manufacturing limitations. Now they only have to project family volumes and average product mixes.

When customers surprise them with last minute changes, some of everything will be available every day. With this kind of mix flexibility, customer needs can be served without disrupting the manufacturing floor or incurring extra costs. This is a tremendous competitive advantage which, when properly exploited, can lead to increased sales volumes.

Less "Hassle"

Not only does level loading make resource planning easier and cycle time make the coordination of supporting requirements faster, there is less "hassle" involved in the whole process. Equipment balancing in the feeder links is simplified when material flows through the shop instead of coming in "tidal waves." Material control becomes a regulation function instead of being driven by transactions or events. There is even less material handling required since the reduced lot sizes can usually be handled manually.

The "pulse" of the shop floor is less erratic when production flows. Daily scheduling is no longer needed since every day during the month is planned to be the same. Like a well-oiled machine, manufacturing can "hum" instead of "coughing and sputtering."

No Learning Curve

When jobs are set up and run once a month or less frequently, it usually takes the operators some time to remember how to do them and to get "back up to speed." Since work standards are based on "full speed" activities, the difference between those and the actual rates during the job start up is called a *learning curve*. It's a recognized cost in the traditional shop. Perhaps one of the most surprising benefits of uniform scheduling is the virtual elimination of the learning curve.

People don't usually lose their skills over night. When every part of their entire scope of work is practiced every day, they don't have to contend with a learning curve. The productivity benefits are immediate and go straight to the bottom line.

Much Less Inventory

The smoothness of a uniform schedule requires much less inventory on the shop floor. Figure 10-11 graphically shows just how much less we're talking about. Materials management people will recognize it as the classic "saw tooth" curve.

The area under the large triangle represents the amount of inventory we would have on hand if we placed a 10-day lot of material in stock and used it up over a 10-day period. As you may recall from high school geometry, the formula for the area of a triangle is ½ times the base times the height. For this example, half of a 10 day lot times 10 days in the period would be 50 days² of inventory ($½ \times 10 \times 10 = 50$). Dividing that figure by the number of days in the period gives us the *average inventory for each day in the period*. In this case it is 50 days² over 10 days, or five days of inventory.

The small triangles represent the amount of inventory we would have on hand if we placed a one-day lot of material in stock every day and used it up each day. Using the same formula, the total inventory for the same period is $\frac{1}{2} \times 1 \times 1 \times 10$ (there are 10 triangles in the period), or 5 days^2. Since there are 10 days in the period, the average inventory for each day is 5/10 or a half-day of inventory.

Notice the relationship between the lot sizes and the average inventories. They are directly proportional. Cutting the lot size from 10 days to one day reduces the average inventory from a five-day supply to a half-day supply, a 10:1 ratio *in both cases*. It's a mathematical certainty. Cut your manufacturing lot sizes and your work-in-process will be reduced by the same percentage. Our example was only 10:1. Think about how many products you're making in 30, 60 or 90 day lot sizes today. This is the reason why JUST-IN-TIME plants using uniform scheduling can cut work-in-process inventories by 90% or more and still be more flexible and productive than traditional manufacturing businesses.

UNIFORM SCHEDULING AND MRP

The benefits of uniform scheduling are so overwhelming that many people wonder if they should consider "throwing out" their current planning system. If you have an operating Manufacturing Resource Planning (MRP) System in place, I would suggest you think long and hard before taking such a precipitous action, for a number of reasons.

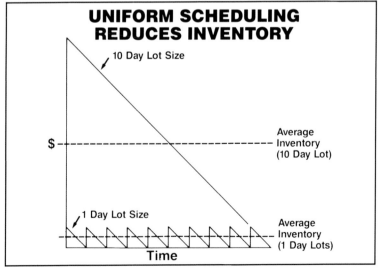

Figure 10-11

- Good planning requires accurate information about the way we build products and how items interact. MRP data base files meet this need.
- Both uniform scheduling and MRP start with a production plan. MRP planning bills make this job easier.
- During the transition to plant-wide uniform scheduling, which could take years, a hybrid system will be required. For some companies it may always be needed.
- The final assembly schedule, which starts the execution chain in uniform scheduling, is a "bear" to maintain manually. MRP logic can be used for this task.

In this section we will explore the rationale behind these statements and establish a "best of both worlds" framework. Some of the terminology may sound unfamiliar, but it's the "language" of MRP. If you run across some words that puzzle you, check with someone in your materials department or consult the American Production and Inventory Control Society (APICS) Dictionary.

The "P" Stands for Planning

During its early stages of development, MRP meant *Material Requirements Planning*. It was a systematic way to determine the time-phased needs for components and raw material ("dependent" items) in a job shop environment. It was driven by a detailed master schedule for end products and took into account actions already taken. Later, it was recognized that a higher level of input, the production plan, was needed to make the system effective so MRP was broadened in scope and renamed *Manufacturing Resource Planning*. It is interesting to note that the only word that survived the translation was *PLANNING*. That is what MRP always did and still does best.

Despite all the educational and promotional efforts during the last two decades, less than five percent of the MRP installations in America ever reached and maintained "Class A" status, which means they delivered what was expected when the systems were authorized. I believe there are three major reasons for that disappointing record:

1. *The environment was too complicated.* We tried to make the systems manage existing complex processes instead of simplifying the processes first. It resulted in the same confusion, only at the speed of light.

2. *In some cases, we distorted the business to fit the system.* Since discrete order MRP was the "only game in town," we tried to turn naturally repetitive flow shops into pseudo job shops to utilize the system. Rate-based MRP systems have appeared recently but conversion costs have deterred many companies from switching to them.

3. *We tried to make MRP do too much.* It was conceived as a planning system but we tried to use it for execution control as well. In truth, what we did was record events and compare them to the plan; and when things got out of hand, we made a new plan. Frequent replanning created a "nervous" environment which disenchanted the users. They responded by ignoring the system.

Let me give you an example of what that does to the supplier base. The following is a summary of weekly releases from a customer to a very confused supplier during a four-month period:

	Beginning of Month	End of Month
September	48,268	38,640
October	62,872	39,000
November	34,610	38,880
December	47,837	40,601

The difference between the four month totals in the two columns is equal to a whole month of production. Yet the actual end of month requirements were very consistent. The reaction from the supplier was understandable when he said, "To be quite honest, we don't believe them and we can't trust them, which is a very bad position to be in."

The Strengths of MRP

For all of that, it is important to remember that some companies did achieve Class A and found MRP to be a powerful tool when properly applied. It is those strengths that we want to couple with uniform scheduling in an ideal "marriage."

First and foremost is the information base or data base. JUST-IN-TIME makes no provision for contingencies, so all the information we use has to be 100% accurate and everyone must work from the same information. If you have thousands of part numbers in your files, there is no way all the needed manufacturing data can be maintained in a timely and accurate manner without a computer and a data management system. MRP does that very well.

Manufacturing planning involves so many elements that it is extremely difficult to do it without mechanical assistance. Computers are great number crunchers. MRP software has many features that let you take advantage of that ability to "massage" data and do a better planning job with less effort.

On the other hand, with that kind of facility, it's also easy to crank out too much information. Any information in excess of the minimum that is needed to do the job is a waste. That's the trap most people have fallen into with MRP. The trick is to find the right balance.

The strengths of MRP are data base organization, integrated planning capability, interactive information updating and time phasing. JIT adds process simplification, flow production and uniform scheduling. Combining them can give us a better planning system than either one by itself.

Production Planning

The common starting point for either JIT uniform scheduling or classic MRP planning is the production plan. It is a "macro" plan for product families in monthly time periods ("buckets") over the cumulative (manufacturing plus procurement) leadtime horizon. These are the "chunks" of the business that top management can rationally discuss without getting bogged down in part number detail. The plan matches production to expected customer demand in the aggregate and verifies that the needed resources will be available.

The "doability" of the production plan must be agreed upon by the key managers at the manufacturing location. Such agreement can only be reached by periodic face-to-face meetings (usually monthly) between those people, as shown in Figure 10-12. The participants should always include:

- The *general manager,* who chairs the meeting, insures that the plan conforms to the business plan and established policies, and resolves conflicts between the other disciplines.
- Marketing, who brings the sales forecast, market intelligence and the voice of the customer to the table.
- Engineering, who manages the product definition and, most importantly, can describe impending changes that will impact the ability to produce to the plan.
- Manufacturing, who knows the people and machine constraints that will affect the production targets.

- Materials Management, who drafts and administers the plan, brings material availability information and uses the final plan to prepare a master schedule.
- Finance, who converts the plan into profit and investment projections.

There could be other participants from time to time. For example, *Human Resources* might be required if the plan requires significant overtime or subcontracting activities that are covered in a labor contract.

At the meeting, information is refined (materials management might have more recent information about customer intentions than marketing as a result of daily interface), conflicting objectives are discussed and resolved (marketing may want more of a given product family than there is capacity to produce), and a "best compromise" is negotiated. The result is a production plan that everyone believes will work and *is committed to help make it work.*

If you're not doing production planning in your company now, you should start. It will significantly improve your manufacturing performance, no matter what kind of planning system you use and regardless of your type of business (e.g., make-to-stock, assemble-to-order or make-to-order). When you move to JUST-IN-TIME, a production plan is a must as it drives the entire uniform scheduling process. (For more information about how to implement production planning, see Appendix I.)

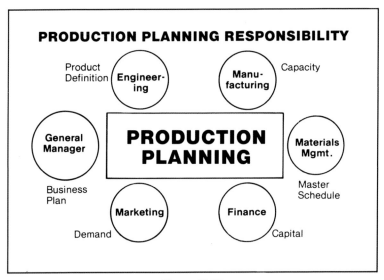

Figure 10-12

Translating the Production Plan

The production plan, stated in terms of product families and monthly buckets of time, establishes the production envelope. The next step is to translate those generalities into specific product numbers that can be manufactured. Here's where MRP can provide a big assist.

Most MRP systems have a feature called a Planning Bill of Material. It identifies all the products that comprise a family and the percentage of that family each product represents (the product mix). A graphic sample of a planning bill is shown in Figure 10-13. In this case, Product Family P is composed of products P1, P2, P3, P4, and P5. The numbers above each product are their percentage of the family — 10%, 20%, 50%, 10% and 10%, respectively.

The percentages can be developed from a forecast, as shown in the figure, or from historical usage. Sometimes they're the same thing. I once attended a forecasting seminar where the instructor told us that "Naive Forecast #1," which says "whatever we did yesterday we'll do tomorrow," is still one of the best short-term forecasting methods known. In either case, the numbers should be updated regularly to reflect the latest situation.

Since each product has a specific bill of material, the family quantity in the production plan can be converted to product number quantities which, in turn, can be exploded and summarized by MRP into the component and raw material requirements. If you wished, those numbers

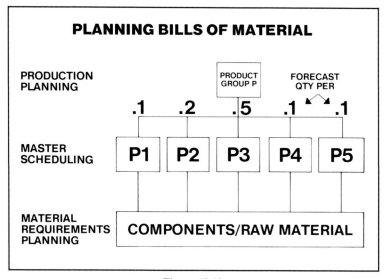

Figure 10-13

could be sent to the supply network for resource planning instead of using cycle time. So long as you use gross numbers, without leadtime offsets or netting, both approaches are compatible.

The three levels in the planning bill tie the production plan (family) to the items to be master scheduled (specific product numbers) to the gross material requirements (component part and raw material numbers) *in monthly increments*. The next step is to break the month into planned production intervals.

Here, again, the MRP planning bill is put to use. When we define the production periods, the system will crunch the numbers to smoothly allocate production among those periods, as shown in Figure 10-14. (Although daily production would be the parameter for uniform scheduling, weekly periods are shown here to simplify the example.) The production plan for Month 1 calls for a quantity of 400 units of Product Group (family) P. The individual product numbers (P1 through P5) and their associated percentages of the family are shown in the first two columns. The far right-hand column shows the total quantity required for each product in Month 1. (For Product P1, .1 X 400 = 40 units.) Each total is evenly distributed among the number of production periods in the month (10 per period for P1).

Notice the smooth, level load proposed by the computer. This is the input a traditional master scheduler would receive as the *starting point* for his or her reconciliation process. But, since every period is like every

PLANNING BILL LOGIC

PRODUCTION PLAN		MONTHS 1				
PRODUCT GROUP P		**400**				

PLANNING BILL	QTY PER	WEEKS 1	2	3	4	TOTAL
PRODUCT P1	**.1**	**10**	**10**	**10**	**10**	**40**
PRODUCT P2	**.2**	**20**	**20**	**20**	**20**	**80**
PRODUCT P3	**.5**	**50**	**50**	**50**	**50**	**200**
PRODUCT P4	**.1**	**10**	**10**	**10**	**10**	**40**
PRODUCT P5	**.1**	**10**	**10**	**10**	**10**	**40**

Figure 10-14

every other period in the month, it is the *ending point* for uniform scheduling. This is where the two planning approaches begin to digress.

Traditional Master Scheduling

In a traditional MRP environment, the master scheduling process is a series of steps designed to translate the production plan into a valid driver for the material requirements planning module. The master scheduler must create a detailed plan by product number that conforms to the envelope of the production plan while dealing with all the constraints of the manufacturing process, such as lot sizes, leadtimes and workcenter capacities. Few people realize just how difficult that job can be. In fact, there are those who say a master scheduler's career objective is to "get out of being a master scheduler!"

The master scheduler's problems start with the production plan. While JUST-IN-TIME equates shipments and production in a given month and changes the total from month to month, the traditional manufacturing approach is to level production as far into the future as possible. The difference between production and shipments is absorbed in finished goods inventory, which must be managed by the master scheduler, as shown in the left-hand side of Figure 10-15. This means that the input numbers to the planning bill of material usually won't be the same as the original figures in the production plan.

Next, the smooth schedule proposed by the computer for each prod-

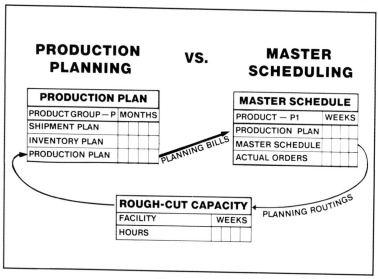

Figure 10-15

product number has to be modified to conform to manufacturing limitations. Remember that nice smooth schedule for P1 that was developed in Figure 10-14? It might be ideal to make 10 units per period; but if the system says that the minimum lot size is 50 units, then more than is needed must be scheduled (a waste) and all of them must be built in the same period (creating a "lump"). That's how a suggestion of 10-10-10-10 gets translated to a decision for 50-0-0-0. To make matters worse, that lump often gets moved around, depending on actual customer orders received.

Then, capacity has to be verified. The production plan said there was enough average capacity to build the product family during the month, but is there enough to do it all in Period 1? That's why a rough-cut capacity check, based on planning routings, must be made. If not, the lump gets moved again.

All the preceding steps had to be taken for one product number. They must be repeated for every other part number in Product Group P and for every other product group in the production plan. And just about the time everything is reasonably balanced, a hot customer request arrives and the whole thing has to be redone. Is it any wonder that master schedulers get a little "testy" sometimes?

As vital as that job is in a traditional shop, all the steps are a waste under JUST-IN-TIME. With uniform scheduling, you can actually run with the output from the planning bill module. The role of the master scheduler under uniform scheduling changes to the development and maintenance of the final assembly schedule, which will be discussed later in this chapter.

A Hybrid System

Realistically, nobody moves to uniform scheduling over night. It's a gradual process. Consequently, both JIT and MRP will have to coexist during the transition period. In addition, some parts of your business may never be repetitive and will continue to require a time-phased, event-driven control system. Finally, even repetitive production has a start-up and phase-out period which doesn't lend itself to uniform scheduling. Is there a hybrid approach that can accommodate all these requirements? I believe the answer is yes.

To put it into perspective, let's look at the product structure shown in the left side of Figure 10-16. In this case, Product A is comprised of two Part B's (they could be subassemblies) and other parts which we haven't shown. Part B, in turn, contains two Part C's and some other items which aren't shown either. It's a fairly typical product structure.

Moving to the right portion of the figure, let's say that a master schedule for Product A calls for the production of 10 units in each period from #3 to #8. To make A's, we have to have some B's and C's, which must be made earlier in the process. If the leadtime for each component is one period, then 20 B's will have to be made in period #2 to support the 10 A's in period #3, 20 B's will be made in period #3 to support the A's in period #4, etc. Similarly, the production of 20 B's requires 40 C's one period earlier. The resulting picture is the classic stair-step requirements schedule produced by a gross MRP explosion with leadtime offsets.

Look closely at Periods #3 through #6. Each one is exactly the same. The fact that the 40 C's in Period #3 are slated for incorporation in the 10 A's in Period #5 is of little interest to the shop floor. What they care about is *what has to be made* in each production period. And it's the same once the build-up has been achieved. Periods #3 through #6 are really a steady state, level-loaded condition. Now the question is, how can we get the MRP system to tell us that without going through all the number crunching required for time-critical events?

The solution lies in the management of the status codes in the product structure. Most MRP systems provide space for a status code to identify the nature of a part number; i.e., is it a final assembly, a subassembly, a purchased part, etc.? One of those codes is called a "phantom." It was originally developed to identify transitional sub-

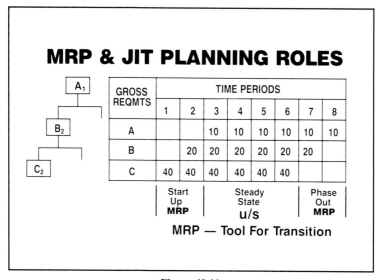

MRP & JIT PLANNING ROLES

GROSS REQMTS	TIME PERIODS							
	1	2	3	4	5	6	7	8
A			10	10	10	10	10	10
B		20	20	20	20	20	20	
C	40	40	40	40	40	40		

Start Up MRP | Steady State u/s | Phase Out MRP

MRP — Tool For Transition

Figure 10-16

assemblies that only existed for an instant in time (like a bolt and washer, just before they are threaded into a nut). A phantom code tells the computer to ignore that item during the explosion process and to presume that its component parts belong to the next higher level in the structure. It becomes invisible to the system. When every item in the product structure, except lowest-level parts, is given a phantom code, it effectively collapses the product structure into a "pile of parts," or a single-level bill of material.

With systems that have on-line data file maintenance, this task can be accomplished in minutes. This means that JIT product families can be exploded into gross requirements at the same time that other products are going through the normal off-setting and netting, all in the same run. (Under steady-state JIT, all we want is a "get ready" plan. Leadtimes, on-hand, on-order and work-in-process tracking are unnecessary.) It also means that parts of product structures can be collapsed to conform to new manufacturing processes, like group technology, while the rest of the structure can be treated the "old way." This gives you maximum flexibility while you are transforming the plant to uniform scheduling, still provides for those items that may always be unique builds, and lets you continue to plan with a single, integrated system.

The features of MRP can even be used to plan the start-up or closeout of a JIT product family. During start-up, the first event at every level is time-critical, so it can be planned and tracked in the usual fashion. When a steady-state condition has been reached, the phantom codes can be inserted and uniform scheduling will apply. When it's time to closeout the product, a physical inventory will be taken, on-hand balances and open orders will be reloaded, and the original status codes will be reinserted. This will reactivate the leadtime offsets and netting features of MRP so "final events" can be planned and tracked.

It will probably only work in your system if the status codes are resident in the product structure file. You need the flexibility of being able to change the configuration of one structure without affecting others. If the status codes are in the item master file, a single change will affect every product structure that uses the part, whether you want it to or not. If your system has to be changed, the experts tell me it's a relatively straightforward modification.

*I must warn you, though, that **this hybrid has not yet actually been implemented** by any of my clients. Since this is the first thing in this book that isn't "tried and true," it is important to make that distinction.* I also realize that there are routing, labor reporting and costing ramifications that will require further exploration. What I've tried to do here is show how a hybrid system could be used to universally plan production, without getting into peripheral MRP applications.

Uniform scheduling is the best tool for steady-state conditions which we are striving to achieve under JUST-IN-TIME. MRP is still the best tool for transition, which will occur at times in every shop. A hybrid planning system, employing the strengths of each, should give you the best of both worlds.

MRP/JIT System Requirements

The MRP/JIT hybrid planning system may sound good to you and I believe it will work, but there's no such thing as a "free lunch," so it will require effort to "make it happen." Some fundamentals apply to both pieces while others are quite different in the two systems. Figure 10-17 summarizes those relationships.

Both MRP and JIT require a ***production plan*** as the common starting point. Despite the fact that it is a requirement to achieve "Class A" MRP status, it's amazing to me how many companies still haven't figured out that no system will ever produce the benefits they expected without this up-front management involvement. JIT uniform scheduling is impossible without a valid production plan.

An equally valid ***master schedule*** is necessary for MRP and we have already seen how difficult it is to develop and maintain one. The fewer

PLANNING CHECKLIST

	MRP	JIT
• PRODUCTION PLAN	✓	✓
• MASTER SCHEDULE	✓	u/s
• BILLS OF MATERIAL	✓	✓
• ON HAND	✓	n.a.
• ON ORDER	✓	n.a.
• ORDER QUANTITIES	✓	→ 1
• LEADTIMES	✓	→ 0

Figure 10-17

parts that have to be scheduled this way, the easier the job will be. Instead of the traditional master schedule, JIT employs the uniform schedule, which is nothing more than a daily slice of the production plan.

Accurate *bills of material* are vital in both approaches. If anything, they are even more important under JIT since there are no provisions for any contingencies. If the bill is wrong, there can be no production whatsoever. The accuracy target has to be at least 99.99%.

On-hand and on-order quantities are important to MRP because they are netted against gross requirements to calculate further needs. They will continue to be important for first-time, last-time and any other time-critical events. Under steady-state JIT, those balances are ignored. Gross requirements establish the planned flow and the Pull System manages that flow.

Order quantities, whether production lot sizes or purchasing "price breaks," must be maintained in an MRP system, as they define the limitations of the current process. When those constraints are eliminated, MRP can be run under the one-for-one option built into most systems. Then it will approach JIT, where everything is one-for-one.

Leadtimes in an MRP system must be timely and accurate if the system is to have any chance at all of producing a plan that reflects the real world. When they are too "fat," MRP asks for too much, too soon and the process will get clogged with excess material. If they are not frequently updated, you can also end up with too little, too late. As leadtimes get shorter, they become less critical. The continuous improvements of JIT drive leadtimes closer and closer to zero. Then, even start-up and phase-out operations become less critical issues.

PLANNING VERSUS EXECUTION

Up to now, we have been building a plan to marshal the needed resources to get ready to produce, using either pure uniform scheduling or a hybrid MRP/JIT planning system. Sooner or later, though, commitments have to be made and some version of that plan has to be executed. The departure from traditional practices is that we will only *commit to an envelope* of production, instead of specific products and component parts, and will launch the actual execution of the plan details with a *final assembly schedule.*

Envelope Commitments

Traditional methods have always required that commitments be made by part number over the leadtime for those parts. If a supplier says the leadtime is three months, we must order specific parts three months in advance of our needs. The supplier, in turn, makes commitments and takes actions based on those orders. If we change the order, even within 30 days of placing the order, we are usually liable for the supplier's material costs. In the second month after placing the order, fabrication and machining costs get added, increasing the cost of change. As the delivery date approaches, the liability for change or cancellation gets close to the full purchase price. This stair-stepping increase in cost liability is shown by the dashed lines in Figure 10-18.

The problem grows as leadtimes get longer. It's nearly impossible to determine precisely what the part number requirements will be six months or more into the future. On the other hand, we're much more accurate when it comes to forecasting families of parts, or an envelope of requirements, just like we're better at projecting families of products. It's the mix that usually causes all the grief.

Some people in the purchasing community figured this out years ago and began to *buy capacity* instead of committing to specific parts. They learned that most of the supplier leadtime was consumed by orders waiting in line to be worked on, or queue time. By reserving a fixed portion of the supplier's capacity for a family of parts and guaranteeing to pay for it, the customer gave the supplier a base level of business that could be counted on to absorb certain fixed costs. The customer could

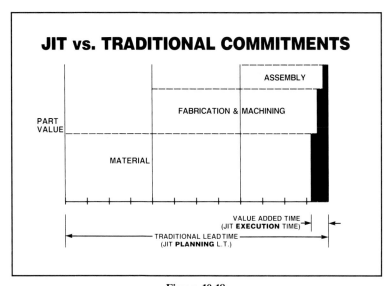

Figure 10-18

then make mix changes without penalty so long as they were within the envelope of the part family, the reserved capacity and the actual manufacturing time, which was a small fraction of the quoted leadtime.

Many years ago, when casting leadtimes were around 26 weeks, I tried it out and it worked just as advertised. Given a one year contract, the supplier reserved certain machines for my company's parts and was able to deliver material one week after we provided the specific part numbers to produce. Our production control manager scheduled that capacity by calling the supplier every day with the requirements for that same day the following week. The same raw material was used for all the parts in the family, so it was easy for the supplier to schedule it based on the average volume which turned out to be very steady. While others were trying to forecast specifics 26 weeks in advance, we were getting a one-week turnaround.

What we did then, and what we do now under JUST-IN-TIME, is shown by the black bars in Figure 10-18. The actual commitment by part number is only made for the time it takes to execute that job after everything else is already in place. That's JIT execution time (which should approach the value added time). The capacity commitment for a family of parts gives the supplier the visibility needed to get resources ready over the total cumulative leadtime horizon. That's JIT planning leadtime. We'll commit to an envelope but won't specify part number requirements until the very last minute.

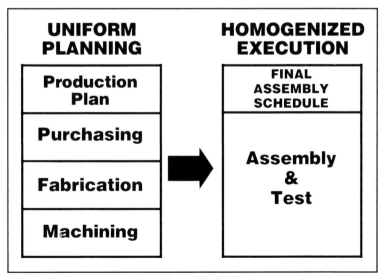

Figure 10-19

The Final Assembly Schedule

At this point we have established a uniform plan, where every working day in a month is an identical slice of the production plan, and communicated those requirements to all the inside feeder operations, like machining and fabrication, as well as the outside suppliers. We have committed to family envelope requirements so resources can be readied for production. It is now time to execute the plan. The relationship between uniform planning and homogenized execution, which finally gets us to a uniform schedule, is shown in Figure 10-19. To insure that the execution of the plan is as homogenized as possible, it will be launched by a *final assembly schedule*.

A final assembly schedule is not a master schedule. Both do relate to final products by part number, but the master schedule horizon covers the entire cumulative leadtime, so it is driven by both customer orders and forecasts. The final assembly schedule horizon is only as long as it *has to be* to logistically support final assembly, and it can never be longer than the order backlog, since only real customer orders are scheduled. Typically, we're talking days here instead of weeks or months.

The objective of a final assembly schedule is to match actual customer orders as closely as possible to the uniform plan that the network has prepared itself to produce. This becomes the new role for the master scheduler that was mentioned earlier in this chapter. By carefully "massaging" the order backlog, he or she can keep the uniform schedule and "exact customer demand" in harmony with one another.

This is illustrated by the example shown in Figure 10-20. It is a final assembly schedule for Product P2. The top line shows the uniform plan for that product as it was developed in Figure 10-14, which was 20 units per period. As customer orders are received for Product P2, the master scheduler slots them in the schedule to "consume" the plan.

The slotted orders *must not exceed* the plan. As shown in the example, the whole Acme order for 15 units can be scheduled in Period #1, but the next order, from Brand X, has to be split between Periods #1 and #2 because there is not enough capacity to produce 25 P2's in Period #1. Similarly, the order from Miscellaneous Manufacturing has to be split between Periods #2 and #3. Priority is given to the "hottest" customer orders, as determined by the sales department, but *you can't overload any period.*

It's important to keep the horizon of the final assembly schedule as short as possible so you can do some "juggling" when it becomes necessary. Suppose the cut-off point for the schedule in Figure 10-20 was three periods and you had to release it now. There are only customer orders for 10 units, but the uniform plan calls for 20. Do you build 20 anyway? Under JUST-IN-TIME you can *only build what the customers order.* But, since the uniform plan is based on families of products, you can examine the backlog for other products in the family to find something to "pull in." As shown in the bottom portion of the figure, there are orders for 5 P1's and 30 P3's in Period #4. The simplest move might appear to be pulling 10 P3's into Period #3 to fill the envelope of the family (Product Group P), but that's too "lumpy." It would be better to pull in proportionally to the average mix in the plan. In this case, pulling 2 P1's and 8 P3's would give you the lowest percentage change for all of the part numbers in the family.

Don't try to force the accumulated build back into balance in the next period. Sometimes this will happen naturally, but the goal is to make each day the same as the plan; so when the mix for one day changes, just "chalk it up" as history. It's better to have one period out of "synch" than to force two or three more out, trying to "catch up."

The final assembly schedule is, in the final analysis, the best compromise between real customer demand and the uniform plan. The Final Assembly Department will work to this schedule, consuming component parts as they build products. The actual consumption of those parts will trigger execution signals for supporting operations to replenish them. They, in turn, will be managed by the Pull System, described in Chapter 11.

FINAL ASSEMBLY SCHEDULE

Family: **P**		PERIOD				
Product: **P2**		1	2	3	4	5
UNIFORM PLAN		20	20	20	20	20

CUSTOMER	QTY.					
Acme Co.	15	15				
Brand X	10	5	5			
Misc. Mfg.	25		15	10		
AVAILABLE		0	0	10	20	20

Other "P"	P1	10	10	10	5	0
Orders	P3	50	50	50	30	0

Figure 10-20

SUMMARY

Uniform scheduling is a planning method for resource allocation that is faster, easier and more effective than traditional scheduling techniques. It is also quite different. It starts with a production plan and levelloads a shop by making every working day in a month the same. Eventually, mixed model scheduling is employed to make every hour the same. Yet, production levels will change from month to month to match customer demand. It uses cycle time as the communication vehicle to rapidly advise the supporting feeder operations how to "get ready" but does not authorize the execution of any part of that plan until the last possible moment. It works great in a JUST-IN-TIME, variable-flow production environment but is totally unsuitable for scheduling "lumpy" manufacturing activities in a job shop.

Manufacturing Resource Planning (MRP) is able to plan for "lumps" of production where time-phased events are important. It is still the best manufacturing data base management tool that I know of and has many features than can make uniform scheduling easier to do. It can be an important planning tool during the migration of a business from traditional manufacturing methods to JIT production and may always be needed for portions of some businesses.

The "best of both worlds" planning system may well be a hybrid of JIT and MRP, where JIT uniform scheduling is used for steady-state conditions and MRP is used as the tool for transition. Techniques are available to integrate the two in a single planning system, with a common data base, that can generate plans in either mode during one pass through the computer and let you change modes as needed.

Commitments made under uniform scheduling are limited to capacity reservations for product and part family envelopes. While the planned product mix for the entire cumulative leadtime horizon is shared with the supply base, it is used only for planning purposes. Execution authorizations are provided by the Pull System.

The "get ready" plan developed under uniform scheduling is launched into execution by a final assembly schedule. It manages the customer order backlog on a daily basis to find the best compromise between exact customer demand and smooth production. It is the only document in the uniform planning process that authorizes action to be taken by specific product number.

Uniform scheduling enables a manufacturing company to immediately respond to urgent customer needs with at least a "partial" of any product made. It is less complicated than traditional scheduling methods and fosters productivity improvements, even to the point of eliminating the learning curve. It can help your company cut manufacturing lead-times and work-in-process inventories by 90% or more. But, it will only work when your manufacturing lot sizes have been reduced to the point that you have real flow production in your plant. It will work best when you are capable of producing every part every day.

THE PULL
SYSTEM

CHAPTER 11

*"The Pull System is an execution system
driven by actual consumption
and controlled by
synchronized replenishment signals."*

During Uniform Scheduling, the planning activities were isolated from execution in order to concentrate on developing a smooth, homogenized game plan that enabled the marshaling of resources to meet the average demand. Execution was launched by a final assembly schedule, which provided the best possible match between the desired uniform plan and real customer orders at the last possible moment. The consumption of material by final assembly will trigger a whole series of execution authorizations for all the supporting activities in the feeder network. This signaling network is called a *Pull System.*

The Pull System quickly responds to real world deviations and variations from the uniform plan as they arise. It advises everyone in the support network what each must do next to keep all of the manufacturing activities synchronized. It enables a higher level of manufacturing activity control and inventory management than any other system that I have seen. Yet, it is so simple, so highly visible and so cost effective you may not even believe it at the beginning. Nevertheless, it is all of those things and, best of all, it really works.

MOVING TO FLEXIBLE EXECUTION

Traditional manufacturing activity control strategies are driven by "just-in-case" considerations, instead of JUST-IN-TIME, and are hampered by the constraints of established practices, like large lot sizes. When these considerations and constraints are removed, using the methods described in this book, a totally new approach to production control can be taken. Like uniform scheduling, the Pull System is based on the variable flow concept of production because *change is easier to manage when it is a variation on a theme, rather than a brand new melody.*

The inspiration for the Pull System came from American supermarkets. It is just one example of how manufacturing companies can make major improvements when they "borrow" from other industries. Of course, significant enhancements were made to adapt the original version to manufacturing, resulting in an even better control system. You can select from a number of options which will be described in this chapter to refine the basic system even further to tailor it to your specific production processes and your stage of JIT development.

Traditional Manufacturing Control

To appreciate why such a change is worthwhile, it is often helpful to remind ourselves where we are today and what we're getting for our efforts. In most traditional plants, manufacturing is accomplished in *stages* with "rest stops" between those stages. Those rest stops are buffer zones of inventory. They are hedges against failure to perform. They exist because supply and demand can't be matched, because we are afraid to trust the supply activities or because we have little faith in the scheduling process itself.

It starts with raw material. As shown in Figure 11-1, we buffer ourselves from outside suppliers because we can't trust them to deliver on time; and if they do, we're not sure the material will be acceptable. At the other end, we buffer ourselves from customers because they give us erratic demands and make major changes at the last minute, so we can't trust them either. That's not good, but it's understood as a "way of life" in a traditional environment.

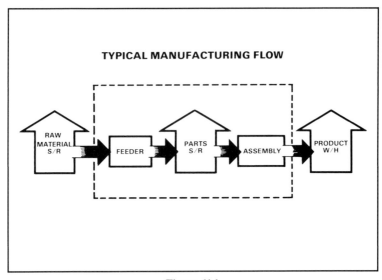

Figure 11-1

What's not so understandable, however, is what we see when we look inside the dotted outline in the figure. That's our own plant. It's one thing not to trust the outside world, but we buffer our assembly operations from our feeder operations because we can't seem to find the courage to trust ourselves either!

Conventional "Push" System

A major part of that situation is caused by the fact that our conventional scheduling and releasing system *pushes* orders through the shop, making it difficult to synchronize the diverse activities required to produce the end products. When a "lumpy" master schedule, as described in Chapter 10, is exploded into its component requirements and lumped even further by large lot size constraints, the resulting job orders or component schedules are anything but smooth. They are launched at the lead-off operation and, when completed there, are pushed to the next operation. The procedure repeats itself at every successive operation until the parts are completed.

If the world never changed, it might work. But, in truth, the schedules for those orders are usually invalid by the time the ink dries on them. Despite our best efforts to adjust the priorities at the workcenters, a discouraging number of those parts arrive at the storage location late and some of them are even early. The result of that process is shown in the upper portion of Figure 11-2. We typically end up with so many

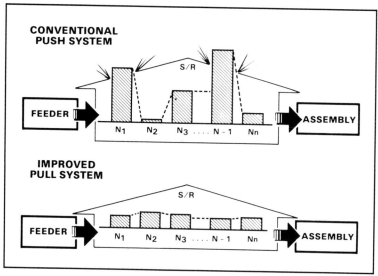

Figure 11-2

of some parts that we run out of storage space while others are in short supply or even out of stock. (Those are the ones the expediters have to chase after.) You can verify this for yourself by taking a look at a physical inventory report or one of your stock status reports. Nothing seems to match up.

The Pain From "Pushing" Parts

To make money, most us need *sets of parts* to assemble into salable products. Imbalances between part numbers increase the inventory investment while simultaneously decreasing the ability to ship, the worst of both worlds. If the final assembly in Figure 11-2 required one each of the components shown, production would be limited by the number of N2's available. All the rest of that inventory would be a waste.

What is needed is less total stock with a much better balance between part numbers, as shown in the lower half of the figure. If we could establish a minimum, balanced inventory and *keep it that way* by replenishing parts only when they are consumed by assembly, we would be *pulling* parts through the system, as needed, in a synchronized manner. Making more final product with less investment is a productivity improvement, a basic goal of JUST-IN-TIME. The Pull System makes it possible.

A Borrowed Idea

The birthplace of the Pull System was the American supermarket. It not only introduced the whole idea of economical "self-service," which is prevalent in so many industries today, but was based on many of the principles embraced by JIT, starting with response to exact customer demand. The type of merchandise carried was based on sales history and projections, but floor stock was replenished only as consumed.

Consider the layout and organization of the store. If you want to buy a can of tomato soup, there is only one aisle where soup can be found (housekeeping) and it is clearly labeled with a sign (visibility management). All the brands and flavors are next to one another making it easy to find your choice. Each item has a fixed, predetermined amount of shelf space assigned to it based on the planned sales rate (uniform scheduling).

As you help yourself to some tomato soup, and others do the same, a roving stockperson will note the depletion and bring back a replacement case, or cases, to bring the stock back to the predetermined level. The more that people buy, the faster it is replenished. If nobody buys tomato soup, no more is brought out. It is a simple, visible system that has worked for a long time.

Improving the Original

Taiichi Ohno, former Vice President of Operations for Toyota Motor Co., claims he was inspired to apply the same concepts to manufacturing when he saw our supermarkets early in his career. There were, of course, some modifications required to adapt it to a shop floor. He started in a machine shop in 1953, and by 1962 it had been adopted company-wide as the Toyota Kanban System.

What sort of modifications were required? First of all, a roving stock person is too "chancey" for a shop. A "run" on tomato soup could lead to a shortage before the next stock check. What was needed was a positive signal to alert the replenisher each time a consumer removed a can of soup. Imagine attaching an identification card to each can of soup with a rubber band. When a can was removed from the shelf, this signal could be sent to the replenisher, eliminating the need for making stock check "rounds." It would also provide up-to-the-minute information about consumption.

The next issue was inventory. In a supermarket, the stock person replenishes from a warehouse. In a JUST-IN-TIME plant, we don't want any more inventory than is absolutely necessary, so we'd like to link the consumer to a producer. Suppose there was a soup machine in the back of the store — one with instant setup capability. Then, upon receipt of a signal card for a can of tomato soup, the producer could move the dial on the machine from "mushroom" to "tomato," produce the can of soup and send it to the assigned place in the store. This is the modification that made it conceivable to design a real-world manufacturing system that could *produce* to exact customer demand.

PULL SYSTEM CHARACTERISTICS

Like uniform scheduling, the Pull System is founded on the premise that variable flow manufacturing principles will be employed in the plant. High volume production is not necessary, but repetition must be the norm. If products cannot be manufactured at least once a month, it will be difficult to apply the Pull System to that part of the business. Conversely, the more frequently products can be made (the target is every day), the better the system will work.

The traditional "push" approach to manufacturing can be characterized as, *"Ready or not, here I come."* The Pull System is exactly the opposite. It can be thought of as, *"Don't call me, I'll call you."* But, more than that, it links every process in the entire manufacturing network, both inside and outside the plant, using simple signals to synchronize production in accordance with changing demands.

Universal Application

The same kinds of signals are used to advise outside suppliers as are used for inside workcenters. Instead of separate shop floor control systems and purchasing release systems, the Pull System integrates the two into a universal execution network. Most workcenters in the system function in both "customer" and "supplier" modes, so having a common methodology makes it easier to manage production.

Manual Simplicity

The Pull System does not require any computer terminals on the shop floor. It employs recirculating signals, usually cards, to automatically authorize the production or movement of material, based on actual consumption. The number of signals in the system is derived from the production plan and controls the level of work-in-process. Yet, since material must be consumed in order to release a signal card, it responds to real-world changes and is self-regulating.

Two Kinds of Signals

There are two broad classes of execution authorizations in manufacturing — instructions to produce or permission to consume. The Pull System has a signal for each of them. As shown in Figure 11-3, a *production signal* authorizes the machine center to manufacture parts that have been taken from the storage area next to it. (In this case, a quantity of Part "a.") This is comparable to the "soup" analogy used in the supermarket example.

But, to maintain control in a production shop, the consumer must also have an authorization to take Part "a" away in the first place. This is called a *withdrawal signal.* This way, both supply and demand activities can be managed on the floor in conformance to the production game plan. This will be developed in more detail later in this chapter.

Standard Lot Sizes

Typically, the Pull System employs standard containers that are "person-moveable." (OSHA suggests that a container full of material should not exceed 44 pounds in total weight.) In addition, the ideal container quantity should be no more than 1/10 of a day's usage of the part. Although there will be exceptions to this ideal, especially at the beginning, the objective is to be able to make small adjustments to the WIP levels on the production floor. That's a bit difficult to do when a container holds several days or weeks worth of material.

The quantity in a container is a fixed number for a given part. In other words, if you decide to put ten of Part "a" in a container, every container of that part must always have exactly ten pieces in it. That's significant, because all the calculations in the system are based on the presumption that standard container quantities will be observed. It's a far cry from the traditional practice of filling tubs to the top with random quantities.

Visual Control

Another reason for standard container quantities is to enhance visual control on the floor. For example, when you see three containers of Part "a" in a staging area, you know there are 30 parts available, not 29 or 31. This sets the stage for a "precision" mentality, which is very important in JUST-IN-TIME.

Completed parts are stored at the producing workcenter, as shown in Figure 11-3. That way, if there is a breakdown in the system for any reason, it becomes obvious when parts are depleted without the receipt of any replenishment signals. Similarly, overproduction stacks up at the

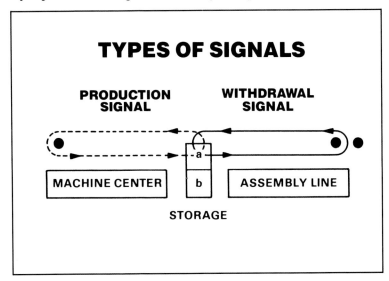

Figure 11-3

producing workcenter. There is simply no place to hide excesses. Production problems also become very obvious. A roving supervisor or fellow workers can tell at a glance whether or not the parts stored at the workcenter are in balance. Attention can then be given to rapidly fixing the problem before it becomes a major catastrophe.

Requires Discipline

The Pull System authorizes activities in the precise order that they are to be executed, so priorities are automatically maintained. However, if individuals fail to respond to those signals or try to "second guess" the system for any reason, *the system will fail.* Instructions must be carried out "to the letter" to insure that the entire network remains synchronized and balanced.

This will be one of the most difficult issues you will face when implementing a Pull System at your company. Old habits, historical distrust of the previous system, a "safety stock" mentality and local prioritizing, to make the "numbers" look good, will cripple the system. On the other hand, when these hurdles are overcome, the Pull System almost becomes a "no brainer." The right parts will be in the right place at the right time with a minimal investment in inventory and administrative effort.

CONNECTING WORKCENTERS

Pull signals connect two points in the production network — a supplier and a consumer. In a JIT shop, group technology workcenters are organized to manufacture complete parts so it's a straightforward "maker — user" relationship. To better understand the process steps, let's walk through an example, based on the graphic shown in Figure 11-3, for Parts "a" and "b" between a machining center and assembly.

Production Signals

The number of production signals is derived from the production plan through a formula which we'll review later. For the moment, let's just say that the calculations told us we would need five production cards for Part "a" and another five cards for Part "b." Immediately, that tells us that the planned mix for those two part numbers is 50-50.

Since uniform scheduling calls for smooth, homogenized production and, hopefully, our setup reduction activities have made this possible, the next step is to interlace the deck of ten cards. (The sequence would be A-B-A-B-A-B-A-B-A-B.) The deck is then taken to the machining center and placed in its "dispatch box." The ten production authorizations in the box are now arranged *in the precise order they are to be made.* As the machining center completes each container of parts, the production card is placed in the container (or attached to it in a plastic sleeve) and stored next to the workcenter in a clearly marked location (squares "a" and "b" in the diagram). Parts "a" and "b" will be alternately manufactured until all the cards are used up. If nobody takes any of those parts away, the workcenter must shut down because there are no more production authorizations. Each of the ten cards is now attached to a container of completed parts.

Withdrawal Signals

That rarely happens, of course, because assembly is also issued some cards to authorize withdrawal of Parts "a" and "b." The quantity of withdrawal cards is usually much lower than the number of production cards because assembly only needs enough to keep the resupply chain flowing. In this case, the formula tells us that two withdrawal cards are needed for Part "a" and another two are required for Part "b." Those cards can be taken to the machine center storage area and will authorize the removal of two containers of each part number for assembly stock.

Back at assembly, as soon as the first part is removed from the first container, that withdrawal card can be sent to the machine center to pull another container of parts for assembly. This provides enough material in circulation (solid line loop in the right side of the figure) to cover the normal resupply time. Every time a container of material is removed from the machine center, the withdrawal card is substituted for the production card as visible evidence that this is an authorized movement. This way, every container of material in the system must have some kind of card attached to it to be "legal."

Automatic Priorities

The production card, which was attached to that container, is placed in the machine center dispatch box, at the rear of the deck. This authorizes the production of one more container of parts to replace the ones just taken. (The travel path of the production card is shown by the dotted line loop in the left side of the figure.) Thus, as each container of material is removed, a replacement container is automatically ordered. Production will follow the same sequence as the removals, simply by making parts in the order the cards are lined up in the dispatch box.

If parts are removed in a slightly different mix than the original 50-50 plan, it doesn't matter. The machine center will just follow the priorities in the dispatch box. By taking parts as needed (and authorized), a value adder in assembly is communicating directly with a value adder in machining about what has to be done next. There is no need for schedulers, expediters or other "helpers" to make the system work. It self-adjusts.

Limited Obsolescence

Even under the most extreme mix changes, the Pull System provides automatic protection. In our example, what if the mix shifted to 100% Part "a" and the demand for Part "b" fell to zero? There are only five cards in the system for Part "b" so, once they are all attached to full containers of parts, no more Part "b" can be manufactured. This puts a guaranteed limit on the amount of obsolete products that can be produced, no matter how subtle the demand shift might be.

A "Chained" Network

Mix changes are often just short term fluctuations. However, even if they are permanent, the Pull System will accommodate them and will communicate the changes faster than any replanning system. For example, if the mix at the machining center changed to 60% Part "a" and 40% Part "b," more material for Part "a" would be required. That's

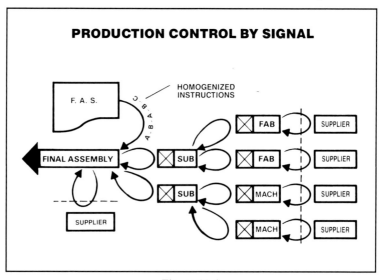

Figure 11-4

no problem. The machining center has withdrawal cards for its raw material, just like assembly has withdrawal cards to take parts away from the machining center in the first place. Therefore, the faster usage of "a" raw material will be automatically communicated to the machine center's suppliers by the faster turnaround of those cards.

Eventually, every workcenter in the network gets connected by Pull System signal loops as shown in Figure 11-4. Each workcenter automatically communicates with its "customers" and its "suppliers" (both inside and outside the plant) as actual consumption occurs. Production control information cascades through the entire network via the signal cards, and nobody has to fill out a single form or make an entry on a data terminal.

Reaction to change happens on a container by container basis, which means "ripples" flow through the network instead of the "tidal waves" that you may be used to seeing. With the Pull System, there is no need to evaluate trend data, make value judgments and issue new schedules or priority lists during the month to respond to change. It's automatic, yet it's manual.

SENDING THE SIGNALS

The signal cards that connect customers and suppliers in a Pull System must contain enough information to allow everyone to do the job required. On the other hand, too much data can just confuse the situation. Therefore, only the minimum needed should be included. Since the cards recirculate, and the only variable is the number of cards in the system at any point in time, most of the information on the cards can be preprinted.

Signal Card Information Elements

Figure 11-5 shows a layout for a typical signal card. As you can see, there is surprisingly little information required. At the top is the *part number* and the *name* of the part that will be produced and transported. It tells you WHAT is needed.

Moving clockwise around the card, the *lot quantity* designates HOW MANY are required in a single container. It is a fixed number for a given part, based on the part size, lot weight, and flexibility goal (less than 1/10 of a day's demand). In a "pure" Pull System, where you can make one container at a time, it also represents the production quantity. During the transition to the ideal system you may have to produce multiple containers of material in one run, so think of one container of material as a "transfer" lot.

The blocks in the lower right portion of the card describe WHERE FROM and WHERE TO. The *preceding process* (FROM) could be a workcenter, a storage location or an outside supplier. Similarly, the *succeeding process* (TO) could be the user department or an interim staging location, like a supplier delivery station. Some people even put a color coded stripe (visibility management) on the left edge of the card to identify the provider and another one on the right edge of the card to designate the consumer. This helps insure that the cards don't get mixed up or sent to the wrong place.

The *signal number* is the CONTROL MECHANISM. It is a unique identifier for this card and also shows the total number of cards for this part number that are in circulation (e.g., #3 of 5). It is especially useful for tracking down missing cards, implementing an engineering change or phasing out a production item. It is the only spot on the card that isn't preprinted since the numbers will vary to correspond with changing production levels.

The *container* identification is needed to tell the producer WHAT PACKAGE is needed for the parts. If you have hundreds or thousands of part numbers in your system, you certainly wouldn't want an equal number of unique containers for them. The Pull System works best when you have a minimum number of container sizes so each can be used for a variety of part numbers. It gives you the most flexibility with the least

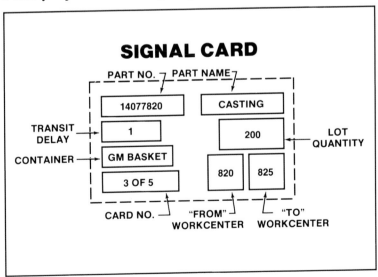

Figure 11-5

investment. Yet, the space for that container of parts at the user location may be carefully designed, so it is important that the parts be in the correct container to fit into the allocated space.

The *transit delay* only applies to withdrawal cards. It is used when there is a regularly scheduled pick up and delivery cycle inside the plant and it is particularly useful for outside suppliers. Since it comes from a variation of the standard formula used to calculate the number of cards required, it will be explained in that section.

The Problem With Cards

On the surface, there is a lot of similarity between a signal card in the Pull System and a *move ticket* in the traditional shop. They do carry much of the same information and the move ticket can authorize the transfer of material, but that's where the similarity ends.

Move tickets are usually throw-away documents. If you've been using them, and that's what people are used to doing with them, those habits can easily carry over to the Pull System. Signal cards are never thrown away. Doing so will result in parts shortages, confusion and discouragement on the shop floor.

Signal cards must not only recirculate, but also they are the action authorizations required to keep everything synchronized. Losing one is like losing a paycheck because we have to "cash it in" to keep the system in balance.

To minimize this problem, three things are required. First, make your signal cards look as different from the move tickets as possible. (Remember, during the transition you may be using both of them at the same time.) Second, encase the signal cards in a plastic coating or envelope to give them a "look" of permanence. Most people hesitate before throwing something like that away. The covering also protects the signal card. Finally, train everyone who might come in contact with one of these cards, including operators, material handlers, storeroom people and janitorial service personnel. When everybody understands the importance of the cards, the system has the best chance of working right from the beginning.

Other Kinds of Signals

Pull System signals don't have to be cards. I have seen a variety of other devices, some of which are shown in Figure 11-6. One workcenter used triangular metal plates (that's *really* permanent) painted a different color for each part number. Instead of using a dispatch box, they dropped the plates in a slotted slide, tilted downward, so the entire queue of work was visible to everyone from a distance. A similar approach, used at another workcenter, employed colored metal washers, or "donuts," which slid down a narrow trough. At one particularly long workcenter, I saw a pneumatic tube used to convey colored golf balls from the completed parts staging area to the starting point in the center. The final segment of the tube was made of clear plexiglas so this work queue was also very visible.

Each of the variations worked well for the people in those areas because the signals were production authorizations which remained in the workcenters. Some people have also come up with unique approaches to withdrawal signals, as well, and to combinations of the two. Figure 11-7 shows a special cart developed by Fisher-Guide in Detroit, Michigan. The special cart is designed to hold precisely 80 sets of brackets and hardware, which will be welded into subassemblies by the operator on the right. When she finishes them all, the empty cart will be taken back to the bracket workcenter to be refilled (a production signal). The cart also serves as a withdrawal authorization, as an empty one must be exchanged for a full one.

Special purpose signals like that one can be quite useful, especially at the beginning when you are trying to get everyone to understand the concepts behind the Pull System. The drawback is that the container becomes the signal, which can get expensive when a plant-wide im-

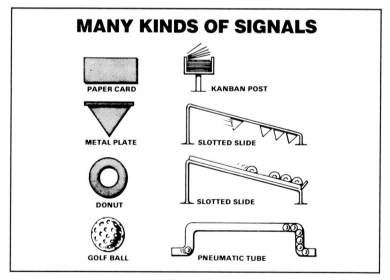

MANY KINDS OF SIGNALS

PAPER CARD

KANBAN POST

METAL PLATE

SLOTTED SLIDE

DONUT

SLOTTED SLIDE

GOLF BALL

PNEUMATIC TUBE

Figure 11-6

plementation is undertaken. For withdrawal signals, in particular, it is usually better to use signal cards to maximize flexibility, minimize costs, and establish uniformity throughout the network.

HOW MANY CARDS?

Sooner or later, somebody has to do a little arithmetic to determine the number of signal cards that are needed to support the production plan. There is only one basic formula, although it is used in two different forms to match real-world situations. Materials Management people will recognize it as the "old" reorder point formula, which fell out of favor many years ago when it was recognized that dependent demand wasn't smooth and linear in most job shops. In a JUST-IN-TIME business, however, we go to great lengths to insure that the demand is smooth and linear, so the formula is very appropriate for this environment.

The formula isn't difficult to apply; but knowing how some people just hate to "crunch numbers," I'll try to keep this section simple and to the point. I do believe it's important that you understand where the numbers come from so you can have confidence in them.

Production Cards

The first thing that has to be done is to determine the number of production cards required to support each part number at a workcenter.

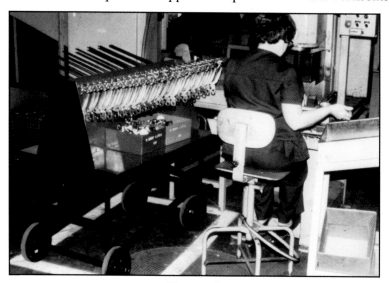

Figure 11-7

The formula for the number of *production cards* is:

$$\# \text{ CARDS } = \frac{\text{AD (WT + PT) (1 + SS)}}{\text{CQ}}$$

Where:

AD = Average Daily Demand during the month for the part number, as determined by the uniform schedule.

WT = Waiting Time at the workcenter for the card to get from the "back" of the dispatch box to the "front."

PT = Processing Time, including setup, for one container of parts.

CQ = Container Quantity, always a fixed number and limited to 1/10 of a day's demand, where possible.

SS = Safety Stock, usually no more than 10% of one day's demand; i.e., one extra container of parts.

All of the time elements in the formula are expressed as decimal portions of a working day. Thus, for a single shift operation, two hours would be .250 days (2/8); while for a two shift plant, two hours would be .125 days (2/16).

Let's take another look at the machining center example used in Figure 11-3 to see how we determined that five production cards for Part "a" were required:

• From the uniform schedule, the average daily demand was 1000 units.

• The processing time for one container of parts was one hour in a single shift operation, or .125 days.

• Since Part "a" and Part "b" were alternated, the work center waiting time was also one hour, or .125 days.

• The container quantity was 50 units.

• There was no safety stock allowance (ideal condition).

Plugging those numbers into the formula gave us:

$$\# \text{ CARDS } = \frac{1000 \ (.125 + .125) \ (1 + 0)}{50} = \frac{250}{50} = 5$$

In the real world, of course, the numbers rarely come out even. You have to "round up" to the next whole number, which automatically adds some safety stock. That's why I always like to do the first calculation with zero safety stock in the formula.

Withdrawal Cards

The identical formula is used to calculate the number of withdrawal cards needed in the plant. In this case, though, the user expects to find some parts in the supplier's staging area so the process time, PT, is set to zero. The only time factor to be considered is the transport time required to take the card to the supplier workcenter and return with the container of parts. In most plants, it is relatively short. That's why there are usually fewer withdrawal cards for a given part number than there are production cards.

For the assembly operation in Figure 11-3, it was determined that a replacement container of parts could be obtained within 30 minutes (.0625 days). The formula then gave us:

$$\# \text{ CARDS } = \frac{1000 \ (.0625 \ + \ 0) \ (1 \ + \ 0)}{50} = \frac{62.5}{50} = 1.25$$

Since we can't issue fractions of cards, the next whole number is two cards, the number that was prepared. Notice that, even though zero safety sock was used in the formula, we ended up with 3//4 of an extra container anyway to cover contingencies.

Outside Supplier Cards

The basic formula presumes that you can send for more material any time you need it. However, in very large plants and especially when dealing with outside suppliers, you may have to depend on regularly scheduled pickups and deliveries. This means a card that "just misses" one pickup will have to wait until the next scheduled time to begin its cycle. The basic formula is modified to incorporate these presumptions when calculating the number of supplier cards required, as follows:

$$\# \text{ CARDS } = \frac{\text{AD} \ (2 \ + \ \text{TD}) \ (1 \ + \ \text{SS})}{\text{DD X CQ}}$$

Where:

AD = Average Daily Demand from the uniform schedule.

2 = The minimum number of scheduled trips required to complete a transaction (one to pick up the card and one to return with material).

TD = Transit Delay, the number of additional scheduled trips that will take place between the one when the card is picked up and the actual material delivery.

DD = Deliveries per Day currently scheduled.
CQ = Container Quantity.
SS = Safety Stock, up to 20% of one day's demand.

The only new elements in the modified formula are the constant (2), the number of daily deliveries that are scheduled (DD) and the transit delays (TD). The constant simply means that its takes a minimum of two "visits" from a supplier to complete a pull transaction — one to pick up the card and a second to return the card with the required parts. However, if the supplier is a long distance away or can't immediately comply with the instructions on the card, it introduces a delay which is highlighted and quantified by the size of TD.

Suppose you had a supplier who was delivering once a day (so DD would be 1) and had a two delivery transit delay (TD = 2). If the supplier picked up a card for a container of Part "a" on Monday, as shown in Figure 11-8, the earliest time you could expect to receive those parts would be on the next delivery, which is scheduled for Tuesday. But, with a transit delay of two, that won't happen. When the truck comes in on Tuesday, it may have other material on it, but not the Part "a" you're looking for. That's the first transit delay. The second transit delay occurs on Wednesday, which means you will finally see Part "a" on the

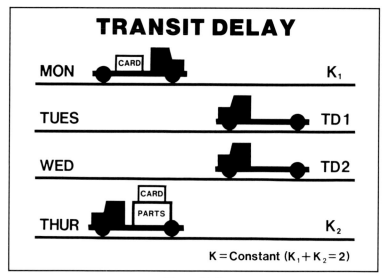

TRANSIT DELAY

MON   K₁

TUES   TD 1

WED   TD 2

THUR   K₂

K = Constant (K₁ + K₂ = 2)

Figure 11-8

Thursday truck. The constant plus the transit delay (2 + TD) always adds up to the total number of scheduled deliveries required to complete the pull transaction.

As you've probably noticed by now, the only difference between the production card formula and the supplier card formula is the manner in which leadtime is expressed. A comparison is shown in Figure 11-9. Either one can be used for in-plant withdrawal cards, depending upon whether the resupply is provided on demand or on a fixed schedule. For outside suppliers, it almost has to be on a fixed schedule so the supplier version is better.

The Value of Frequent Deliveries

The supplier formula also gives us a clear picture of the value of frequent deliveries. Suppose an outside supplier was producing Part "a" instead of the machine center. The average daily demand would still be 1000 units (AD = 1000) and there would still be 50 units in each container (CQ = 50). With one delivery per day (DD = 1), a transit delay of two (TD = 2) and a 20% allowance for safety stock (SS = .2) "just in case the truck breaks down," the number of cards required would be:

$$\# \text{ CARDS} = \frac{1000 \ (2 + 2) \ (1 + .2)}{1 \times 50} = \frac{4800}{50} = 96$$

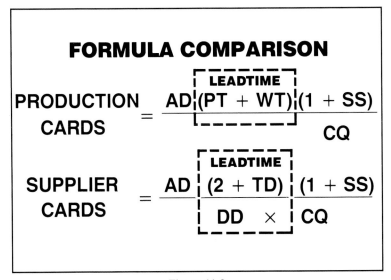

FORMULA COMPARISON

$$\text{PRODUCTION CARDS} = \frac{\text{AD} \overbrace{(\text{PT} + \text{WT})}^{\text{LEADTIME}} (1 + \text{SS})}{\text{CQ}}$$

$$\text{SUPPLIER CARDS} = \frac{\text{AD} \overbrace{\dfrac{(2 + \text{TD})}{\text{DD}}}^{\text{LEADTIME}} \times (1 + \text{SS})}{\text{CQ}}$$

Figure 11-9

That's more than 13 times the number of cards required to make Part "a" internally (5 production cards + 2 withdrawal cards). Although most of the cards will be in "float" at the supplier or on the "road," the potential inventory (and obsolescence) is 4800 units, almost a week's worth of material.

Increasing the delivery frequency would make a dramatic improvement. Four deliveries per day would drive the number of cards down to 24. That's an improvement but still too high. To get to the level afforded by internal manufacturing, the material would have to be delivered every hour, or eight times a day and the transit delay would have to be driven to zero. Then the formula would give us:

$$\# \text{ CARDS } = \frac{1000 \ (2 \ + \ 0) \ (1 \ + \ .2)}{8 \ \times \ 50} = \frac{2400}{400} = 6$$

That's a maximum of 300 units (6 × 50) in the system, or 30% of a one-day supply. It is a typical number for an advanced JIT company like Toyota which is turning its inventories 80 to 100 times per year.

The supplier version of the formula puts two issues into perspective for the planner. First, as the number of daily deliveries increases, the number of cards required is going to be reduced proportionately. Second, the longer the transit delay, the more cards (and, therefore, the more inventory) will be required to keep the system going. That's why JIT puts so much emphasis on selecting suppliers who are near the user plant.

Production Control, At Last

The development and maintenance of the cards required for the Pull System is the responsibility of the production control organization. My friend and associate, Howard Weston, keeps a list of what he calls "mutually exclusive" terms and says that production control, like military intelligence, belongs on the list. Based on my experience in traditional shops, I can see how he reached that conclusion. We never really *controlled* anything. We made plans and issued schedules, but things seldom turned out the way we planned for them to be.

The Pull System gives production control the opportunity to *live up to its name.* Do you want 10% less inventory? Take 10% of the cards from the shop floor and the results are guaranteed. Are you tired of expediting workcenters in an effort to keep the production floor coordinated? When the shop follows the card priorities, production will always be synchronized. How many times do you run out of parts due to schedule changes? Under the Pull System, shortages are the exception instead of the rule.

Of course, you first have to do some work to realize these benefits. You begin by calculating the card requirements for each part number loop in the system and creating the cards. This information is then entered in a log book. The number of cards may change from month to month as production levels change, so the log is the master control record. In its simplest form, the log will include the loop identifier (part number/from/to) and the number of cards authorized for each planning month.

If the current month calculation calls for more cards than last month, the additional cards are prepared and delivered to the appropriate workcenter. When fewer cards are needed, the extra ones from last month are physically removed from the respective workcenters. Once the card levels are set for the new month, production control drops out of the loop. All the execution actions are handled by value adders on the shop floor.

The calculated levels can be reduced, on an experimental basis, to see if the system will work with less work-in-process. This is equivalent to "lowering the water level in the river" to see how far you can go before the first "rock," or problem, appears. The workcenter supervisor conducts the "test" so some of the cards can be immediately reinserted in the system when a problem is discovered. After it has been demonstrated that a given loop can function with fewer cards than the calculations suggested, the excess cards are returned to production control. The quantity of returned cards is entered into the log book as a "minus factor" for future calculations. This becomes an ongoing activity in the quest for continuous improvement.

VARIATIONS TO GET STARTED

The best, most flexible Pull System will employ two types of signals, production and withdrawal, and every container of material will have one of these types of cards attached to them. At the beginning, however, you may have parts that can't be produced one-container-at-a-time because your setup reduction program has not yet reached the point to make it economically feasible. Until that happens, you can use *multiple container signal cards* or accumulate cards until you have enough for a predetermined *multiple card production lot*.

There will also be times when there is no room to stage completed parts at the production workcenter, forcing you to store them at the user workcenter. In that case, a *one-card system* can be used to authorize both production and delivery of the material. It complicates the calculations, which bothers some people at the beginning, so there is a *"rough cut"* approach you can use that is less intimidating to them.

This section will give you some insight into each of these variations. Please remember, though, that they are *interim* solutions. The ultimate objective is still to produce one-at-a-time.

Multiple Container Signal Cards

A multiple container (lot type) signal card is a production authorization. In addition to the standard information, this card defines the number of containers of material that will be manufactured in a single production lot. Instead of one card per container, this card is attached to one particular container in a "stack" which represents the reorder point. That number must also be specified on the card.

In Figure 11-10, the stack of six containers represents the minimum manufacturing lot size for this part. The lot type signal card is attached to the fourth container from the top. When the first and second containers of parts are removed from the stack, no action is necessary. Removal of the third container "exposes" the signal card, which means it's time to send it to the "supplier" workcenter to authorize the production of another lot of six containers of parts. The length of time it should

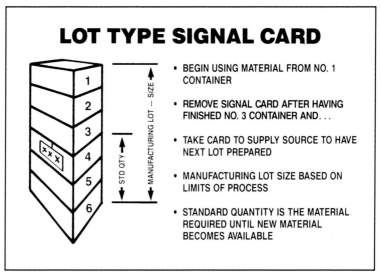

LOT TYPE SIGNAL CARD

- BEGIN USING MATERIAL FROM NO. 1 CONTAINER

- REMOVE SIGNAL CARD AFTER HAVING FINISHED NO. 3 CONTAINER AND...

- TAKE CARD TO SUPPLY SOURCE TO HAVE NEXT LOT PREPARED

- MANUFACTURING LOT SIZE BASED ON LIMITS OF PROCESS

- STANDARD QUANTITY IS THE MATERIAL REQUIRED UNTIL NEW MATERIAL BECOMES AVAILABLE

Figure 11-10

take to consume the fourth, fifth and sixth containers is the leadtime required for the new lot of six containers to arrive. The "standard" quantity or, as you probably know it better, the reorder point quantity is therefore three containers, which is specified on the signal card.

As production rates change, the reorder point will change accordingly. Higher production levels will require moving the card higher in the stack, perhaps to the third container. Conversely, lower production levels will call for moving the card down the stack, possibly to the second container. The proper number must be shown on the card, so this becomes a variable item that may have to be changed from month to month.

The production card formula can be used to calculate the standard quantity. However, the processing time (PT) must be modified to include the entire lot of material. (The basic formula presumes you are going to produce just one container of parts.) This, coupled with the minimum production lot size, is going to add inventory to the system so don't get too liberal with safety stock allowances.

Be sure that the lot type signal card has a completely different "look" from the one-for-one cards so people don't get them confused. If the normal card is rectangular, give this one a different shape, like a triangle, a different size or a special color. Having to work with signals that mean different things is one of the drawbacks of using lot type cards.

Multiple Card Production Lots

Even when multiple container lot sizes are necessary, I believe that it is better to start with and stay with a one-card-for-each-container system. It provides consistency and uniformity on the shop floor, which is not only simpler but also more "fail safe." In this environment, an authorization for multiple container production can be triggered when a "set" of cards, equal to the minimum run size, is accumulated.

There are several ways to do this. One of the easiest is to erect a display board at the work center that lists every part number manufactured there, with a nail beside each one. Above the nail you write the number of cards required before a production run can be started. As material is taken away from the workcenter storage area, the released production cards are hung on the corresponding nails. When the accumulation of cards reaches the minimum-run quantity, that "deck" goes into the dispatch box (as though it was a single card in the ideal system). That way, each part number can have a different run quantity, but the priorities for the decks in the box are maintained.

To avoid having to count the cards on the nail each time a new one is added, a more visible approach can be used, like the one shown in Figure 11-11. In this workcenter, old time card racks are used to accumulate the cards, with one slot for each card. The production trigger is identified by a red band (slot "A" in the figure). Thus, as parts are consumed, the slots are filled with cards until the trigger point is reached. It's easy to see which part will probably be run next. (It looks like it will be Part #4.) But, because cards accumulate as the result of actual consumption, up to the minute priorities are maintained and the next run could well be for Part #2 or Part #3.

Having individual slots for each card also provides a way to tie production priorities and raw material reordering together. The slot marked "B" in Figure 11-11 usually holds a signal card for the raw material needed for this part. When the accumulated production cards reach this slot, the material withdrawal card is pulled out and sent to the "supplier" workcenter. The number of slots between "A" and "B" is the standard quantity, or reorder point quantity, for this item. By the time the production cards reach slot "A," the material should arrive at the workcenter, ready to be processed.

A One Card System

There will be times when the producing workcenter does not have the

Figure 11-11

space to stage even a small quantity of finished units. Then they will have to be stored at the user location. In that case, a combination withdrawal/production card can be used.

Referring back to Figure 11-3, you can see that the two loops shown there would be combined into one long loop. When the first piece was removed from a container at assembly, the card would have to go all the way back to the machine center dispatch box, since there wouldn't be any inventory storage at the machine center. (All the finished material would be at assembly.) When the machine center did complete a container of parts, it (and the signal card) would be sent directly to assembly.

At first glance, this might look like an easier system to develop and manage. After all, there would be fewer cards to contend with. The trouble is that you will have to contend with a longer time frame for the longer loop, which increases the opportunity for unnoticed problems to arise. In addition, the "fail-safe" feature of visible finished stock at the producer workcenter will not be there as a "back up." It does work, though, especially in smaller plants and focused factories where distances are relatively short. And, it will help you work around the storage problem until you can change the layouts.

Use a modified production card formula to determine the number needed each month. In this case, the waiting time (WT) must include the transit time to get the card back to the "supplier" workcenter and to get the parts from there back to the user. If you use the one-card system to reorder minimum lot sizes, the processing time (PT) must also be changed, as was described in that section. Remember, the user will have to store all those parts so keep the lot sizes as small as possible at the beginning and keep working on reducing them.

"Rough Cut" Calculations

When I first started working with clients to help them install the Pull System, despite carefully reviewing the calculation techniques with them and "walking through" the first few with them, many people never seemed to get the "hang" of it. Later, I learned that there were two main reasons for this, especially at smaller plants in remote locations.

First, a formula almost 'terrorizes' some people but their pride won't let them admit it. Those were the ones who were "too busy" to finish the calculations between my visits. Second, the detailed time intervals called for in the formula were not known or available in any file, so the job of compiling them seemed overwhelming, and didn't get done. Yet these same people knew their business extremely well and could quote part numbers, leadtimes, machine capabilities and bottleneck areas right off the "tops of their heads." It became apparent that an even more simplified approach was needed to get people started.

It seemed that most everybody was used to filling out forms, so this would be a very non-threatening way to get some numbers on paper. Knowing, too, that leadtimes were going to be "ball park" estimates, at least initially, it made sense to combine them into a single number for a one-card system, where most of my clients usually started. Finally, since just about everybody seems to be able to use a pocket calculator, a "follow the columns" set of math function instructions was in order.

The result is shown in Figure 11-12. Only four bits of information are needed for each part number. The math symbols remind the person what to do between columns to get to the final answer and the definitions for each column heading are on the single-page review sheet shown in the figure. It's rough, it includes too much safety stock, in my opinion, but it works!

The important thing is it gets people over that first hurdle of concern so they can begin implementing the Pull System in earnest. Once they see the system in operation they will want to fine tune it. That's when they will go back to the formula. Only then, there will be less pressure, more familiarity and greater motivation to try something a bit more sophisticated.

SPECIAL PURPOSE SIGNALS

The Pull System is based on the principle of smooth flow between workcenters that produce complete products or parts. As you get into plant-wide application of the system, all sorts of exceptions will arise. There may be cases when *expedite signals* will seem necessary. *Temporary signals* may be required to handle non-flow conditions or short-term disruptions. Unique operations may have to be tied to integrated workcenters with *process signals*. For outside suppliers, in particular, the distance penalty can be reduced by using *electronic signals*. These are standard variations to the basic system which will be reviewed in this section. As time goes by, you may well invent others to suit your own special circumstances.

Expedite Signals

When the product mix changes significantly, the increased demand for a given item could cause the normal buffer stock to run out. To avoid

PULL SYSTEM WORK SHEET

COMPANY			USER LOCATION		
DIVISION/PLANT			SOURCE OF SUPPLY		

PART NUMBER	AVERAGE DAILY DEMAND $\times$	LEAD TIME DAYS $+$	MINIMUM LOT SIZE $\div$	STANDARD CONTAINER QUANTITY $=$	NUMBER OF SIGNAL CARDS

AVERAGE DAILY DEMAND - Monthly production quantity divided by the number of working days in the month.

LEAD TIME DAYS - The number of working days from the time a card is sent to the source of supply to the moment the card returns to the user location, attached to a container of parts. A working day includes all shift hours normally worked. Therefore, a four hour lead time would be 0.5 days in a single-shift plant, but 0.25 days in a two-shift plant.

MINIMUM LOT SIZE - The minimum production quantity that can be run with one setup or the minimum shipping quantity that an outside supplier has agreed to send. This number should get smaller as setup reductions are implemented.

STANDARD CONTAINER QUANTITY - The number of pieces to be placed in one reusable container. This quantity should be fixed. The minimum lot size may have many containers of parts in it. The ideal container size is 1/10 of the daily demand. Try to avoid anything larger than one full day's demand, even for small parts.

NUMBER OF CARDS - The calculation will give you the number of cards needed to support the average daily demand in Column #2. Round the answer up to the next whole number. *CAUTION: This calculation includes one full container of safety stock plus the rounded up portion of another. If your container sizes are large (more than 1/2 of a day's demand) you may wish to subtract one card from the calculated answer.*

Ken Wantuck Associates
24655 Southfield Road, Suite 207, Southfield, MI 48075

Date _____ Page ___ of ___

Figure 11-12

this, one of the cards in the set (for a given part number loop) can be given a special color (like red) and attached to the last container of parts. When this last container of parts is taken away, the red expedite card is placed in the *front* of the dispatch box, instead of the rear, automatically giving it the top priority. If the time to set up and run a container of parts is greater than the time in which one container will be consumed, use the lot type signal calculation to determine which container should hold the expedite signal.

The expedite signal is particularly useful when a one card system is employed, since the producer has no visual control of the completed stock on hand. A version of this is shown in Figure 11-13. The stack of pre-cut material on the shelf is used to manufacture seat covers at a Ford plant in Saarbruken, West Germany. The top card is a lot type reorder card. The amount of material between it and the lower card (the expedite card) is the standard quantity to cover normal replenishment leadtime. The material below the expedite card is safety stock. If material consumption exposes the expedite card, which is colored pink, it is sent to the supplier department. There, the pink card initiates a search of the dispatch box to find the matching reorder card that was previously sent. The two cards are clipped together and placed in the front of the dispatch box to give that order top priority.

Try to hold the number of expedite signals in your system to a minimum. Otherwise, they'll become as commonplace as "hot tickets" in a

Figure 11-13

traditional shop. Also, make sure everybody truly understands exactly how the system is intended to work. Sending out expedite signals before the time they are supposed to be used can "foul up" the entire priority system.

Temporary Signals

Short-term deviations from normal production can be planned and executed by using temporary signals. Typically, they would be issued for such things as:
- A "bump" in demand for a given part number caused by a significant shift in product mix.
- A build-up of inventory to cover a planned shutdown for things like machine overhaul or model changeover.
- A limited production run for a new product.
- A phase-out/phase-in for a part revision.

Temporary cards are *one-time-only* signals. They are issued by production control, sent to the appropriate workcenter, go through one "life cycle", and are returned to production control, which monitors the returns and records them in the log book. For example, if it was determined that 20 temporary cards would be needed to cover a two-day shutdown of a workcenter, they would be issued to that workcenter and interspersed with the other jobs in the dispatch box, to keep the flow as smooth as possible. As these extra parts were taken away, the temporary cards would *not* be placed in the dispatch box. Instead, they would be sent to production control. By recording the returns, production control can insure that the temporary cards don't stay on the shop floor, inflating work-in-process longer than necessary.

Here, again, these signals should look different from the others so they will be handled differently. A unique color, a diagonal stripe across the card, or just leaving off the plastic covering are possibilities. Because temporary cards are only issued for special reasons, many companies require that the reason be written on the card or attached to the card on a separate piece of paper. It's a good way to tell people not only what to do, but also why they are being asked to do it.

Phasing in a part revision is trickier, but it can also be handled with temporary signals. In this case, production control starts at the lead-off operation by replacing the "old revision" cards in the dispatch box with "permanent" revised ones. Then, they affix old revision temporary cards to the finished material in the workcenter storage area. Next, they proceed to the customer workcenter and, knowing how many temporary cards are in the supplier workcenter, place a compatible number of temporary cards in the supplier dispatch box. Any remaining cards in the dispatch box are replaced by permanent cards for the new revision. Similarly, all the cards attached to finished material in this workcenter are replaced with old revision temporary ones. This procedure is repeated at all the downstream workcenters in the process chain.

Back in the office, production control will have a record of how many temporary cards are on the floor for each loop in the system. They will also have an equivalent number of permanent cards for the new revision. As each temporary card comes in from the floor, a permanent replacement will be sent out. Equilibrium will be reached when all the temporary cards have been returned.

Process Signals

Pull System signals are intended to connect integrated workcenters that manufacture complete products or parts. Sometimes, one or more key operations cannot be included in a workcenter. To connect them to the rest of the network, a *"push-pull"* combination signal can be used. It is called a process signal.

A process signal is activated by the consumption of material. That's the *pull* part. It is sent to the lead-off operation of the "mini" process, from which it follows each operation, in sequence, through the respective workcenters, as if it was a traditional routing sheet. That's the *push* part. For short sequences, it's a dandy compromise to handle special cases. For long sequences, it is only slightly better than an order launching system. (It does at least control the launch, based on actual material usage.)

A good application of a process signal is one that connects only a few operations. That's what was done for the JCI Linden focused factory, described previously in Figure 7-4. Some of the parts used in the assembly cells required stamping, sanding, broaching and heat treating in four different locations before they could be used. The alternatives were to create four sets of pull signals (assembly to heat treating, heat treating to broaching, broaching to sanding and sanding to stamping) and establish four storage areas for semi-finished parts, or to use a process signal. The latter option was chosen.

Cards were issued to assembly, based on the one-card system calculations. Each card showed the usual basic information, but the from/to items were replaced by the routing for all the operations the parts were to undergo. Assembly sent the card to stamping in the usual fashion. The completed lot of stampings was forwarded (pushed) to sanding, along with the card. The sander was physically moved next to the broach, creating a "mini" group technology cell, so those two operations could be done in sequence. The parts and the card were then sent to heat treating and were finally pushed on to assembly.

This type of signal worked for JCI because there were only a few process steps, the operations were fast and this was an exception, not the rule. Remember, the "push" part of a process signal is like pushing on a stiff rope. If it's short, you've got some degree of control. The longer it gets, the less likely will be your ability to even influence it.

Electronic Signals

Some form of waiting time is involved for every type of pull signal that may be used. The longer the time, the more signals (and inventory) will be needed to keep the system going. This can place outside suppliers who are located a great distance from the customer plant at a significant disadvantage. However, the waiting time can be cut almost in half if some form of electronic transmission is used to send requirement "cards" to the supplier instead of sending them with the truck driver.

The simplest way to do this is by telephone. Whoever does order releasing in your plant can serve as the interface between the internal card system and the outside supplier. He or she will place telephone releases for predetermined lot sizes when internal consumption signals reach a trigger point. The information flow is shown in Figure 11-14.

The store of material from the previous supplier shipment is shown at the top. Each container has a reorder card attached to it. When the customer workcenter removes a container from the stores area, the reorder card is placed in a collection box. The cards are picked up by production control every hour or so. In the production control office, the cards are sorted into piles by part number and placed in accumulation boxes or "pigeon holes." When enough cards have been accumulated to reach a trigger point (reorder point), production control calls the supplier to release the next shipment.

By prior agreement, the supplier has one lot available (usually a skid load of containers) and will ship it upon receiving the call. That shipment, in turn, will initiate a replenishment order at the supplier plant which should be available for the next telephone call.

Production control sends the deck of cards which triggered the supplier call to the receiving department, where the cards now become an authorization to accept material. When it arrives, receiving attaches a card from the deck to each container in the shipment and sends the material to the storage location. This completes the replenishment cycle.

Each person in the process receives automatic authorization to take a specific action, yet nobody has to generate a single piece of paper. To people inside the plant, it's "business as usual" since everything they see is controlled by cards. As long as the number of phone calls is manageable, this very basic approach for electronic pull signaling is quite effective.

Electronic Data Interchange (EDI)

When the number of transactions grows to the point where it becomes a burden, Electronic Data Interchange (EDI) can be employed to automate the information flow. There are many systems available today which can link customer and supplier computers together to

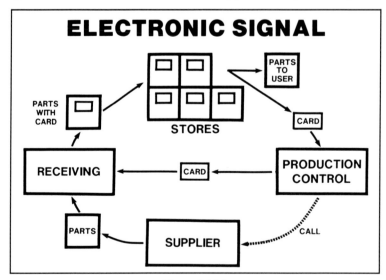

Figure 11-14

exchange vital information. Some trade associations, like the Automotive Industry Action Group (AIAG), have already developed and published standards to simplify the use of this tool throughout a supply network. When tied together with bar coding, an EDI pull signal network could eliminate thousands of manual transactions and telephone calls. Production control would not even have to bother with replenishment signals.

The system would work in a very similar fashion to the one previously described in Figure 11-14, except the block marked *Production Control* would be replaced by an *EDI Terminal*, which could be located in the receiving department. Instead of production control picking up the cards, receiving would pick them up on regularly scheduled basis. The cards would be run through a bar code reader to record the part number and the serial number on the card. Then the cards would be placed in the appropriate "pigeon holes" in receiving to await the arrival of the material.

Within the computer, the part number would be linked to a file that contained all the rest of the information on the card, including the number of cards required to trigger a signal to the supplier. When that point was reached, the system would automatically send a transmission to the supplier to authorize the shipment of a standard lot of material. The cards in receiving would still be the authorization to receive material and send it to stores as before, but they would also be run through the bar code reader to register the material receipt in the system.

That transaction would not only update the system records, but would also make it "fail safe." That's where the serial number comes into play. The first time the card is read it will be placed in a supplier order file in the computer, by serial number. First, however, the serial number will be checked against the file to make sure it isn't already there. If so, the transaction will be rejected and duplicate entries will be impossible. When material is received, the second bar code reading will clear the serial number from the file, allowing it to be entered again the next time around.

To make the system work, production control will have to enter its log book data in the computer so the authorized levels and serial numbers are available for control purposes. The system could also be tied to the payment system, making it possible to cut checks to the supplier without the necessity of matching invoices, purchase orders and receiving reports. Some companies are already doing this today.

EDI provides some powerful, "high-tech" opportunities to extend the Pull System to every supplier in the network, no matter where they are located. The important thing to remember, though, is to keep it simple and don't clutter it up with any "bells and whistles" that aren't really necessary.

SUMMARY

The Pull System is the execution companion system to uniform scheduling. Originally patterned after American supermarkets, it is simple, flexible, visible, responsive to real-world changes in customer demands, and is self-regulating. It is applicable to both inside work-centers and outside suppliers. Yet, for all of that, it can be completely manual in its basic application.

The system is intended to regulate mix changes in a flow manu-facturing environment. It "pulls" replenishment production through a shop as the result of actual consumption. Pull System supply "loops" are the connectors between producers and consumers that can integrate every workcenter in an entire supply network, as shown in Figure 11-4. It responds extremely well to variations on a theme (the uniform schedule) but does not lend itself to "lumpy" manufacturing.

Production is controlled under the Pull System by the number of authorization signals issued for both usage and supply. The signals are usually cards, although other types of signals can be used. A modified reorder point formula is used to determine the quantity of cards in the system for any level of production. Many variations can be em-ployed to get the system started and to handle special situations, like expediting, temporary conditions and engineering changes. It can be tied in with Electronic Data Interchange (EDI) to communicate with distant suppliers.

The Achilles Heel of the system is lack of discipline. The Pull System maintains up to the minute priorities for all of the workcenters and suppliers in the network when everyone follows the authorization signals explicitly. When the signals are lost, ignored or "second guessed," the system will fail.

The Pull System provides better production control for less cost. It lets value adders communicate their needs directly to each another, eliminating the necessity for an "army" of helpers and complex systems. This was vividly demonstrated by an analysis I made while studying three plants making the same products. Two were traditional plants and the third was a JUST-IN-TIME plant with a Pull System. There was a remarkable difference between the direct to indirect labor ratios at the three plants. The traditional plants ranged from 1.33:1 to 1.45:1, while the JIT plant had a ratio of 4.45:1. In other words, the JIT plant had only had *one-third as many indirect people* as did the traditional plants. On top of that, they had fewer "directs" per unit output, as well.

The control aspects of the Pull System are demonstrated by an experience that took place at JKC, the Bendix affiliate mentioned in Chapter 8. As shown in Figure 11-15, their annual inventory turnover rate rose from 11.2 to 30.5 in just nine quarters. If you look carefully, you'll see that the ninth quarter jumped by almost seven turns. That made people nervous. They wondered if they were going to stretch the system to the point where it would "break the rubber band" as was discussed in Chapter 2. So they decided to add back a little inventory to relieve some of the stress.

By adding more pull signals to the shop floor in a very controlled fashion, they slowly brought the turnover down to 25.6. (After all these years, I still have a hard time getting used to thinking about getting turnover *down* to 25.) That part was OK, but there was a disastrous side effect from that "cure." JKC's *quality and productivity went down along with the turns.* While I've been saying over and over again that lowering inventory is the key to higher quality and

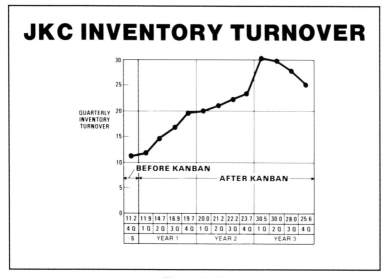

Figure 11-15

productivity, here is at least one case where the converse of that was also true — higher inventory lowered the quality and productivity. Needless to say, JKC changed its strategy and went back to "stretching the system" by pulling some signal cards off the floor. At last report, they were exceeding 38 inventory turns per year, and the end was not in sight.

That's the beauty of the Pull System. It's a cost effective way to give you more real production control than you've ever had before. When coupled with uniform scheduling, it provides the "nuts and bolts" to plan an effective manufacturing enterprise, execute that plan while still responding to real-world changes in customer demand, and improve the business by lowering inventory in a controlled manner to expose and fix problems. When you extend the Pull System to the supplier base, you can "pull" production through the entire network.

SUPPLIER
RELATIONS

CHAPTER 12

"JIT supplier relations are long-term partnerships
with single-source suppliers
who provide certified quality material
while continuously reducing costs."

The JUST-IN-TIME strategy encompasses the entire production process, from mining raw material to delivery of the end product to the final customer. The first 11 chapters of this book concentrated on the plant, the "inside" shop. The purchasing function, management of the "outside shop," has been saved until now for two very important reasons:

1. It doesn't make sense to ask suppliers to do something you don't know how to do yourself.

2. Frequent, small lot deliveries won't do you much good if you haven't changed your production system to make use of them.

However, once the transformation of your internal shop is underway, JIT must be extended to the supplier network to obtain the full benefit of the strategy. Like the internal elements already discussed, JIT supplier relations encompass a new set of values, many of which are *completely contrary to present practices*. Nevertheless, they work and JUST-IN-TIME can't be completely effective until the suppliers are brought into the "family."

SUPPLIER PARTNERSHIPS

Webster defines a partner as a *"sharer"* and a *"player on the same side."* That is exactly what is being sought in a JIT supplier partnership. Admittedly, it is a far cry from the guarded relationships that exist between many customers and suppliers today. Partnerships require equal consideration, fairness, risk sharing and mutual trust. It's going to take some "doing" to get from where we are to where we want to go. It won't be easy, either.

Shared Control

Contrary to what many people think, JUST-IN-TIME can be implemented at a plant in relative isolation. You can buffer yourself from both your customers and suppliers with inventory. As shown in Figure 12-1, raw material and purchased parts stores can buffer the plant from the impact of "unreliable" supplier deliveries or quality. Finished goods can buffer the plant from "unreliable" customers, who keep changing their minds and dropping last minute "bombs" on the plant. Inside those two buffer zones the plant can not only practice JIT, but also the users are in total control of their manufacturing process.

The bad news is that those buffer inventories are a waste in JUST-IN-TIME and need to be eliminated. To remove the raw material and purchased parts stock, the supplier network must be directly tied to the users, as shown in Figure 12-2. However, this increases the risk and the potential complexity. Control is now shared by two parties, the customer and the supplier, who must intimately communicate with one another if there are to be no provisions for contingencies.

At the beginning, the buffer inventory may just shift to the supplier's finished goods stock. That's hardly a solution. It is, at best, a temporary stop-gap. There is no way a supplier can increase inventories and reduce costs at the same time. The only answer is for the supplier to also implement JIT production and, in turn, extend JIT to its supplier base. This needs to be repeated all the way through the entire supply network until the excess inventory is literally pushed "back into the ground." Then, all the partners can share the savings.

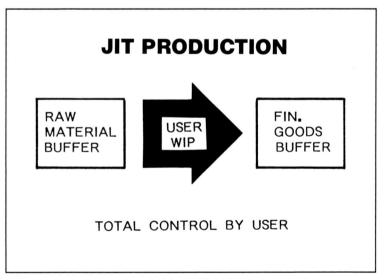

Figure 12-1

Suppliers Are People

Corporations are legally considered to be "persons," but they are artificial entities. Dealings between those companies are conducted by real people. In JUST-IN-TIME supplier partnerships those people place more emphasis on relationships than they do on contractual details. That is not to say contracts aren't important. They must be so for legal reasons, if no other. But, true partners will "make it right" no matter what is written on paper. It is a very *personal* relationship.

The partnership has to be beneficial to both parties. In contract law, this is called "equal consideration." Another way of looking at it is a "win-win" relationship. The past practices of "seeing what we could squeeze out of a supplier'" or "seeing how much we could get out of a customer" must be replaced by a *partnership for mutual prosperity.* It is a different perspective and it will be difficult for some to accept, especially if your purchasing people don't "buy into" the concept.

The "bottom line" is that JIT people policies and practices will have to be extended to the people in the supply network. It's the key to continuous improvement, which makes it possible to eliminate contingencies and reduce costs. Suppliers must be instilled with the same team spirit, mutual objectives, mutual dependence and trust that is called for among your own people. It can't happen if they are treated as unimportant "outsiders," to be dealt with at arms length. That's why they have to become part of their "family."

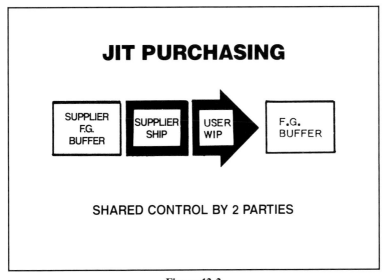

Figure 12-2

BREAKING WITH TRADITION

JIT supplier relations call for *"long-term* partnerships with *single-source* suppliers who provide *certified quality* material while continuously *reducing costs."* Each of the highlighted terms flies in the face of traditional practices. In some cases they are even contrary to government procurement regulations. Since the old way is based on the premise of *no trust,* it may be understandable in the old environment. But, when a customer-supplier relationship is a genuine partnership, the willingness to rely on one another provides a golden opportunity to break away from many of the wasteful traditional practices.

Long-Term Partnerships

Purchasing has long been a short-term business. In many companies each procurement is a separate transaction, usually authorized by an approved requisition. Some people call these "spot buys." A long-term contract is considered by many to be an annual buy, against which periodic releases are issued to the supplier. Only in major aerospace or defense programs is it common to see a multi-year buy and even that is circumstantial, as it is tied to a long-running program. (Each item is still a single purchase for a single program.)

Partnerships are intended to last a lifetime. Partners are not supposed to "dangle on a string," living from job to job, any more than our employees should. There has to be some degree of security so the supplier can make long-term commitments for technology, quality and cost improvements to support the customer. A JIT supplier partnership is much like a marriage. It is expected to last forever, even if it doesn't always end up that way.

Single-Source Suppliers

In the traditional purchasing world, suppliers bid against one another to customer-prepared drawings and specifications. It has always been the way to make sure we "get what we want" and to foster "healthy" competition. In many businesses, a minimum of three bids is required before any purchase can be made. In addition, some companies split their purchases for each part number in the system between two or three suppliers, "just-in-case" somebody doesn't deliver.

A JIT supplier-partner is the only source the customer has, not just for a given part number, but for a whole family of those parts. (A "marriage" is not only supposed to be for life but it should also be *monogamous.*) Both partners are taking a risk and each has to trust the other to make it work.

The supplier should be the "expert" about the technology and processes used to make that part family, so that knowledge should be put to work. (After all, if we knew that much about it, we'd probably make the parts ourselves.) This gives the customer the opportunity to incorporate that expertise into the product during the design stage instead of an "afterthought" cost reduction.

Since single-sourcing places all the business for a given part family in one set of hands, the supplier gets more volume, which should be reflected in lower prices. Knowing that there is no backup, the supplier also feels a heightened sense of responsibility to the customer. It is, however, still a risky business. With all the "eggs in one basket," the customer has nowhere to turn if the supplier fails to deliver. Yet, it's no different than the strategy being followed on the shop floor. Having duplicate suppliers is like having duplicate departments in the plant. You can't afford the cost of either one.

Certified Quality Material

When the material arrives, it has to be good. Today, we try to insure that by checking incoming material in receiving inspection. It is not only a costly exercise but is also time consuming and as was shown in Chapter 3, not particularly effective. One of the reasons for moving to single-source suppliers is to eliminate receiving inspection.

The JIT supplier's manufacturing processes must be under statistical process control and their capability should be certified by the customer. Parts produced under these conditions need not be inspected. Instead, they can be delivered directly to the place where they will be used by the customer. SPC charts serve as the documentation to assure that the process stayed in control during the time the parts were made.

Reducing Costs and Prices

Without multiple suppliers or competitive bidding, how can a customer prevent being "taken" by a single-source supplier? The answer is surprisingly simple. First, remember that a major objective of the partnership is to *reduce costs,* not to "hold increases in line," so the savings can be shared with the customer. Prices are negotiated based on a joint analysis of those costs.

At first blush, the thought of allowing a customer to see a supplier's "books" might seem like heresy. Actually, it's really "no big deal."

Anyone who has been involved with government contracts should be very familiar with negotiating prices based on incurred costs. Despite all the "red tape" and arguments with the auditors, the defense industry still makes money. It just takes some time to get used to it.

Indirect costs will also be significantly reduced, especially paperwork. When nobody trusts anybody else, multiple bids are required for every purchase, there are several suppliers for every part, everything has to be inspected and material must be identified to know who made what, a "ton" of paper is required to keep it all straight. It takes many people to fill out and track all that paperwork, which is a waste. Perhaps this can best be illustrated by an actual company experience.

Several years ago, Hoover Universal Seating Division, headquartered in Saline, Michigan, was awarded a contract as the sole source for a family of truck seats to Nissan, in Smyrna, Tennessee. During the "button-up" negotiations, Hoover asked Nissan for a mailing address for the invoices. Nissan responded, "We don't accept invoices." Hoover then asked, "How are we going to get paid?" Nissan replied, "In all the years we've been manufacturing pick-up trucks, we've never shipped one without a set of seats. You are our only seat supplier. As each truck goes out the door, we know exactly which seats are in it. We will keep track of those shipments and send you a check every ten days."

Hoover was nonplused but had little alternative. Needless to say, they kept their own tally of the seats sent to Nissan. Except for minor discrepancies due to cut-off times, the figures always agreed. Hoover got its money and both companies avoided a lot of useless paperwork.

JIT SUPPLIER ISSUES

With the stakes as high as they are, it should be easy to see why JIT suppliers must be carefully selected. In fact, it usually requires a multi-disciplined team to make that determination. Although production capability and competitive prices are musts, they only establish the first plateau for selection. Many other criteria will enter into the picture before a partnership can be established. The key JIT issues are:

- Quality Assurance
- Responsiveness
- Continuous improvement
- Frequent, small lot shipments
- Timely communications
- JIT production

Quality Assurance

The first and foremost issue that will *make or break* any supplier in a JUST-IN-TIME network is quality assurance. The basic concepts of Quality at the Source, described in Chapter 3, must be understood, accepted and implemented in order to qualify. With no provisions for contingencies, the customer will have to shut down if the material, delivered at the "last minute," does not work. There is no escape from this awesome responsibility.

Statistical process control is mandatory. Impressive training numbers and charts on the wall won't be enough. SPC is going to have to be an integral part of the work routine at a JIT supplier. Control charts will be the "language" of quality assurance, enabling a customer to know exactly how well the process by which the parts were made was working. That's why JIT customers are, and will continue to be, so insistent on this particular issue.

Beyond control limits, a JIT supplier is expected to produce products that are as good as they can be, regardless of what the specification says. What counts is not whether the part "passes" but rather how compatible it is with the customer's application. This also applies to product reliability. Parts must be "right," not just when they are delivered, but long after they have been assembled into the customer's product. The more "perfect" the supplier's parts are, the better the customer's products will, in turn, satisfy its customers and the more business everyone can expect to share.

Responsiveness

A JUST-IN-TIME supplier-partner must *respond to exact customer demand,* within the framework of uniform scheduling and the pull system. Container quantities must be precise. "Standard industry practices" of shipping ordered quantities ± 10% are not acceptable. Delivery dates and times are crucial, so they must be honored, not just to the "spirit" but to the "letter" of the requirements.

There is no way a JIT supplier can expect to receive a "frozen" schedule, by part number, from the customer. The monthly production envelope for a family of parts will be honored to utilize reserved capacity, but mix changes will occur every day and immediate response will be expected. Similarly, engineering change orders (which hopefully reflect product improvement and cost reductions) will call for immediate implementation. A JIT customer won't want to hear about the three months of inventory that was "built ahead" of the releases.

Relying on the expertise of the single-source supplier, the JIT customer will expect design assistance in a timely fashion. Many suppliers will have to add engineering talent to their payrolls to complement their process knowledge so they can provide a total support package to the customer. Problem solving will be a part of that responsibility, as well. There will be no time to worry about "whose fault" it might be. Immediate response to trouble calls is a hallmark of a JIT supplier.

Continuous Improvement

The management team at a JIT supplier must believe in and work for the principle of continuous improvement. The supplier evaluation team will be looking for an attitude that says, "Yes, we will provide the increasingly higher quality levels you seek; yes, we believe that productivity can be continuously improved so prices can be reduced; and yes, we intend to respond even faster with each passing year." This management attitude must already be in place for the supplier to be successful. The customer can teach the supplier the techniques of SPC, group technology, setup reduction, the pull system, etc., but the customer can't change inherent supplier management attitudes. That "rock" is too big.

That's why the evaluation team will undoubtedly ask for some evidence to demonstrate the supplier's commitment to JIT. What tools are in place? Are value analysis or value engineering projects underway? What sort of results have been seen? Is there a quality circle program? What ideas have been developed? The proof will be in the doing. Otherwise, the concern will be that the "nice round words" spoken at the negotiation table may not be reflected in later actions.

Continuous improvement is the foundation of continuous price reductions. (If they come from the supplier's "hide," it certainly won't be a win-win situation.) Improvements made between negotiations should belong to the supplier. At negotiation time, they should be *shared with* (not totally taken by) the customer. Then, the cycle will repeat itself. That's a partnership at work.

Frequent, Small Lot Shipments

JUST-IN-TIME customers will be using flow manufacturing in their plants which will require a *flow of material* into those facilities. A JIT supplier will be expected to support the flow with frequent, small lot shipments which can be used immediately by the customer. This gives rise to all kinds of transportation issues which will be addressed in Chapter 13. But first, it is the "mindset" of the supplier that is the issue.

This requirement is exactly the opposite of traditional practices, which entailed infrequent, large lot shipments. It's very different, but it's also beneficial to both the customer and the supplier.

This happened at Plasti-Line, Inc., a custom sign builder in Knoxville, Tennessee. The company originally had three hardware suppliers for a wide variety of items used in their products. Replacement stock was ordered from a cardex system, called in to one of the suppliers, processed through receiving when it arrived, stored in the stockroom, pulled when a requisition was received from the floor and delivered to the user location. A typical scenario.

Plasti-Line decided to consolidate its hardware family with a single-source supplier, who was to deliver parts every day, as needed. A number of floor stock racks, like the ones shown in Figure 12-3, were strategically placed in the shop. Each day, a supplier representative came into the plant, resupplied each rack with the hardware that had been used the previous day, made a list of those items and left it with material control as he left the plant. There was no ordering, no receiving, no stockroom and no material handling work that had to be done by Plasti-Line. Yet, the consolidation netted them lower hardware prices to boot. On top of that, with regular deliveries every day, they never ran out of stock because somebody forgot to place an order. Both Plasti-Line and the supplier ended up as "winners."

Figure 12-3

Timely Communications

A JIT supplier must keep the customer informed about all events that can impact performance, *just like a department of the customer's plant*. In effect, that's what it is. With no contingencies in the system, a single-source supplier must not hide bad news from the customer or even delay it. That could certainly shut down the customer's operation. Timely communications will at least alert the customer to potential disruptions and provide an opportunity to help solve the problem. Communications must not only be more frequent but also more honest than they may have been in the past. It should be a mutual concern.

The linkage could be as basic as telephone calls between key people at each plant. By this, I mean predetermined "doers," not "brass." The time available to take corrective action will be short so it must not be wasted by "going through channels." More sophisticated communication systems, like Electronic Data Interchange (EDI), should also be considered to make the job as fast and easy as possible. Timely communications can overcome many of the concerns people have about dealing with "remote" suppliers in a JIT world.

JUST-IN-TIME Production

In the final analysis, *a JIT supplier will have to become a JIT producer.* The ultimate objective is not to pass costs down to the supplier. It is to push costs out of the network. But, a supplier who tries to "look" like a JIT supplier to its customer while clinging to its traditional production methods will have to incur higher costs for finished goods inventory if nothing else. Sooner or later, those costs will become oppressive, especially with the pressure to continually reduce prices. A supplier can absorb those costs for the short-term while the conversion to JIT production is taking place, but to try to do it for the long-term would be a self-defeating strategy.

JIT SUPPLIER CHALLENGE

Pressures to do things "differently" are already being seen in the marketplace. Today, suppliers are besieged by a bewildering array of new proposals under the name of JUST-IN-TIME. Sometimes, they are the "real" thing. In other cases, the customers are well intentioned but still don't understand the ramifications of a true JIT customer/supplier partnership. In still others (hopefully very few), customers are selecting the features of JIT that suit them without "signing up" for the commensurate responsibilities that a partnership demands. In every case, new opportunities are changing the marketplace. If you haven't already been approached, you soon will be. It is important that you be able to recognize what is happening, what customers are getting and what suppliers have a right to expect, because things will never be the same again.

Price Decreases

The "word is out" that some suppliers are accepting multi-year contracts with built-in price decreases of as much as five percent per year. Too many of those suppliers don't have the "foggiest" notion how they're going to reduce their costs proportionately. The threat of losing all that customer's business for the next five years probably drove them to accept the contract now and worry about costs later. Unfortunately, this is starting a "muscle mentality" in some quarters that can hurt everyone. Some of those suppliers are going to "fold up" before their contracts expire, leaving their customers in the lurch and the market permanently disrupted. Nothing is going to change that.

On the other hand, genuine JIT customer/supplier partnerships are being built today. Of course, they include continuous price reductions, but they are based on the mutual cost reduction efforts and cost-based negotiations discussed in this chapter. In most cases, they are still experimental relationships because neither partner has ever done this sort of thing before. Many of them are starting with "half a loaf" and working their way toward a permanent partnership. There's nothing wrong with that, so long as there is a mutual understanding of the end goal.

Fewer Suppliers

Supplier consolidation, by whatever means, has been underway in some industries for a number of years. Automotive plants who used to have more than a thousand suppliers are taking a page from Toyota's book which calls for only 300 suppliers to a given plant. In fact, shrinking the supplier base to about one-third of its former size seems to be the typical target. With fewer suppliers and more business for each of the remaining suppliers, the stakes are getting higher every year.

Since JIT implementation is still relatively new in this country (even though we've been talking about it for a decade), some suppliers are simply refusing to consider a JIT customer/supplier partnership. Perhaps the change is too great for them or they just don't see the long-range benefits to their companies. Needless to say, they are the ones who get "weeded out" early in the game. Others, though, want to adapt to the new strategy, but not even all of them can be survivors. Only those who "commit and do" will be winners.

To be successful, a supplier must also qualify a customer. Customers who want the advantages of JIT supplier relations but show no inclination to change the way they run their own businesses are not likely to be good partners. Part of the problem is that too many people, on both sides of the negotiating table, still don't know what JIT is all about. That can be helped by education. However, to survive in this new environment, it is vital that a supplier be able to recognize the difference between the real thing and somebody who is playing "screw the supplier" and calling it JUST-IN-TIME.

CUSTOMER PREREQUISITES

A prerequisite is "something necessary to do something subsequent." Customer prerequisites in a JIT supplier relationship are those things that should be in place *before* trying to forge a partnership. Remember, it is the customer who is asking the supplier to do something different than the old arrangement. It is the customer who will first benefit from the new partnership. It is also the customer who has the initial leverage and therefore needs to understand that a one-sided relationship is not a partnership.

All of the customer prerequisites have been previously introduced, but the specific implications of the responsibilities need some reinforcement. The key ones are:
- Long-term commitments
- Stable production plan
- Families of parts sourcing
- Small incremental changes
- Timely communications

Long-Term Commitments

A partnership is *expected to last forever.* Whether it does or not depends on how well each partner lives up to the original commitments. Nobody really expects a customer to issue a lifetime contract to a JIT supplier partner, not at the beginning, for sure, and probably not ever. What the supplier does need to see, however, is an expression of good faith that is markedly different from past practices.

As a starting point, I suggest that you at least double the length of the longest contract you ever offered that supplier before. It will get some attention and demonstrate that this is a "different" situation. The follow-on contract should be even longer. Eventually, five to ten-year contracts should be commonplace. The longer the relationship is sustained, the less important the actual contract will become.

A long-term commitment encourages a supplier to make long-term investments to improve quality and productivity. Without them it's difficult, if not impossible, to sustain continuous price reductions. Similarly, if the supplier is expected to be an "expert" in its field, ongoing technology investments will also be required. The more secure the relationship becomes, the more initiative and risk a supplier will be willing to take to preserve and enhance the partnership.

Stable Production Plan

A JIT customer-supplier partnership is intended to be a *stable relationship*. The customer gets a steady, reliable source of supply, and the supplier gets a solid customer base upon which the rest of the business can be built. The greater the percentage of the total business the JIT customer represents, the more stable it needs to be.

That is not to say that the relationship won't have to weather economic ups and downs because it certainly will. But, those cycles happen gradually. Month-to-month changes in the production plan, as was discussed under uniform scheduling, will accommodate those changes. Once the production envelope for next month has been set, however, the customer must honor that consumption level to protect the resources committed by the supplier. (Remember, pricing was based on the premise that those resources would be effectively utilized). Changes to subsequent monthly envelopes should be gradual (in order of 10% per month) to give the supplier time to reallocate resources.

A stable production plan should not be confused with a "frozen schedule" by part number. A JIT supplier is expected to react to mix changes within a production envelope every single day. If the supplier is producing in small lots and responding to pull signals, those changes will not cause any difficulties. What the supplier cannot tolerate is sudden changes in the production level for a current month or large changes in subsequent months. Replacing "last minute surprises" with gradual adjustments is what a stable production plan is really all about.

Families of Parts Sourcing

Placing an entire family of parts with one supplier makes it easier for them to react to mix changes while still maintaining productivity targets. Typically, we're a lot "smarter" about our overall production levels than we are about the mix of products within that envelope. When one supplier has the whole family, mix changes can, and usually do, offset one another to minimize the disruption.

Suppose you had a part family comprised of just two numbers, A and B, but each of them was placed with a different supplier. Now imagine that the requirements for those two parts changed so that you needed 20% more A's and 20% fewer B's. You would have to issue two change orders to the two suppliers, both of which would cause them problems. The one making A's would have to "scramble" to find the capacity to build the increase, while the one building B's would be "stuck" with extra capacity. This is shown in the left side of Figure 12-4.

Contrast that with the right hand portion of the figure. In this case, the same supplier has both parts, so only one communication would be necessary. The increase in Part A would be offset by the decrease in Part B, so the supplier's resources could still be fully utilized because the production envelope would remain unchanged. This is the key to achieving both flexibility and productivity at the same time.

Small Incremental Changes

Mix-change instructions to a JIT supplier should be expected frequently, but each one must be a small increment of the monthly total. The idea is to eliminate shock waves in the network and to replace them

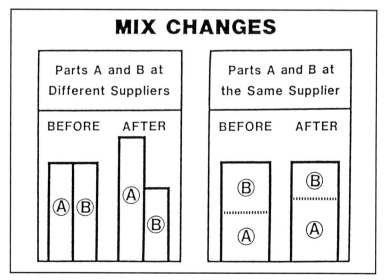

Figure 12-4

with *ripples of change.* It extends the variable flow concept of manufacturing to the entire supply network so outside suppliers can have the same advantages as inside departments.

This is where pull signals become so important. Envision your current purchase order change system and imagine how much paperwork would be required to make small changes every day. It would never "play." You'd have to hire the "Pharaoh's army" to do it. Even an automated releasing system would be burdened with this many changes. Yet, by using pull signals, daily and even hourly changes can be transmitted without any administrative intervention. (If you skipped over Chapter 11 because you weren't particularly interested in "production control," this would be a good time to go back and read it. The Pull System is also the mechanism used for JIT supplier change control.)

Timely Communications

A JIT customer has the same responsibility to communicate with its supplier-partners as they do. For all the efforts to smooth production and protect the envelope, "hitches" are going to happen from time to time. Immediate notification of plant disruptions, temporary shut-down plans or anticipated engineering changes will at least give the supplier an opportunity to make adjustments. It makes it clear that the supplier is really considered a member of the family.

Similarly, by sharing future plans with the suppliers the customer can give them valuable visibility to help guide their capital investments and technology acquisitions. They don't need the intimate details of the five-year business plan, but overall volume projections and major product revampings would certainly help. Closer in, a "peek" at the planned orders in the MRP system will provide a more detailed outlook over a broader horizon than the supplier usually sees. That's because the customer's cumulative leadtime is much longer than the supplier's delivery leadtime. These projections aren't "promises." They are *plans* being shared with a partner. This sharing of information will also help forge an even stronger partnership.

JIT PURCHASING CHALLENGE

The full benefits of JUST-IN-TIME won't be seen until it is extended throughout the supplier network. Only then will a real closed loop system become a reality. Improved customer service (responding to "exact customer demand") coupled with lower plant costs and inventory investment (the elimination of waste) will be optimized when the entire network is integrated, as shown in Figure 12-5. By now, you have seen how the "theoretical ideal' of linking internal processes to the "outside world" can be achieved in very practical terms. The purchasing function can't do it alone but must assume the leadership role.

Today's supply base must be made aware of your intentions to move toward JIT customer-supplier partnerships and "sold" on the idea. To do that, you'll have to help them understand what JIT is all about. A new supplier qualification process will have to be developed and implemented. The role of the buyer is going to change dramatically from the traditional one. It is going to be a major undertaking that will take years to accomplish. But, it will be well worth the effort because the "bottom line" contribution will be as great, if not greater, than all the shop improvements put together.

Communicating Intentions

If you plan to establish a JIT supply network and are willing to enter into customer-supplier partnerships, the first thing you have to do is alert the present supply base of your intentions. A "nice" letter won't do it. Many of the suppliers won't even know what you're talking about. (It's taken hundreds of pages to describe JIT in this book.) Besides, if you're serious about getting into "personal" relationships with JIT suppliers, there's no better place to start than at the beginning.

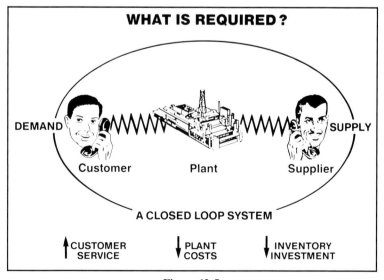

Figure 12-5

You'll need to organize and conduct a series of conferences with those suppliers to explain your new direction face-to-face. I would suggest you restrict the attendance at these meetings to chief operating officers (plus a key aide or two) from each supplier location you deal with. As different as these ideas are, there's no way a sales representative will be able to convey the full meaning of your intentions to the people "back home." You'll need policy makers there.

At the meeting, you should explain what it is you're trying to do, why you're doing it, what will be expected of your supplier-partners, what you will do in return, how partners will be selected, and what the timetable will be. You might as well be "up front" with them about the fact that your supply base is going to shrink as new partners are signed up. With this perspective, the suppliers can consider their options.

Educating Suppliers

One of the best things you can do at your supplier meetings is to show them what you have done in your own plant. Seeing is not only believing but also the key to understanding. If you don't have anything to show them yet, it may be a bit premature to start building your JIT supplier network. You can, however, still let them know of your intentions for the long-run.

In a case like that, you can hold a JIT training session for the suppliers. My firm has conducted many JIT seminars for supplier groups to "kick off" such programs. The operating executives who normally "don't have the time" to attend a training seminar will do so when "invited" by an important customer. Once they understand what JIT is all about and how serious you are about implementing it, the bridge to the rest of the "players" at the supplier location will be in place.

Later, when the partnership is established in principle, you will undoubtedly have to send some people to help the suppliers get their own internal training programs underway. They, in turn, have to assume the responsibility of training their suppliers. And so it will go, until the entire network is converted to JUST-IN-TIME supply.

Qualifying Partners

Deciding which of several suppliers is going to become the single-source supplier-partner for an entire family of parts is a major undertaking. It will require a thorough process, carefully followed by a multi-disciplined evaluation team. Purchasing will lead the team, which should include representatives from quality, process engineering and production or material control as a minimum. Using the list of Supplier Issues as a starting point, the team will visit the supplier and evaluate it, not as a vendor, but as a potential partner.

You can't do everything at once, so you'll be tempted to begin with your "A" suppliers. That's fine, if they are receptive to the message delivered at your supplier meetings. On the other hand, some "B" suppliers will express a sincere interest to "give it a try," and it's a lot easier to start the learning process with a willing partner. Once the "bugs" are worked out and you've got it down to a "science," you'll have better luck "courting" the more reluctant suppliers.

Not every supplier is going to sign up, at least not at first. You may have a key supplier, say in the primary metals business, that "flat-out refuses" to change anything. That's an exception, albeit an important one, that you'll have to contend with the "old" way while you build the rest of your partnerships. As more suppliers come on board, that exception is going to be a "thorn in your side," and you'll be motivated to do something about it. You may find a brand new supplier in that industry who is willing to try something new. You could even end up designing that material out of your products. The point is, if you think creatively, you'll be able to overcome even the most difficult obstacles, so don't let the exceptions discourage you.

New Role For The Buyer

A popular misconception about the purchasing profession is that "a buyer is a person who sends out requests for quotation to three sources of supply and then goes to lunch with the low bidder!" As one who spent a number of years in the field, I consider that to be a "bad rap." What a traditional buyer *has been,* however, is a sourcing expert. Whatever you needed, that person knew where to get it and at a good price. Once a JIT supply network has been established, the need for sourcing experts will diminish. It will be replaced by a growing need for *supplier experts* in the purchasing department.

With the vast number of suppliers most companies have, it is difficult for a buyer to really know very much about any of them. In a JIT network, each buyer will have fewer suppliers to work with, but will have to know them intimately. The buyer will have to visit each supplier to understand exactly how the suppliers' processes work. He or she is going to be the interface for all supplier cost improvement projects and will put this knowledge to work when negotiating the periodic price decreases. That's an exciting new role.

The best part, in my mind, is that this kind of buyer will have a much better perspective of genuine cost reduction. No more should a five-cent reduction in the purchase price result in a ten-cent increase in manufacturing cost. Process understanding and involvement will make the difference.

Bottom Line Contribution

In most companies, purchased materials and services account for *more than half of the sales dollar.* A typical income statement is shown in Figure 12-6. Up to now, all of the JIT improvements discussed have addressed the less-than-50% portion of the sales dollar represented by "inside" costs. Purchasing savings can exceed all the rest put together.

For the example shown, consider the impact of a five-percent reduction in purchased material cost. Five percent of 50% is two and a half percent, which would drop straight to the bottom line. Adding that to the 10% profit shown would raise the total to 12.5%, which is a *25% increase in profit* (2.5/10). Try this with your own company income statement. The potential improvement is incredible.

SUMMARY

Once internal JIT manufacturing is underway, it must be extended to the supplier network to obtain the full benefit of the strategy. JIT

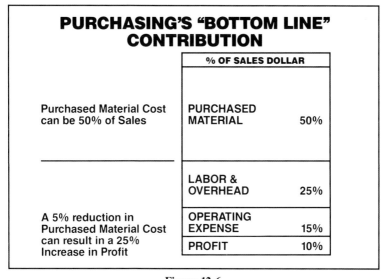

Figure 12-6

supplier relations encompass a new set of values, many of which are *completely contrary to present practices.* They call for *"long-term* partnerships with single-source suppliers who provide *certified quality* material while continuously *reducing costs."* While different, these values are necessary to forge the customer-supplier partnerships that will make JIT supply work. JUST-IN-TIME can't be completely effective until the suppliers are brought into the "family."

Like a marriage, a partnership is intended to be monogamous and to last forever. With "all the eggs in one basket," the relationship must be based on mutual trust. If it goes sour and a "divorce" ensues, it is unlikely that those two partners will enter into a new union again.

JIT suppliers must be carefully selected. It usually requires a multidisciplined team to make that determination. Critical supplier issues include quality assurance, responsiveness, continuous improvement, frequent small lot shipments, timely communications and JIT production by the supplier.

Supplier consolidation has been underway in some industries for a number of years. Shrinking the supplier base to about one-third of its former size seems to be the typical target. With fewer suppliers and more business for each of the remaining suppliers, the stakes are getting higher every year.

There are a number of customer prerequisites that should be in place *before* trying to forge a JIT supplier-partnership. The customer is the one who is asking the supplier to change the old arrangement, who will first benefit from the new partnership, and since it wields the initial leverage, must understand that a one-sided relationship is not a partnership. Prerequisites include long-term commitments, a stable production plan, family of parts sourcing, small incremental changes and timely communications.

The elimination of waste will be optimized only when the entire network is integrated. The purchasing function can't do it alone but must assume the leadership role. The challenge is to communicate those intentions, educate the suppliers and qualify new partners. This will entail a new role for the buyer which will make a significant contribution to the bottom line.

You can't tap that gold mine, though, until you get your own "ducks" lined up. Continuous price reductions are dependent on supplier cost reductions which, in turn, are dependent upon your implementation of JUST-IN-TIME. That's the starting point.

TRANSPORT
INNOVATION

CHAPTER 13

*"Transport innovation is a new way
to achieve frequent, predictable delivery
of small quantities to the point of use
at the lowest total cost."*

Transport innovation is the execution portion of JUST-IN-TIME purchasing. It is the physical linkage between the inside and the outside processes. Of all the aspects of JIT, there are probably more misconceptions about transportation than any other. Respected publications have raised all sorts of concerns about the "extra costs" of JUST-IN-TIME delivery and speculated that they could offset all the benefits derived from JIT production.

This might be true if all the options were confined to traditional approaches like commercial carriage. However, when ingenuity is applied to this field, just as it has been to all the other parts of the production network, it opens new vistas for continuous improvement. The first step is to overcome any preconceptions so you can take a fresh look at transportation from a totally new perspective.

JIT TRANSPORT PERSPECTIVE

Perspective can only be gained when you take a step back to see the whole "forest," not just some of the "trees." Typically, transportation has been viewed by manufacturing industries as "putting products on a truck, train, plane or bus." But that's just one "tree" in the overall effort to get the right material to the right place at the right time. JUST-IN-TIME transport issues include *every step that is required to move material from the **hand** of the last value adder at a supplier location to the **hand** of the first value adder at a customer location.*

This requires an examination of the *"what,"* the *"who"* and the *"how"* issues of material movement. The *"what"* turns out to be much broader in scope than traditional transportation. The *"who"* will entail the establishment of JIT transport-partners and new working relationships. The *"how"* will require that traditional transportation *"givens"* be *"retired"* and replaced by new concepts and methods.

Wider Scope

When you look at the dictionary definition of *transportation,* "the act or means of conveyance from one place to another," it's fairly broad in scope. Historically, though, the real-world application has been much narrower. In recognition of this, many practitioners in the field, including professional societies, have changed their names to include *logistics,* a term borrowed from the military. However, that word is defined as the "procurement, transportation, maintenance and supply of people, equipment and facilities," which makes it a bit too broad for this topic as it applies of JUST-IN-TIME.

What we're concerned here is every step in the process between the moment the last value adder at a supplier location finishes working on a product to the time the first value adder at the customer location picks it up to add more value. I've chosen the word, *transport,* which means "to carry from one place to another," to describe this JIT segment. It is intended to be broader than traditional transportation (which focuses on external conveyance) but narrower than logistics (which includes procurement and staffing).

JIT transport is a process that starts at a supplier location and ends at a customer location. A typical sequence of events for LTL (less than full truck-load) shipments could include the following:

By the supplier. . .
• Move material to packaging
• Package
• Store
• Pick for shipment
∗ Move to dock
• Palletize
∗ Load carrier

By the carrier. . .
• Move load to local terminal
• Unload and consolidate by destination
• Reload
• Move to enroute breakbulk terminal
• Unload and consolidate by destination
• Reload
• Move load to destination city
• Unload and consolidate by customer

- Reload
* Move load to customer location
- Drop trailer at customer "bullpen," or
  drop trailer at customer dock, or
  wait for customer to unload trailer
* Return empty trailer to terminal

By the customer...
- Move trailer from bullpen to dock
* Unload
- Move empty trailer to bullpen
- Receive material into inventory
- Inspect material
- Move to stores
- Unload, store and record location
- Pull from stores upon demand
* Move to assigned floor location
- Remove expendables (cardboard, wood, etc.)
- Move expendables to trash area
- Compress trash
- Load trash truck

There are 32 steps in this process. Yours may be shorter, but it could just as easily be longer. Most of those steps are a waste. Only the six with asterisks are absolutely necessary to get material from the supplier value adder to the customer value adder. The others just add time and cost to the process.

Some of the steps, like terminal consolidations, are taken to optimize local performance or because they are required by the "system." Transport innovation is aimed at eliminating as many of those steps as possible by providing a *new way to achieve frequent, predictable deliveries of small quantities to the point of use at the lowest total cost.* When all of the parties involved work together to optimize the entire process, not just parts of it, significant reductions in cost will accrue and delivery times will decrease dramatically.

Transport-Partners

JUST-IN-TIME transport innovation requires that all three parties, the supplier, the carrier and the customer, work together more closely than ever before. With three parties, communications are going to be more complex unless a "super-simple" system is established. As shown in Figure 13-1, control of the total process is shared and a breakdown by any one of the three can stop the flow. To be effective, each must be a partner in a common "cause."

That means transport partnerships will have to be forged, just like the supplier partnerships discussed in Chapter 12. You will have fewer carriers than you do today, each will be a single source for a "family" of business, and they will be treated as a part of your operation, as though they were "in-house" carriers.

Frequent, predictable deliveries of small quantities to the points of use are different parameters than those established for carriers in the past. A different relationship will be needed to achieve them. Quality assurance, responsiveness, continuous improvement and close communications will be key issues for transport partner selection. Long-term, exclusive contracts, stable schedules, small incremental changes and equally close communications will be required from the customer. This partnership, too, must be a "win-win" situation for mutual prosperity.

New Concepts

When you consider a total process, it often turns out that optimizing one segment of it can be detrimental to the total. By the same token, sub-optimizing one segment can often improve the total. With three partners involved in the JUST-IN-TIME transport process, each must

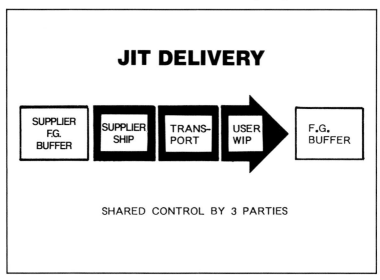

Figure 13-1

understand the objectives of the whole and how their part is expected to support the total process. That's how a new perspective is gained and new concepts can be introduced.

A very large part of the total transport process is containerization. Huge amounts of cost, far beyond purchase costs, can be eliminated by replacing expendables with *reusable containers.* To support JIT flow manufacturing, *frequent, time-of-day deliveries* will be mandatory. This will entail not only a redefinition of "on-time," but will also require new types of equipment to make it feasible. Traffic at both the supplier and the customer plants will increase dramatically, creating a demand for *rapid load/unload capabilities.*

Transport partnerships will require much closer cooperation and communication than is reasonable to expect from traditional commercial carriage. Instead, *dedicated contract carriage* will be employed. These relationships can also be expanded to apply innovative solutions to seemingly insurmountable problems like *overcoming distance issues.*

There is no end to the new ways that can be implemented when "old" issues are viewed from a new perspective. The highlighted concepts in the preceding paragraphs are just the nucleus to get you started, but they do provide a solid foundation for JIT transport. Let's take a look at each of them in more depth.

REUSABLE CONTAINERS

In the ideal JIT network, each value adder hands completed work to the next value adder, one-at-a-time. When distances or production lot sizes make that impossible, completed work must be accumulated in containers which can be transported to the next value adder. Historically, those containers were usually disposable devices because it was unthinkable to pay shipping costs to return the containers. While concentrating on the narrow issue of shipping costs, many people overlooked the huge initial costs, the handling costs, the breakage costs and the disposal costs associated with expendable containers.

The Cost of Cardboard

Cardboard and wood containers are not cheap. Many companies know the unit cost for their expendable packaging (to five decimal places) but don't know what the aggregate costs are. For larger plants, it can be millions of dollars per year. There are many hidden costs like those incurred by the supplier to repack the material from internal containers to cardboard boxes. These end up as part of the material unit cost. This extra handling also provides more opportunities to damage the material.

Expendable containers often fail to provide sufficient protection to the material they are transporting. How many times have you seen boxes in your receiving department that looked like the one in Figure 13-2? Damaged material will show up in scrap or rework. Even if compensation is received from the shipper, the customer will incur indirect costs just to handle the problem and process the necessary paperwork. The supplier will often have to "eat" the costs required to expedite replacements. In a JIT shop it could also stop production.

Inside the customer plant, cardboard containers and packing material introduce clutter to the shop floor, foiling housekeeping efforts and impairing visibility management. Empty boxes and salvage material must be collected, removed from the floor and disposed of, requiring more customer indirect costs. These show up as plant overhead and are rarely tied back to material costs.

When all those costs are accumulated, the result can be staggering. My firm did a study for the Ford Motor Company, Wixom, plant in 1984 that came up with a $6,000,000 annual figure ($1 million of which were disposal costs). Two years later, a follow-up study by Ford people increased that estimate to between $8 and $10 million every year. That's a lot of opportunity for improvement. You'll find similar opportunities in your system when you look at the total transport process.

Figure 13-2

Available Reusables

Reusable containers are available in almost every conceivable shape and size, so most of your needs can be met without any tooling expenditures. The simplest of these is a *plastic tub* that is person movable when full of material. Some of them come with hinged or snap-on lids to protect the material during transit, as shown in Figure 13-3. Others are designed to stack so the bottom of one serves as the top for the one below it. (When rotated 180 degrees, they will nest together so empty containers will require less space than full ones.) Most have slots molded in them so permanent dividers can be inserted to separate the parts inside. The vast majority of requirements can be met by the plastic tub category of container. Even low-cost items, like hardware, that are usually "bulk packed" are better off in a reusable container. (Think about what dumping a carton of bolts does to carefully machined threads.)

Larger, ungainly parts can be shipped on plastic pallets with reusable pallet dividers that are molded to conform to the shape of the parts. They afford much better protection for the parts and will also nest together for return shipment. When large, pallet-size tubs are absolutely necessary, they can be obtained in high-strength plastic at only one-quarter the weight of comparable steel tubs. Many of them can be collapsed to about one-third of their original size. (The value of the nesting or collapsing features of these containers is not so much to save space on return shipments, as will be shown later, as it is to save

Figure 13-3

space in the staging areas at your plant where the "empties" will have to be marshaled for return to the suppliers.)

Minimum Variety

Simplification is the byword of JUST-IN-TIME. The fewer types and sizes of reusable containers in your system, the less complicated it will be to manage. As always, the ideal JIT number is *one*. It may not seem feasible for your operation, but it certainly is possible.

Figure 13-4 shows an incoming material staging area for a JIT company that actually has only one size of reusable container in its system. Empty containers are accumulated on the roller conveyer in the right side of the figure. When a supplier drops off six containers of material, he picks up six empty containers. There is no paperwork involved.

The price paid for container simplicity is breaking the cardinal rule of the transportation industry, which is, *"Thou shalt not ship air!."* Notice that the containers of material in the lower part of the figure are not full. How then, you may be wondering, is it possible to reduce transport costs when the "cube" volume per shipment is not maximized? The answer has two parts. First, remember that the objective is to reduce the total cost of the transport process, even if one segment has to be de-optimized. However, we're not going to stop there. There is also a better way to ship when reusable containers are employed, which will be covered in the Contract Carriage section.

Figure 13-4

Maximum Flexibility

You should not only have a minimum variety of container types, but they should also be capable of being "mixed and matched." With more frequent shipments, there will be smaller quantities of each part number per shipment. A pallet, however, will still be a unit load for material handling. The best way to solve this dilemma is to be able to mix different part numbers, and therefore different size containers, on the same pallet. It will only work if the containers are designed that way. At least one organization, the Automotive Industry Action Group (AIAG), has already developed container standards to meet this need.

Whatever variety of reusable containers you employ, they'll all have one thing in common. The last value adder at the supplier location will place the material in the container and no one else will touch it before the first value adder at the customer location does. With all the superfluous handling and damage potential removed, the transport process can concentrate on moving the full container to its destination in the fastest, most cost-effective way possible.

FREQUENT TIME-OF-DAY DELIVERIES

Time is a critical JIT transport issue, not only because leadtimes are so important to flow production, but also because longer delivery cycles will require more reusable containers in the system "float." When the cycles are short, you should be able to buy all the reusable containers you need for less than you now spend for cardboard in one year. On the other hand, you could go "broke" trying to support a bloated system with reusable containers.

With a minimum number of containers in the system and keeping in mind the need to maintain a flow of material into the customer plant, frequent deliveries will have to be made on a very tight schedule. This literally means receipts at a specific customer location on specific days at specific times during those days. For many in the transportation field, that is not just a new thought, it's a *radical* idea.

The "Cube" Mentality

The cost to move a trailer, a boxcar or a cargohold from one point to another is a known, fixed number in the transportation business. The more material that can be "stuffed" into the enclosure, the lower will be the cost per unit shipped. As a result, much time, energy and talent is expended to fill the available cubic volume (the "cube") for every trip.

In the trucking industry, the first emphasis is to ship a full trailer of material from a point of origin to the final destination. Full truckload shipments (TL) are priced very competitively. When less than a truckload (LTL) is shipped by one customer, the trucking company tries to combine it with other partial loads to fill up the truck. To do that, a series of consolidation terminals, with transit "legs" between them, is used (much like airline "hops" between major cities). At each terminal, trailers are unloaded and reloaded to maximize the cube volume for each leg. To the trucker, the extra costs associated with the terminal operations are more than offset by the fuller utilization of trailer capacities and the higher prices that can be charged for LTL shipments.

The drawback to the customer, besides the higher prices, is that LTL shipments take longer to reach their destination. It's much like the difference between taking a plane trip that makes several stops on its way to your destination instead of taking a non-stop. To further compound the problem, the traffic in and out of a terminal is subject to many fluctuations (again, much like an airport) which can delay outbound shipments. One thing you can be fairly certain of is that a trailer will be held as long as possible, even if it means a schedule delay, in order to fill it up. Is it any wonder, then, that LTL deliveries are usually approximations? There must be a better way.

Learning From History

Back in the days when I was in purchasing, we used to schedule our incoming material with "week of. . ." dates, hoping it would arrive by Friday. JIT deliveries, by contrast, must be *precise and predictable* because any provisions for contingencies would be considered a waste. Not only must it arrive on the right *day* but also at the correct *hour.* This idea, while new to some and inconceivable to others, is not new at all.

In the early sixties, I participated in a plant tour of the Carling Brewery in Baltimore, Maryland. The tour was educational and the free samples were even better, but what really intrigued me was the scheduling system they used for incoming trucks. The plant had no space to store either empty bottles or full ones, so each inbound truck (carrying empty bottles) was assigned a precise arrival time *to the minute.* After the empties were unloaded, the truck was reloaded with full cases of beer and was on its way in a matter of minutes. The system was based on frequent, predictable deliveries, with no provisions for contingencies, and it was working before anybody in this country ever heard of JUST-IN-TIME production.

Consolidating On Wheels

Carling broke with traditional concepts because it had a particular need that could not be met by them. JIT has specific needs that cannot be met by traditional concepts either. In order to ship smaller amounts more frequently to precise schedules, something better than traditional LTL must be found to avoid the extra handling, cost and time delays. The solution that seems to be working best is to consolidate on wheels.

Side-loading trucks, like the one shown in Figure 13-5, (a friend calls this one a "DeLorean") are used to pick up material from several suppliers for delivery to one customer. Since any part of the load can be reached from either side, both material and empty containers can be mixed in any combination at any time. The size of the vehicle varies according to the volume and distances to be traveled. General Motors, for example, is using large side-loading trailers (made by Fruehauf) to transport foam products and soft-sided trailers (made by Tautliner) to ship tires one way and new cars in the other direction.

In some cases, especially for nearby suppliers, the best bet turns out to be direct delivery by a supplier-owned small truck or van. I know of instances where a supplier was asked to deliver material to a consolidation terminal and had to pass right by the customer plant to do it! That happened, of course, because one segment of the transport process was trying to optimize its individual portion. When the cost of the entire JIT transport process is considered, direct supplier deliveries

Figure 13-5

begin to make a lot of sense, especially for small quantities.

Regular Schedules

Predictable also means repeatable. Without uniform scheduling by the customer, as discussed in Chapter 10, there is little likelihood of making JIT transport work. With more frequent deliveries, truck traffic at the customer plant is going to increase dramatically. A smooth flow of incoming vehicles will be necessary to handle such a volume. That can't be done by picking up the phone at the last minute to order a truck, or concentrating deliveries early in the month or "bunching" inputs on Mondays. A regular schedule, based on smooth demands for material, is the foundation for predictable deliveries.

The Chrysler Corporation has been providing such schedules to its assembly plant suppliers since the early eighties. Nearby suppliers are given specific delivery times several times each day. Even distant suppliers are delivering daily at specific times. In every case, however, the volume per delivery is roughly the same (small incremental changes) and the schedule horizon is sufficiently long to cover the transportation time. A Bendix plant in Virginia was able to make daily shipments to an assembly plant in Windsor, Ontario (a distance of almost a thousand miles) from this kind of schedule.

RAPID LOAD/UNLOAD

Smoothing the flow of heavier inbound traffic is only half of the "battle." Unless those vehicles are "turned around" and cleared from the area as quickly as possible, you could end up with a real "traffic jam" at your plant. Therefore, deliveries must be thought of not just as arrival times but also as departure times. This gives rise to the concept of *delivery windows*. Rapid loading and unloading during these windows can be enhanced by point-of-use doors, driver self-unloading and some innovative equipment.

Point-Of-Use Doors

No matter how many truck wells you have at your plant today, it's probably an insufficient number to handle the higher traffic volume you'll experience with JIT transport. Besides, those wells are usually in one corner of the building, which means long travel distances for your material handlers to get the incoming material to the point where it will be used. If you're going to add more receiving points, they might as well be close to the material point-of-use.

The idea is to strategically place point-of-use doors around the periphery of plant, as illustrated in Figure 13-6. When material is unloaded, it can be placed in an assigned staging location near the door or taken directly to the point of use. (Remember, the supplier is shipping certified quality material, so no receiving inspection should be needed.) By getting the delivery truck as close as possible to the point-of-use, in-plant material handling distances are minimized. In fact, I have even seen cases where the delivery truck was driven inside the plant and the material was unloaded right at the user workcenter.

The new doors should be simple, roll-up types. Truck wells are very expensive and aren't necessary with side-loading vehicles. They can easily be unloaded from ground level with a standard fork-lift truck.

Initial reactions to this idea are almost always negative. Concerns range all the way from the aesthetic impact on the plant appearance to fears that these uncontrolled access points could lead to major thefts by "outsiders." Those concerns can be overcome by a recognition of the tremendous cost advantages of point-of-use delivery. In addition, the trucker will be a transport-partner, a member of the family that we need to trust.

The Ford Motor Company assembly plant in Wixom, Michigan went through this "soul-searching" exercise back in 1984, when they first considered point-of-use doors. At that time the proposal was to add eleven

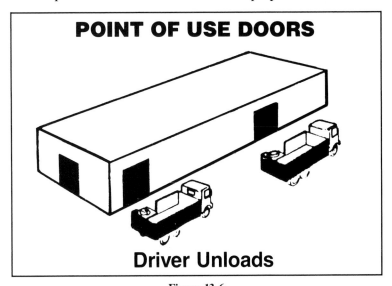

POINT OF USE DOORS

Driver Unloads

Figure 13-6

of them at very key locations. They did it and it worked so well they expanded to 24 doors. That, in turn, led to 48 doors. They'd like to add even more but are beginning to wonder if there will be enough remaining wall space to support the roof!

Driver Unloading

The additional JIT deliveries to all of those point-of-use doors could call for more material handling at your plant, even though some of it would be offset by shorter in-plant travel distances. However, that would add cost to the system, which is contrary to the JIT principle of eliminating waste. On the other hand, there are many opportunities to cut those costs when the process is examined with an eye toward waste elimination.

When the material handler waits for the truck driver to arrive and position the vehicle at the loading dock, that's idle time — a waste. When the driver waits while the material handler unloads the truck, it's more waste. Only one person is busy at a time, so only one person should be needed in total. The driver is already in the truck when it arrives, so he or she is the logical candidate to unload it.

The driver will park the truck at the assigned door, unload the specified material, take it to the assigned drop location in the plant, collect empty containers, load them in the truck and drive away, with *no action required by customer personnel.* If material handling equipment is needed, the driver will take it from a customer pool and return it when the job is done. (Licensing and insurance issues will be handled the same way they are for plant employees.) This is, without a doubt, the most cost-effective way to transfer material from the supplier to the hand of the value adder at the customer plant, and it's being done every day.

That is not to say that drivers, especially Teamsters, won't object to their new role at the beginning. After all, they're being asked to do something that wasn't in their job description in the past, at least not in the industrial sector. However, the food industry has been doing it for a long time. Watch the procedure at your own supermarket some morning. As each beverage, bread and milk truck pulls in, the driver unloads it, takes the products into the store, places them on the appropriate shelf or in the cooler, removes outdated products, collects empty containers, prepares a delivery receipt for the store manager's signature, and even collects money when it's a COD delivery. That flexible worker is usually a Teamster and that process has been followed for more than 50 years! The precedent has long been set. People are just beginning to recognize that this is the way of the future for industrial companies as well.

Innovative Equipment

As was mentioned earlier, the easiest trucks to unload are side-loaders. However, there aren't that many of them around yet; and until they become the "norm," you'll have to contend with the traditional end-loading trailer. There are a number of innovative approaches that can be applied to utilize these trailers during the transition period.

End-loading trailers and ground-level point-of-use doors are not compatible. However, you can employ portable ramps, like the one shown in Figure 13-7. (Notice the simple doors in the background.) They are relatively inexpensive and still give you a lot of flexibility.

Another way to get more mileage out of end-loaders is to use "truck strippers" at your existing truck wells. These hydraulic devices reach into the trailer (under the pallets) all the way to the nose and extract the entire load onto a roller conveyer in one movement. They're more expensive but provide a way to substantially increase the traffic at a limited number of wells.

Yet another innovation can be "borrowed" from the beverage industry. They equip their trailers with roller tracks on the floor (usually two tracks for each pallet width) and a hydraulic lifter on the trailer nose. When the truck is being loaded, the nose is pulled down so gravity can

Figure 13-7

be employed to allow a person to "walk" a pallet into the trailer instead of using a fork-lift. This is not only fast, but also reduces the damage that often occurs when trying to maneuver a fork-lift in a 40 foot trailer. At the destination, the lifter pushes the trailer nose up so the pallets can slide out, as if they were in a magazine.

These were just a few examples. There are many ways to use innovative equipment to overcome what might otherwise seem to be insurmountable obstacles. And that's just the point. Don't let anyone tell you that JIT transport might work for somebody else but won't apply to your company because of your "unique" situation. The chances are high that somebody else has already faced and solved a very similar problem.

DEDICATED CONTRACT CARRIAGE

The concepts of reusable containers, frequent time-of-day deliveries and rapid load/unload were introduced first to set the stage for the development of transport-partner relationships that really work. To appreciate how the new approach, called *dedicated contract carriage,* can benefit everyone involved, first consider traditional commercial carriage.

Eliminating Traditional Wastes

Using commercial carriage to transport material has a lot of similarities to riding in a taxicab. The cab owner has made an investment in equipment and people, and is burning up fuel while the cab "cruises" in search of a fare. When you step into the taxi, you're going to pay not only for the time and distance required to get you to your destination but also for a share of the time when nobody was using the cab. It's the same when you call a trucking company terminal and order a truck to be at your dock at three o'clock in the afternoon. That is only possible if the vehicle was idle at the time, waiting for a "fare." Commercial carriage prices are higher, therefore, because higher investments must be made to respond to unknown and erratic demand. It's the price one has to pay to get "sudden service."

On the other hand, when demand is predictable and smooth, regular, repeatable transport routes can be established, making it a totally different "ball game." That's when *contract carriage* becomes an extremely attractive alternative to traditional practices. In this mode, you will lease a truck and driver to pick up and deliver material along routes that you will design. With a long-term contract, your transport-partner can purchase the type of equipment you need (like side-loading trailers). With known costs for consistent requirements and less risk for the trucker, prices will be lower than you can imagine; yet both partners will "win" because the wastes of the traditional system will have been eliminated.

Designing Closed Loops

The customer designs closed-loop transportation systems to take advantage of the repetitive nature of the supply plan. A typical loop is shown in Figure 13-8. Here, the leased truck arrives at the customer plant first thing in the morning to load empty containers. It then proceeds to Supplier A, where it arrives at a specified time to drop off empties and load today's shipment. It then proceeds to Supplier B, where the same process is repeated, and finally to Supplier C, where empties are dropped and today's shipment is loaded. The full truck then returns to the customer plant to unload. Due to its repeatability, this type of transportation loop is often called a "milk run."

The ideal situation is to have every day for a given closed loop the same as every other day. Many times, though, current volumes won't support that frequency. In those cases, it may be possible to design loops where Mondays, Wednesdays and Fridays are run along one route while Tuesdays and Thursdays are on a different one. At the very least, every Monday should be like every other Monday, every Tuesday like every other Tuesday, etc.

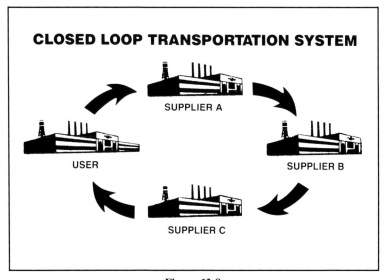

CLOSED LOOP TRANSPORTATION SYSTEM

SUPPLIER A

USER

SUPPLIER B

SUPPLIER C

Figure 13-8

Members Of The "Family"

A contract carriage transport-partner will even paint your company name on the side of the vehicle used to service the closed-loop transportation system. The regular driver, who is on a regular route, will become an extension of your own company as daily contacts are made with suppliers. Many service companies have long recognized that the best salesperson is a familiar face. United Parcel Service (UPS) is a good example. When "Charlie" walks in the door asking, "Any UPS today?" he *is* UPS to you. When he's on vacation or ill and a replacement walks in, the first inclination is to ask, "Where's Charlie today?"

The value of this human interaction cannot be overstated. Remember, these are the people who will be entering your plant to "do their thing" without any supervision by plant personnel. It requires a lot of mutual trust. While I'm quite familiar with the expression, "familiarity breeds contempt," it's also a fact of life that it is easier to trust a familiar face. In addition, it's harder for one human being to "fleece" another when they have to look each other in the eye every day.

OVERCOMING THE DISTANCE ISSUE

Many people believe that a supplier must be located right "next door" to a customer for JUST-IN-TIME delivery to work. There's no doubt that it helps, but it isn't mandatory. The key issue is not geography. It's the amount of leadtime a customer can give a supplier, in relation to the necessary transportation time. If the leadtime is long enough, distance is not a problem and closed-loop combinations can be employed. If the leadtime is less than the transportation time, it's a big problem, but all is not necessarily lost. There are some innovative approaches, like JIT process centers, that can still save the business even if they aren't "perfect" solutions.

Geography Versus Leadtime

My first exposure to the geography issue came when I was studying the JIT system used by Jidosha Kiki Corporation (JKC) in Japan. They had only one plant complex, located in the northwestern suburbs of Tokyo, yet they made frequent deliveries to every one of the eleven vehicle manufacturers in the country. Fourteen deliveries per day were made to Toyota, located some 250 miles "down the road" near Nagoya, and daily shipments were made to Mazda, 650 miles away in Hiroshima. This certainly wasn't the typical "supplier next door to the customer" scenario I had heard so much about before going there. The travel time for those JKC trucks was very slow by U.S. standards. The road system doesn't compare to our interstate highways, it has to follow a mountain chain that forms the center of the island, and is clogged bumper-to-bumper with trucks (the people travel mostly on the "bullet train"). In fact, a truck on a U.S. road can travel two miles in the same amount of time that JKC could travel one mile. When you translate that to American geography, as shown in Figure 13-9, a mile-for-mile equivalent from the city of Chicago would cover a substantial portion of the industrial heartland of our country. A time-for-time equivalent (1300 miles) includes all of the continental U.S. but four states and parts of two others, plus most of southern Canada. Distance is not a "big deal" so long as there is sufficient notification leadtime to travel that distance.

Mixed Mode Transport

Closed-loop transportation systems, or milk runs, can be combined with long-haul carriers to provide effective mixed-mode transport. For example, the NUMMI plant in Fremont, California, gets a high percentage of its domestic parts from the midwest. A series of milk runs collects material from the suppliers, and it is consolidated in a trailer at a terminal. The trailer is then hauled to Chicago, where it is transferred to a "piggy-back" rail car and transported to California. Upon arrival

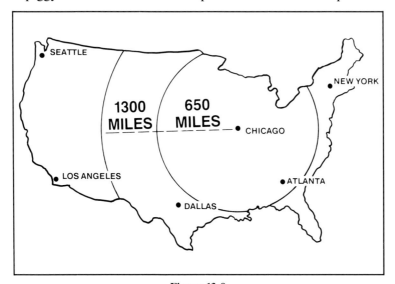

Figure 13-9

there, a tractor hauls the trailer the rest of the way to the plant. A stylized version of this combination is shown in Figure 13-10.

You may be surprised to hear that rail transportation can be employed in a JUST-IN-TIME network, especially with the jurisdictional, political and work-rules problems faced by that industry. There's no doubt that those things make it harder to establish a JIT transport partnership with a rail carrier. Yet, by meeting the preconditions and schedule stability discussed earlier, others are indeed incorporating rail as part of JIT delivery.

One of those companies is SnoKist Growers, a Yakima, Washington food cooperative that ships local fresh and canned fruit throughout the United States. Their transport partnership with Burlington Northern Railroad enables them to ship boxcars of fruit to any one of twelve participating independent public warehouses located throughout the railroad's service territory. There, the boxcar is unloaded and portions of it can be picked up by the customer or trucked to the customer. SnoKist claims it can "make its products available to market within 24 to 48 hours and deliver within a half-hour window." Besides improved customer service, SnoKist has lowered its transportation costs. The bottom line is that they are seeing a 40% sales increase in 1988 over the previous year.

JIT Process Center
There will be times when the customer notification leadtime has to

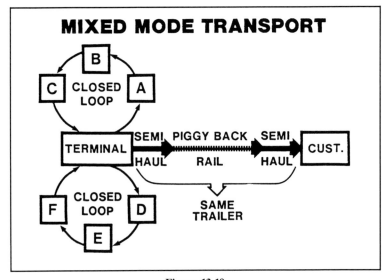

Figure 13-10

be shorter than the transportation time. The supplier will then have to consider two options:

1. Give up the business
2. Build a plant near the customer

The first is unthinkable if it's an important segment of the supplier's business and the second may be too expensive, although a number of companies have opted for this strategy. There is a third option, shown in Figure 13-11, called a JIT process center.

The strategy here is to move only the last operation of the process near the customer instead of building a new plant. It certainly isn't ideal because it introduces additional transport steps (the remote operation(s) and the shuttle service to the customer). On the other hand, it usually beats the first two options "hands down." In addition, the work done at a JIT process center can be done by a third party as part of the transport partnership agreement.

By shipping semi-finished units to the process center (which is located close to the customer), the supplier can comply with shorter notification leadtimes. This is especially advantageous when the final operation determines the finished part number, allowing the supplier to "assemble to order" in a flexible, responsive manner. The final operation can even be the sequencing of various finished units in a specific order as is being required by some customers in the auto and appliance industries today.

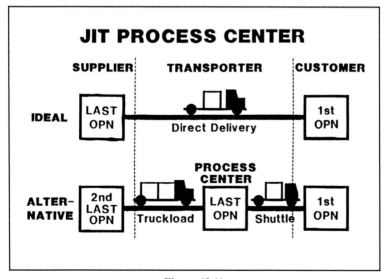

Figure 13-11

A JIT process center is usually established in leased space with a minimum of capital equipment or "high-tech" skills needed. It can be set up rapidly and at a relatively low cost, especially when compared to new plant construction. The key word here is *process*. It is not intended to be a warehouse. A process center should never have more than one to two days of inventory on hand.

For some suppliers, where the key issue is not so much transport leadtime as it is inability to respond to JIT schedules "back at the ranch," a process center can serve as an interim solution to keep the business. It is often faster and easier to set up a new operation with new concepts at a remote location. It is a way to "buy some time" until the manufacturing plant can be converted to JUST-IN-TIME production.

Delco Experience

The Delco Division of General Motors was one of the first companies in the U.S. to use a process center to compensate for inadequate transport leadtime. The division, located in Dayton, Ohio, had been a long-time supplier of strut components to the Oldsmobile assembly plant in Lansing, Michigan, some 240 miles away. However, when Oldsmobile introduced a new model vehicle, it decided to purchase modular strut assemblies and to bring them into the assembly plant in the precise sequence that finished cars were being assembled. That sequence wouldn't be known until the cars came out of the painting operation which was

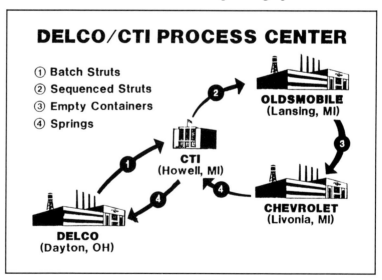

Figure 13-12

only seven hours before they were needed. Delco's dilemma was the potential for new business (assembling 128 varieties of modular struts) and a 240-mile distance problem.

Their solution, as shown in Figure 13-12, was to establish a JIT process center in Howell, Michigan. It was about 30 minutes away from the Oldsmobile plant and also about a half-hour away from the Chevrolet plant in Livonia, Michigan, where the springs for the struts were manufactured. A contract carrier, Customized Transportation, Inc. (CTI), was engaged to provide both the transportation and the JIT process center management.

Two closed-loop delivery systems were designed. The first tractor started at the process center with a trailer full of sequenced modular struts, delivered them to the Oldsmobile plant, picked up empty containers, dropped them off at Chevrolet, picked up full containers of springs, brought them back to the center, and dropped the full trailer in the process center yard. This was done four times a day. In the second loop, a tractor carried a trailer full of springs down to Delco and returned with containers of modular struts, one part number per container. Several vehicles were used for this loop.

Inside the process center, the containers of struts were arranged on the floor, by part number, much like a supermarket. Roughly every minute, Oldsmobile transmitted a requirement for a pair of modular struts to CTI. When 20 instructions (the container quantity) were accumulated, an operator with a towmotor pulling two containers (one for right-hand and one for left-hand struts) went up and down the aisles of parts, picking the designated ones and placing them in the correct location in each container. Verification stickers were placed on each strut and a part- location matrix was placed on the outside of the container. Full containers were then double checked for accuracy, staged and loaded on a trailer. Typically, they arrived at Oldsmobile about two hours before they were needed on the assembly line.

Delco's solution was far from ordinary. But, it took something that creative to keep important business that would otherwise have been lost. While it wasn't a "perfect" JIT transport situation, it was an outstanding compromise to meet conditions beyond their control. There is no limit to what can be done when innovation replaces conventional wisdom.

SUMMARY

JUST-IN-TIME transport is a process that includes every step required to move material from the hand of the last value adder at a supplier to the hand of the first value adder at a customer. When innovative concepts are applied to the total process instead of trying to optimize portions of it, frequent, predictable deliveries of small quantities of material to the point of use can be achieved at substantially lower total costs than by traditional methods. Transport partnerships with a smaller number of carriers will be necessary to make it happen.

Transport innovation includes the replacement of expendable packaging with reusable containers to simplify handling and to provide better protection to the transported material. Frequent, time-of-day deliveries will be made to the point-of-use at a customer plant to provide a flow of incoming material to match the flow of the customer's JIT production. Regular, repeatable schedules will be required from the customer to make this possible. Heavier traffic will demand rapid loading and unloading of vehicles within thirty to sixty-minute time windows. Drivers will unload their own trucks and innovative equipment, like side-loading trailers, will make the job easier.

Long-term, dedicated contract carriage will replace commercial carriage as the primary mode of transportation. The role of customer traffic personnel will change from commodity rate expertise and the ability to "get a truck" on demand to the design and management of closed-loop transportation systems to support JIT flow production. Long-distance issues will be handled by mixed-mode transport when there is enough notification leadtime and by JIT process centers when there isn't.

JIT transport innovation will relentlessly pursue the elimination of waste inherent in traditional transportation systems. It will establish a responsive network that will provide more frequent, faster, reliable deliveries with substantially less material handling and system inventory. With fewer, dedicated transport partners in the network, even paperwork requirements will be reduced. As the execution arm of JIT purchasing, JIT transport innovation is a practical, achievable way to provide more deliveries for less total cost.

*"JIT implementation is the means of ACTION
that takes you from where you are
to world-class performance."*

You have seen all the segments of JUST-IN-TIME and how they fit together. The JIT anchor chart, which was introduced in Chapter 1 and is shown again in Figure 14-1, should be very meaningful to you now. You've also seen the incredible improvement opportunities that JIT offers. The issue is, what do you intend to do with all this new knowledge?

There's an old adage that says, "If you don't use it, you'll lose it." Webster defines implementation as "providing the means to put into practice." That's the job to be done if you plan to become Number 1 in the world in your industry. JIT implementation is *the means of action to take you from where you are today to world-class performance.*

In this book, I've described the goal-where you should want to go. In order to proceed, you first have to take a hard look at where you

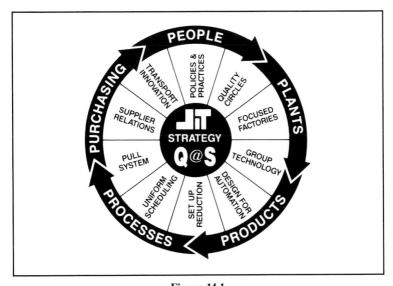

Figure 14-1

are today and then develop an action plan to reach the goal. It is like the equation shown in Figure 14-2. If A represents where you are now and B is the goal, but you can't *"see"* how to get from A to B, it doesn't matter how good the goal is because you're never going to get there. That's why C, implementation, is equally important to the goal you are trying to reach and why this chapter may be the most crucial one in the book.

IMPLEMENTATION SEQUENCES

Where does one start? There is no way to simultaneously implement all the elements on the JIT anchor chart and still stay in business. It's like eating an elephant. You can only do it "one bite at a time." But, which bite should be first and what should be the order of the others?

There is no one best answer. The JIT Strategy and the People elements are company culture changes that will be evolutionary in nature. Quality at the Source will apply "across the board," as well as to specific JIT implementation projects. For the rest of the elements the JIT anchor chart is like a clock, in that dependent items follow prerequisite ones in a clockwise direction. Even so, there are plenty of choices, depending on your type of business, manufacturing processes, and stage of JIT development. Three effective sequences that work are the "full commitment," the "back door" and the "vertical slice" approaches.

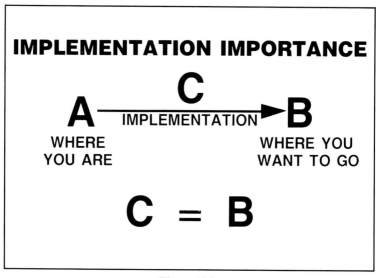

Figure 14-2

Full Commitment

If you think of your plant as divided into three broad classes of activity — final assembly, feeder operations (there could be several levels of these) and lead-off operations (the first time value is added to incoming material) — the most effective place to start is final assembly, as shown in Figure 14-3. That's because the application of uniform scheduling at final assembly will set the desired pace and flow for every other operation in the process.

You may recall that the two main components of uniform scheduling were level loading and cycle time communication which are shown in the first column in the figure. Also shown in that column is quick changeover (achieved by setup reduction activities). While you may not be able to make every part every day at the beginning, it needs to be a key objective of this first phase. The idea is to create the smoothest, most homogenized possible consumption of component parts.

Pull signals can then be used to draw material from those feeder operations and outside suppliers who deliver to the JIT final assembly area. At the beginning, none of them are likely to be able to respond as desired, so you will continue to use inventory as a "buffer" until they achieve this capability. In the meantime, final assembly will be drawing material very smoothly from this inventory bank and the inventory level will be a measure of how well (or poorly) the feeder operations are coming "on board" with their JIT implementation.

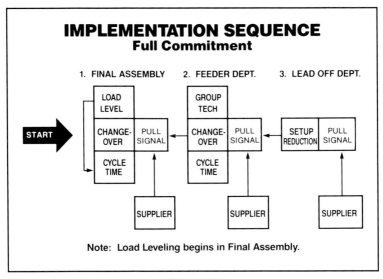

Figure 14-3

Internal feeder operations will need to do four basic things in order to support final assembly. First, they will have to organize into group technology cells so they can supply completed units instead of having to route parts through a myriad of operations in different departments. Next, setup reduction must be applied to those GT cells so they can respond quickly to changes in part number mix and manufacture small lot sizes to resupply final assembly. When they can do this, they should be able to respond directly to the pull signals from final assembly, eliminating the need for buffer inventory between the two (except for the amount in the pull signal calculations). Finally, they should be able to extend the pull signal system to their supplier operations, both inside and outside the plant. Like final assembly, they will work from buffer inventories until they first "get their own acts together" and then bring each of their supply agencies on board.

This series of actions will be repeated until every level of manufacturing in the plant, right back to the lead-off operations, has been linked together. At lead-off, the main issue will be to implement setup reduction. This is significant because lead-off operations are often considered as "roughing" activities (such as blanking, chucking and forging in the metal moving business or lead tinning, component sequencing and cable preparation in the electronics field) which service many secondary work centers and may be excluded from feeder GT cells. Even so, those operations must be able to economically manufacture in small lot sizes, be able to respond to pull signals and be able to generate pull signals for their raw material suppliers.

The full commitment approach, then, starts at final assembly and *cascades **up** the supply chain* until everything in the process is included. It is the quickest way to get bottom-line results because uniform scheduling is introduced at the place where it will do the most good and will help each successive level by making it easier to respond to "exact customer demand."

Back Door Approach

Sometimes, people are hesitant to begin a JIT implementation at the stage of production that is "right next to the customer." The up-front commitment is not as strong and there is a genuine fear that something will go wrong and impact customer deliveries. The back door approach, which is just the reverse of the full commitment approach, helps allay these concerns by starting as far away from the customer as possible and by establishing an early success to build management confidence.

It starts with setup reduction (which is the fastest, easiest JIT element to implement) in the lead-off operations, as shown in Figure 14-4. Quick successes here generate enthusiasm for the program and are able to demonstrate, even to the "timid," that JUST-IN-TIME really does work. It's a confidence builder.

With lower setup times, the lead-off operations can produce in smaller lot sizes and consume raw material in smaller batches. This, in turn, means tying the raw material suppliers to the new process. While pull signals can be easily be generated to do this, the suppliers must also have advance notice to marshal the necessary resources to do the job. Since final assembly is not yet in the picture, it is not generating a uniform demand nor a uniform schedule for the supply network. Therefore, a "pseudo" uniform schedule with a level load (shown by the dotted box in Figure 14-4) must be issued to the raw material suppliers involved with those lead-off operations. This starts a smooth flow of inputs to the plant.

The output from the lead-off operations initially flows into an inventory bank because the feeder departments are still consuming material in large lots. It does, however, provide the stimulus to begin converting those operations to GT cells, as was described in the full-commitment approach. As they begin to consume material more smoothly, the "pseudo" uniform scheduling activity is transferred to this stage of the process, covering all upstream operations and applicable suppliers.

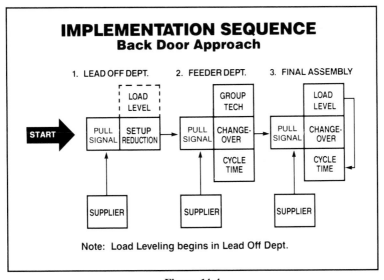

Figure 14-4

Pull signals are then used to trigger actual requirements. Reduction of the inventory banks becomes the measure of how well it is working.

Finally, when all the upstream operations are engaged in flow production, the final assembly department can be brought "on board." Uniform scheduling is transferred to the spot where it belonged in the first place, pull signals are used to call for replenishment parts and outside component suppliers are tied into the system. The end result is the same as was achieved via the full-commitment approach but the back-door approach *cascades* **down** *the supply chain.* It just takes a bit longer to complete the implementation and to see the bottom-line results.

Vertical Slice Approach

The best approach, in my opinion, is to implement JIT in a vertical slice of the business. To do this, you have to be able to segregate all of the functions in the plant that pertain to one product family, as you would in a focused factory. It's easy enough to do on paper but is not always mechanically feasible.

The first step is to analyze your current product families, using the implementation grid shown in Figure 14-5. This gives a perspective of the interactions between the families and the plant activity classes. The full-commitment approach is shown by the solid horizontal arrow lines and the back-door approach is represented by the dashed ones. In both cases an entire class of activity is converted to JIT before the next one is started.

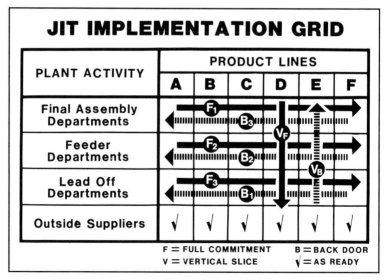

Figure 14-5

The vertical arrow lines show the two alternatives available for vertical slice implementation. Here, one product family at a time is transformed to JIT. The solid vertical arrow line shows the full-commitment version and the dashed vertical arrow line is the back-door vertical-slice approach.

The biggest advantage of the vertical-slice approach is that it lets you implement all the interconnecting facets of JIT, for a portion of your business in the shortest length of time. Much of the tailoring has to be applied to the interconnections, and it's easier to transfer the lessons learned in a limited application area to the other product lines. The product line P & L statement will give you a good indicator of how well the entire business will perform when JIT is implemented plant-wide.

IMPLEMENTATION GUIDELINES

There is no "only way" to implement JUST-IN-TIME. While some are faster than others, each of the sequences described has been successfully used. Whichever one is employed, all share the same objective and should be governed by the JIT principles that have been discussed in this book. In addition, there are some suggestions and caveats that should be kept in mind when designing your implementation program to help insure its success.

Implementation Suggestions

First of all, always use a *pilot approach* to get JIT started at your company. There is no way you can implement all the elements at once nor can you do it plant-wide in a "crash" program. There's just too much to do and the resources required would be staggering. A pilot program will focus your efforts in line with available resources and let you "learn as you do." The experience gained can then be applied to subsequent efforts so each can be increasingly effective.

The first pilot must be successful. It will serve as the springboard to establish momentum for the rest of the implementation program. Therefore, *pick the area with the best people* to "stack the deck" in your favor. Good people with positive attitudes can overcome the initial mistakes that often occur. Many companies want to do the first pilot in an area where they can achieve the "biggest bang for the buck," but this area may also be the riskiest. A successful pilot is more important than the size of initial returns. You may not get a second chance if the first one fails.

It is important that everyone involved with the pilot should *understand the principles* involved or else the project won't make any sense to them. Understanding is the key to success. On the other hand, *don't study it to death.* I once had a client who took a whole year to evaluate an implementation proposal before finally deciding to proceed. Lengthy studies are often just a ploy to postpone action. No matter how thoroughly you plan, there are bound to be changes during the pilot implementation as unforeseen events occur. A basic understanding is sufficient to get started.

Since the proof is in the doing, try to *start doing something as soon as possible.* Action creates interest and generates enthusiasm. Doing the implementation develops the experience that can be utilized to adapt the principles to your environment. Don't expect it to be perfect the first time. Instead, get started and then *go for continuous small improvements.* Otherwise you may never get off first base.

Implementation Caveats

Caveat emptor is a Latin phrase that means, "Let the buyer beware." There are some key items you should be aware of and beware of, so they don't sidetrack your JIT implementation or, worse yet, undermine your efforts. These things have cropped up repeatedly in programs I've been involved with so they're based on real-world situations, not just speculation. Remember, Caesar received a caveat about the Ides of March, but he chose to ignore it. Please keep the following issues in mind as you proceed.

Your first pilot, regardless of the implementation sequence chosen, will undoubtedly include some setup reduction activity. Although it's been said many times already, it's worth repeating that the objective is *to reduce lot sizes, not setup people.* If you can cut setup times in half, cut the lot sizes in half and double the number of runs. Take your return out of inventory reduction, not people reduction. You need their input. Some of the operations managers don't fully understand this at first and it's critical that it be accepted if you expect your pilot to succeed.

Don't be satisfied with early successes. One of the saddest lessons I learned early in my JIT career was that some people will rise to the challenge of a JIT pilot just to prove they can do it. Afterward, the tendency is to pat each other on the back for a job well done and then go back to "business as usual." While JIT implementation can be thought of as a program or a project, JUST-IN-TIME has to become a way of life throughout the company if you expect to achieve world-class manufacturing capability.

When selecting the implementation sequence that's best for you, remember that *full benefits won't be realized until uniform scheduling is installed.* Uniform scheduling is the key to variable-flow production, which allows you to respond to changes in product mix while still maximizing people productivity. You'll see it on the bottom line. Until then, you'll have to rely on other measures, such as setup time reduction, leadtime reduction, lower scrap rates or work-in-process inventory reductions to demonstrate the benefits of the JIT pilot project.

Don't involve suppliers until your in-house system is in order. In each of the recommended sequences, only those suppliers who would be delivering to JIT workcenters were incorporated in the plan and only at the time the workcenter was ready to consume material in a smooth uniform manner. To do so any sooner would be a waste of effort and could destroy your credibility as a JUST-IN-TIME customer-partner.

10-STEP GAME PLAN FOR CHANGE

A successful pilot project, then, is vital to the implementation of JUST-IN-TIME on a plant-wide basis. It is the measure of applicability to a given plant and the promotional medium for the balance of the facility. Usually, you get only one chance to succeed, so the area selected is crucial and the program needs to be a formal one to maximize the probability of success. (This is not the time to "fly by the seat of your pants.") The approach I recommend follows classic project management procedures but includes some "twists" that have been learned from a lot of "ups and downs" over the years. Like a good recipe, it works well if you include all the ingredients and follow the process. It is called the *10-Step Game Plan for Change.*

Step 1: Top Management Leadership

JIT implementation won't happen unless top management at the facility both understands and fully supports it. A manager who understands the power of JIT will be able to convey to others the message that "we believe JIT will work for us." A "champion" is needed to gain the attention of the work force and to give those people the inspiration to make the needed changes. That's what leadership is all about. Managers "handle things," but *leaders take us to places we've never been.*

The leader must make a clearly *visible commitment to JIT,* which obviously involves some risk. But, the difference between "commitment" and arms-length 'involvement' is significant. (If you had bacon and eggs for breakfast this morning, the hen was "involved" but the pig was "committed"!)

A clear *directive to proceed* should be issued by top management, preferably in writing, to insure that the message is clearly understood by everybody as it makes its way through the organization. (It could be some other sign, like moving the project leader into an office adjacent to the key executive who is promoting the project.) In follow-up actions the importance of the project should be reinforced to maintain its priority. This may appear to be overkill to some, but experience has shown that winning projects always seem to have this degree of top management commitment and support.

Organizationally, a *steering committee* should be formed to formulate policy and guide the project. It should include the department heads who will have to provide resources to the project and, therefore, need to be a part of it. If you have a labor union at your plant, there should be *union representation* on the steering committee, preferably the highest ranking official available. JIT requires total involvement by all the people, so it just makes good sense to bring them in "up-front" to share in the project development and to see first-hand how both the company and the employees will benefit from JUST-IN-TIME.

A final, vital issue in this category is the *protection of the employees* who will be asked to participate in the project. You don't have to immediately embark upon a program of "full employment," but those employees who are involved in the pilot must be assured that they will not lose their jobs with the company if their efforts result in position eliminations. It will be difficult to gain their support without such a commitment and employee inputs are the key to JUST-IN-TIME production.

Step 2: The Steering Committee

The steering committee has a number of responsibilities, the most important of which are to provide project guidance and support. It provides a forum for discussion of project progress and establishes a peer group to help insure the support of department managers when assistance from their areas is needed.

One of the key responsibilities of the steering committee is the *selection of the pilot area.* As has been mentioned previously, it is vital that one with the best chance of success be picked. The members of the steering committee should have the experience and business judgment to make the best selection.

The next issue is the *selection of the project leader.* This should be a full-time job for a dynamic person who understands the principles of JUST-IN-TIME, can work well with people, can interface with technical support activities, can train those who will be involved in the project, and can serve as an all-around "cheerleader" to keep the project going. It works best if the project manager comes from a manufacturing-related department so everyone clearly understands that this is a manufacturing project rather than an inventory-reduction program.

The steering committee should also be involved in the *selection of the project team members,* who are usually involved on a part-time basis. The team should be comprised of eight to ten persons (much larger than ten gets unwieldy). At least half of them should come from the shop floor. They are the "experts" about what we do now. Supervisory and technical members; e.g., industrial engineering, are also needed. The goal is to have a nicely balanced team that isn't "overpowered" by any one discipline and gives the shop floor members an opportunity to contribute. The ability to work together, enthusiasm for the project, and the respect of co-workers are key qualifications.

The steering committee *provides the resources* for the project since the members usually control the "purse strings" at the facility. JIT implementation doesn't require a big, up-front capital outlay, but it does require people resources and some expense money. In addition to team members, technical experts may have to be "loaned" to the project for limited periods of time. Expense moneys can include travel, education, equipment rearrangement and modification costs.

Last, but not least, the steering committee should conduct *periodic reviews* of the project to insure that it is on track and to provide an entree to those areas where functional support is needed. The project team is motivated to action when it knows the reports have to be made. The committee helps keep the focus on the original objectives so the team doesn't start to "wander." The review meetings also provide a "peer-pressure" forum to help insure that resource promises are kept. The reviews should be held frequently, once a month at least.

Step 3: Education Program

JUST-IN-TIME is so far-reaching and so different from traditional practices that it will eventually impact every person in the organization. It will entail the most widespread education effort you have ever undertaken. However, it can be done in phases, parallel to the implementation.

There are three broad categories of people who will need the education. First is the *management team*. They must understand the concepts of JIT and "buy into" them to even get a project off the ground. Otherwise, the whole thing could be put "on hold." Next is the *project team,* who will become your in-house JIT "experts." They will have to understand JIT technology in much greater detail than is required by management because they have to turn concepts into a practical reality at your company. Finally, there is the *critical mass,* which is really everybody else. However, this group starts out with the people in the pilot area (and those who interface with the pilot area) and expands through the work force as more projects are initiated.

There are many avenues available to achieve this education. For management and the project team, *live seminars* are an ideal way to absorb a concentration of information in a short period of time without distractions. They can be tailored to fit individual businesses and questions can be answered on the spot. They are an effective way to introduce JIT to a location and to spur the development of a management action plan for JIT implementation.

Videotape courses are a very cost-effective method to bring JIT education in-house for the balance of the organization. (My 30 hour JIT course, which parallels this book, is distributed by The Forum, Ltd., Milwaukee, Wisconsin.) Videotape courses can be taught in short, easy-to-absorb modules over a period of time and the case studies provide a good picture of how others are implementing JIT. They are also a handy reference source for the review of key points or for training new employees who join the company after the first wave of JIT education has been completed.

There is a wealth of JUST-IN-TIME *books and literature* on the maret to supplement the live and video education. Some of these have already been mentioned in this text. A suggested reading list can be found in Appendix II. It is not all inclusive but is certainly representative of the good material that is available. The project team will need this depth of material to develop the level of JIT expertise they will need.

The best education for the project team would be to have them *visit a plant that is implementing JIT.* There is no substitute for watching JIT implementation in real-time and talking to those who are experiencing the transformation. The problem is that those plants aren't in the "tour business" and will often refuse requests to visit because they are felt to be disruptive. On the other hand, if one of your suppliers is a

JIT plant, they will probably be very pleased to show you their facility.

Step 4: Pilot Project Planning

Once the project team has been selected and educated, the next step is to develop an implementation plan for the pilot project. It is extremely important that the project team have a feeling of ownership for the pilot, even though the steering committee will have selected the pilot area and may already have set some specific goals and objectives during its deliberations. This is where the team-building skills of the project leader will be vital. The team should be led in a manner that allows them to naturally reach the same conclusions as did the steering committee. For the first few team meetings, it often proves beneficial to have an experienced consultant assist the project leader.

The project team will be asked to *recommend the JIT elements* (like setup reduction, group technology, uniform scheduling, pull system, etc.) which should be included in the pilot. We've already established that they can't all be done at once. The elements selected should support the overall objective of the pilot project but must still be a manageable task. Usually three or four is plenty.

Putting one team member in charge of each element, much like a subcommittee chairperson, and assigning the other team members to one or more of the task groups, has proved to be a very effective method of team organization. A sample of this is shown in Figure 14-6. Here, a

JIT PILOT TEAM

TEAM MEMBERS	JIT ELEMENTS			
	S/U	GT	U/S	PULL
Setup Person	C			
Press Oper.- Days	X			
Press Oper.- Nites	X			
Maintenance Supv.	X	X		X
Indust. Engineer	X	X		X
Ass'y Supv.- Days		C	X	X
Assembler – Days		X		
Ass'y Supv.- Nites		X	X	C
Assembler – Nites		X		
Production Planner			C	X

Figure 14-6

10-person team is distributed among three JIT element sub-groups. (The project leader works with each group as a facilitator.) Notice that many members "pull double duty," but each task team is focused on a single element with no more than six members on it.

Next, *measurable improvement goals* must be set which reflect the initial project objectives. It's the commitment to "how much better" the pilot will be than the traditional process. By the time the project team has reached this point, they usually understand their workcenter better than they ever have before but may still be cautious when it comes to goal setting. However, it is not a critical issue since JUST-IN-TIME is based on continuous improvement. If the initial goals are easily met, the team can simply re-establish new ones (which usually happens).

To measure improvement, you have to *know the starting point.* Ideally, the improvement measures selected can be gathered from the current reporting system. However if such is not the case, the basis for data collection and performance calculations must be established up front. For example, if reduced production leadtime is the goal, you may have to track job close outs or trace a specially marked part through the process to establish both the baseline and later improvements. (Be ready for anything here. I had one client who launched a part painted red into the "system" that never came out the other end!)

You should also make it a point to *take pictures of the original process.* The first pilot will be a model for future projects and you will undoubtedly be called upon to explain what you have done to other parts of the company. Pictures of the "before" and "after" situations will make the numerical improvements "come to life."

Next *develop a work plan for each JIT element,* along with a target schedule. Each task group will have to establish a detailed schedule for its JIT element that includes who will do what and when it will be completed. Then those schedules must be coordinated with the other task groups to insure that they fit together. Several tries will probably be required before the project team comes up with what they consider to be an integrated, workable plan. With help from accounting, the costs and benefits of the plan should be calculated and it will then be ready for presentation to the steering committee.

Step 5: Steering Committee Approval

While steering committee reviews have already been discussed, this first one is so important it is given a separate step number. This formal review is the first presentation given by the project team to top management. It should be approached by both groups with care and preparation since the objective is to secure *formal project approval.*

To make this work, the steering committee must be receptive. This is best achieved if the *project leader "pre-sells"* the proposal by sending up "trial balloons" to key steering committee members during the project-planning phase to see how they "fly" and feeding back any significant concerns to the project team. Modifications can then be incorporated ahead of time so that formal approval is almost guaranteed.

It should be a team presentation. If feasible, each member of the project team should be given an opportunity to speak, even if it is only a short segment. For example, task group chairpersons would be expected to report on the portions for which they were responsible. Although some of the team members will be nervous about the meeting, they will feel a real sense of accomplishment (and obligation to perform) when the ordeal is over. Management, in turn, will see just how good the team is, get an appreciation for the value of the project and should be just as committed to its success.

Step 6: Employee Training

The project team serves as the information and training base for the pilot and must be able to convey this information to fellow employees on both a formal and informal basis. Otherwise, the plant will never become totally self-sufficient in JUST-IN-TIME.

After the project implementation plan has been approved by the steering committee, the project team must give the employees in the pilot area sufficient training to enable them to understand the project and enough *JIT perspective* to contribute to it. The intensity need not be as great as was the project team's education, but there should be enough to give the employees the tools they need to get involved.

The most critical portion is the explanation of the project detail to the employees. This is the time when *participation by the employees* and suggestions from them should be encouraged, even though it means modifying the implementation plan. (Those people like a little ownership, too.) The team must not get caught in the "not-invented-here" trap. Rather, it should *review the work plan* with the employees, step by step, and actively encourage suggestions for change. It is even worth "priming the pump" by leaving out a fairly obvious item to get the feedback process started. The amount of involvement generated during this implementation step will have a major bearing on the success of the pilot project.

Employee training also means conveying an understanding of the *employee benefits* that will come from the JIT pilot. While an improved competitive position for the company will enhance job security, there are personal benefits as well. For example, no employee likes to do rework jobs. The potential to reduce rework by 90% or more is very meaningful. Similarly, waiting for maintenance to repair an inoperative machine can be a major source of frustration, especially if it means being "sent home" for a time. A JIT pilot gets priority service from maintenance (you should negotiate a 15-minute guarantee) which does wonders for the "quality of work life" of those employees. When they appreciate the personal benefits from the pilot they will take a more personal interest in its success.

Step 7: Pilot Implementation

As the actual implementation begins, people are going to wonder, "What is going on over there?" It's important to keep them informed because if you don't, the "rumor mill" will invent something. Issue a simple, one-page *newsletter* periodically, or write special articles for your company newspaper, if you have one. This effort will not only communicate the "real story" but will also generate interest and enthusiasm for future JIT implementation projects.

Implementation starts with an emphasis on *housekeeping.* The floors should be cleaned and refinished, if necessary. Every piece of equipment should be repainted. Prepare signs that draw attention to the pilot project. A neat, clean working environment sets the attitude and makes it clear that JIT is different from "business as usual." The housekeeping organization steps demonstrate the productivity values associated with having the right things in the right place at the right time, and nothing more. The concept of "visibility management," where everything that is right or wrong within the workplace is easy for the employees to understand, will help pave the way for the scheduled improvements.

The pilot plan for each *JIT element is then executed.* This can be done in parallel, but time should be provided for coordination as this should be an integrated implementation. The project team should meet frequently, if only for a short time, to avoid going off in separate directions. Progress should be monitored and recorded. (Figure 14-7 shows an easy way to do this.) As *feedback* develops, *revisions* to the plan should be made to take advantage of this information. (For example, I have yet to see a group technology layout that didn't get changed several times before it satisfied everyone in the workcenter.)

One more caveat should be stated at this point. The project team needs to be *mentally prepared to solve any problem* which may arise, especially during the first pilot project in a plant. If this mental readiness has not been instilled by the project leader, it can lead to major discouragement on the part of the team members. Anticipated problems, however, can be turned into opportunities since they reflect the real-world environment and their solutions will improve the pilot project. When the team is prepared for a major disaster, real problems will seem small and manageable by comparison.

Step 8: Pilot Post-Mortem

While JUST-IN-TIME is expected to last forever, a pilot project must come to an end. The project team will "hand off" to the operations people and return to their regular jobs. A lot of time and money will have been invested to develop expertise that is resident in team members' heads and may soon be forgotten. It is extremely important to capture that information in a form that will be useful for other applications.

Loosely interpreted, a post-mortem is "an examination of the deceased (project) to learn about causes and effects." A *written record* of this study can be passed on to other project teams as a set of guidelines to make their paths a little easier. Although there will undoubtedly be "tons" of schedules, meeting minutes, etc. in the files, it will be difficult for a newcomer to make much sense out of the jumble of

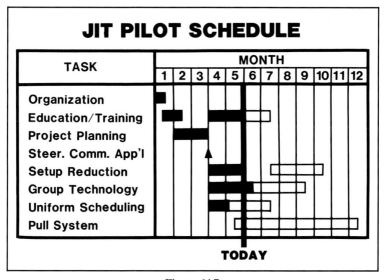

Figure 14-7

information. What is needed is a narrative — a "story" about the birth, life and completion of the pilot project.

As the project begins to wind down, the project should be reviewed in detail by the team members. Thought should be given to *how the project was organized* and assignments were made. The rationale behind the selection of improvement goals and how they were measured should be discussed. A summary of the major *problems encountered* and how they were solved is very useful. Most important of all are the *lessons learned.* In other words, what would the team have done differently if this information had been available to them at the start of the project?

Finally, the post-mortem should include the *benefits achieved.* What were the original targets and what are the results to date? What is the projection for the next year? This is the bottom line that management wants to hear about.

Step 9: Feedback to Steering Committee

The last act of the project team is to deliver the post-mortem document to the steering committee and to make a *formal presentation* of its contents. Just as formal project approval (Step 5) was a critical first milestone for the pilot, this step *forces the post-mortem* to happen. It insures that the lessons learned from the pilot will be communicated to management for transmission to other project teams. It also insures that management will hear the message, whether or not they actually read the final report.

The presentation meeting becomes the *formal pilot close-out* session. Too many projects start out with a big "bang" and die with a "whimper." This project started big and should finish big. It is also an excellent occasion for the steering committee to give the project team a well-deserved *"pat on the back"* for a job well done. A symbolic memento is very much in order. I've seen everything from engraved watches or wall plaques to embroidered jackets or caps presented. Whatever you select, it should be a pleasant reminder of the contributions made by this group of JUST-IN-TIME pioneers to your company.

Step 10: Expansion to Next Project

The tenth step is to do it all over again. Building on the knowledge gained from the first pilot, the process is now ready to repeat itself. You don't have to wait until the first pilot has been completed before a new project is selected, but it is strongly recommended that you wait to initiate it until the first pilot is well enough along to feel confident about a successful conclusion. Above all, don't dilute the initial pilot effort by spreading your resources too thin.

New project leaders and members may well come from the first pilot program. They can bring both JIT expertise and experience with them. In some cases, the leading candidates for new project leaders will be wearing blue collars. JIT implementation will provide you with a wealth of people development opportunities.

If you have the resources, *consider parallel programs* for subsequent implementation projects. Once the initial pilot has "broken the ground" and you have a core of in-house experts, follow on projects are usually easier and faster. (You may recall that the Ferro focused factory implementation, described in Chapter 6, improved from ten weeks for the first line to four weeks for the last line.) I've had clients who even started three parallel programs, once the initial pilot had proved itself.

Each successive project should be better than its predecessors. That's how education, experience and the post-mortem process will pay off for you. It's really just the JIT principle of continuous improvement at work. Don't stop, though, until JUST-IN-TIME is truly a way of life throughout your company.

THE PATHWAY TO CHANGE

Changing to a new way of living is no easy task. At the very least, change is uncomfortable. In some cases, it can even be painful. Yet, I hope I have shown you that changing to JUST-IN-TIME is not only a logical, practical way to become a world-class competitor, it may well be the *only way* for many of us.

If you are one of the first people at your location to think that JIT is the answer, your fellow workers will not necessarily greet you with "open arms." To the contrary, many will scoff because they are uninformed or misinformed. Others will resist any change from traditional practices because they fear the unknown. ("Let's stick with what has worked in the past.") If one of those is your plant manager or general manager, it will be even more difficult. Yet, someone has to start the ball rolling. If you believe (as I do) what you have read in this book, then you can become an instrument for that change at your company.

The pathway to such significant change is much like a journey through four separate and distinct regions. The names of the regions are: *Attitude, Knowledge, Practice and Skill.* Each must be traversed and mastered, in sequence, before change can be successfully and permanently achieved. The Dale Carnegie Institute visualizes the regions as quadrants of a circle, as shown in Figure 14-8, which they call the *Circle of Change*. It is very applicable to JUST-IN-TIME.

Attitude

Without the right "mind-set," change cannot happen. That's why *attitude* has been addressed in so many of the chapters in this book. Changing a negative attitude about JIT to a positive one requires that you surmount not one, but four thresholds.

It begins with *"I need."* Recognition of the need for change starts the ball rolling. If you believe your competitive position is secure or that you've got a "lock" on the market, there's no motivation to change and you never will. At the other extreme, if off-shore competition has almost put you out of business, you don't have to be convinced of the need. For most companies, it is the forward thinkers, who can look beyond the tips of their noses to see what's coming down the road, who must jolt the rest of the organization out of its complacency to see the need for JIT. But even that is not enough.

The second threshold is *"I want."* Needing and wanting are light-years apart. Overweight people know they need to shed some pounds. Their doctors, friends and common sense tell them this. Yet, until they decide that they really want the benefits of being "in shape," they'll never even consider a diet. It may be the same thing for you regarding

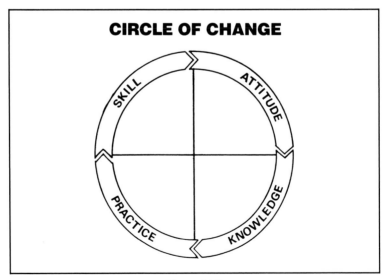

CIRCLE OF CHANGE

Figure 14-8

JUST-IN-TIME. If you view it as unpleasant "medicine," it may never happen. On the other hand, if you can envision not only the practical benefits of JIT but also the sweeping improvements to the quality of work-life that are within your grasp, it is hard not to want it. Yet, when you decide you really do want JIT, it's still not enough.

The most difficult threshold is *"I can."* It requires that you overcome the PLOM Syndrome ("Poor Little Old Me"), in which you see yourself as a victim of uncontrollable circumstances. "Our plant and equipment are too old to convert to JIT," or "Our business is different and not compatible with JIT," or "I'd love to adopt JIT at my plant but *they* won't let it happen," are typical PLOM statements. Let's face it, if they wanted JIT you'd already be doing it. But you can change their minds, and you can make JIT work for your business once you make up your mind that it is a possible, although formidable, task. Even that, however, falls short of the mark.

The final threshold is the commitment that *"I will."* This is where you have to take some risk. Believing you can, but failing to take any action, won't help your company one bit. You have to resolve to carry the JIT banner to the decision-makers who hold the keys to making JUST-IN-TIME a reality in your business. It's a difficult job, but somebody has to become a "champion" to start the ball rolling. If you don't, who will?

Knowledge

A change in attitude must be supported by the knowledge of what to change to. That's what this book has been all about. It contains a lot of information that can be of immense use to your JIT implementation, provided that it has been understandable.

Knowledge alone, though, is like a "core dump" from a computer. It can be a confusing jumble of information that doesn't seem to make much sense, even though the data is completely accurate. It can lead people to the wrong conclusions like, "JIT is an inventory control system." Knowledge must be organized to clearly show both the "big picture" and the relationships of the component parts. Only then can it be transformed to *understanding,* which will support the attitude change.

Knowledge is the key to understanding, but understanding is the key to success. Everyone in the organization must understand what to do, why it is necessary and how to do it. When they believe and they understand, you are half-way home.

Practice

Theory becomes reality through practice. "Doing" JIT, not just talking about it, produces the benefits of the change. The 10-step game plan for JIT pilot implementation was designed to help you take that first step toward a new way of living.

Pilot implementation lets you gain hands-on *experience* with JUST-IN-TIME. That's how you pick up the nuances and subtleties of JIT as it relates to your specific business. That's also how you develop the core of expertise to expand the pilot effort to a plant-wide change in running the business.

JIT experience must be earned. You can't hire somebody to do it for you. Change can't happen unless you personally live through it. That's the experience no amount of money can buy.

Skill

A one-time experience will not usually change your way of living. It's too easy to slip back to the "old way" of doing things. On the other hand, repeated experiences reinforce the "new way" and help you turn it into a skill. That's the difference between an apprentice and a journeyman.

Skilled athletes make their sports look easy. That's because they have practiced so long and so diligently that what they do has really become a habit. They can almost do it "in their sleep." However, there are good habits and bad habits. It is the *good habits* you want to develop, by changing to JUST-IN-TIME, that will make you a world-class competitor. To get there, you have to eliminate the *bad habits* that have accumulated over a long period of time.

That's what gives the Circle of Change its shape. It is a continuous process of converting bad habits to good ones by changing the mind-set (attitude), understanding what to do (knowledge), gaining experience by doing it (practice), and honing that experience into a new skill. But, for it to do your company any good, you'll have to start the "wheel" rolling.

SUMMARY

JUST-IN-TIME implementation is the means of action to take you from where you are today to world-class performance. No matter how good the goal of achieving JIT may be, if you can't see how to get there, you never will. That's why implementation is just as important as the goal itself.

There is no one best way to implement JIT. The JIT Strategy and the People elements are company-culture changes that will be evolutionary in nature. Quality at the Source will apply "across the board," as well as to specific JIT implementation projects. For the rest of the elements the JIT anchor chart (shown in Figure 14-1) is like a clock, in that dependent items follow prerequisite ones in a clockwise direction. Even so, there are plenty of choices, depending on your type of business, manufacturing processes, and stage of JIT development. Three effective sequences that work well are the "full-commitment," the "backdoor" and the "vertical-slice" approaches.

While some are faster than others, each of the sequences has been successfully used. Whichever one is employed, all share the same objective and should be governed by the JIT principles that have been discussed in this book. It is recommended that a pilot project be initiated in the area with the best people to gain experience. It is important that they understand the JIT principles, but don't study it to death. Get started as soon as possible and make continuous improvements as you go. Remember, the objective is to achieve variable-flow production, so reduce your lot sizes, not the number of setup people in your plant. Don't be satisfied with a single early success. Implementation must be plant-wide, and uniform scheduling must be employed before the full benefits of JIT will be realized. Bring your suppliers "on board" as you implement but don't ask them to deliver JUST-IN-TIME until you're ready to consume that way.

The 10-Step Game Plan for Change is a "recipe" for successful JIT implementation. The steps include:
1. Top management leadership
2. A steering committee
3. An education program
4. Pilot project planning
5. Steering committee approval
6. Employee training
7. Pilot implementation
8. A pilot post-mortem
9. Feedback to the steering committee
10. Expansion to the next project.

Like any good recipe, it works well if you use all the ingredients and follow the prescribed process.

The bottom line is change, which can be uncomfortable to many and even painful to some. JUST-IN-TIME requires wide-spread changes that will affect everyone in the organization. Attitudes must change first. You have to accept the need for JIT, want it, believe you can do it and commit that you will do it before it can happen. JIT knowledge must be translated to understanding and put into practice via implementation projects. Only then can it become a skill and a new way of living.

JUST-IN-TIME implementation starts with a banner carrier who has the vision and the courage to carry the message to the decision makers who may not want to hear about it. You could perform the service of a lifetime for your company if you accept that challenge. Are you ready?

JIT
MEASUREMENTS

CHAPTER 15

"Measurements are the yardsticks
that tell us how we've done
and motivate us to perform."

The implementation of JUST-IN-TIME will create major changes in your business which will probably not be accurately reflected by your current system of measurements. That's significant because, let's face it, *we work the way we are measured.* Measurements are the yardsticks that tell us how we've done and motivate us to perform. If they give the wrong signals, management may not want to implement JUST-IN-TIME. The problem is that some of today's measurements could make it look like you're doing worse under JIT instead of better.

Most performance measures are derived from cost accounting information, the fundamental premises of which are more than a half century old. To make matters worse, there has been a growing tendency over the years to make what were originally intended to be *internal* measurements conform to *external* reporting conventions and regulations. As a result, useless and often misleading performance information, as well as cost data, has been provided to operating management.

As more American companies begin to adopt JIT, the drawbacks of the old measures are becoming increasingly apparent, both to operating management and to their financial organizations. Just like the barriers of traditional practices in the shop, there are traditional mindsets in the accounting community which will have to be overcome. But, since traditional cost accounting measurements simply do not reflect the new conditions created by JIT, new measurements *must* be developed. This chapter will cover a number of measurements which are very compatible with JIT and which will give you valid performance and cost indicators.

WHY TODAY'S MEASUREMENTS DON'T WORK

The textbooks tells us that *financial accounting* is mainly concerned with the "historical, custodial and stewardship aspects of external reporting." *Cost accounting,* on the other hand, is supposed to involve the "gathering, objective analysis, and rational interpretation of relevant information to help management exercise considered judgment in planning and controlling the business." Cost accounting is also charged with costing products for inventory valuation and income determination. Unfortunately, the second responsibility has become the cost accounting driver due to the growing need to report standardized information on inventories and costs to external entities, like the Internal Revenue Service (IRS) and The Securities and Exchange Commission (SEC), or to satisfy independent auditors who are governed by rules of the Financial Accounting Standards Board (FASB).

To avoid keeping two sets of books, cost accounting usually provides operations management with combinations of "standard" data for performance measurement and control. The trouble with that data is that it is based on out-dated, often-irrelevant assumptions that, while suitable for tax reporting and book balancing, may have no relationship to real product costs or real operations performance. In truth, the numbers being generated today provide little useful guidance for managerial decisions and can even *drive management to do the wrong things.*

Acme Corporation Example

To illustrate the validity of that rather strong statement, consider the following example, which was published in an article by Robert S. Kaplan entitled, "Yesterday's Accounting Undermines Production" (Harvard Business Review, July-August, 1984).

"During Richard Thompson's two years as manager of the Industrial Products Division of the Acme Corporation, the division enjoyed such greatly improved profitability that he was promoted to more senior corporate responsibility. Thompson's replacement, however, found the division's manufacturing capability greatly eroded and a plunge in profitability inevitable.

Careful analysis of the operations during Thompson's tenure revealed:
- Increased profitability had been largely caused by an unexpected jump in demand that permitted the division's facilities to operate near capacity.
- Despite this expansion, the division's market share had actually decreased.
- Costs had been reduced by not maintaining equipment, by operating it beyond rated capacity, by not investing in new equipment or product development, and by imposing stress on workers to the point of alienating them.

• Many costs had been absorbed into bloated inventory levels. By this time, however, Thompson was secure in his senior position and was still receiving credit for the high profits Industrial Products had earned under his direction."

Where were the performance measurements that should have alerted Acme Corporation management to those problems? Was Thompson actually driven to do **wrong** things so he could "look good" by an inappropriate yardstick? If so, what should be done?

Changes in Manufacturing

We need to start by recognizing that manufacturing today is already undergoing a considerable change even without JIT. As companies move to automation and Computer Integrated Manufacturing, the baselines all change as well. Our cost accounting concepts were developed early in this century when technology was low, production was long and stable, and direct labor represented half of the value added in the manufacturing process. In those days, it made sense to concentrate on measurements like direct labor efficiency and machine utilization as indicators of future profit generation.

Today, those premises no longer apply. As American factories have become more automated, the ratio between direct labor and overhead costs has shifted from 1:1 to 1:3, as shown in Figure 15-1, and is projected to go to 1:4 by the year 2000. In some companies, that number

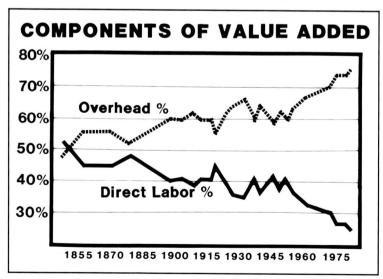

Figure 15-1

is already 1:12. In addition, the real dollars for overhead costs have risen because of the additional support costs associated with running and maintaining the sophisticated automated equipment and the huge numbers of transactions that must be recorded to keep track of our complex manufacturing activities.

JUST-IN-TIME Changes

JUST-IN-TIME further accentuates this trend. First, because it stresses simplification and rationalization of production processes, it leads to lower direct labor requirements. Second, because of the drive to maximize operator self-sufficiency, many traditional indirect functions like material handling, inspection, machine maintenance, scheduling and job processing are at least partially transferred to operator responsibilities. Third, because JIT principles call for the reduction of inventories to expose and fix problems, the resulting high turnovers offset the traditional needs for complex inventory accounting procedures.

In the relentless quest to continuously improve quality and productivity, JIT also changes many other traditional manufacturing practices. We find ourselves shifting from big is better to small is beautiful, from inventory is an asset to inventory is a liability that covers up problems, from specialized, limited-scope workers to flexible "do-it-yourselfers," from inevitable rejects to doing it right the first time, from high-inertia, slow-reaction manufacturing to fast response to exact customer demand and from comfort contingencies to the elimination of all waste.

Performance measurements need to reflect and encourage these trends. Cost measurements must likewise reflect these changes so we can eliminate unnecessary transactions and accurately gauge true product costs. It's a new ball game which requires a new view of today's measurements and replacements for some of them.

THE PRO'S AND CON'S OF ROI

The most popular macro measure used today is Return On Investment (ROI). Developed by the Du Pont Company prior to 1919, it is an ingenious measurement that relates the profit and loss statement to the balance sheet in a single number. The component parts of the Du Pont ROI formula are shown in Figure 15-2. The upper chain develops earnings as a percent of sales while the lower chain calculates investment turnover as related to sales. When the two factors are multiplied together, the result is the return on investment, expressed as a ratio. Since sales cancel each other out in the final calculation, ROI can also be computed as earnings divided by the total investment.

ROI is a handy indicator of how effectively a given business is providing investors a return on their money which is what free enterprise is all about. It can be compared to the interest that might be received from a bank for the same investment. As you can see from the elements in the chart, it is most applicable to business units that are self-contained profit centers.

ROI as a Performance Measure

The original intent of ROI at Du Pont was to help determine where best to invest capital among the various business opportunities in the company. Later, ROI was also used as a performance measure for the general manager at each business unit. In this case, however, it was modified slightly to charge the general manager with gross operating investment and earnings *net* of depreciation (cash profits). In their words, ". . . it would be inappropriate to consider that operating management was responsible for earning a return on only the net operating investment. The capital, liability and reserve positions of an enterprise are largely a reflection of the philosophy of top management as to how the business should be financed. The Du Pont Company believes that operating management should be responsible for turning in a profit on capital assigned to that management regardless of how the capital was raised."

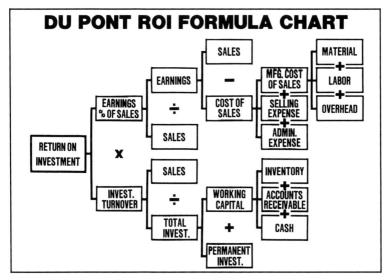

Figure 15-2

Note that the tone and the context of those statements are long-term. Capital investments are not made for the short run. Yet, somehow ROI has come to be used as a short-term performance measure by many companies today. They *live or die by the monthly ROI.* Some are even trying to use ROI to measure cost centers by allocating sales and capital to them. This is where an otherwise effective measure begins to break down because, at this level of detail, it's inaccurate, irrelevant and too easy to "beat."

Beating ROI in the Short-Term

Suppose you were running a manufacturing operation that had an annual budget of $1 million for direct labor and $4 million for overhead costs. (Some people call the latter item manufacturing burden costs.) In order to make the cost accounting easier, those two numbers are tied together in a ratio that says, "every time a dollar of direct labor is spent, four dollars of overhead cost will be attached to it." That translates to an overhead rate of 400%. If everything goes according to the plan, spending $1 million for direct labor by the end of the year will "absorb" the $4 million of overhead. That's the long-term goal.

In the short-term, however, let's say you needed some extra profit this month to make your ROS and ROI look good. By working on a Saturday, you would spend more direct labor hours than originally planned and therefore absorb more overhead into inventory than planned. Since the system has to presume that the work was necessary, the standard amount of labor and overhead would get charged to the inventory account. The overtime premium would be an unfavorable manufacturing variance, but it would be offset by the extra overhead absorption, most of which would be "funny money" because the actual overhead costs would hardly change at all. The difference between absorbed overhead and actual overhead would show up as a *favorable* manufacturing variance, which would flow straight to the bottom line. Presto, you'd have instant "profits."

That's just one of the things Richard Thompson did at Acme. (I've seen it done many times myself. I bet you may have, too.) Yet it's so *wrong.* Bringing people in on an overtime basis to make things that we don't even need now and consuming material that most likely was acquired to be used elsewhere for something that was needed is the grossest of wastes. But, it will certainly improve the monthly ROS and ROI. Even though everybody knows it is "wrong" they still do it because they are driven by a measurement system that focuses on *today.* All you have to do to make today look good is mortgage the future.

Negative Influences on ROI

Using a long-term measurement to monitor short-term performance is just part of the problem. Distortions are accentuated by a number of other driving forces. In their wonderful book, *Relevance Lost* (HBS Press, 1987), H. Thomas Johnson and Robert S. Kaplan describe six of them:

1. Short-term performance pressures from upper management and outside investors discourage long-term investments by company managers.

2. Faster promotions these days also discourage investments which just "pave the way" for successors.

3. Larger, more-decentralized organizations today provide more opportunities to take "dysfunctional" actions which may go unnoticed.

4. Fewer senior managers today really understand their company's products and processes, choosing instead to manage only "by the numbers."

5. Executive bonuses are primarily based on short-term accounting figures.

6. The manufacturing environment has changed so dramatically it is unreasonable to expect sixty-year old measurement systems to still be useful.

It's the combination, then, of a long-term measure with a short-term mentality, coupled with management's inability or unwillingness to "read between the lines" that has degraded the effectiveness of ROI as the key performance measurement. To let JIT "take hold," ROI must be supplemented with valid short-term measurements that will motivate managers to do the "right things."

JIT PERFORMANCE MEASUREMENTS

The key to effective JIT measurement is inherent in the fundamental definition, "JUST-IN-TIME is a production strategy with a new set of values to continuously improve quality and productivity." In particular, measurements need to reflect:

1. The value of time,
2. The new JIT values,
3. An emphasis on continuous improvement,
4. A new quality mindset, and
5. Total people productivity.

No single measurement can effectively cover all of these bases, so a compatible series will be necessary.

Baseline JIT Values

JUST-IN-TIME is the embodiment of the adage, "Time is money." There has been a great deal of emphasis placed on the *value of time* in this book through the reduction of time elements like customer response time, manufacturing leadtime, process control feedback time, setup time, supplier reorder leadtime, and transport time. With few exceptions, the measurement system should reward things that are done faster and penalize things that take longer to accomplish.

The methodology of JUST-IN-TIME embraces *new values.* It centers on the elimination of waste, especially in terms of non-value added activities and unnecessary investments. Instead of a trade-off philosophy (How can I justify this investment?), it is a relentless reduction effort (How can I eliminate this waste?) Eliminating contingencies and driving production lot sizes down to the lowest possible level (ideally, one) are vital to the reduction of response time. The measurements should encourage these approaches and discourage trade-off ratios which foster contingency investments or "creative accounting."

A fundamental principle of JIT is *continuous improvement* until perfection is attained. Measurements should be more concerned with relative performance over time for a given operation than with the absolute numbers themselves. In addition, every operation is different, so trying to use performance data that is meaningful at the local level to compare one business to another can be like trying to equate apples to oranges. For example, a highly-engineered, assembled-product facility is going to produce significantly different performance numbers than a capital-intensive, commodity-type manufacturing operation. If you want to compare operations for relative investment considerations, use ROI. If you want to know if JIT is working in the short-term, look at the performance measures for each separate facility and monitor the rate of improvement over time. Eventually it will show up in the ROI figure as well.

Quality and Productivity Emphasis

The JIT quality target is perfection. That's a far cry from today's results and requires a *new quality mindset.* Quality performance measures need to reflect this goal, both as a reminder of the target and as a method to reorient the thinking of the work force toward its viability. In addition, remember the second corollary of Q@S Principle #1 which says quality improvements should not be more expensive. Those costs need to be monitored in conjunction with quality performance data to give a true picture of the quality progress at a location.

JUST-IN-TIME changes everybody's job to enhance *total people productivity*. The traditional lines of demarcation between direct and indirect labor, between salary and hourly jobs, and between "professional" and "non-professional" activities become blurred. The only valid measure of people productivity in a JIT environment is one which includes all of them. That way, tradeoffs (like those between direct labor employees and salaried technicians needed to support high-tech equipment) will always be taken into account. There should be no way to move people costs from one "pocket" to another just to make a given measure look better.

Key Performance Measurements
The foregoing criteria can be met by three broad categories of short-term performance measurements. They are:
- People Productivity
- Product Quality
- Inventory Utilization

Specific recommendations for each category are described in the following sections.

PEOPLE PRODUCTIVITY

What is productivity? In its simplest form, it is getting more output for a given level of input. Just about everybody can agree with that much. It's the next level of detail that starts all the debate. What is output? Is it what we make, even if we don't sell it? While some might argue to the contrary, the JIT answer is quite clear. When you are trying to produce to *exact customer demand,* there is no benefit and should be no credit for production in excess of the sales demand. Thus, only that which is actually sold should be considered output.

Inputs can also be interpreted many ways. People, equipment, total assets and energy are commonly used bases of input. Each has more or less importance to specific businesses; e.g., energy is a major input in many process industries, depending upon the product produced.

Thus, output per person, per machine-hour, per asset dollar or per kilowatt-hour are often used. In many cases, companies have tried to combine all of them into a consolidated productivity measurement. That can get very complicated and often requires data that is not readily available through normal collection channels. In addition, the resulting ratio can be so nebulous that people will have a hard time relating to it. The best productivity measurement will be one that is simple and understandable even if it doesn't include *everything*.

Sales Per Person

The most significant short-term variable in the majority of manufacturing activities is the number of people involved. I once had a boss who insisted that all other costs "magically" increased or decreased in direct proportion to the number of people on the payroll, regardless of the control measures employed. He was simply applying the Pareto Principle to separate the important item from the "trivial many." The fact is that people spend money and more people spend more money. I must admit that with rare exceptions it proved to be a good rule-of-thumb.

It may explain why the most popular productivity measurement used in the United States today is *sales dollars per person on the payroll*. According to the American Productivity Center in Houston, Texas, about 80% of American companies use it. Sales dollars per person is simple, understandable and easily attainable. It only gives credit for actual customer shipments and includes the entire payroll. Its drawbacks, however, include the fact that inflation will distort the sales dollars from year to year, that overtime or "temporary" employees may not be accounted

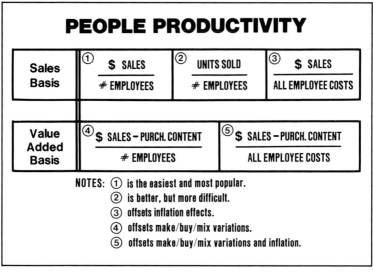

Figure 15-3

for, and that vertically integrated businesses will suffer when compared to pure assembly businesses. (The way to "beat" this measurement is to subcontract everything.)

The inflation issue can be overcome by measuring *unit sales per person on the payroll*. If your production output can be stated in terms of pounds, gallons, square feet, etc., it is the most stable, simple measurement of people productivity. Product mix variations can be handled by equating the output to "standard" units of measure, which will complicate things a bit.

On the other hand, if you use *sales dollars per payroll dollar* as the productivity measurement, the inflationary effects on sales and costs will tend to cancel each other out. If the payroll costs include fringes, overtime, and temporary employees, it will be pretty hard to beat this measurement. The only thing it doesn't account for is the degree of vertical integration.

Value Added Per Person

That problem can be solved by measuring the amount of value *added per person on the payroll*. In this case, purchased content costs are subtracted from sales dollars. The difference is the value that is added as a result of your company's efforts. When divided by the number of people on the payroll, the resulting ratio will be more stable for a variety of businesses because more value added content will generally require more people, and vice-versa. Inflation is still an issue, though.

The best measure of people productivity, in my opinion, is *value added dollars per payroll dollar*. It's a dollar for dollar ratio which cancels out the effects of inflation, especially in fast turnover operations like JIT shops. Higher labor costs for vertically integrated operations are offset by a higher value added factor in the numerator of the ratio. Similarly, greater factory margins for highly-engineered assembled products are offset by the increased engineering costs in the denominator of the equation. Shifts in personnel costs from operations to technical support are accounted for as well. Best of all, it answers the overall question, "How are we benefiting by having this combination of people on the payroll?"

The five people productivity measures discussed in this section are recapped in Figure 15-3. They will provide you with varying degrees of visibility depending upon the information you have or are willing to develop. What's important is that the one you select be consistently applied and that the emphasis be placed on relative improvement over time.

PRODUCT QUALITY

The ultimate goal of Quality at the Source is *perfect parts every time.* The pathway to get there is continuous improvement. The measurement of progress must keep that goal in focus while also accounting for the *decreasing cost of quality.* This dual objective is similar to the safety reporting system most companies use in which the frequency of accidents and their severity are both important. It's the combination of defect rates and quality costs that gives a true measure of total quality performance.

Defects Per Million

Everybody in the organization needs to start thinking about defect rates in terms of parts per million. You have already seen examples in this book of companies who are achieving 100, 60 and even 20 parts per million customer reject rates. Internally, of course, the numbers may be much higher. The important thing, though, is to orient everyone's mindset to this significantly higher level of performance requirements.

At the beginning, it can be discouraging. A one percent defect rate will translate to 10,000 parts per million. However, it will clearly establish how far you have to go to become a world-class competitor. On the positive side, the improvements made will appear to be much more significant because every tenth of a percent gain will net you 1,000 parts per million.

The baseline for measurement should be physical volume (parts, gallons, pounds, etc.) as opposed to a labor base (defects per hour), dollar base (percent dollars defective) or some other compound ratio. The idea is to keep the measurement as simple and "pure" as possible. It should clearly answer the question, "How good are we?"

There are two broad areas of concern. The first is how well customer expectations are being met. There are many things we can do internally, as discussed in Chapter 3, to help assure that only good products leave the plant. Shipped products represent the net effect of the entire Quality at the Source effort on the external world. Customer reject rates, then, are the first ones that we should realistically expect to achieve parts per million performance.

Internal defect rates are usually monitored by operation, by machine, by workcenter, etc. In fact, you probably already have so much data now it is hard to get anybody outside of the quality department to even look at it. Too much information can be almost as bad as too little. The best way to keep everyone's focus on internal quality is to combine the defect rates into a single number for each product line (focused factory) and again for the whole plant. The absolute numbers may be frightening at first and may even increase for awhile as quality standards tighten. But these are "handles" that management can relate to and which can be easily tracked to give them a "big picture" look at the progress of the internal quality program.

Another reason external and internal defect rates should be monitored separately is that the information you receive about them will be on different time bases. Internal data will be almost real-time, allowing you to react quickly with corrective actions. External feedback will lag behind the causes of those customer rejects by weeks and even months. Trying to combine both in one period, like a month or a quarter, will produce an artificial measurement of questionable value.

A good way to maintain defect rate information is on a statistical control chart, just like the SPC charts discussed in Chapter 3. The data can be averaged, plotted and used to calculate control limits, which will establish the expected range of the defect rate information. That way you will know when month-to-month changes are normal variations or are something requiring investigation. It can save you a lot of "wheel spinning" time trying to chase down explanations for minor variances that aren't even statistically relevant.

Cost of Quality

Defects represent failures of the production system to meet expectations. They are expensive, perhaps even more so than many people realize. Everybody tracks scrap and rework costs, which represent the bulk of *internal failures,* but there are many other ones which seldom get recorded. For example, the "fire fighting" time spent by engineers and supervision on reject problems is buried in department expenses. Retesting reworked material is rarely segregated from normal inspection. The cost of the material review storage area and its maintenance are part of the plant overhead. When added together, these hidden costs can equal or exceed your scrap and rework costs.

For all of that, customer rejects are the most costly, not only from an expense standpoint but also because of their potential impact on future business. These are *external failures.* Warranty and field service costs would be unnecessary if these failures did not occur. In addition, customer service activities to handle complaints are a quality failure expense but are likely to be absorbed in the sales department's budget.

Similarly, all the customer "hand-holding" trips that are taken by sales and engineering people to correct field problems fall into this category. External failure costs can easily double or triple the internal failure costs unless we find them first.

The money we spend to find discrepancies before they are shipped to the customer is classified as the cost of *appraisal*. This includes such things as in-process and final inspection, testing, measurement equipment calibration and maintenance, receiving inspection, supplier dock audits, and related administrative expenses. Quality conscious companies have invested heavily in this area because it is generally believed that one dollar of investment here can save two to five dollars of scrap and rework cost. Even so, this category typically amounts to half of the failure costs. It has not been effective because it happens after the quality, or lack thereof, has been built into the product.

Investments that are aimed at keeping defects from occurring in the first place are called *prevention* costs. They include things like design for manufacturability efforts, process improvements, "fail-safe" mechanisms, SPC training and implementation, supplier evaluation, selection and development, etc. Current industry estimates are that a dollar spent here will save four to seven dollars in appraisal and failure costs. In other words, this is the category that makes it possible to improve product quality while simultaneously decreasing the cost of quality. It is also the least applied in most companies.

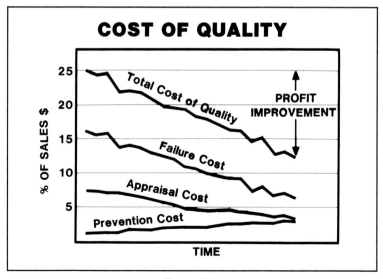

Figure 15-4

When the costs of failure, appraisal and prevention are summarized, it is not unusual to find that the total cost of quality can be *20% to 25% of the sales dollar.* That is a "big piece of change." A well-designed and implemented prevention program can eventually take this figure down to the 2% to 3% range. It is an incredible opportunity for profit improvement but don't expect it to happen "overnight." This is a change in company culture which will take time to achieve.

A good way to track the component costs of quality is shown in Figure 15-4. In this example, the total cost per sales dollar was cut in half and the relative proportions of the categories changed significantly. (Failure costs went from 65% to 50% of the total, appraisal costs dropped from 30% to 25% and prevention costs increased from 5% to 25%.) Couple this with your defect rate control charts and you'll have a clear picture of how good you're getting and how much you're saving.

For more information about setting up and implementing a quality cost system at your company, I recommend two booklets published by the American Society for Quality Control (ASQC), *Principles of Quality Costs* and *Guide for Reducing Quality Costs.*

INVENTORY UTILIZATION

After people productivity and product quality. the next key issue is how well a production center is utilizing the assets assigned to it. As stated earlier, permanent assets (like plants and equipment) are long-term investments that are best measured by ROI or a modification of ROI which yields return on permanent assets only. Short-term performance measurements should be applied to working capital which are the only assets that can be affected by operating management in the short-term.

Why Inventory?

The biggest part of working capital and, in fact, the largest element of the entire asset base for most manufacturing companies is inventory. For many businesses it can amount to half to two-thirds of the total investment base. The Pareto Principle would definitely classify inventory as an "A" item.

Coincidentally, it is also the "asset" that JUST-IN-TIME has identified as a *liability* which inhibits people productivity and product quality. So, while we want those two sets of numbers to go *up,* we want to encourage inventory levels to go *down.* This is especially true for work-in-process (WIP), the inventory on the shop floor.

To effectively control inventory, you should be able to separate it into three major categories: finished goods, WIP and raw materials or purchased components (material). At the beginning, there may be some valid arguments for maintaining finished goods to support customer service and for material to buffer unreliable suppliers, but there is no justification for high WIP inventory. Since your JIT implementation will start on the shop floor, with supplier and customer interfaces coming later, you will need to be able to track the progress of each segment separately. In the "perfect" JIT shop there will be no finished goods or material inventory and very little WIP.

Inventory Turnover

The dollar value of inventory, while important from a cash-flow standpoint, is not nearly as significant as its relationship to the volume of production it supports. A million-dollar inventory is a big investment; but if it supports four million dollars of output, it is a much better investment than if it only supports two million dollars of output. While this relationship, called inventory turnover, has long been recognized as a materials management measurement, it is the best short-term measurement of operating management's utilization of its biggest asset.

This can be clearly seen by taking another look at the Du Pont ROI chart in Figure 15-2. Of all the elements in the income stream (the top chain), the biggest and most controllable by operating management is the *manufacturing cost of sales (MCOS),* which consists of material, labor and overhead. That statement is equally valid for a profit center or for a cost center. The biggest element in the investment base (the lower chain) is the *inventory.* When MCOS for a period is analyzed and divided by the average inventory level during that period, the resulting figure tells how many times that inventory will rotate in a year to support the output level (hence the term, inventory *turnover).*

Notice that no credit is given for what is produced, only what is sold. That reinforces the JIT principle to produce only to exact customer demand and discourages building inventory to make the production numbers look good. This measurement is not intended to show a return on the inventory investment, but rather how well the investment is being managed to accomplish the sales goals of the operating unit. It also supports the value of time in a JIT environment because the faster the throughput time in the shop, the lower the WIP and the higher the turnover becomes.

Inventory turnover is usually calculated on a monthly, quarterly or annual basis, as shown in the top portion of Figure 15-5. In each case, the manufacturing cost of sales for the period is annualized and the inventory is averaged. Monthly figures will be probably be unstable unless your sales are very consistent. Quarterly data will be much more representative of your progress, and like the productivity and quality measurements, it is the trend that really counts.

Inventory Days On Hand

Inventory utilization can also be expressed as the number of days of sales (in MCOS dollars) that the inventory will support. Many people prefer this measurement because it is easier to visualize than a turnover ratio. For example, having 90 days worth of inventory on hand when your manufacturing throughput time is supposed to be 30 days clearly indicates that there's too much of something around.

The key decision point for this measurement is whether a day is a calendar day or a production day. Those who worry about the time value of the inventory investment will argue that it is on hand on weekends as well as work days, so calendar days should be used. On the other hand, that "day" of inventory would not support a full production day, so it would not be as meaningful to operations people. My preference is to state the inventory in terms of production days to maximize its utility as a reference.

Since the number of production days will vary from month-to-month

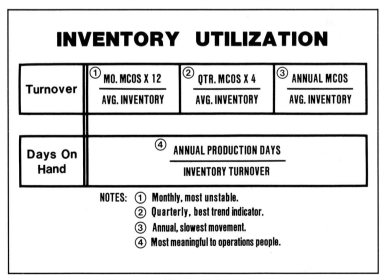

Figure 15-5

and with overtime, the only way to stabilize this measurement is to pick the number of production days you expect to work in a year and stick with it. That way, you can convert any turnover figure into inventory days on hand by simply dividing the number of annual production days by the inventory turnover as shown in the bottom of Figure 15-5.

Manufacturing Throughput Days

If you're willing to make one more set of calculations, inventory days on hand can be used to give you a very good approximation of your manufacturing throughput time. The aggregate days on hand figure can't do that for you because it is a combination of material in storage, work-in-process and finished goods, each of which has a different dollar value for one "day" of inventory. By computing a separate figure for each segment, you can tell how long it takes for the average part or product to get through that segment. Summing them will give you the total manufacturing throughput time for the whole plant, portal to portal.

The first step is to establish the relative inventory values in each segment so you can compute *inventory factors*. As inventory flows through a plant, it picks up cost and, hopefully, value like the diagram shown in Figure 15-6. In this case, it has only the material content value while it sits in raw material stores for ten days. Next, labor (and overhead) get added during the ten days it takes to go through the manufacturing process. Finally, the completed product sits in finished

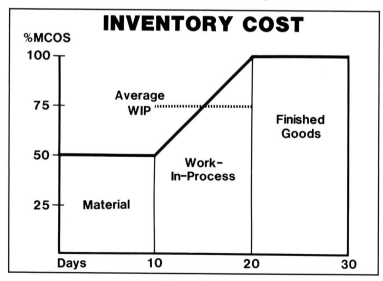

Figure 15-6

goods inventory at full MCOS value for another ten days before it is shipped to a customer. The total throughput time in the plant is 30 days. The problem is that inventory days on hand are always computed at full MCOS but the only segment that carries that value is finished goods. As a result, days on hand is always less than actual throughput time. That's where the inventory factors come in.

By computing a factor for each inventory segment, based on its relative MCOS value, you can easily determine the "real" average throughput time for your plant. In each case, the factor is the fraction of full MCOS represented by that segment, which can be taken from your monthly P&L (or cost) statement. In our example, material is 50% of MCOS so the factor would be 0.5. For work-in-process, the factor is material content (50%) plus *half* of the labor and overhead content (the average amount in WIP, as shown in Figure 15-6) which adds up to 75%, or a factor of 0.75. Finished goods is valued at full MCOS, so its factor would be 1.00.

The inventory value in each segment is then divided by its factor to raise it to full MCOS value. This, in turn, is divided by the average daily shipments (in MCOS dollars) to arrive at manufacturing throughput days (leadtime days). Then, you can convert any days on hand inventory report to leadtime days like the following example:

Inventories:		FACTOR	EQUIV. MCOS	LT DAYS
Raw Material	$1,000,000	0.50	$2,000,000	20
Work-In-Process	750,000	0.75	1,000,000	10
Finished Goods	1,000,000	1.00	1,000,000	10
Total	$2,750,000			40

Average Daily MCOS $100,000
Inventory Days On Hand   27.5

Clearly, you can see that the equivalent manufacturing throughput time of 40 days is substantially longer than the inventory days on hand figure of 27.5 days. There's nothing wrong with using the aggregate days on hand number to monitor continuous improvement in inventory utilization. However, if you want to know how long it is really taking to process material through your plant, the extra step to get to throughput days or leadtime days is well worth the effort.

REPLACING OLD PERFORMANCE MEASUREMENTS

People productivity, product quality, and inventory utilization should be the "Big 3" performance measurements used in a JIT business. Ideally, sub-optimal measurements, like labor efficiency and machine utilization, should be eliminated. However, that may be too traumatic for many, especially if they have been the primary shop performance measurements up to now. To help ease the transition, I'd like to suggest two replacement measurements, *labor effectiveness and machine performance,* which will at least support the JUST-IN-TIME objectives.

Labor Effectiveness

The implementation of JIT creates major changes in the shop. Many indirect activities (inspection, material handling, setup, minor maintenance, etc.) are reduced by new layouts and process improvements and others are absorbed into operator responsibilities. As a result, direct labor efficiency rarely reflects the actual situation.

While direct labor efficiency takes advantage of time standards to account for product mix when measuring actual expenditures against the targets, it has little relationship to potential profitability because:
- It does not account for indirect labor.
- If often drives us to over produce (when we're on a "roll") or to make the wrong (easy) parts, neither of which may be shippable in the current period.
- It can make us look "bad" even when we are doing the "right" things, like absorbing indirect activities into direct labor functions and reducing total headcount.

By the simple expedient of adding indirect labor costs to the denominator of the direct labor efficiency equation, a more meaningful short-term measure is created. Called Labor Effectiveness, the formula is:

$$\text{Labor Effectiveness} = \frac{\text{Standard Hours Earned}}{\text{Total Hours (D.L. + I.L. Worked)}}$$

It offers the following advantages:
- Better tracking to the "bottom line,"
- More comprehensive measurement,
- Shows JIT improvements,
- Still uses standards to reflect product mix.

These claims may not be readily apparent when you look at historical data in a traditional shop. I believe it is because we have tended to hire indirect labor in proportion to direct labor based on previously budgeted ratios. Only when JIT implementation forces changes in the ratios does the value of Labor Effectiveness as a measure become clearly visible.

JCI Linden Experience

The implementation of JIT at Johnson Control's Linden plant produced some eye-opening improvements, many of which have been discussed in this book. As the results began showing up on the bottom line, the accounting department became concerned that the direct labor efficiency numbers did not reflect the same improvement. In fact, they wondered whether the plant was "playing games" with the numbers.

To convince them that the progress was real, and to offer a better short-term measure, a study was conducted to compare Labor Effectiveness with Direct Labor Efficiency. Data for an 18-month period were analyzed as shown in Figure 15-7. The timeframe includes seven months before JIT and eleven months of partial JIT implementation. The correlation was remarkable:

- During the seven months before JIT, Direct Labor Efficiency and Labor Effectiveness tracked each other; but neither one tracked actual variable margin.

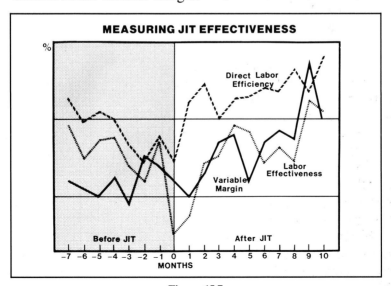

Figure 15-7

- With JIT implementation, a series of significant events occurred, including the first departmental rearrangement, a physical inventory, and the elimination of press room overtime. Both measures reflected this, but Labor Effectiveness was much more sensitive to the changes.
- In JIT Months 1 and 2, both measures tracked the improvements in the new Assembly Department, plus the elimination of overtime in the Primary Press Department and the Tool Room.
- In JIT Month 3, the elimination of a labor-intensive product line improved margins but was reflected by a *lower* Labor Efficiency rating. Labor Effectiveness went up like the Variable Margin.
- In Month 5, Variable Margin and Labor Effectiveness dropped while Labor Efficiency actually went up a bit.
- In Month 6, the change in Labor Effectiveness was contrary to the change in Variable Margin. This was the only occurance.
- In JIT Months 8, 9 and 10, Labor Effectiveness tracked Variable Margin while Labor Efficiency went in the *opposite direction each time.*

In short, while there is no doubt that Labor Effectiveness is far from a perfect measure, it stands head and shoulders above Direct Labor Efficiency in this JIT environment. It reflects whether we're making any money and seldom (only once in this study) provides a contrary signal.

Machine Performance

The traditional measurement of machine utilization impels us to keep a machine busy whether the parts are needed or not. While it is important to know whether or not a machine is paying for itself according to its purchase rationale, and also whether we have extra capacity, using machine utilization as a performance measurement is contrary to JIT principles. First, there should be no incentive to produce more than the scheduled quantity as JIT calls for producing to exact demand. Second, when machines are dedicated to focused factories or group technology cells, their capacity is dependent on the combined capability of all the machines in the cluster.

What we should do is measure machine running hours for *scheduled production only.* This will give us a handle on how well the equipment performs when called upon. It is the measurement of JIT Principle #7, which states that machines must always be ready.

The formula for machine performance is:

$$\frac{\text{Machine}}{\text{Performance}} = \frac{\textbf{Run Hours For Scheduled Production}}{\substack{\textbf{Standard Hours for} \\ \textbf{Scheduled Production}}}$$

This measurement only gives credit for running scheduled production. The ideal number is 1. When the ratio is less than 1, it is an indicator of unplanned downtime so it serves as a productive maintenance monitor. When the number is greater than 1, it means it took more hours than planned to accomplish the schedule (a quality problem) or else unauthorized production was run, so it is also serving as a schedule adherence monitor.

The classic utilization figure (machine running hours divided by available hours) should only be used as a measure of potential capacity for capital planning purposes. Even there, if the machine is a non-bottleneck unit in a GT cell, its capacity will be paced by the capacity of the bottleneck equipment.

BETTER PRODUCT COSTS

Once we get past the issue of performance measurements, we still have to know what our actual product costs are so we can price them to make money. Here, again, JUST-IN-TIME changes all the old perspectives. Today's cost systems are complex and require large volumes of input transactions because the manufacturing processes are complicated. That, coupled with arbitrary allocations and questionable allocation bases (like direct labor), has resulted in less than optimal product cost information. JIT simplifies things. Focused factories, group technology, operator self-reliance, less material handling, etc., make it easier to tie expenses directly to product families.

As a minimum, the traditional approach of establishing operations standards and accumulating costs by operation will shift to *process standards* for product and part families. A large part of today's overhead costs will shift to direct expenses and the remaining portion will be allocated based on time, which some people call *velocity costing*. The ultimate simplicity will be to *direct cost* everything, which becomes feasible when inventory turnovers begin to exceed 12 times per year. The result of these changes is more accurate costing information that is far earier and less expensive to obtain.

Direct Costing at Hewlett-Packard

While most companies are hesitant to make such major changes at first, you should know that precedents have already been set. Hewlett-Packard, for example, took a bold new approach when implementing JIT at its Boise and Disc Memory Divisions. The changes included:

1. *Eliminate the direct labor cost category.*

H-P determined that since direct labor represented only 3% to 5% of its product cost and that variances were more dependent on how well a process was working than on worker efficiency, it made little sense to track direct labor separately.

2. *Treat manufacturing overhead as an expense.*

With dramatically improved inventory turnovers as a result of JIT, virtually all overhead costs incurred each month flowed through to the cost of goods sold the same month. Thus, no useful information was provided by tracking these costs through inventory accounts.

3. *Reduce accounting for scrap and rework.*

Less inventory between workcenters also meant less potential scrap. Since defective product was discovered almost immediately, elaborate tracking procedures were not needed.

The bottom line is that H-P's simplified accounting approach has saved them an estimated 100,000 journal entries per month at Disc Memory Division alone. At Boise Division, one accountant using a microcomputer handles all the cost reporting that took three accountants and a fully automated cost system to operate in the traditional manner. Even better, H-P reports that, "Production line managers can now understand the simpler reports provided by the accounting department and actually use the information in those reports."

Process Standards

Most companies don't have the daring shown by H-P. This is especially true when top management and their financial advisors don't yet fully understand JIT. They have to take it one step at a time. The first step for them is recognizing that operations standards will not be applicable in a JUST-IN-TIME environment.

Operations standards, long considered the lowest common denominator for costing purposes, address individual steps and individual performance in a "random" shop. This isn't the case under JIT where the focus is on the total process required to make a component/product including all of the links. When the factory floor is reorganized into product oriented workcenters with cross-trained operators who can and do perform every operation in the process, individual performance by operation is meaningless. Furthermore, the sequence of operations is fixed by dedicated equipment, so the flow is definitely not random. Besides, measurements based on operations standards require too much detail, too many transactions and too much complexity.

Under JIT, operations standards are replaced by process standards, which are summations of all the operations required to manufacture the product or component in a contiguous workcenter. Individual performance measurements are replaced by group or team performance measurements. The emphasis changes from meeting the engineered standard to continuous improvement over previous performance.

Data collection is really simplified. Consider the example shown in Figure 15-8. Suppose that a shop had only five products and each one was routed through five departments in its manufacturing process. To determine the cost for product P3, five bits of information would be needed. Similarly, five inputs would be needed to determine the performance of the department performing Operation #3. Twenty-five bits of information would have to be collected and summarized ten different ways to determine the cost for all five products and the performance of each department.

When all the operations are connected, as in a GT cell, the product

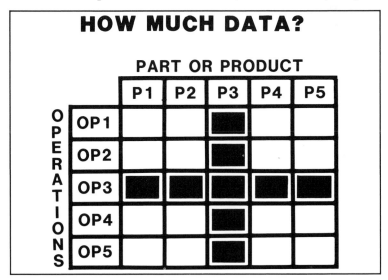

Figure 15-8

cost information and the workcenter performance are one and the same. They are collected at only one point. In effect, the data collection and processing efforts have been cut by 80%. Not only is this less complicated, it requires fewer accountants to "massage" all that information.

MANUFACTURING OVERHEAD

Manufacturing overhead distorts true product costs in a JIT environment because it is allocated on the wrong basis (direct labor cost, machine hours or material dollars); and when applied under the full absorption standard cost method, it drives us to overproduce so we can overabsorb. In addition, there is so much arbitrary allocation of shared costs among product families that the accuracy of the resulting "product cost" is highly suspect, even in a traditional operating environment.

Of all the product cost elements, manufacturing overhead is the second largest, after material, and is usually two to ten times larger than direct labor. It is defined as "all the direct and allocated costs of manufacturing other than direct labor and purchased materials." Once upon a time, this "all other" category was less than the direct labor content, so rough approximations did not hinder reasonable cost data. Today, the sheer magnitude of overhead demands better apportionment.

This is easier in a JIT environment because equipment is dedicated to specific product families in focused factories or to component/sub-

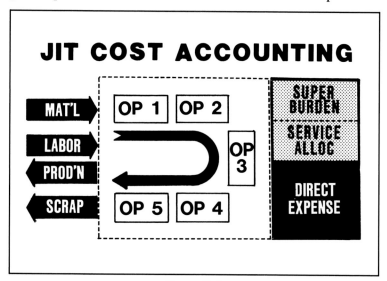

Figure 15-9

assembly families in group technology cells, as shown within the dotted lines in Figure 15-9. Since many indirect functions are now performed by the value adders in the workcenter, many costs in today's overhead pools will be part of the production process and won't need to be be allocated. (This is the lower block on the right side of the figure.)

JIT Overhead Elements

As a result, the JIT overhead pool will be smaller, as shown by the upper block on the right side of the figure. It, in turn, can be subdivided into two categories:

1. *Service allocations,* which are based on direct value added service or floor space used.

2. *Super-burden expenses,* which include unused floor space and plantwide administrative costs. These categories and their major components are summarized in Figure 15-10.

Many support activities can be directly charged to workcenters based on direct services rendered, because the workcenters are product related, not operations oriented. This is especially important in such areas as equipment maintenance, quality assurance, manufacturing engineering, material stores and handling, production planning and manufacturing systems activities. Each can be examined during the budgeting process to determine whether it is a "value added" service to a

JIT OVERHEAD ELEMENTS

SERVICE ALLOC.	"Value-added" support by: • Direct service • Actual space used
SUPER BURDEN	Remaining overhead costs: • Unused space • Administrative

Figure 15-10

product/component family for which the users are willing to pay. If not, it is probably a "waste" caused by the system and should be eliminated.

Some of those costs may not be directly chargeable but can be related to physical space used. They can be allocated based on the percentage of *space actually used for productive work.* For example, if the identifiable space for all workcenters and dedicated stores is 80,000 square feet out of 100,000 square feet of available manufacturing space, then direct allocations for 80% of the area-related costs should be made against the 80,000 square-foot base. The remaining 20% of those costs should be part of the super-burden category which contains plant-wide costs to keep the doors open. As workcenters condense, using less and less space, the overhead costs for those product areas will decrease, with the excess transferring to super-burden costs. In this manner, you can always see what the true costs of a product workcenter are (or would be if they had no other overhead to support).

The super-burden cost pool contains the applicable costs for the *unused space plus plantwide administrative costs,* like personnel administration, cost accounting, purchasing, plant security, insurance and utilities. Super-burden shows us both how much the superstructure is costing and where we have areas of opportunity to bring in new production to utilize some of the excess space. Every general storeroom and aisle that can be converted to a workcenter is a potential source of more output from the existing physical resource. The question is, "How can we allocate super-burden expenses to best reflect true product costs while encouraging JUST-IN-TIME values?"

Velocity Costing

Overhead costs have traditionally been allocated based on direct labor, material cost or some combination of the two. None of them reflects true product costs, especially under JIT. The best basis for the allocation of the super-burden is time. We all pay rent based on the size of our facility and the length of time it is used. The longer a manufacturing facility is used for production, the more the product should pay. Conversely, since JIT strives to shorten manufacturing throughput (lead) times, there should be a cost incentive to do so. This concept is called Velocity Costing.

Each part in the system should pay *"rent"* for the time it is using the facility. Long leadtime parts literally consume resources for a longer time than short leadtime parts. In this manner, a truer allocation of super-burden can be determined while motivating everyone to reduce leadtimes to obtain cost benefits.

The allocation of super-burden under velocity costing is based on leadtime days. For a given component, it is the total elapsed time from the moment it (or its raw material constituent) arrives at the plant to the time it is shipped out the door as part of a final product. Therefore, in-house manufactured components will carry more overhead than purchased components which are only final assembled.

As a starting point, you can use the "rolled up" leadtimes in your MRP system, which should include all setup, run, move and queue (or storage) times. A gross explosion of the Production Plan or a Master Schedule will provide the quantities of parts that are planned for the leadtime horizon. (You may have to supplement it with a forecast because a whole year of planned production is needed.) The number of parts times the quantity of each part times the leadtime per part is then summarized to develop the total number of planned leadtime days for the year. When total budgeted costs for super-burden elements are divided by the total leadtime days for all the products to be made, the result is the "standard" cost per leadtime day.

Figure 15-11 shows how these data would be developed for one product. Product A is composed of one Part B and two of Part C. Part B, in turn, contains two of Part D and one Part E. The leadtimes for each are shown by length of the vertical lines under each part, measured against the scale on the left side. The table on the right shows how

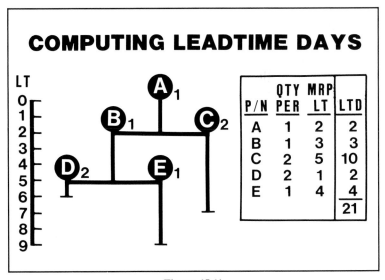

Figure 15-11

the total number of leadtime days for the product would be developed. For example, Part C has a leadtime of five days (it extends from 2 to 7 on the scale) and there are two of them in the product structure, so there would be 10 standard leadtime days for this part. The summation of all the part leadtimes in the structure (including the top level assembly time) results in 21 leadtime days for Product A. That number becomes the cost basis (base LTD) for overhead allocation. The planned rolled up leadtime (nine days for Product A) is the velocity standard for that product.

Super-burden is charged to a product based on the ratio of actual days required to build the product divided by the planned leadtime days (velocity standard) times the cost basis (the base number of leadtime days for the product times the cost per leadtime day). The formula is:

$$\text{Chargeable Super-burden} = \frac{\textbf{Actual Rolled Up LT}}{\textbf{Planned Rolled Up LT}} \times \textbf{Base LTD} \times \frac{\textbf{Std. Cost}}{\textbf{LT Day}}$$

Actual leadtimes are easy to obtain in a job-order environment. In a flow shop, it will be necessary to do gateway reporting to get this information. It's worth it, though, because it is amazing how conscious everyone in the shop becomes of throughput times and works to reduce them. It will also give you a totally new perspective of your product costs which may surprise you.

Velocity Costing at Plasti-Line

Plasti-Line, Inc. in Knoxville, Tennessee, has been wrestling with the implementation of velocity costing since 1987. (Plasti-Line is the leading producer of illuminated signs in the United States). When the company was in the early stages of JUST-IN-TIME implementation, Steve Newton, the Controller, wanted to develop a cost-accounting system that would support:

1. Critical success factors established by management
   a) Being the low cost producer
   b) Reducing manufacturing leadtimes
   c) Eliminating non-value added actions
   d) Controlling materials
   e) Providing the right strategic information
2. Performance improvement at different operational levels
3. Variance reporting to highlight key performance indicators

Initially, Plasti-Line could not accurately measure leadtime days from the receipt of material, due to a significant raw materials stores level and varying storage times per part number. Consequently, a separate overhead pool for material was established which included all acquisition, shipping and storage costs and was allocated against material value.

Plasti-Line's new cost-accounting system was defined as "a standard manufacturing cost-accounting system with the following attributes:

1. Absorption of manufacturing overhead costs based upon a fixed-dollar rate per standard leadtime day with the difference between absorbed and actual overhead expense incurred reported as a variance;

2. Absorption of material overhead costs; i.e. vendor scheduling, purchasing, receiving, raw material warehouse costs, etc., based upon a percentage of standard cost of materials purchased with the difference between absorbed and actual expenses incurred reported as a variance;

3. Finished goods inventories and sales cost at a current standard with all cost improvements made through value analysis to be reported on a monthly basis;

4. Sales cost for standard cost of sales plus distribution department costs applied as a percentage of sales (sales being defined as product shipments) with the difference between actual cost incurred and that absorbed to cost of sales being charged freight variance."

There are a number of differences between Plasti-Line's new cost-accounting system and previous procedures. They include:

1. Emphasis on reducing leadtime by absorbing manufacturing overhead on leadtime days rather than labor dollars;

2. De-emphasizing direct labor measurement by adding this cost element to manufacturing overhead;

3. Recording inventory transactions from the MRP transactions file;

4. Setting up a separate overhead pool for a "material overhead";

5. Setting up a separation cost of sales line item for the distribution department costs;

6. Emphasizing control of materials by measuring material usage variance;

7. Maintaining more accurate cost data by revising standards quarterly rather than on an annual basis.

Item 7 turned out to be an understatement, as Steve had to revise his standards four times during the first six months of operation under his standards four times during the first six months of operation under the new system. In retrospect, he attributes this to setting up the cost system before the leadtime reductions took place. As a result, the rapid changes in the shop required more frequent updates to the system than were anticipated. It is vital, however that the leadtime changes be incorporated so the cost system can reflect "true" costs.

Management had to adjust its thinking considerably as a result of the new cost system. All the numbers looked "funny" at first because they were so different from previous data. In some cases the figures were met with disbelief and long arguments ensued. Yet, as things settled down and people became more familiar and comfortable with the new approach, the cost system provided undeniable pointers toward volume and cost variances which were not apparent in the past.

Steve looks at Plasti-Line's experience from a "good news-bad news" perspective. The good news is that the project, which included ten operations people on the development team, had to completely rethink management's objectives so a measurement system could be designed to support them. This unified the management team. The bad news arises as Steve looks ahead while reflecting on the difficulty and expense involved in installing the new system. He says, "In another year or two I can see us changing to a much more simplified, less expensive, period-costing system. Was all this really necessary? On the other hand, could we ever get to JIT without going through this stage first?"

Steve's question embodies the dilemma faced by almost every company trying to implement JIT today. It's much like the "chicken and egg" issue . . . which came first? One thing is for certain though, we work the way we're measured. It's hard enough to initiate the changes in traditional manufacturing practices called for by JIT without fighting a measurement system that sends out contrary signals. That's why it is such an important issue.

SUMMARY

Measurements are vital to everyone, not just the accountants. They are the yardsticks that tell us how we've done and motivate us to perform. If they give contrary signals to the JIT principles you are trying to implement, you will lose your support because *we work the way we are measured*.

Today's cost and performance measurements are based on half-century old premises which do not reflect the changes manufacturing has undergone in the last few decades. In addition, they have been distorted over the years to conform to external reporting requirements. In truth, the numbers being generated today provide little useful guidance for managerial decisions and can even *drive management to do the wrong things.*

JUST-IN-TIME further accentuates this problem by introducing even more changes to manufacturing. By focusing on the simplification and rationalization of production processes, it reduces direct labor requirements, shifts many indirect functions to operator responsibilities and eliminates the need for complex inventory accounting procedures. It's a new ball game which requires a new view of today's measurements and replacements for some of them.

For example, Return On Investment (ROI) is a good long-term indicator of how effectively a given business is providing investors a return on their money, but somehow ROI has come to be used as a short-term performance measure by many companies today. They *live or die by the monthly ROI.* To let JIT "take hold," ROI must be supplemented with valid short-term measurements that will motivate managers to do the "right things."

The key to effective JIT measurement is inherent in the fundamental definition, "JUST-IN-TIME is a production strategy with a new set of values to continuously improve quality and productivity." In particular, measurements need to reflect the new JIT values and stress quality and productivity. This can best be met by three broad categories of short-term performance measurements, *People Productivity, Product Quality, and Inventory Utilization.*

The most significant short-term variable in the majority of manufacturing activities is the number of people involved. It may explain why the most popular productivity measurement used in the United States today is sales dollars per person on the payroll. *The best measure of people productivity is value added dollars per payroll dollar.* It's a dollar for dollar ratio which includes everybody, offsets the effects of inflation, and is more stable for a wide variety of businesses. Shifts in personnel costs from operations to technical support are accounted for as well. Best of all, it answers the overall question, "How are we benefiting from this combination of people on the payroll?"

A combination of defect rates and quality costs gives a true *measure of total quality performance.* Defect rates need to be measured in parts per million, even though the numbers may be in the tens of thousands at first, to orient everyone's mindset to this significantly higher level of performance requirements. The total cost of quality, which includes failure, appraisal and prevention costs, may represent 20% or more of your sales dollar today. This can be reduced to the 3% range over time, while simultaneously improving product quality, through a relentless prevention program.

The largest segment of the investment base for most companies, and the only one that operating management can affect in the short-term, is inventory. It is also the "asset" that JUST-IN-TIME has identified as a "liability" which inhibits people productivity and product quality. *Inventory utilization is best measured by annualized turnover rates or days supply on hand.* This measurement is not intended to show a return on the inventory investment, but rather how well the investment is being managed to accomplish the sales goals of the operating unit.

People productivity, product quality and inventory utilization should be the "Big 3" performance measurements used in a JIT business. Ideally, sub-optimal measurements, like labor efficiency and machine utilization, should be eliminated. However, to help ease the transition, *labor effectiveness* (a modification to the labor efficiency that includes indirect labor) and *machine performance* (which only gives credit for scheduled production) can be used. These will support the JUST-IN-TIME objectives.

Once we get past the issue of performance measurements, we still have to know what our products actually cost so we can price them to make money. Here, again, JUST-IN-TIME changes all the old perspectives. Today's cost systems are complex and require large volumes of input transactions because the manufacturing processes are complicated. JIT simplifies things. Focused factories, group technology, operator self-reliance, less material handling, etc., make it easier to tie expenses directly to product families.

As a minimum, the traditional approach of establishing operations standards and accumulating costs by operation will shift to *process standards* for product and part families. A large part of today's overhead costs will shift to direct expenses and the remaining portion will be allocated based on time, which some people call *velocity costing*. The ultimate simplicity will be to *direct cost* everything, which becomes feasible when inventory turnovers begin to exceed 12 times per year, and has already been demonstrated by companies like Hewlett-Packard. The result of these changes is more accurate costing information that is far easier and less expensive to obtain.

In measurement, as in all phases of JUST-IN-TIME, the key principle is continuous improvement. Transition is always the most difficult time, but it can also be a learning experience which helps everyone grow. Why build a "temporary" bridge to the future when it may not be the ultimate solution? Because it lets you start now, will give you valuable experience to improve upon, and will begin to weld the whole team together in pursuit of common objectives. It's the JUST-IN-TIME way.

PRODUCTION PLANNING

A Production Plan is management's game plan for the conduct of a manufacturing business. It is a specific, validated management-level statement of the production levels at which a company is to operate, considering customer requirements, sales goals, inventory investment and profit objectives. Its purpose is to provide a unified plan, discussed and agreed upon by all concerned, which optimally balances the sometimes conflicting objectives of maximum customer service, minimum investment, stable production, low production cost and maximum profit, shown by the Circle of Conflict in Figure A-1.

HOW PRODUCTION PLANNING IS DIFFERENT

All production operations do some type of production planning. However, there are three key elements which differentiate a formal Production Plan from most other planning processes:

1. The *integration* of the manufacturing operations plan with the other plans of the business.
2. A *formal committee* which approves and commits to

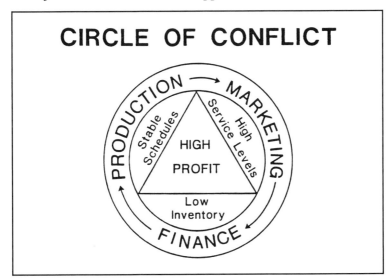

Figure A-1

achieving the Plan.

3. A *compatible master schedule* which is developed within the parameters of the Plan.

A Production Plan is *not* a long-range strategic plan, an annual budget, a master schedule, the customer order backlog, the shipment schedule, or a sales forecast. Rather, it is a separate document which integrates the last four of these with all other factors impacting production into a concise master plan for the conduct of manufacturing operations.

Plan Integration

It takes many types of plans, at varying levels of detail, to effectively manage a business. Without careful integration, they can easily conflict and work at cross-purposes. Figure A-2 illustrates how demand information should be consolidated upward in large, composite families in order to provide the summary data management requires. The output from the production planning process flows downward through several planning levels to the lowest component. Each of these plans must complement the others if the organization is to be effective. A structural look at the planning process is shown in Figure A-3. The inventory plan can be developed from an explosion of the master schedule. The final validation of a Production Plan ultimately becomes:

• Can your customers rely on the delivery commitments?

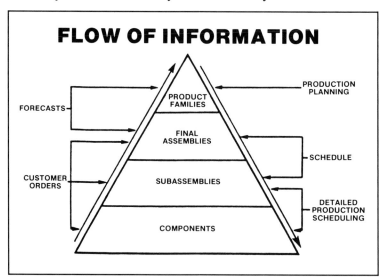

Figure A-2

- Will management accept the profit projection as the internal baseline projection?

Formal Planning Committee

All functional disciplines which impact the achievement of the plan must be represented on the Production Planning Committee by the highest ranking person in each discipline at that location. Membership may vary from business to business; e.g., engineering may not be required in a make-to-stock environment; and from time to time; e.g., Industrial Relations may be required when the plan envisions a significant change in the size of the work force. Typically, the formal committee would be composed of the following:

MEMBER	RESPONSIBILITIES
• General Manager	• Policy, plan approval, resolve conflicts
• Marketing	• Sales forecasts/customer orders
• Manufacturing	• Machine & manpower considerations
• Materials	• Draft plans, material inputs, shortages, shipments, master schedule

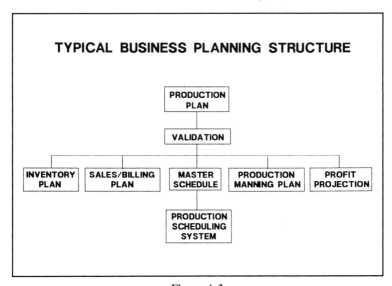

Figure A-3

- Controller
- Engineering

- Inventory and profit plans
- Major product changes, custom product releases

The necessity for formal procedures and meetings cannot be over-emphasized. Production Planning will only be successful if it is recognized by everybody as the official game plan for the operation, and each contributing discipline executes its part of the Plan without any modification or second guessing.

Compatible Master Schedule

The Master Schedule is subordinate to the Production Plan but is a very vital element. It must always be developed within the general parameters of the Plan. While the Production Plan is stated in terms of product families and monthly periods, the master schedule addresses specific product numbers in weekly or daily periods. It is normally prepared by the master scheduler after the Production Plan has been approved, and care must be taken to insure that it reflects the intent of the Production Plan. In rare cases, such as long-term government contracts for a single item, the Production Plan and the master schedule could become synonymous. Otherwise, they're very different.

PRODUCTION PLANNING CHECKLIST

Production Planning is a process. It will vary some by type of business, but there are certain characteristics which are fundamental to all businesses. Figure A-4 is a checklist of the key items. It consists of seventeen line items grouped into Management, Document and Administration categories. Most items are self-explanatory, but the following items merit special emphasis:

Monthly Meetings

The plan must be updated at least monthly. Production Planning is an iterative process, so an out-of-date plan is useless, and may actually be harmful. The time periods or "buckets" used should be monthly, close in, but can be larger; e.g., quarterly further into the future.

Commitment

The General Manager and all the members of the committee must review and must commit themselves to the plan. In this connection, the

PRODUCTION PLANNING CHECKLIST

MANAGEMENT ELEMENTS

☐ FORMAL MPP COMMITTEE, WHICH INCLUDES THE GENERAL MANAGER, CONTROLLER AND FUNCTIONAL DIRECTORS (I.E., MARKETING, MANUFACTURING, MATERIAL, ETC.)

☐ MONTHLY REVIEW MEETINGS TO REVISE AND UPDATE THE MPP

☐ COMMITMENT FROM DIRECTORS THAT THE MPP WILL BE FOLLOWED

☐ SIGNATURE APPROVAL BY THE GENERAL MANAGER

☐ USED AS THE BASIS FOR BUDGETING AND FINANCIAL FORECASTING

☐ USED AS THE BASIS FOR DOWNSTREAM MASTER SCHEDULES AND CUSTOMER COMMITMENTS

☐ REQUIRES MPP COMMITTEE APPROVAL FOR CHANGES IN SCOPE

MPP DOCUMENT ELEMENTS

☐ CONTAINS THE MINIMUM NUMBER OF PRODUCT FAMILIES THAT FULLY DESCRIBE THE BUSINESS (INCLUDING SPARES AND REPAIRS)

☐ COVERS A TIME PERIOD (PLANNING HORIZON) EQUAL TO OR GREATER THAN THE LONGEST PRODUCT FAMILY LEAD TIME (PROCUREMENT TIME + MANUFACTURING TIME)

☐ IS SUBDIVIDED INTO MONTHLY PERIODS, AS A MINIMUM

☐ RECONCILES SALES FORECASTS AND CUSTOMER ORDERS TO REALISTIC SHIPPING PLANS, SHOWING RESULTING SHORTAGES/SURPLUS

☐ DESCRIBES THE ACTUAL PRODUCTION PLAN, WHICH USUALLY DIFFERS FROM THE SHIPPNG PLANS

☐ HAS BEEN VALIDATED WITH RESPECT TO REALISTIC:
  - MACHINE CAPACITY
  - LABOR SHIFT/OVERTIME PLAN
  - VENDOR CAPACITY AND LEAD TIME
  - MATERIAL AVAILABILITY

ADMINISTRATIVE ELEMENTS

☐ CONVERTED TO A MASTER SCHEDULE, BY PART NUMBER, IN WEEKLY TIME PERIODS, WHICH CONFORMS TO THE MPP

☐ ADMINISTERED BY A MASTER SCHEDULER, WHO MAY ONLY MAKE MIX CHANGES WITHIN THE SCOPE OF THE MPP

☐ PERFORMANCE MEASURED AT LEAST WEEKLY AND REPORTED TO THE GENERAL MANAGER

☐ UNCOMPLETED WORK RESCHEDULED INTO FUTURE TIME PERIODS, SUBJECT TO MPP SCOPE RESTRAINTS

Figure A-4

commitment does not necessarily mean everyone is in absolute agreement with the Plan; rather, it means the Plan has been discussed, conflicting objectives have been resolved in the manner indicated by the Plan, and everyone is now committed to its achievement.

Signature

The commitment must be evidenced by the General Manager's signature on the plan, and many companies also require the signature of every member of the Committee. Unsigned Production Plans, or those signed by one staff member or a department head, do not receive the same attention. This has been proved many times in actual practice.

Product Families

The Production Plan should be stated in terms of product families or product lines, not shippable end items with specific part numbers. Product families are the natural groupings of similar items; and in most businesses, management has already identified these families and used them to analyze other parts of the business. They usually relate to marketing groupings, physical production lines, etc. They should be relatively broad; don't get involved in too much detail at this level.

Horizon

The planning horizon used for the Plan must be sufficient to cover the longest cumulative leadtime; i.e., purchase leadtime plus manufacturing time as a minimum. It may have to be even longer to encompass personnel adjustments, subcontracting strategies and capital equipment acquisitions.

Validation

A positive determination must be made that the Production Plan is achievable in terms of the resources required and is not just a "wish list" of things management would like to have happen. Validation of the Plan requires a rough-cut look at available capacity in terms of the material, machines and personnel that can be applied to its achievement within the Production Plan horizon.

Measurement

The results of the planning process must be measured and recorded weekly. It is the only way to tell how well the Plan is executed. The Plan may be quantified in terms of equivalent units, dollars, standard hours, board feet of lumber or anything else meaningful to the management of the business.

Rescheduling

Products may be "past due" to a customer or past due from a previous plan, but products can't be manufactured yesterday. A Production Plan which shows a past due column for production is not valid. By the same token, a front-end production "bubble" in the first month of the Plan, which exceeds available capacity, is also invalid. On the other hand, customer orders which are past due should be compared to realistically planned production to show when recovery is expected. Comparing customer demand and planned production will also show potential surplus.

THE PLANNING SEQUENCE

The planning cycle will normally extend over several days. Most companies will find it useful to conduct a series of preliminary meetings at which the basic information required for Production Plan is developed, such as the sales forecast or open-order status reports. These meetings are commonly conducted by subordinates of the Planning Committee. However, the final review and approval of the plan requires the personal involvement of the committee members, including the General Manager.

A typical planning sequence would include:
1. Preliminary meeting to review customer demand (orders, releases, forecasts, etc.)
2. Draft plan to meet demand (End Of Month - 8 days)
3. Preliminary meeting to compare available personnel, material and capacity to draft plan
4. Revise plan if required (EOM - 6 days)
5. Prepare an inventory plan that corresponds to the revised draft Production Plan, including:
   - Purchased material input
   - Direct labor and burden input
   - Shipment plan/finished goods balances
6. Calculate labor costs, overtime, manufacturing expenses, burden absorption, etc.
7. Develop a profit projection (EOM - 4 days)
8. Conduct the final Production Planning Committee meeting to review the proposed Plan, modify it if necessary and approve the final Plan (EOM - 2 Days)

TYPICAL PLANS

The format of the Production Planning document must be tailored to fit the individual business. In some cases, the same company may have format variations for diverse product families.

A sample layout for a company manufacturing products against customer releases is shown in Figure A-5. This is typical for a repetitive manufacturing operation. The management forecast line is a plus/minus quantity that factors in the consensus judgment of the Committee in relation to what customer releases and/or the sales forecast says demand will be. The format for a make-to-stock business would be very similar except that open stock orders would replace customer releases.

The other end of the spectrum is shown in Figure A-6 for custom-engineered products. Here, different measurements are used. Since these products are usually quoted based on estimated costs and may have no standards, the planning and tracking of gross margins and production hours is crucial.

Whichever format is used, a separate plan should be prepared for each product family and it should be confined to one page.

IMPLEMENTATION

Getting the Production Planning process going is a major under-taking, especially if interdisciplinary communications and coordination have been minimal. However, after the initial efforts to get it started, the job gets easier because subsequent iterations are just updates and the process gets smoother as the participants become familiar with it. To help you get started, the following is offered as a guide:

Establish Your Baseline
- Review the Production Planning Checklist.
- Establish an action plan to incorporate missing elements into your Production Planning process.

Organize For Results
- Form a Production Planning Project Team.
- Appoint a top notch Project Leader.
- Establish target milestones for implementation.

Establish Project Tasks
- Decide who should sit on the Planning Committee.

SAMPLE FORMAT
CUSTOMER RELEASES
PRODUCT LINE A
(000's OF UNITS)

	PAST DUE	CURRENT MONTH	+1	+2	+3	+N
REQUIREMENTS						
CUSTOMER RELEASED						
CUSTOMER FORECAST						
MANAGEMENT FORECAST						
TOTAL REQUIREMENTS						
PRODUCTION/SHIPMENTS	XXX					
BEGINNING F.G. INVENTORY	XXX					
PLANNED PRODUCTION	XXX					
TOTAL AVAILABLE	XXX					
SHIPMENTS	XXX					
ENDING F.G. INVENTORY	XXX					
CUSTOMER POSITION	XXX					
MANPOWER	XXX					
PRODUCTION DAYS	XXX					
DAILY RATE	XXX					
# LINES / # SHIFTS	XXX					
HEADCOUNT	XXX					
OVERTIME	XXX					

Figure A-5

SAMPLE FORMAT
CUSTOM ENGINEERED INDIVIDUAL UNITS
PRODUCT LINE A

	PAST DUE	CURRENT MONTH	+1	+2	+3	+N
CUSTOMER ORDERS						
NUMBER OF UNITS						
SELLING PRICE						
GROSS MARGIN						
COST OF SALES						
ESTIMATED HOURS						
PRODUCTION						
BEGINNING WIP-HOURS	XXX					
PLANNED PRODUCTION-HOURS	XXX					
SHIPMENTS-HOURS	XXX					
ENDING WIP-HOURS	XXX					
SHIPMENTS						
NUMBER OF UNITS	XXX					
SELLING PRICE	XXX					
GROSS MARGIN	XXX					
CUSTOMER POSITION						
NUMBER OF UNITS	XXX					
SELLING PRICE	XXX					
ESTIMATED HOURS	XXX					
MANPOWER						
PRODUCTION DAYS	XXX					
HEADCOUNT	XXX					
UTILIZATION	XXX					
EFFICIENCY	XXX					
OVERTIME	XXX					

Figure A-6

- Define your product groups.
- Determine the planning horizon for each group.
- Review your product structures, for Production Planning compatibility.
- Reformat the product structures, if necessary.
- Define your Production Plan inputs and responsibilities.
- Establish a procedure for the sequence of events.
- Determine the frequency of events (monthly milestones).
- Define how the Production Plan will be translated into a master schedule.

Phase-In Production Planning
- Educate all the participants.
- Select a pilot product group and run it through all the planning phases.
- Expand until all product groups are covered by a Production Plan.

PRODUCTION PLANNING BENEFITS

Is it worth it? Without question, a properly executed Production Plan can improve productivity and customer service levels while decreasing expediting, premium transportation costs, setups and inventory levels. You really have to experience it, though, to fully appreciate its value.

In the early 1980's, The Bendix Corporation decided to implement Production Planning at every manufacturing location. A corporate-wide program was undertaken to establish a minimum standard, communicate the basic criteria throughout the world-wide organization, measure compliance to the standard, and correct deficiencies. A number of success stories were recorded:

- A European subsidiary improved productivity by 9% and increased inventory turnover by 30% in three years.
- A domestic automotive component division was able to maintain favorable investment ratios despite reductions of more than 30% in customer orders.
- A Canadian subsidiary reduced its inventories by $4 million while improving customer service within the first year of implementation.

Production Planning is by no means a panacea. Like any good tool, it must be conscientiously applied by knowledgeable users to be effective.

SUGGESTED READING

As JIT implementation project teams get into the "nitty gritty" details of putting JUST-IN-TIME to work and as bosses begin to ask more far reaching questions than can be answered in just one volume, you'll need to expand your reference resources. While there are scores, if not hundreds of books available on JIT topics, the following list contains a core group that we at Ken Wantuck Associates have read and believe will be of value in your quest for more JIT knowledge. Where possible, we have sorted them into categories that correspond to the chapters in this book. It doesn't necessarily mean that is the only topic covered in the reference, but rather it means that topic is covered particularly well, in our opinion.

MANAGEMENT OVERVIEW

Abegglan, James, and Stalk, George, Jr. *Kaisha, The Japanese Corporation.* New York: Basic Books, 1986.

Halberstam, David. *The Reckoning.* New York: William Morrow & Co., 1986.

Imai, Masaaki. *Kaizen: The Key to Japan's Competitive Success.* New York: Random House, 1986.

Karatsu, Hajime. *Tough Words for American Industry.* PHP Institute, Inc., 1985.

Lu, David J. *Inside Corporate Japan.* Cambridge, MA: Productivity Press, 1987.

Ohmae, Kenichi. *Triad Power, The Coming Shape of Global Competition.* New York: The Free Press, 1985.

Pascale, Richard T., and Athos, Anthony G. *The Art of Japanese Management: Applications for American Executives.* New York: Simon & Shuster, 1981.

Vogel, Ezra. *Japan as Number One, Lessons for America.* Boston, MA: Harvard University Press, 1980.

JIT STRATEGY

Ford, Henry. *Today and Tomorrow.* Republication
of original 1926 autobiography. Cambridge, MA:
Productivity Press, 1988.

Ohno, Taiichi. *Toyota Production System.* (English
translation) Cambridge, MA: Productivity Press, 1988.

QUALITY AT THE SOURCE

Crosby, Philip. *Quality Is Free.* New York:
McGraw-Hill, 1979.

Feigenbaum, Armand V. *Total Quality Control.*
New York: McGraw-Hill, 1961.

Fukuda, Ryuji. *Managerial Engineering.* Cambridge,
MA: Productivity Press, 1983.

Ishikawa, K. *What Is Total Quality Control The Japanese
Way?* New Jersey: Englewood Cliffs, Prentice Hall, 1985.

Karatsu, Hajime. *TQC Wisdom Of Japan.* Cambridge, MA:
Productivity Press, 1988.

Mizuno, Shigeru (editor). *Management For Quality
Improvememt.* Cambridge, MA: Productivity Press, 1988.

Patton, Joseph, Jr. *Preventive Maintenance.* Research
Triangle Park, NC: Society of America, 1983.

Shingo, Shigeo. *Zero Quality Control: Source Inspection &
The Poka-Yoke System.* Cambridge, MA: Productivity
Press, 1986.

Western Electric Handbook Committee. *Statistical Quality
Control Handbook.* Western Electric, 1956.

PEOPLE POLICIES & PRACTICES

Hatakeyama, Yoshio. *Manager Revolution!* Cambridge,
MA: Productivity Press, 1985.

Posner, Barry, and Kouzens, James. *The Leadership Challenge.*
San Franisco: Jossey-Bass, 1988.

Ouchi, William. *Theory Z.* Reading, MA:
Addison Wesley, 1981.

Rosenthal, Edward C., and Burton, Cynthia. *Mutual Gains.* New York, NY: Praeger Publishers, 1987.

Tichey, Noel M., and DeVanna, Mary Ann. *The Transformational Leader.* New York, NY: John Wiley & Sons, 1981.

QUALITY CIRCLES

Crocker, Olga L., Charney, Cyril and Chiu, Johnny Sik Laung. *Quality Circles.* New York, NY: Mentor Books, 1984.

Komatsu, Ltd. *QC Handbook.* Cambridge, MA: Productivity Press.

GROUP TECHNOLOGY

Computer & Automated Systems Association of SME. *Capabilities Of Group Technology.* Dearborn, MI: Society of Manufacturing Engineers, 1987.

DESIGN FOR AUTOMATION

Bernardo, Francisco P. Jr. *Design & Implementation Of Low Cost Automation.* Hong Kong: Asian Productivity Organization, 1972.

SETUP REDUCTION

Shingo, Shigeo. *A Revolution In Manufacturing.* Cambridge, MA: Productivity Press, 1985.

IMPLEMENTATION

Christopher, Robert. *Second To None, American Companies In Japan.* New York, NY: Ballantine Books, 1986.

Japan Management Association. *Canon Production System.* Cambridge, MA: Productivity Press, 1986.

Shingo, Shigeo. *Study of Toyota Production System. From Industrial Engineering Viewpoint.* Cambridge, MA: Productivity Press, 1981.

JIT MEASUREMENTS

AME Research Report. *Accounting For Manufacturing Productivity.* West Palatine, IL: Association for Manufacturing Excellence, 1988.

Berliner, Callie, and Brimson, James (editors). *Cost Management For Today's Advanced Manufacturing.* Boston, MA: Harvard Business School Press, 1985.

Burns, William and Kaplan, Robert. *Accounting and Management, Field Study Perspectives.* Boston, MA: Harvard Business School Press, 1987.

Christopher, William. *Productivity Measurement Handbook.* Cambridge, MA: Productivity Press, 1985.

Johnson, H. Thomas, and Kaplan, Robert C. *Relevance Lost, The Rise & Fall Of Managerial Accounting.* Boston, MA: Harvard Business School Press, 1987.

ADDITIONAL SUGGESTED READING

Gunn, Thomas G. *Manufacturing For Competitive Advantage.* Cambridge, MA: Ballinger Publishing Company, 1987.

Hall, Robert W. *Attaining Manufacturing Excellence.* Homewood, IL: Dow Jones-Irwin, 1987.

Hall, Robert W. *Zero Inventories.* Homewood, IL: Dow Jones-Irwin, 1983.

Hay, Edward J. *The JUST-IN-TIME Breakthrough.* New York, NY: John Wiley & Sons, 1988.

Hayes, Robert, and Wheelwright, Steven. *Restoring Our Competitive Edge.* New York: J. Wiley & Sons, 1984.

INDEX